# Lawyers in Society

## THE CIVIL LAW WORLD

D0171184

# Lawyers in Society

## VOLUME TWO
# THE CIVIL LAW WORLD

Edited by
RICHARD L. ABEL
and PHILIP S. C. LEWIS

**UNIVERSITY OF CALIFORNIA PRESS**
*Berkeley / Los Angeles / London*

University of California Press
Berkeley and Los Angeles, California
University of California Press, Ltd.
London, England

LIBRARY OF CONGRESS
Library of Congress Cataloging-in-Publication Data

Abel, Richard L.
Lawyers in society: the civil law world/Richard L. Abel and
Philip Simon Coleman Lewis.
p.    cm.
Includes index.
ISBN 0-520-06263-9 (alk. paper)
1. Lawyers—Congresses.   I. Lewis, Philip Simon Coleman.
II. Title.
K117.A24 1988
340'.023—dc19                              88-1231
                                           CIP

Printed in the United States of America

1   2   3   4   5   6   7   8   9

# Contents

# Preface

This is the second of three volumes on the comparative sociology of legal professions. In the first volume we analyzed the legal professions of the major common law countries of the industrialized world (England and Wales, Scotland, Canada, the United States, Australia, and New Zealand) and that of the most populous common law country in the third world (India). We made no effort to cover other common law systems in Northern Ireland and the Republic of Ireland, the Caribbean, Asia, and Africa because of limitations on our resources and our inability to identify national reporters and because the International Center for Law in Development previously produced a book on several of those countries.* In addition, the Commonwealth Legal Education Association currently is investigating access to legal education and the legal profession in Commonwealth countries, including those of the third world.

The present volume contains studies of eleven civil law professions (Belgium, Brazil, the Federal Republic of Germany, France, Italy, Japan, the Netherlands, Norway, Spain, Switzerland, and Venezuela). This is a broad, though not entirely representative, selection from northern and southern Europe and the Latin American countries influenced by Spain and Portugal. Limited resources and the lack of national reporters prevented us from surveying the legal professions of the socialist and the Islamic worlds (although a Yugoslav colleague did participate in early discussions). The third volume in this series uses these national reports and other sources to draw theoretical and comparative conclusions. All three volumes are the product of the Working Group for Comparative Study of Legal Profes-

---

*Dias, C. J., R. Luckham, D. O. Lynch, and J. C. N. Paul, eds. 1981. *Lawyers in the Third World: Comparative and Developmental Perspectives.* Uppsala: Scandinavian Institute of African Studies; New York: International Center for Law in Development.

sions, which was created by the Research Committee on Sociology of Law, a constituent of the International Sociological Association.

The Working Group was formed in 1980 and met annually thereafter, in Madison (Wisconsin), Oxford, Mexico City, and Antwerp, during the conferences of the Research Committee. These meetings were devoted to discussing theoretical approaches to the legal profession and developing an inventory of information that national reporters were to collect. Drafts of most of the chapters were presented at a week-long meeting at the Villa Serbelloni, the Rockefeller Foundation's Conference Center in Bellagio, Italy, 16–21 July 1984. They have been revised extensively since then, assisted by further discussions during meetings of the Working Group in Aix-en-Provence and New Delhi in conjunction with the annual conferences of the Research Committee.

During the course of such a lengthy project involving so many people we have been assisted by numerous individuals and institutions. The Board of the Research Committee on Sociology of Law consistently offered moral and financial support. Stewart Field, currently on the law faculty at the University of Wales Institute of Science and Technology, Cardiff, took extensive notes on the discussions at Bellagio, which helped all of us to revise our contributions. Pam Taylor of All Souls College, Oxford, typed those notes and retyped many of the contributions. Dorothe Brehove and Marilyn Schroeter, together with other members of the secretarial staff of UCLA Law School, also retyped many contributions. We are grateful to the Rockefeller Foundation for hosting our conference and to the American Bar Foundation for the financial support that made the conference possible. Terence Halliday of the Foundation provided invaluable administrative assistance in organizing that conference and since then has taken responsibility for leading the future activities of the Working Group. Richard Abel would like to thank UCLA Law School for continuing administrative and financial support. Philip Lewis would like to thank the Trustees of the Nuffield Foundation who made possible his participation in the early stages of this project.

Richard L. Abel                                    Philip S. C. Lewis
Los Angeles                                        Oxford

# 1
## Lawyers in the Civil Law World

RICHARD L. ABEL

Readers are likely to approach a book of essays about lawyers in the civil law world with two initial questions: why lawyers, and why the civil law world. Philip Lewis addressed the first question in his introduction to our earlier volume on lawyers in the common law world (Lewis, 1988). We believe that an understanding of the characteristics and practices of lawyers can offer important insights into the workings of legal systems. We also feel that this understanding is best advanced through research that is comparative, sociological, and historical.

The reasons for focusing on the civil law world are more complicated. Very little has been written in English on lawyers outside the common law world. English-speaking students of comparative law (which generally, although not invariably, means civil law) have paid little or no attention to lawyers, although works intended for a more popular audience sometimes offer useful observations (e.g., Burdick, 1939; Bedford, 1961). The leading texts and casebooks ignore the subject entirely or treat it very briefly (e.g., Gutteridge, 1949; von Mehren, 1957; von Mehren & Gordley, 1977; Schlesinger, 1960; Glendon et al., 1982; Barton et al., 1983), although the latest contribution offers a fuller exposition (Glendon et al., 1985). Historical approaches are equally neglectful (e.g., Watson, 1981; but see Clark, 1987). John Henry Wigmore had virtually nothing to say about lawyers in his three-volume *Panorama of the World's Legal Systems* (Wigmore, 1928). René David omitted all coverage of lawyers in the civil law world in the three editions of his *Modern Legal Systems in the World Today* (David & Brierly, 1968; 1978; 1985). The contemporary ten-volume *Modern Legal Systems Cyclopedia* (Redden, 1984) offers only the most general and superficial observations, bereft of empirical data. The seventeen-volume *International Encyclopedia of Comparative Law* (1975–1979) ignores the subject except for brief references to judges and prosecutors in the national reports, and the first eight volumes of the *Compara-*

*tive Law Yearbook* (1977–1984) touched on the subject just once, in a symposium on legal education. In the decade 1976–1985, the leading *American Journal of Comparative Law* published one article on German legal education (Geck, 1977), one on the employment of *avocats* within French law firms (Le, 1981), and one comparing lawyers (Clark, 1981). Its British counterpart, the *International and Comparative Law Quarterly*, published nothing on lawyers in the decade 1974–1983.

I do not want to overstate the neglect, however. Scholars have offered accounts of lawyers in the civil law world in treatises on civil procedure (e.g., Ginsburg & Bruzelius, 1965; Herzog, 1967), overviews of particular civil law systems (e.g., Cappelletti et al., 1967) and of the civil law generally (Merryman, 1969), sociologies of particular legal professions (Lynch, 1981), symposia on legal systems and legal professions (e.g., Magnus, 1929; Union Internationale des Avocats, 1959; Dias et al., 1981; Kötz et al., 1982; Wagner, 1985; Katz, 1986a), comparative statistics on legal professions and legal systems (Johnson et al., 1977; Merryman et al., 1979), comparative sociology of the professions (Conze and Kocka, 1985), and other sources I rely on in this introduction. Nevertheless, there clearly seemed to be a need for more systematic, empirical, coordinated examination of lawyers in the civil law world.

This review of the literature assumes that answers to two questions that really should be antecedent: is there a civil law "world," and what countries exemplify it? There are ample historical grounds for expecting similarities among lawyers *within* each of these two categories—common and civil law—and differences between them. English lawyers founded the legal professions in the colonies that later became the United States, Canada, Australia, and New Zealand. Although Scotland originally had a civil law system and trained its lawyers on the continent, centuries of English political and economic domination wrought a close resemblance between Scottish and English lawyers. In addition, several hundred years of British colonial rule over India superimposed a "common law" profession that coexists uneasily with indigenous institutions and traditional cultures. Historical interconnections also can be traced among civil law countries, if with more branches. The combination of revolutionary example and Napoleonic conquest exported the French legal system throughout much of Europe. Colonial expansion, especially by France, Spain, and Portugal (although also by Belgium, the Netherlands, Germany, and Italy), imposed European legal systems on the Americas, Asia, Africa, and Oceania. After political ties were severed, these links were preserved through economic dependence, cultural influence, education, and language. Even in the absence of colonization, countries as diverse as Japan, Turkey, and Ethiopia adopted European legal systems, in whole or in part.

Each world may be coherent and distinct for another reason as well—because the parts of its social order fit together. This functionalist explanation can be applied to many different social environments, from the nation-state to the smallest of its subsystems. At the highest level of generality, we could explain the characteristics of lawyers in terms of national histories. It has been suggested, for instance, that the sequence in which a powerful state apparatus and an industrial economy emerge strongly affects the relative prominence of lawyers employed by the state vis-à-vis private practitioners (Rueschemeyer, 1973: 7–8; 1978: 112; Clark, 1981). Evan (1968) found a correlation between the proportion of the labor force employed by public bureaucracies and the number of law schools. Others have focused on relationships within the legal system. All students of comparative law are familiar with Weber's (horrified) observations about the differences between England and Germany with respect to the location of legal education, the nature of legal thought, and the openness of the legal system to reform (Weber, 1954: 198–206). Since then, scholars have suggested connections between codification and the role of lawyers (e.g., Cohn, 1960, 1961; Merryman, 1975), between the relative responsibilities of lawyers and judges in developing facts and the characteristics of private practice (Langbein, 1985), and between the nature of authority (hierarchical versus coordinate) and the legal process (Damaska, 1986). In this introduction, I would like to offer a more modest justification for using the analytic category of the civil law world by exploring whether lawyers in these countries actually share traits that distinguish them from those in the common law world and whether these traits are interconnected.

Although I have been speaking of "worlds," our coverage of civil law countries is partial and possibly unrepresentative. I have tried to supplement it with data from other European and Latin American countries. However, I have made no effort to include either socialist countries that built on civil law systems or Islamic countries that had experienced European colonial rule and thus inherited a civil law tradition. The difference between the viewpoints that inform the national reports on one hand and this introduction on the other hand may illuminate the value of these analytic categories. All the authors of the following chapters are participants in the societies, the legal systems, and sometimes also the legal professions that they are describing. As editors, we have tried to preserve the unique perspectives they bring to that inquiry. By contrast, I am an American law teacher asking questions that inevitably are influenced by my very different background. We hope that the interaction between these different versions will provide fresh insights.

# WHAT IS A LEGAL PROFESSION?

## THE PROBLEM OF THE UNIT OF COMPARISON

Those who belong to or study the legal profession in the common law world share an implicit understanding of that concept. It consists of two overlapping criteria: the formal credential that entitles one to represent parties in court; and the functional role of mediating the exercise of state power, whether among private individuals or entities or between them and the state. These criteria are related not only stipulatively but also empirically: most of those who obtain formal qualifications perform the functions of lawyers, and a significant proportion of such functions are performed by those formally qualified. The category is essentially unitary. Its core—historically, numerically, and ideologically—is private practice. Where this is divided between barristers or advocates and solicitors (most sharply in Britain), each branch sees the other as a complement, if also a rival, within a functional whole. Although some lawyers perform their roles as house counsel, prosecutors, government employees, members of legal aid or public defender offices, law teachers, or judges, these categories are smaller and more peripheral; furthermore, they both see themselves and are perceived as constituents of a single legal profession. They share the same formal qualification, and lawyers move fairly freely between the categories. Therefore, it is relatively unproblematic to "compare" legal professions in different common law countries.

The civil law world is dramatically different from its common law counterpart in every respect. To begin with, there is no "legal profession." Indeed, the very title of this chapter is an ethnocentric misnomer. The common law folk concept of "lawyer" has no counterpart in European languages, except through such awkward literal translations as *homme de droit*. Instead, civil law countries recognize two categories, one more inclusive than the common law concept and the other less so. The first is the jurist: to acquire a university degree in law is to attain an honored status (if one devalued by credential inflation in recent decades). Many such graduates (sometimes a majority) pursue occupations unrelated to law, however, and possession of a degree does not constitute a corporate group. The second category is the private practitioner—a concept with clear equivalents in all European languages and sharply defined boundaries. However, the latter emphatically is *not* the core of any notional legal profession. Rather, other subsets of law graduates take precedence—historically, numerically, and ideologically. These include the magistracy (judges and prosecutors, often combined in a way that is inconceivable to the common law), civil servants, law professors, and lawyers employed in commerce and industry. In some civil law countries the list of "legal occupations" includes roles performed in the common law world by those without any legal training: notaries everywhere, police chiefs in Norway and Brazil, and bailiffs and process servers in France. None of these occupations sees itself as part of a larger whole that also contains private practitioners. Each may demand its own formal qualifications in addition to the law degree, and there is little lateral mobility among them. Voluntary associations tend to be limited to a single occupational category (and even to proliferate within each).

Comparisons between common and civil law worlds thus become acutely problematic because the common law legal profession is not equivalent to either civil law folk category—jurist or private practitioner— and the congeries of legal occupations in the civil law world is not itself a folk category. One illustration of this difficulty is the repeated tendency of Western observers to exaggerate the population per lawyer in Japan—10,056 in 1982—by counting only *bengoshi* (private practitioners who have graduated from the Institute of Legal Training and Research). If the calculation is expanded to include all those who perform functions comparable to that of the lawyer in Western countries—law professors, judges, public prosecutors, in-house counsel, judicial scriveners, administrative scriveners, patent attorneys, tax attorneys, and foreign lawyers— the ratio becomes 1,239:1, which is not very different from that of other Western European countries (Brown, 1983: 479, 484).

The historical dominance of common law legal professions by private practitioners is symbolized by the appointment of their most senior and respected members to the bench. England represents the most extreme example: privately practicing barristers were briefed as prosecutors by the government (even the attorney general and the solicitor general retained their private practices until the end of the nineteenth century); practicing barristers and solicitors did most of the law teaching in both university law faculties and private courses designed to prepare students for the professional examinations until after World War II; private practitioners rather than salaried lawyers still deliver virtually all legal aid (which is administered by the Law Society, a private body); and privately practicing barristers often serve as part-time judges.

In much of the civil law world, by contrast, lawyers were state employees first and private practitioners only later. Japan, for instance, created a judiciary and a prosecutorial staff in the nineteenth century, which had to undergo rigorous training and examinations. By contrast, private practitioners were required to submit to a much easier examination only in 1893, they received no practical training, and many qualified under a grandfather clause; not until 1933 were they required to take the same examination as judges and prosecutors, and not until after World War II did they receive the same training (Brown, 1983: 266–267). In sev-

eral European countries, notably France and Switzerland, the eighteenth-
and nineteenth-century revolutions attacked and temporarily abolished
the "feudal" privileges of guilds of private practitioners. Norwegian
judges and prosecutors were required to obtain university law degrees in
Denmark, whereas private practitioners were required to learn only local
Norwegian laws and customs and could be examined at home. Indeed, all
Norwegian private practitioners actually were made government officials
between 1809 and 1848.

Even after private practice acquired a distinct identity within civil law
systems, states monitored it closely, fearful of challenges to their sovereignty. Throughout the eighteenth and nineteenth centuries, the German states restricted the number of advocates, who formally were part of
the judicial service. Prussia even abolished private practice between 1780
and 1783, appointing civil servants to a quasijudicial role to advise litigants. Most dramatically, the Nazis expelled Jewish advocates and
judges—whom they also identified as left-wing opponents; because earlier discrimination had excluded Jews from the more prestigious careers in
the judiciary, forcing them to enter private practice, the ratio of judges to
advocates increased from 9,943:19,276 (0.52:1) in 1933 to 16,000:12,000
(1.33:1) in 1943 (Reifner, 1986: 104).

The relative significance of private practitioners within the two worlds
also is revealed by the numerical ratios between them and other professional categories: judges and prosecutors, legally qualified civil servants,
and lawyers employed in business. Despite the considerable difficulties of
categorization and the incomplete and sometimes approximate statistics,
the differences between the two worlds are clear (see table 1.1). Throughout the common law world there are between two and seven judges per
100 private practitioners. The ratio in the civil law world always is higher
(with the exception of Spain), generally many times higher. In Germany
in 1962, there were ninety judges for every 100 private practitioners—
more than twenty times the ratio in the United States. If we add prosecutors (whom civil law countries include in the same category), the ratio
increases still further. In Britain and the United States, the ratio of lawyer
civil servants to private practitioners never exceeds 20:100. Again it is
much higher throughout the civil law world (except Colombia); and in
most of the countries for which I have statistics the two categories are
roughly comparable. Finally, there are fewer than ten lawyers employed
in business for every 100 private practitioners in the common law world
(except the United States, which had sixteen in 1980); however, the ratio
was far higher throughout the civil law world, where lawyers employed in
business usually *outnumbered* private practitioners. In Italy in the 1960s,
half of all law graduates became either civil servants or employees in
private businesses (Cappelletti et al., 1967: 91).

In the civil law world, the judiciary (and to a lesser degree prosecutors and civil servants) are at least the equals of private practitioners in terms of prestige and income and, generally, their superiors. In the common law world, successful private practitioners always earn far more than judges, prosecutors, or civil servants and often are reluctant to relinquish these material rewards, even for the status and power enjoyed by the highest positions in the judiciary or the executive. In Germany, both judges and private practitioners acknowledge the greater prestige of the former (Rueschemeyer, 1973: 119; Geck, 1977: 106). During the course of their legal education, the proportion of German students interested in becoming judges increases (Rueschemeyer, 1973: 104). A study of German *Referendäre* (apprentices) in the early 1980s revealed that of those who expressed a preference, 40 percent wanted to become judges or civil servants, 23 percent wanted to become *Anwälte* (private practitioners), and 10 percent wanted to become company employees. Among Italian private practitioners who responded to a 1966 survey, 42 percent gladly would have accepted salaried employment at the same income; twelve years later, a similar proportion of Lombard private practitioners (38 percent) were prepared to make such a change (Prandstraller, 1967, 1981). Throughout the civil law world, only those law students with the best academic records can enter the judiciary (e.g., Italy; see Certoma [1985: 72]). In Sweden, only half of the applicants are accepted by the training school for judges, prosecutors, and sheriffs (Bogdan, 1981: 141). In France in 1978, the Ecole Nationale de la Magistrature accepted only 154 of the 962 applicants, selecting on the basis of their performance on the *Certificat d'aptitude à la profession d'avocat* (CAPA) examination (Nagourney, 1981: 64). Indeed, as the production of law graduates has increased, the private economy has stagnated, and the fiscal crisis of the state has retarded the growth of public sector jobs, the attractions of the latter have increased and competition to obtain them has intensified. The common law world has experienced a similar divergence between the attractions of public employment and private practice but to the advantage of the latter: in 1972, large New York law firms paid beginning lawyers only slightly more than the federal government or state prosecutor ($16,000 vs. $13,300 and $12,500); by 1986, employees of the former began at two to three times the salaries of the latter ($65,000 vs. $27,000 and $25,000) (Lewin, 1987).

In the common law world there is considerable mobility among the categories of practice during the careers of many lawyers. In Chicago in the mid-1970s, for example, two-thirds of government lawyers had been in private practice, a fifth of large firm lawyers had worked in government, and two-fifths of house counsel had been in private practice; only a third of those who began as government lawyers remained civil servants (the

lowest rate of retention of any first job) (Heinz & Laumann, 1982: 195).
And, of course, all common law judges have been private practitioners,
government lawyers, or law professors (often occupying several of these
roles in succession).

In the civil law world, by contrast, law students make a fairly irrevoc-
able decision about which category to enter at graduation or shortly
thereafter. In many countries they then receive additional formal training
or a specialized apprenticeship, and subsequent career changes are rare. In
Germany in 1979, for instance, a quarter of all judges were under thirty-
five years old, indicating the early career choice (as well as the recent
expansion of the judiciary) (Wagner, 1985: 675). It is important not to
exaggerate the rigidity of these categories, however. The boundary
between private practice and business employment may be uncertain:
"employed" lawyers may have private clients, and private practitioners
eagerly seek retainers from major companies. In the Netherlands, private
practitioners may become judges in midcareer; in Japan, judges may retire
to enter private practice. In Italy, lawyers often act as honorary judges,
*giudici conciliatori*, and *vicepretori*; in Germany, law professors serve as
part-time judges (Geck, 1977: 107). In third world countries such as Chile
(Lowenstein, 1970), Colombia (Lynch, 1981: 54), Venezuela, and Brazil,
the remuneration from public sector jobs may not be sufficient to retain
the ambitious; indeed, public lawyers may simultaneously be compelled to
work for private clients in order to earn sufficient income. Yet with all
these qualifications, the compartments still are far less permeable in civil
law than in common law countries, and these divisions are compounded
by rules of incompatibility, separate professional associations, and even
patterns of socializing, all of which can cause problems of communication
between them (Merryman, 1969: 110). The continued strength of these
divisions is confirmed by the failure of France to unite them into a single
legal profession during the reforms of 1971.

## THE THEORETICAL FRAMEWORK

Much recent work within the English-speaking world on the
professions—medicine as well as law—has been informed by a theoretical framework drawn from critical sociology (e.g., Freidson, 1970; Larson,
1977) and economics (for an overview, see Abel [1988: chap. 1]). This
theory argues that an occupational category of private practitioners who
wish to professionalize must seek control over the market within which
they sell their services and simultaneously assert and enhance their status.
They can pursue market control (and its concomitant economic advantages) by regulating both the production *of* producers (entry into the pro-

fession) and production *by* producers (demarcation of the boundaries of the monopoly and restrictions on competition within it). They can pursue status in many different ways: controlling *who* enters the profession (and not just how many), denying their own interest in pecuniary gain, allying themselves with powerful and prestigious clients, asserting their independence from the state, engaging in conspicuous altruism, and attaining and defending self-regulation. The vehicle for this project is the voluntary private association. Many of the contributors to the first volume in this series, *The Common Law World* (Abel & Lewis, 1988), found this theory illuminating, and even those who rejected it felt the need to demonstrate that their legal profession was exceptional.

Clearly, an observer who began by seeking to understand lawyers in the civil law world never would construct such a theory. Their experience is different in almost every respect. The core members of that occupational category are employed by the state (and an increasing proportion are employed by private enterprise); these jurists are not concerned with controlling supply—their employers do that for them. Nor are they obsessed with market relations. They derive their status from membership in a university-educated elite and from the respect accorded civil servants (and the employees of large companies). Legally qualified civil servants pride themselves on their *loyalty* to the state, not on their independence from it. As employees, they are regulated by the bureaucratic structure within which they work. Associations are likely to be local, compulsory, and official and to exercise less authority.

If the theory of the "professional project" illuminates the civil law world at all, it will be most useful in understanding those law graduates who resemble the core of the common law professions—namely, private practitioners. In the following sections, therefore, I will discuss the ways in which that theory must be adapted to account for the very different configuration of legal occupations in the civil law world and the fact that private practitioners are only a subcategory—historically, numerically, economically, and socially inferior to jurists employed by the state.

## CONTROL OVER ENTRY

In the common law world, private practitioners organized themselves into voluntary associations, a central goal of which was to control entry into practice and competition among practitioners. In the civil law world, by contrast, the state historically controlled entry into the core of the profession by appointing judges, prosecutors, state attorneys, and civil servants. I noted above that the financial rewards, security, and status of state employment always have been sufficient to attract the best law graduates, who compete vigorously for the prize of becoming state employees. Once they have attained this goal (typically early in their careers, through examination), they are guaranteed lifetime employment, with advancement largely (but not exclusively) determined by seniority. Few leave, and those who remain are not threatened by the lateral entry of potential competitors.

These characteristics do not sharply distinguish civil and common law worlds, for the state everywhere controls the number of judges, prosecutors, and lawyer civil servants (if these roles are more central to civil law professions). What does distinguish the civil law world is the fact that the state also controls entry to positions that are subject to market forces in the common law world. Many legal occupations, although economically dependent on the fees of private parties rather than on state salaries, were and still are protected by a *numerus clausus* (admission quota). In Germany, some states controlled the number of private practitioners (Anwälte) until 1879. The economic significance of this restriction was manifest in two ways. First, the financial rewards of private practice were so high prior to 1879 that even judges jumped at the opportunity to enter it whenever positions were available, notwithstanding the prestige of a judicial career. Second, the population per Anwalt was 12,000 in Prussia in 1867, although it was only 1,000 to 2,000 in other European countries and in German states without a numerus clausus. When the Prussian restriction was lifted, growth was dramatic. Berlin, which had ninety to one hundred *Justizkommissare* before 1879, contained more than 1,000 Anwälte in 1906. Throughout Germany, the number of Anwälte increased threefold between 1880 and 1913 (from 4,122 to 12,324), while the population per lawyer fell by half (from 10,970 to 5,346) (Rueschemeyer, 1973: 165 n.52, 175 n.75).

In Italy, the office of *procuratore* was governed by a numerus clausus as late as 1950 (Sereni, 1950: 1001). In many European countries, a numerus clausus still limits entry to the notariat and to the small category of lawyers qualified to appear before the highest courts. In Chile, the number of notaries increased only 26 percent between 1945 and 1970 (from 114 to 144), while the number of lawyers increased by 357 percent (from 943 to 4,306); in Italy, notaries increased by 36 percent during this period (from 2,559 to 3,490), while lawyers increased by 62 percent (from 25,642 to 41,639) (Merryman et al., 1979: 466–467, 470–471); in the Netherlands, the number of notaries remained constant between 1900 and 1986, while the number of advocaten increased sevenfold.

France preserved the most elaborate restrictions. The state controls the numbers of all *officiers ministériels*: *avoués* (official representatives of parties responsible for procedural formalities in litigation in courts of appeal), *notaires* (notaries), *huissiers* (bailiffs), and *greffiers* (court clerks). The holder of such an office can sell it on retirement. Some notion of the worth of such state-created scarcity can be gained from the fact that greffiers have been able to obtain as much as eight times their annual incomes in such sales; and when the state merged avoués (in the lower courts) with avocats (advocates) in 1971, it paid the former between four and five and a half times their annual incomes for loss of the right to sell their offices (David & de Vries, 1958: 24; Herzog, 1967: 83; Herzog & Herzog, 1973: 470). Further evidence of the imbalance between supply and demand is the fact that individual office-holders have been allowed to form professional civil societies, thereby increasing the number of practitioners while maintaining the fiction that the number of offices remains constant—exactly what happened in England when the numbers of people actually performing the functions of the "Six Clerks in Chancery" gradually multiplied (Holdsworth, 1926: 369).

The state directly determines how many jurists it will employ and the size of those categories still ruled by a numerus clausus. It is another institution—the university (generally also public)—that mediates entry to private practice in civil law countries. Here, again, the divergence between the two worlds is marked. Common lawyers traditionally qualified through apprenticeship. (Scotland is the exception that proves the rule, since the role of university education reflects its civil law heritage.) English universities taught no English law until the last quarter of the nineteenth century. In the United States, Canada, Australia, and New Zealand, few universities taught *any* law until the twentieth century. Even after law faculties were established, American lawyers did not begin attending them in significant numbers until the early 1900s, and in the other common law countries, the shift from apprenticeship occurred only after World War II.

By contrast, a university law degree long has been essential for almost all legal occupations in civil law countries (Ranieri, 1985). Law (together with theology and medicine) was one of the first faculties established by European (and Latin American) universities, many of which are very old—Bologna celebrated its nine-hundredth anniversary in 1988. Requiring this credential substantially limited entry because only a tiny proportion of the population traditionally attended the elite secondary schools that prepared for university and had the financial resources to survive the many years it took to obtain a university degree. In Germany in the early 1960s, between 2.5 percent and 4 percent of the relevant age cohort went to university (Rueschemeyer, 1973: 66 n. 6). In Sweden in 1960, 13 percent of those between ages eighteen and twenty-four were in some form of higher education, but the three law faculties were producing only about 200 graduates per year in 1950 (Ginsburg & Bruzelius, 1965: 51 n. 5, 53 n. 12). In France in the early 1960s, only about 100,000 students were enrolled in any form of higher education (Herzog, 1967:69 n. 14). In third world countries the proportion remains very low: Only 4.6 percent of the Brazilian age cohort were attending university as late as 1980, and only 3.7 percent were doing so in Colombia in 1965–1967 (Lynch, 1981:27).

If universities in the civil law world were exclusive until the 1960s, law was one of the least selective subjects. Because law faculties did not offer vocational training for private practice but rather granted a degree that conferred generalized status and entree to public and private administration, they attracted a very large proportion of undergraduates. In the Netherlands in 1850, 46 percent of all undergraduates were studying law; in Colombia between 1937 and 1941, 54 percent were doing so (Lynch, 1981:27). Everywhere this proportion appears to have declined over time: to 7 percent in the Netherlands in 1960 (before returning to 13 percent in 1979), to 15 percent in Colombia between 1965 and 1967 (ibid.), from 21 percent to 9 percent in Italy between 1957 and 1968 (Merryman et al., 1979:426), and from 23.7 percent in Brazil in 1961 to 9 percent in 1980. Even so, the proportion remains much higher than in the common law world: nearly half of all Spanish undergraduates (but see Lancaster & Giles [1986:370]—only 12.7 percent in 1972/73), 14 percent in Italy in 1977, 11 percent in Austria in 1980 (Schreuer, 1981:17), 7 percent in El Salvador in 1977 (MacDonald, 1986:197), 5.7 percent in Venezuela in 1981/82, and 6.5 percent in Germany in 1980. Two-thirds of Brazilian law students questioned stated that they wanted a law degree in order to pursue *other* professional careers, and another tenth wanted it for the associated status; only half of all law graduates ultimately entered legal occupations.

University legal education in the two worlds differs in content as well as numbers. Everywhere in the civil law world it is an undergraduate degree, whereas in the United States it is exclusively graduate, and in Canada, Australia, and New Zealand it generally is combined with undergraduate education in another subject (mixed degrees also are available in England). The organized legal profession (i.e., the association of private practitioners) strongly influences the content of legal education in the common law world, either directly or by controlling professional examinations. In the civil law world, the state plays a much larger role in determining the curriculum, even in private universities (which are a minority in Italy, Spain, and Portugal, a majority in Japan, Brazil, and Colombia). Although many common law faculties relied heavily on private practitioners teaching part time until after World War II, today virtually all their instructors teach full time; they are paid close to the median lawyer income but do not enjoy the wealth or status they could attain in private practice (given their generally strong academic backgrounds). In northern Europe, law professors earn high salaries and receive the highest prestige of any legal professional (Geck, 1977: 106). In southern Europe and Latin America, they also enjoy considerable status (Cappelletti et al., 1967: 87); but their low salaries compel them to spend most of their time in private practice—95.5 percent of Colombian law professors teach part time (Lynch, 1981: 28 n. 125). In Brazil, it is necessary to teach seven class hours per *day* (in several different schools) in order to make a living wage. Yet, paradoxically, the full-time academics in common law faculties offer a fairly vocational training, whereas the full-time practitioners who teach part time in civil law faculties are intensely theoretical (perhaps because the former see themselves as preparing for private practice, whereas the latter educate students for the magistracy and civil service).

Whereas the student:faculty ratio in most common law faculties is about 20:1, it is more than 100:1 in Germany, whose law faculties range from 1,200 to 4,000 students (Geck, 1977); and other civil law faculties are incredibly large: 14,476 in Madrid in 1978/79, 11,559 in Barcelona, 16,290 in Naples in 1974, 15,275 in Rome, 11,163 in Bari, and 8,870 in Palermo. In Italy in 1970, there were 151 students for each tenured professor and 92 students for each professor (tenured and nontenured); in Spain, there were 106 law students for each professor (Merryman et al., 1979: 427, 429, 433–434). All these students could not attend class even if they wanted to do so. In Austria, fewer than half of all students regularly attend classes (Scheuer, 1981: 22). Three-quarters of Brazilian students work six to eight hours per day to support themselves, at jobs usually unrelated to law. In Colombia, 65 percent of students worked part time, and 15 percent worked full time (Lynch, 1981: 52). The reasons for this lack of academic commitment are not just economic but also pedagogic: students find the lectures uninteresting and unrelated to the examinations they must pass. German professors (and those in many other civil law faculties) regard themselves primarily as scholars, who also happen to teach (Geck, 1977: 106). As a result, students rely heavily on private crammers—in 1980, two-thirds of all German students used the notes of a single firm (Weyrauch, 1964: 96–120).

Common and civil law educational institutions also exercise their gatekeeping functions differently. Until after World War II, entry to law faculties in the common law world was relatively uncompetitive. In the United States, unaccredited part-time evening schools unaffiliated with universities admitted anyone who could pay the low tuition; even elite schools such as Harvard accepted most college graduates who were capable of paying the much higher tuition. English law faculties were equally undiscriminating. In the last few decades, however, competition to enter law faculties has become intense in both countries. Moreover, because faculties within each country vary greatly in prestige, admission to high-status schools is an important means of controlling access to the most desirable professional careers. Once students are admitted, however, virtually all graduate, at least at the more elite institutions.

The situation in the civil law world is the inverse. Until the mid-1960s, entry to university was limited to the tiny socioeconomic elite who attended academic secondary schools. The educational reforms of that decade opened the university to *all* secondary school graduates, greatly expanding existing universities and establishing new ones. In Germany, for instance, 25 percent of the relevant age cohort attended university in 1981, compared to only 2 to 4 percent in 1960. Because these institutions vary much less in prestige than those in the United States or England, most students attend the one nearest their home in order to minimize living expenses.

Yet if admission to university law faculties is not a barrier, many students fail to complete their degrees—often because of lack of interest rather than academic difficulties, sometimes for economic reasons. Just half of all entrants receive law degrees in Argentina (MacDonald, 1986: 200), Austria (Schreuer, 1981: 20, 23), and Belgium; only 40 percent do so in Norway and less than 20 percent in Venezuela. Half of German law students do not complete the course, and a quarter of those who take the first state examination fail. In Italy, only 7,718 law degrees were awarded in 1980—5 percent of the 144,869 students enrolled; 25 percent should have graduated if students were completing their academic work in the expected four years (de Francisis, 1986: 159). The Faculty of Law and Political Science of Paris awarded only 1,309 *licenses* and 600 other law degrees in 1953/54—10 percent of the 19,509 students enrolled in the three- to four-year course; it awarded only 792 licenses and 167 other degrees in 1958/59—7 percent of the 14,165 students enrolled (Herzog, 1967: 70 n. 18). In 1978, three-quarters of nonrepeating French law students failed their first-year examinations, and only 35 percent of entrants ever obtained *maîtrises* (master's degrees) (Nagourney, 1981: 67). In Spain, only 5 to 7 percent of enrolled law students graduate each year, compared to the 20 percent who should complete the five-year course. At the other extreme, the three Swedish law faculties graduated 70 percent of their entrants in the 1960s, perhaps because the numbers were small (200 graduates per year) and students took separate examinations in each subject, whenever they were ready to do so, and could repeat up to four times (Ginsburg & Bruzelius, 1965: 51 n. 5, 56 n. 21, 57 n. 28).

In common law countries, associations of private practitioners successfully campaigned for professional examinations, required by the state but administered by the profession. In nineteenth-century England, where most barristers did not read law at university and most solicitors did not attend university at all, professional examinations became an important barrier to entry. In the United States, they encouraged entrants to abandon apprenticeship for formal education, which better prepared them for the bar examination; and they curtailed entry during the Great Depression of the 1930s, when the profession feared "overcrowding." In Australia, however, the law degree qualifies for practice; and almost all law graduates in Canada and New Zealand pass the professional examination at first attempt.

In civil law countries, examinations play a different role. Given the importance of the university as gatekeeper, further examinations often were superfluous. Law graduates did not have to take professional examinations until 1925 in Switzerland and 1963 in Brazil. In Norway, the Netherlands, Belgium, Spain, and Colombia (Lynch, 1981: 91 n. 15), there still are no requirements beyond a university law degree. Where examinations are required, they are administered by the university itself (as in Norway or the first examination in Germany) or by the state, not by the profession. (Yet, where examinations are administered by a regional rather than a national government, the local profession may be able to influence the pass rate—why else does it vary between 13 percent and 70 percent in Italy and by substantial amounts in Brazil?) Examinations often were introduced as a means of selecting judges and prosecutors from among aspiring law graduates and were extended to private practitioners only later—the time lag was 35 years in France and even longer in Japan. Besides, the large proportion of law graduates who seek employment in the civil service or in private enterprise often need not take these examinations.

There is substantial national variation in the difficulty of the examinations. In Germany, although half of all beginning law students drop out before the first state examination, 75 percent to 80 percent of those who take it pass the first time, half of the failures repeat, and half of the repeaters also pass, so that nearly 85 percent ultimately pass; more than 90 percent of those who sit for the second state examination (at the end of their apprenticeship) pass (Geck, 1977: 95; Braun & Birk, 1981: 74–75, 77). In France, by contrast, less than 20 percent of those obtaining a law degree in the mid-1960s passed the entrance examination for the institutes of professional training (Herzog, 1967: 73), although virtually all who began the training program obtained the CAPA. The most extreme example is Japan: even after completing a law degree and preparing for an additional three to five years, only 2 percent of those taking the entrance examination for the Institute of Legal Training and Research (ILTR) are admitted (and can become judges, prosecutors, or private practitioners).

In the common law world, apprenticeship with a private practitioner long performed the gatekeeping and training functions of the university in the civil law world: in the United States until the early 1900s, in England, Canada, Australia, and New Zealand until the 1960s. England, again, was the extreme: the five years of articles required of aspiring solicitors who had not attended university and the year of pupillage expected of barristers—for both of which apprentices had to pay substantial premiums and work without pay—remained substantial obstacles to entry at least until the 1950s.

Given the centrality of the university in the civil law world, it is not surprising that apprenticeship is less important and structured quite differently. In Brazil and Venezuela, it is optional and informal; only students with good family connections are able to arrange an apprenticeship; in Colombia, a year was required only in 1977 (Lynch, 1981: 91 n. 15). In France, the Netherlands, and Austria (Schreuer, 1981: 24–25), apprenticeship is the point at which legal careers diverge: judges and prosecutors take one path and private practitioners another. Even when several legal occupations share a common apprenticeship, the magistracy dominates the experience. In Germany, where all those who pass the first state examination are eligible for a two-and-a-half-year paid apprenticeship (*Referendarzeit*) administered by the state, most of the time is spent in civil and criminal courts, with prosecutors, and as civil servants and only a small portion with private practitioners. In Sweden in the 1960s, only 40 percent of law graduates could obtain apprenticeships, which were mandatory for judges and prosecutors but merely desirable for advocates (Ginsburg & Bruzelius, 1965: 57 n. 28). Only in a few countries, such as Belgium, France, and Italy, does the mandatory apprenticeship with a private practitioner allow local bars to control who enters private practice and how many do so.

Furthermore, universities resist efforts to expand apprenticeship—Brazilian law schools successfully opposed the Brazilian Bar Association's campaign to require apprenticeship, and there is a tendency to formalize postuniversity training—French avocats copied the institute created by the magistracy, although local bars retained control over instruction. Several German universities actually incorporated the Referendarzeit within their curricula during the reforms of the 1970s, although these experiments since have been terminated by the state. Several Dutch universities recently created one-year postgraduate professional training programs. Because students at such institutes typically are supported by the state (sometimes with a contribution from the profession), the requirement does not constitute the kind of economic barrier that apprenticeship long represented in England. An important exception is a private postgraduate law school established by Dutch corporations and law professors to prepare for international business practice, whose students pay a tuition ten times as high as that of Dutch law faculties.

The last obstacle to entering the profession is actually beginning to work. England, again, is the most extreme example of control by private practitioners. Barristers must obtain a tenancy in an existing chambers; the scarcity of physical space within the Inns of Court in London poses a major obstacle for all; women and racial minorities also encounter discrimination. Solicitors must be employed as assistants for at least three years before setting up practice on their own or in partnership. The hiring decisions of American law firms also limit entry to that sector, although nothing prevents those who pass the bar examination from practicing individually. In the civil law world, the number of entry-level positions as judges, prosecutors, and civil servants represents the single greatest constraint. As we will see below, civil law countries have had a strong (and distinctive) ideological antipathy to both large partnerships and the employment of private practitioners. Consequently, law graduates often enter private practice on their own, although they remain dependent on referrals from established lawyers (with whom they may share office space). Only a few countries place nominal limits on the activities of younger practitioners. In Italy, a lawyer must serve several years as a procuratore, with limited rights of audience, before becoming an avvocato. The Sveriges advokatsamfund (Swedish Lawyers' Association) requires five years of experience in private practice before admitting lawyers to membership, which is essential for appointment as a criminal defense counsel and for a successful civil practice (Ginsburg & Bruzelius, 1965: 65–66).

The very different structure of the legal professions in the common and civil law worlds is clearly reflected in the process by which entrants qualify. In the common law world, voluntary associations of private practitioners vigorously sought to control entry to private practice. In the civil law world, the state directly controlled employment in the magistracy and civil service. In the common law world, the organized private profession exercised control through apprenticeship, professional examinations, and limits on entry to private practice. In the civil law world, the state controlled entry to the university, and university and state examinations determined who could obtain employment in the public sector. In the common law world, formal education, whether by the private profession or the university, was vocational. In the civil law world, education at university (and even by private crammers) was highly abstract. In the common law world, entry to law faculties was relatively unrestricted until the 1960s but has become intensely competitive since then. In the civil law world, entry to university law faculties was extremely limited until the 1960s but has been opened to virtually all secondary-school graduates since then. Attrition is low in common law faculties, high in civil law faculties. Thus, the civil law world does not display the "professional project" so characteristic of the common law. Rather, the state is interested in obtaining highly qualified lawyer employees while controlling costs, and the university is torn between the desire to expand and the need to maintain educational quality. The size of the private profession is little more than an accidental by-product of these forces.

## THE STRUCTURE OF PRIVATE PRACTICE

We have seen how difficult it is to compare "legal professions" in the common and civil law worlds because they differ in terms of external boundaries, internal divisions, and foci. For the same reasons control over entry, which preoccupies the "professional project" in the common law world, assumes a very different form and significance in the civil law world. Even if we confine our attention to the sphere of private practice, which both worlds share, we should not be surprised to find considerable divergence between them, given the different location of private practice within the two worlds, as well as the different legal and social environments. The distinctiveness of the civil law world in this respect reflects its narrower, more traditional conception of private practice, which is manifest in the size and structure of law offices, the nature of lawyers' work, relations between lawyers and competing occupations, and the place of lawyers within the system of social stratification.

Lawyers everywhere began by practicing as individuals. In the common law world, some still do so: English barristers, Scottish advocates, Australian barristers in states where the profession is divided de jure or de facto, self-styled barristers sole in New Zealand, and many privately practicing lawyers and solicitors in all those countries, as well as in Canada and the United States. Yet individual practice is declining in the common law world. Although English barristers cannot pool profits, they must practice in chambers that share costs and exchange work; these now contain a median of sixteen barristers in London and twelve in the provinces, and today only about 10 percent of privately practicing solicitors are solo practitioners. At the other extreme, law firms are growing in size and in the proportion of the profession they contain. In the United States, 250 firms have more than 100 lawyers, and the largest have more than 500; 15 percent of private practitioners belong to firms with more than twenty lawyers, 22 percent to firms with more than ten, and 31 percent to firms with more than five.

Private practice in the civil law world recalls the common law world of the nineteenth century. Most lawyers practice alone: 51 percent of those in Lombardy in 1978 (Prandstraller, 1981), 84 percent of all French lawyers in 1981—70 percent even in Paris, 81 percent of Tokyo lawyers in 1962 (Brown, 1983: 276) and 73 percent of Japanese lawyers in the 1980s, 73.5 percent of German lawyers in 1967 (Rueschemeyer, 1973: 41

n. 47), 61 percent of lawyers in Rio de Janeiro, 57 percent of the Swedish Lawyers' Association in 1962 (Ginsburg & Bruzelius, 1965: 67 n. 81), and 40 percent of Dutch lawyers in 1960. Italian lawyers in the 1950s (Sereni, 1950: 1000) and French lawyers today (Le, 1982: 97) often practice out of offices located in their homes. Solo practice does not reflect economic forces so much as persistent loyalty to the ideology of professional "independence" and the desire of private practitioners to differentiate themselves from employed lawyers. Consequently, whereas solo practitioners generally occupy the base of the professional hierarchy in common law countries, they often constitute the elite in the civil law world: *litigantes de prestigio* in Venezuela and jurists, jurisconsults, and *pareceristas* (legal opinion writers) in Brazil.

All common lawyers (other than barristers sole in New Zealand and members of the Bar in the divided professions of England, Scotland, and some Australian states) always have been able to form true partnerships. Civil lawyers were allowed to do so only recently: individual *barreaux* (local professional organizations) could permit associations of up to five lawyers in France in 1954, but true partnerships without a numerical ceiling were allowed only in 1972 (von Mehren & Gordley, 1977: 143); Italian lawyers could not form loose professional associations until 1939 or partnerships until 1973, although busy lawyers always had "substitutes" (Sereni, 1950: 1004).

Even after the relaxation of formal restrictions, civil lawyers have been slow and cautious in forming partnerships. Most associations share only expenses, not profits: only 9 percent of Japanese lawyers in the 1980s belonged to true partnerships. Furthermore, most partnerships remain very small: 36 percent of Italian lawyers in Lombardy in 1978 were associated with only one or two others, compared to only 13 percent in larger firms (the rest practiced alone) (Prandstraller, 1981); in Tokyo in 1962, 13 percent of private practitioners were in firms of two or three, compared to only 5 percent in larger firms (Brown, 1983: 276); only 8 percent of law firms in Rio de Janeiro in 1980 contained more than five lawyers; partnerships in Germany emerged only in the 1960s; in 1967, 94 percent contained only two or three partners, and only 2 percent contained more than four lawyers; 20 percent of the firms consisted of relatives (Rueschemeyer, 1973: 42, 43 n.51); in 1985, 83 percent of all German firms still had fewer than four partners; in Sweden in the 1960s, most firms contained two to four lawyers (Ginsburg & Bruzelius, 1965: 52); in the Netherlands, 44 percent of all private practitioners were in firms of two to four lawyers in 1960, and 35 percent still were found in firms of this size in 1979; and in the early 1960s there were only 30 partnerships (containing a total of 70 lawyers) in Paris, compared to the 1,930 solo practitioners in that city, and there were only twenty other partnerships in the rest of France (Herzog,

1967: 81). The largest firms remained small by common law standards: no more than about twenty in Lombardy in 1978 (Prandstraller, 1981); a maximum of twenty by law in Spain; perhaps 300 lawyers in firms larger than five in Venezuela, only 10 of which have more than ten and the largest just thirty; only three Tokyo firms with more than ten lawyers in 1962, the largest of which contained fifteen (Brown, 1983: 276), and only about twenty that large today; only forty-seven firms with more than five members in Germany in 1972 (Wagner, 1985: 669) and no firm larger than nine in 1967 and only forty-two that large in 1985.

One reason for the slow growth is principled opposition to the employment of private practitioners. French avocats still maintain that the collaborateur (salaried lawyer) who has completed the stage (apprenticeship) is not an employee (Le, 1981). Whereas a fourth of all American private practitioners were associates (employees) in 1980, only 18 percent of Japanese bengoshi were in that category (Isoro, or apprentice lawyers); in France in 1968, a third of all private practitioners had no lawyer employees, and another third had only one (Herzog & Herzog, 1973: 464 n. 8); and in Sweden in 1961, only 128 out of the 1,138 members of the Sveriges Advocatsamfund (11 percent) were salaried employees in advocates' offices (Ginsburg & Bruzelius, 1965: 67 n. 81). Yet economic forces appear to be eroding this aversion to growth: some Brazilian firms contain as many as fifty lawyers; the proportion of German lawyers practicing alone fell from 50 percent in 1967 to 29 percent in 1985; 26 percent of Dutch private practitioners were in firms with more than nine in 1979 and 19 percent in firms with more than fifteen (one of these contained sixty-one lawyers).

The structure of law offices in the civil law world is closely connected to what those lawyers do. Here, again, ideology is a powerful force. Private practitioners are concerned, even obsessed, with a need to demonstrate their independence from the state, perhaps because it seems so dominant. As we have seen, judges, prosecutors, and civil servants represent the core of the profession. In Greece, even private practitioners are viewed as nonsalaried civil servants (OECD, 1984: 14). In civil law countries, the state generally creates and funds law faculties, sets curricula and examinations, regulates and funds apprenticeships, and even establishes professional associations. In reaction against this dominance, German lawyers define the essence of a professional as a private practitioner, and French lawyers stress their independence (ibid., 6–7). Civil lawyers do this, typically, by emphasizing their role as advocates, particularly as criminal defense counsel. Prior to 1972, the French division between the lower-court avoué (who was an officier ministériel) and the avocat (who belonged to a profession libérale) was partly a distinction between an officer of the court subordinated to the state and an independent practitioner totally committed to representing a client.

This ideological identification with advocacy is consistent with the distribution of work across substantive areas: French avocats in 1973/74 devoted 18 percent of their time to family law, 14 percent to personal injuries, 14 percent to commercial law, 10 percent to criminal law, and 8 percent to labor law (Karpik, 1985: 575); Japanese bengoshi spend more than a quarter of their time on debt collection and another 14 percent on damage claims. Few lawyers are able to specialize. Individuals and small businesses form a relatively large proportion of their clientele—80 percent in Colombia (Lynch, 1981: 93)—partly because larger businesses tend to employ law graduates to provide legal advice, negotiate, and draft documents. Perhaps because civil lawyers provide a narrower range of services, the public consults them less often: only 14 percent of a Norwegian sample in 1966 ever had used a lawyer, compared to 39 percent in Scotland (Royal Commission, 1980, 2: 55), 57 percent in England and Wales (Royal Commission, 1979, 2: 188), 66 percent in the United States (Curran, 1977: 185), and 74 percent in New Zealand. In third world countries such as Brazil and Venezuela, the poverty of most people prevents them from consulting lawyers.

As a result of all these factors, the caseloads of civil lawyers seem low: 334 matters per year in Germany (of which only 130 are litigated), 250 in the Netherlands (of which only 134 are completed), 37 open cases at a time in Japan, and an amazing 4.9 civil cases filed per lawyer per year in Italy—even fewer in central and southern Italy. Civil lawyers also may work fewer hours than their common law counterparts: 1,200 billable hours per year in Norway (1,800 working hours), compared to as many as 2,000 billable hours in the United States. Yet a recent survey of Bavarian Anwälte revealed that they worked an average of fifty to fifty-five hours per week, 48 weeks per year.

This powerful self-conception of private practitioners as advocates affects their relations with competing occupations. On one hand, they have sought to oust potential competitors from advocacy, especially during periods when the supply of lawyers has been increasing. In 1981 Germany refused to issue any further licenses to the Rechtsbeistände (legal advisers who lack a law degree but can appear in local courts), although the remaining 3,500 were allowed to practice until they retired; and Brazil has seen the disappearance of provisional lawyers, who previously practiced in primary courts. In contrast, civil lawyers have allowed competitors to encroach on functions that fall outside their narrow self-definition. In France, nonlawyers dominate the labor court (conseil des prud'hommes) and justices of the peace (Herzog, 1967: 66–67); in Germany, they may appear in tax, administrative, social insurance, and labor courts. Everywhere private practitioners have lost the counseling function to others: notaries in all countries, Syndici (house counsel) in Germany, conseils juridiques and juristes d'entreprises in France, bachelors of commerce and accountants in Norway, *dottori commercialisti* in Italy (Certoma, 1985: 59–61), *despachantes* in Brazil, and a host of occupations in Japan— judicial scriveners, administrative scriveners, patent attorneys, tax attorneys, and even illegal accident specialists (Ramseyer, 1986; Brown, 1983). In some countries, such as France and Switzerland, relinquishing the role of counselor was a conscious decision. In France, the Syndicat national des avocats accused the rival Confédération syndicale des avocats of the unforgiveable sin of "modernism"—encouraging avocats to abandon their traditional role as "auxiliaires de justice" for the compromised role of "auxiliaires d'enterprise" (Le, 1982: 102).

The structure of law offices, the functions performed, the nature of the clientele, and the division of labor with other occupations all affect the location of private practitioners within the system of professional and social stratification. In the common law world, private practitioners tend to bifurcate into a small elite, consisting of large firm lawyers serving a corporate clientele (together with the most successful advocates in the divided professions) and a large base of solo and small-firm practitioners serving individuals and smaller businesses. These two "hemispheres" (Heinz & Laumann, 1982) often come from different backgrounds, obtain different legal educations, perform different functions, participate in different professional associations, and enjoy vastly different levels of prestige and income, with the elite earning twenty times as much as the base.

Because most private practitioners in the civil law world perform the same fairly narrow range of functions, practice alone or in small partnerships, and do not extract surplus value from employed lawyers, the spectrum of prestige and income is considerably narrower (Rueschemeyer [1973: 54], but see Karpik [1985]). In Norway, senior lawyers earn only about twice as much as beginners. Civil lawyers as a group appear to do less well economically than common lawyers, compared to the national income distributions: in France in 1976, 316 members of the Paris Bar (7 percent) declared no income, and 3,170 (67 percent) declared less than $20,000 (Le, 1982: 99); in the Netherlands, private practitioners earned less than physicians (whether general practitioners or specialists), pharmacists, notaries, dentists, and even veterinarians. Yet in poorer third world countries such as Brazil, Venezuela, or Colombia (Lynch, 1981: 55–56), private practitioners remain at the very top of the national income scale.

## CONTROL OVER THE MARKET FOR LAWYERS' SERVICES

In the common law world, professions dominated by private practitioners and exposed to market forces sought to control production *by* producers once they had attained sufficient control over the production *of* producers.

In the civil law world, this feature of the "professional project" takes a different form for two reasons. First, the state plays a larger role in the former effort just as it did in the latter. Second, private practitioners in the civil law world seem more concerned to distance themselves from the pursuit of commercial advantage and to preserve their status. Control over the market for lawyers' services takes the form of three kinds of restraint on competition: between those with legal training and those without any, among legal occupations, and within private practice.

We saw above that civil lawyers view themselves primarily as advocates. Consequently, it is not surprising that advocacy is the core of their monopoly, vigorously defended against intruders. Indeed, countries such as Germany, France, Italy (Certoma, 1985: 49), and Venezuela compel litigants to retain a qualified advocate in most matters, prohibiting self-representation. Germany did so during the depression, in a conscious attempt to expand the market for Anwälte (Reifner, 1986: 118). Yet in Sweden, lawyers lack even a monopoly of advocacy (OECD, 1984: 32–33); there were a hundred "juridical bureaus" (juridiska byråer) in Stockholm in the early 1960s, staffed by laypersons or law graduates not admitted to practice and offering legal advice and representation (Ginsburg & Bruzelius, 1965: 50, 52). Only members of the Sveriges advokatsamfund can use the title "advokat" or be appointed as criminal defense counsel and reimbursed by the state (ibid., 63, 66); but when the Sveriges advokatsamfund persuaded private legal expense insurance companies to deny reimbursement to nonmembers, the state struck down the restrictive practice (OECD, 1984: 34). Similarly, the Danish Bar Council was forbidden to require that creditors refer debtors to lawyers for the administration of estates (ibid.). The monopoly of advocacy typically does not apply to lower courts or administrative tribunals (for Germany, see von Mehren & Gordley [1977: 148–149]); efforts to extend it in Brazil failed in 1963 and again in 1980. Finally, whereas lawyers in the United States and some Canadian provinces have a formal (if ineffective) monopoly over legal advice, most civil lawyers enjoy no such protection. German lawyers obtained it during the Nazi era (Reifner, 1986: 119), but contemporaneous efforts failed in Norway, as did those by French avocats in the 1950s.

Even in the relatively unitary professions of the common law world there are boundary disputes between barristers and solicitors and between private practitioners and employed lawyers. Given the more numerous divisions within the civil law world and the less dominant role of private practice, it is not surprising that such controversies are more frequent and heated. Because civil lawyers have chosen to defend the core of advocacy while surrendering the periphery of advice, powerful competitors have occupied the latter realm. Although French conseils juridiques are only a third as numerous as avocats, they long have been able to assume a corporate form, and many of these firms have become quite large, whereas avocats only recently began to form small partnerships; sociétés fiduciaires of conseils juridiques may have branch offices in the principal French cities, whereas even professional civil associations of avocats are limited to a single office (Herzog & Herzog, 1973: 464). In Japan, as we have seen, bengoshi have exclusive rights of audience in court, but outside it they confront numerous competitors. In both these countries, the competing occupations have sought to professionalize. The 1971 reform of the French legal professions gave conseils juridiques the exclusive right to use that title, while requiring them to obtain the same law degree as an avocat (license) and complete a similar three-year apprenticeship; it also disqualified them from commercial activities (Herzog & Herzog, 1973: 478–482). In Japan, many of the competing occupations are almost as exclusive as bengoshi. Judicial scriveners, for instance, must take an examination whose pass rate is only 2 percent, are limited to a single office, and were allowed to form partnerships only in 1967 (Brown, 1983: 354–359). Pass rates for tax and patent attorneys are equally low (ibid., 403, 430; Ramseyer, 1986: 508–509).

One response to competition has been to seek unification. The divisions between barrister and solicitor did not survive export to the United States or Canada, although traces are found in New Zealand and some Australian states, but the English Bar has repulsed repeated calls for fusion. The civil law distinction between those who draft pleadings and take formal responsibility for the proceedings (avoués, *procuratori*, *procuradores*) and those who argue in court (avocats, avvocati, *abogados*) has been less resilient. The former category has disappeared everywhere except in the higher French courts and in Spain. Yet the role of notary, which is almost vestigial in the common law world, remains a wholly independent and powerful profession throughout the civil law world. In addition, the ambitious attempt to merge all the French legal professions, begun in the 1950s, terminated in 1971 by incorporating only the avoués in lower courts (whose numbers had declined from 3,500 in 1900 to about 1,500) and the *agréés* in commercial courts (who totaled only 150) (Herzog & Herzog, 1973: 465, 467 n. 25). An important obstacle to absorbing the other occupations was their performance of functions deemed inconsistent with the image of a liberal profession.

The last category of restrictive practices is directed at competition among lawyers. Until recently, virtually all countries, both common and civil law, excluded noncitizens from their legal professions (OECD, 1984: 37–38, 41; Schreuer, 1981: 25–26; Herzog & Herzog, 1973: 475). The European Economic Community (EEC), however, prohibits such obstacles to the free movement of services, including legal services, among member states (although this ruling has not been applied to notarial services) (OECD, 1984: 39). Although a member country still can require foreign nationals who wish to enter its own legal profession to meet all the requirements demanded of citizens, it cannot prevent those who belong to legal professions in other EEC countries from practicing law as long as they correctly identify the profession to which they belong. Consequently, large numbers of foreign lawyers are practicing in Paris as conseils juridiques (Le, 1982: 98). Even in Japan, where the extraordinary difficulty of the ILTR entrance examination, particularly for nonnative speakers, has excluded virtually all foreigners, reciprocal agreements now admit foreign lawyers to practice (Ramseyer, 1986; Farnsworth, 1987); the first three new American lawyers began practice in Tokyo on May 21, 1987 (*New York Times*, 22 May 1987, p. 5).

Restrictions on competition among domestic lawyers appear to be directed almost as much to maintaining a "professional" self-image and preserving social status as they are to securing economic gains. The constraints on "incompatibility" are most striking to an observer from the common law world, where they limit the bar only in divided professions. In the civil law world, by contrast, they apply to all private practitioners and are far more extensive. In Italy in the 1950s and 1960s, private practitioners could not enter any form of employment or be notaries, members of the clergy, merchants, business executives, journalists, judges, prosecutors, or civil servants (Sereni, 1950: 1002; Cappelletti et al., 1967: 93). In France, avocats could not engage in any business activities, accept employment, or hold public office; they could serve as directors of a corporation only with the permission of their barreau and then could not act as legal counsel or advocate for the corporation (Herzog & Herzog, 1973: 472; Le, 1982: 79, 82). German Anwälte who practice as Syndici cannot appear in court if they devote more than half their time to their employment. One reason for this limitation is the greater emphasis that German lawyers (compared to American) place on their independence from clients (Luban, 1984: 266). Yet Norwegian jurists employed full time by private enterprises still can engage in advocacy if they contribute to the bar association damages fund.

A second important restriction is geographic. In federal common law polities (the United States, Canada, and Australia), lawyers can practice only in the states or provinces to which they have been admitted, a limitation justified by local variation in the law. In the unitary civil law polities, similar restrictions lack even this weak justification. In Germany, a lawyer can appear only in a single Landgericht and the Amstgerichte subordinate to it. In France, lawyers can appear only before the courts of the barreau to which they belong, although they can plead anywhere. In Italy, less experienced lawyers are limited geographically (Certoma, 1985: 43–45). In Spain, lawyers may practice only in the courts of their Colegio but may join as many Colegios as they wish. Sometimes the restrictions are vertical as well as horizontal: German lawyers must choose between the Landgericht and the Oberlandgericht; only the more experienced Italian lawyers can appear before the higher courts (ibid.). These limitations on advocacy are supplemented by others on office location (which again have counterparts in divided common law bars). Lawyers in France, Germany, Denmark, and Japan must practice from a single office situated within the local bar to which they belong.

Most legal professions always have prohibited their members from engaging in any form of self-promotion, although the Scandinavian countries have allowed limited advertising (OECD, 1984: 53). In the common law world, the United States was the first to relax this restraint in 1977, quickly followed by England, Scotland, Canada, Australia, and New Zealand. Civil law professions, acutely concerned with their noncommercial image, thus far have resisted this trend, although it is widely acknowledged that clients are channeled to lawyers by numerous intermediaries, including touts, police, insurance companies, and trade unions. Lawyers still might be able to engage in some price competition without resort to advertising. In many civil law countries (such as Germany and Italy), however, this is precluded by extensive state regulation of fees for advocacy. Professional associations often promulgate fee schedules that may cover noncontentious matters as well, although these rarely are binding and sometimes are wholly ineffective (OECD, 1984: 60–61). The Venezuelan legal profession adopted a fee schedule in 1971, and the Paris Bar published an elaborate schedule in 1979 (Le, 1982: 76–78), both presumably in response to the threat of competition that had been intensified by the rapid growth in numbers. Sometimes these schedules are exempt from antitrust scrutiny because of the official status of the professional association (ibid., 18). But in both Denmark and France the state has struck down fee schedules as anticompetitive (ibid., 21).

## THE CREATION OF DEMAND

In the common law world, the erosion of control over supply (which I discuss below) coincided with growing interest in stimulating demand, by both private and public means. I mentioned above the liberalization of rules against individual advertising; professional associations also engaged in collective advertising and established lawyer referral services. True, it was the state, not the profession, that initiated legal aid programs: in England in 1950, in the United States in 1965, and in Canada, Australia, and New Zealand at about the same time. Yet if the profession initially was passive and even suspicious, it soon became an enthusiastic supporter. Everywhere except the United States, many private practitioners now depend on publicly subsidized demand for a significant portion of their incomes; and in the United States, the organized profession has sought to divert federal funds from salaried lawyers to private practitioners (see generally Abel [1985]).

Civil lawyers have been far more conservative about creating demand, just as they have been about other aspects of private practice. No professional association has engaged in collective advertising, and no country has liberalized the rules prohibiting individual advertising (nor have Scandinavian lawyers taken much advantage of their greater freedom to advertise). Because of their strong attachment to the role of advocate, civil lawyers have been reluctant to expand their market as counselors. Indeed, their inaction has conceded much of this market to competitors (both private practitioners and company employees), who are well positioned to retain it in terms of location, structure of practice, skills, and visibility. Yet efforts by French avocats to inform the public of their usefulness as counselors (Le, 1982: 103) and by Belgian notaries to stimulate demand suggest that this passivity may be changing as a result of an oversupply of private practitioners.

With some notable exceptions, civil lawyers have been equally reluctant to seek state subsidies for demand. Here the reasons are more complex and various. Many third world countries lack either the resources or the political will to ensure legal representation for the vast mass of the population too poor to purchase services on the market. In those predominately Catholic countries where divorce is either illegal or socially disapproved (Italy, Spain, and Latin America), the staple of legal aid practice is unavailable. Although divorce is common in Japan, 89 percent of all divorces occur by consent and do not require a lawyer. In the Netherlands, by contrast, the divorce rate rose from 5,000 in 1960 to 70,000 in 1982 (following the liberalization of the law in 1971) and accounts for more than half of all legal aid cases. As a result, the legal aid caseload grew from 18,000 in 1958 (the year after the program was established) to 90,000 in 1980. Nor is it coincidental that French avocats became interested in legal aid when French divorce law was reformed. Civil litigation rates in many of these countries are low not just because the population lacks the money to hire lawyers and divorce is unavailable but also because people lack confidence in the judicial system, perceiving it as intolerably slow and arbitrary.

Several constituencies have been not only indifferent to legal aid but actually hostile. The legal profession has several reasons for suspicion. French lawyers feared that they would lose the "symbolic capital" they generated by offering their services charitably—a burden they were willing to sustain because it had been declining (few clients sought such services) and fell mostly on apprentices. The material significance of such schemes may be judged from the fact that they accounted for only 0.2

percent of civil cases in Italy in 1979. The approximately 32,000 Spanish lawyers handle a total of only 100,000 legally aided criminal cases and 50,000 arraignments per year. Even after the creation of legal aid the Paris Bar continued to require its members to provide free services once a year "in the interest of the public and for the good image of the Paris Bar" (Le, 1982: 101 n. 221). French lawyers also feared that state control of legal aid payments would lead to state control over the fees paid by private clients (Herzog & Herzog, 1973: 487). When private practitioners do endorse legal aid, they naturally want to do the work themselves; the state, by contrast, often prefers to employ lawyers, which facilitates state fiscal and political control. Spain and many Latin American countries already have "public attorneys" with a vested interest in representing the members of dependent groups (the poor, women, children, and ethnic minorities). In the absence of effective systems of state legal aid, trade unions, political parties, and churches advise their members and help them obtain legal representation. These institutions may oppose state action as a threat to the political loyalty that their own assistance engenders. Some of the most innovative programs were established by students and political activists, who remain intensely suspicious of state intervention.

Yet despite this indifference and hostility on the part of both the profession and powerful private entities, some growth of state-funded legal aid seems inevitable. Programs initiated by volunteers eventually decline without external finance and institutional support. The recent rapid growth in the number of lawyers encourages interest in legal aid: surely it is not fortuitous that the Netherlands, which has nearly four times as many lawyers per population as Belgium (which it otherwise resembles in many respects), established a legal aid program nearly twenty years earlier. Once legal aid is introduced, private practitioners quickly become dependent on it—half of the caseload of rural French avocats now consists of legally aided matters (Le, 1982: 101). In the Netherlands, the judicare budget rose from Dutch florin (DFl) 13 million in 1970 to DFl 132 million in 1980, and the total legal aid budget (including staffed offices) reached DFl 225 million in 1982. Legal aid gradually is being extended to both civil and criminal matters, minor crimes as well as major, and advice as well as advocacy. Indeed, the concern of private practitioners becomes how to dissuade the state from cutting costs by delegalizing such matters as divorce.

## PROFESSIONAL ASSOCIATIONS

In the common law world, the association of private practitioners was the indispensable mechanism for limiting entry, enhancing status, restricting competition, and asserting a claim to self-regulation. The English legal profession is virtually synonymous with the Inns of Court (and its post-war complements, the Senate and the General Council of the Bar) and the national and local law societies; the legal profession in the United States is inconceivable without the American Bar Association, state bar associations, and those of cities and counties. In the civil law world, by contrast, professional associations are far less salient to the core of the legal profession—judges, prosecutors, and civil servants—or to the numerous law graduates employed in business. These often have their own organizations, such as the Deutscher Richterbund for German judges and prosecutors. In any case, they are unconcerned with controlling entry, enhancing status, limiting competition, or regulating themselves: their employer (whether public or private) does all this for them. As we have seen, private practitioners in the civil law world also exercise less influence in these respects; the nature of their professional associations is one of the reasons.

In the civil law world, associations of private practitioners began as local guilds and retained this form long after powerful national bodies had emerged in the common law world. In some instances these local organizations were created by and subordinated to the state. French *ordres des avocats* originally were established by the *parlements* (composite legislative, executive, and judicial bodies); even after they gained independence in the eighteenth century, their decisions concerning admission to the bar could be appealed to the courts (Le, 1982: 67 n. 31). When Japanese *bengoshi* were required to join local associations in 1880, these were subordinated to the chief prosecutor of the district (Brown, 1983: 265). Because of their medieval origins and connotations, local guilds were temporarily suppressed by the eighteenth- and nineteenth-century bourgeois revolutions in many countries, including France, Switzerland, and Venezuela. The attempt to create a Brazilian national association in 1880 was rejected by a Chamber of Deputies hostile to professional privilege. Even where local associations survived or revived, they failed to form a national organization for several reasons: the lack of unity in the country itself (e.g., in Italy, Germany, and Spain), the state's concern to forestall potential opposition, and rivalries between the dominant capital and the provincial bars (e.g., in France).

National associations emerged late: in France in 1902, Brazil in 1930, Italy in 1944, the Netherlands in 1952, and Belgium in 1968. Colombia still has none (Lynch, 1981: 24 n. 99). In many instances these were established by and subordinated to the state: for example, Brazil, the Netherlands, Belgium, and Greece (OECD, 1984: 14). The Fascists created the Italian national bar association in 1944 and placed it under the Ministry of Grace and Justice (Certoma, 1985: 46). The only organization that ever encompassed all German jurists was Der Bund Nationalsozialistischer Deutscher Juristen (Rueschemeyer, 1973: 59 n. 90). Unofficial national groups did emerge (sometimes before the official ones), but many were mere umbrellas of local bars (as in France or Venezuela) or concerned largely with cultural and social activities (as in the Institute for the Order of Lawyers in Brazil). Membership varied from as many as two-thirds of all Swedish jurists and three-fourths of all law students in the Sveriges juristforbund in 1961 (Ginsburg & Bruzelius, 1965: 68 n. 88) and about two-thirds of all Germany Anwälte in the Deutsche Anwaltsverein (Rueschemeyer, 1973: 60) to as few as 10 percent of Mexican lawyers (MacDonald, 1986: 208). The state's fear that professional associations might become oppositional foci was confirmed in Spain—where the Colegios of Madrid and Barcelona attacked Franco toward the end of his regime—and in Brazil, where the national bar association criticized military rule and has become an important force for democratization. Yet, the official German bar associations offered virtually no resistance to Nazism, actively collaborating in the exclusion of Jewish lawyers (Rueschemeyer, 1973: 180–182; Reifner, 1986), and the voluntary Deutsche Anwaltverein was suppressed by the Nazis in 1933.

The structure of professional associations shaped the regulation of private practitioners. Local associations used largely informal mechanisms that remained fairly effective as long as those bodies were small (in Germany in 1960, the Anwaltskammern ranged between 100 and 2,300 members) (Rueschemeyer, 1973: 60). With the gradual shift of authority from local private bars to national official associations, regulation has been formalized. Furthermore, the state plays a larger role than it does in the common law world. Although private associations of advocates discipline their members in Denmark, Norway, and Sweden, those penalized can ignore the sanctions unless the state chooses to reinforce them by expelling the offender from practice (OECD, 1984: 14). In Switzerland, Germany, and Italy, disciplinary bodies either are state agencies or contain only a minority of private practitioners. It is interesting (if discouraging) that discipline seems no stricter when imposed by external authorities than when exercised by the profession itself. In Spain, 24 private practitioners were punished in 1983 and 30 in 1984, out of the 10,000 in Madrid; 24 were punished in 1983 and 32 in 1984 out of the 5,000 in Barcelona. In Sweden in 1960, the Sveriges advokatsamfund expelled only 2 of its more than 1,200 members, warned 2 others, and issued reminders to 26 (Ginsburg & Bruzelius, 1965: 68 n. 86). Perhaps because of their preoccupation with advocacy, civil lawyers (like barristers in divided common law professions) have been largely exempt from malpractice liability. In Italy, lawyers are liable only for gross negligence (Sereni, 1950: 1003). In France, avocats were required to obtain malpractice insurance only after they merged with avoués in 1971 and began to handle client funds (Herzog & Herzog, 1973: 471–472). Barcelona lawyers obtained a group malpractice insurance policy only in 1985. If civil lawyers are more thoroughly subordinated to state control than their common law counterparts, that appears to offer them some protection from public scrutiny.

## THE POSTWAR TRANSFORMATION: ARE CIVIL LAW AND COMMON LAW PROFESSIONS CONVERGING?

We have seen that civil and common law legal professions differ in fundamental ways: the very notion of a legal profession, the nature and prominence of internal divisions, influences on the number and characteristics of entrants, the structures of private practice, restraints on competition, interest in stimulating demand, and the form and function of professional associations. In the postwar period, and especially since the mid-1960s, legal professions in both worlds have experienced a profound transformation: numbers have increased rapidly, demographic composition has altered, lawyers have been redistributed across roles, the structure of private practice is being transformed, new professional associations are emerging, and old ones are assuming new tasks. To the extent that similar forces are producing these changes, the historical differences between the two worlds may be diminishing.

### THE NUMBERS EXPLOSION

Almost all capitalist nations have experienced rapid growth in the size of their legal professions in the last two decades. The rate of expansion is particularly noteworthy because it follows a long period of stasis. In Germany, there was virtually no change in the ratio of population to lawyers between the period following the repeal of the numerus clausus in 1879 and the drop in the mid-1960s. In the Netherlands, the population per private practitioner actually increased from 3,700 in 1850 to 7,700 in 1920, and as late as 1970 it had fallen to only 6,200. In France, there were 7,321 avocats in 1937 but only 6,565 in 1960; even more dramatically, the number of *stagiaires* (apprentice private practitioners) had fallen from 2,464 to 923 between these dates (Herzog, 1967: 75 n. 36). Similar stasis characterized the common law world: the ratio of population to lawyers in the United States was the same in 1951 as it had been in 1900; in England, the *number* of solicitors in 1948 was almost exactly what it had been in 1890 despite the substantial increase in population.

Although the university made a major contribution to the growth of the legal profession in both worlds, the reasons were somewhat different. In most common law countries, the university displaced apprenticeship as the gatekeeper to practice only after World War II. (The United States and Scotland are exceptions.) In Australia and Canada this displacement was total; in Scotland, the university recently assumed responsibility for postgraduate vocational training as well. Only in England is apprenticeship still a major barrier. In the civil law world, where the university always had responsibility for legal education, other changes occurred. Entry, which had been limited to the graduates of elite academic secondary schools, was offered to all secondary-school graduates. In Germany, the number who qualified for university rose from 59,000 in 1962 to 104,000 in 1974 (Geck, 1977: 93); whereas 4 percent of the relevant age cohort was enrolled in university in 1960, 25 percent was enrolled in 1981. Existing universities expanded, and new ones were established. This occurred even more rapidly where the private sector participated, as in Japan: the twelve public and twenty-eight private law faculties in 1960 multiplied to twenty-three public and sixty-five private in 1980, while the proportion of students enrolled in public institutions declined from 12 percent to 8 percent (Brown, 1983: 231). There is a striking parallel to the American experience during the first three decades of this century in both the rate of expansion and the role of private institutions.

Public universities charged little or no tuition, and most countries provided means-tested support for living expenses. The rate of increase in law student enrollments often exceeded that in the university as a whole because other popular subjects imposed quotas, forcing many to study law as a second or third choice. Furthermore, as we will see below, law attracted a large proportion of the women who began attending university in increasing numbers during the 1960s. These push factors were complemented by the expansion of both the private economy and the state, which pulled secondary-school graduates into legal careers.

The increase in law student enrollments was unprecedented and extraordinary (see table 1.2). In the common law world it was most dramatic in those countries experiencing a rapid shift from apprenticeship to the university (England and Wales, Canada, Australia, and New Zealand) and somewhat less marked where the university already was the sole mode of entry (the United States—which had displayed a similar increase when the academy displaced apprenticeship in the early twentieth century—and Scotland). Yet even these high rates of increase were dwarfed by those in the civil law world. Although the latter peaked at different times in the years since 1960, depending on the growth of universities, almost everywhere they exceeded the rates of growth in the common law world. (Germany and Japan appear to be exceptions.) In both worlds, larger numbers of entrants rapidly expanded the number of private practitioners (see table 1.3). Because most law graduates in the common law world already were engaged in private practice, the rate of increase there was lower. In the civil law world, the number of places in the magistracy and the civil service remained fairly constant, forcing private practice (and private employment) to expand more rapidly (as in France, Brazil, Belgium, and the Netherlands). Yet it is striking that the number of private practitioners in Italy grew so slowly, perhaps because the market already was saturated, given the low level of confidence in the courts and the paucity of civil cases. In Japan, the difficult entrance examination for the Institute of Legal Training and Research also restrained growth.

The rapid increase in entry inevitably stimulated those already qualified to seek to tighten control over supply. In the common law world, mechanisms to do so already were in place: limits on enrollment in law faculties and sometimes in postgraduate vocational training programs; professional examinations (controlled by private professional associations) and limits on the number of places for apprentices and on the initial jobs or practice opportunities for those fully qualified. Many American states lowered the pass rates on their bar examinations in the 1980s. It is noteworthy that law student enrollments stopped growing in 1976 in the United States, 1978 in Scotland, 1979 in Canada, 1980 in Australia, and 1984 in Auckland, New Zealand.

In the civil law world, the situation may have been more acute because the fiscal crisis of the state precluded any expansion of public sector employment. University enrollments also ceased to grow, less because places were limited than because students lacked the financial means or the economic incentive to earn a degree that offered no job. Germany substituted loans for student grants. Where enrollment was capped, the moving force was not private practitioners protecting their economic interests but university professors seeking to maintain educational quality. When the Norwegian government refused to provide funds to hire additional teachers to meet rising enrollment, the Oslo University Law Faculty cut the number of entering students in half.

Yet there were precedents for private practitioners to seek to control entry. In Germany, associations of private practitioners had responded to the depression by supporting the expulsion of Jewish attorneys (which reduced the number in practice from 19,276 in 1919 to 12,030 in 1933) and urging a numerus clausus and the expulsion of women, younger and older attorneys, and socialists and communists (Reifner, 1986: 114–117). A contemporaneous account in the *New York Times* of 11 December 1932 (quoted without comment but apparent sympathy by the journal of the National Conference of Bar Examiners in the United States) is worth excerpting:

The German bar threatens to become engulfed in a maelstrom of economic depression which is already menacing the other professions. The "proletarianization" of the bar and "radicalization" of the growing body of law students are some of the menaces envisaged by the leaders of the profession.

The German Bar Association has just adopted a resolution demanding that for the next three years there shall be no admissions to the bar and that, when this complete closure has been lifted, in 1936, only a limited number of candidates shall be admitted in any year.... Dr. Rudolf Dix, president of the German Bar Association, frankly admits the proposed measure was dictated by desperation. He defends it as a stern necessity if the legal profession is to be saved from utter pauperization.... One-third of the German lawyers earn less than $1,400 a year and 16 percent earn $600 or less.... Overcrowding the bar is the more distressing because of the jamming of law schools. The number of students has doubled since the war, and it was 20,800 last year.

Dr. Dix contends there is more at stake than the issue of material existence.

"Proletarianization of the bar must inevitably lead to its decay in competence and a loss of integrity," he said. "And if the bar decays justice also decays. This means an end of the lawfully ordered existence of a nation. For Germany especially the independent incorruptible administration of justice is a life-and-death matter." (2 *Bar Examiner* 83–84 [1933])

Several months later the same journal quoted a *New York Times* account of events in Greece:

Forcible reduction of the number of lawyers practicing in Greece is the object of legislation now being worked out by the Minister of Justice.... Greece will try to force its too abundant lawyers into special classes of practice, designated by the courts before which they are licensed to appear. Only a fixed number will be allowed to argue before each tribunal.

Besides limitation of notarial work and the other more or less clerical by-practices of the law, the number of lawyers in the whole country will be limited. At present there are more than 7,000 lawyers in Greece, or about one to every 1,000 inhabitants, the highest percentage in the Balkans. Henceforward retirement from practice will be obligatory after an age is reached that the government, with some difficulty, is now attempting to fix. No limit is to be be placed on the number of students of law, but young law graduates will have to wait for vacancies at the bar of their selected tribunal before they can be begin to practice. (3 *Bar Examiner* 23 [1933])

Even during the postwar boom, when the number of German law students nearly doubled between 1954 and 1959, bar associations mounted a leaflet campaign exaggerating the problem of overcrowding and the low incomes of Anwälte, which resulted in a 69 percent decline in the size of the entering class in 1960 (Rueschemeyer, 1973: 102 n. 83).

Rapid growth since the 1960s has excited similar responses. In France in 1981, the pass rate on the entrance examination for the vocational year required of all private practitioners (the CAPA) fell to 20 percent, reducing the number of entrants by half. The 1983 biannual meeting of the Deutsche Anwaltsverein focused on the "flood of Anwälte" (Anwaltsschwemme), and the association began circulating pamphlets warning school leavers against studying law. The Dutch Bar Association (unsuccessfully) has sought the introduction of a state examination and a mandatory postgraduate course. The Brazilian Bar Association (OAB) persuaded the Federal Council of Education to disapprove the establishment of any law faculties and to freeze the number of places at existing schools. Although this was done in the name of educational quality, it cannot be irrelevant that the number of schools had increased by nearly 50 percent between 1970 and 1980. In Colombia, where sixteen of the twenty-seven law schools were founded after 1950 (eight after 1970), a 1974 presidential decree made it more difficult to create new law faculties (Lynch, 1981: 28 n. 37). One effect of the shared experience of expansion thus was to make civil lawyers resemble their common law counterparts in their interest in controlling supply. Additional consequences are traced in the following sections.

## DEMOGRAPHIC CHANGES

The rapid rate of growth was accompanied by changes in the composition of the legal profession. By far the most dramatic was the entry of women. Until the 1960s, women accounted for an insignificant fraction of the profession. Many countries in both common and civil law worlds excluded them until the beginning of the twentieth century. Germany allowed women to become private practitioners in 1922, but the Nazis expelled them again in 1936. Women were not admitted to the French magistracy until after World War II; the first woman judge in the Netherlands was appointed in 1947; and Italian women could not become judges until 1963 (Cappelletti et al., 1967: 104). Even after the legal barriers fell, social obstacles remained. Two factors have lowered these in the last two decades: the feminist movement, and the university, which displaced or reduced the importance of apprenticeship in much of the common law world and rapidly expanded in both worlds. Because civil law faculties offered a liberal arts education rather than the more vocational training found in common law faculties, women entered the former earlier than the latter. Women represented 8 percent of students in the Faculty of Law and Political Science in Paris in 1953/54 and 26 percent as early as 1958/59 (Herzog, 1967: 70 n. 18). Women represented 21 percent of law students in the Netherlands in 1969. Growth was slower in other countries: women represented 30 percent of university students but only 7 percent of law students in Germany in 1966.

With very few exceptions, women now constitute at least a third of all law students, and in some countries they are more than half. This dramatic transformation has important implications. First, much of the growth in law student enrollments is attributable to the entry of women. The fact that the number of men did not increase proportionally and in some countries remained constant or even declined provides some evidence that university enrollment functioned as a form of supply control (since it is unlikely that the proportion of qualified male secondary-school graduates seeking a law degree actually decreased). Second, the fact that the proportion of women has stabilized suggests that this push factor in the growth of legal professions was self-limiting, a conclusion confirmed by the recent leveling off of the overall rate of growth.

The success of women as law students, however, does not ensure that they will be equally distributed across professional roles. Many who graduate may not enter the profession at all. In Japan, women constituted 3 percent of those passing the entrance examination for the Institute of Legal Training and Research in the 1950s, 5 percent between 1965 and 1975, and still only 10 percent today. They are even less well represented in adjacent occupations: 5 percent of judicial scriveners, less than 3 percent of tax attorneys, and less than 2 percent of patent attorneys (Brown, 1983: 362, 409, 433). By contrast, women represented a third of all French stagiaires in 1960 and a quarter of all avocats in Paris and its suburbs (Herzog, 1967: 82 n. 83); by 1983, they were a third of all avocats; although women constituted only 4 percent of all Italian lawyers in 1966, they made up 41 percent of Italian law students and 35 percent of law graduates in 1980; and in 1978 they represented a third of praticanti procuratori (apprentice private practitioners) in Lombardy and 11 percent of Lombard lawyers (Prandstraller, 1967, 1981; de Francisis, 1986: 159).

In both common and civil law worlds, women appear to prefer employment over private practice (because the hours are limited) and the public sector over the private (because of its greater universalism). Consequently, they remain severely underrepresented in the more prestigious and rewarding forms of private practice: they constituted only 2 percent of Dutch notaries in 1979; there were practically no women avoués in Paris in 1960, when women constituted a quarter of all avocats (Herzog, 1967: 85). Today, women are overrepresented in the Paris suburbs (which generally are poorer than the inner city). Even after a quarter century of significant representation among avocats, they represented only 2 percent of all bâtonniers (heads of local bar associations).

The judiciary lies at the other extreme because of its fixed hours and generous leave policies and, most of all, because recent graduates are appointed on the basis of academic performance in the civil law world (whereas in the common law world judicial appointments reward success in private practice and political connections). Women constituted 32 percent of Dutch apprentice judges in 1979 (compared to 24 percent of apprentice private practitioners) and 21 percent of French judges in 1982 (Ehrmann, 1983: 177). They represented 56 percent of the graduates of the Ecole Nationale de la Magistrature in 1984 and 1985 (Soulez Larivière, 1987: 54). Given the respect accorded judges in the civil law world, women law graduates may be better situated to achieve equality there than they are in the common law world, where private practice remains the route to career success.

Rapid expansion of the profession inevitably has made it more youthful (except in Italy and Japan, where growth has been slower). In the common law world, this has had the greatest impact on private practitioners, with important implications for their professional associations. Age, like gender, has had no effect on the common law judiciary, which still is appointed largely from older male private practitioners. In the civil law world, the most dramatic impact may have been on the judiciary: 44 percent of French judges were less than thirty-five years old in 1982 (Ehrmann, 1983: 177).

These changes in gender and age have not been accompanied by any significant shift in class background. This is particularly noteworthy because an explicit purpose of expanding university enrollment was to reduce class privilege. Yet the fact that as many as half the positions in law faculties were filled by women has preserved the upper-class composition of the profession for two reasons: the social obstacles women still must overcome are more easily surmounted by those from privileged backgrounds, and the intensified competition for entry and advancement is advantageous for those with better educational credentials, which are correlated with class background. Dahrendorf (1967: 236, 238) has commented on the strongly middle class background of German lawyers. In Lombardy in 1978, 32 percent of private practitioners had professional fathers (19 percent were lawyers), another 36 percent had fathers who were white-collar workers, and only 4 percent had fathers who were workers or farmers (Prandstraller, 1981). Still, Belgium, the Netherlands, and France have seen the entry of some lawyers from lower-class backgrounds or religious or linguistic minorities. Furthermore, there may be greater social mobility in third world countries: a high proportion of Brazilian lawyers are the children of parents without any university education, and in Colombia, private night law schools facilitate entry—although 68 percent of the fathers of a sample of lawyers still belonged to the most educated 3 percent of the population (Lynch, 1981: 46).

## CHANGES IN THE DISTRIBUTION OF LAW GRADUATES AND THE STRUCTURE OF PRIVATE PRACTICE

Changes in how many qualify as lawyers and who does so also influence the distribution of law graduates among legal careers and the structure of private practice. In both the common and the civil law worlds, the increased number of graduates has compelled some to enter less favored sectors of the profession, thereby enlarging their relative size. In the common law world, intense competition for positions in private practice (employment in law firms and seats in barristers' chambers) has encouraged many to seek employment in private industry or government. The one-third to one-half of all graduates who are women may have additional reasons for doing so. As a result, the proportion of American lawyers in private practice declined from 89 percent to 68 percent between 1948 and 1980, while the proportion employed in industry or commerce increased from 3 percent to 11 percent, and the proportion employed in government (outside the judiciary) increased from 8 percent to 11 percent. In England and Wales, the proportion of solicitors holding practicing certificates and employed full time in commerce, industry, nationalized enterprises, or other private sector activities increased from 4 percent to 7 percent between 1957 and 1984 (and many other privately employed solicitors do not take out practicing certificates). In both countries, the ratio of house counsel to private practitioners increased between the 1950s and the 1980s (see table 1.1). This push factor has been reinforced by the desire of commercial consumers of legal services to cut expenses by substituting less expensive in-house counsel for more expensive private firms. India may represent the most extreme example of a common law country: only 10 percent of law students will ever enter private practice. Although the ratio of judges to private practitioners has worsened, common law judges are beginning to take a more active role in managing litigation, partly in emulation of their civil law counterparts (Langbein, 1985: 858–866).

In the civil law world, the pressure of numbers has had the opposite effect. Jobs for law graduates outside private practice have grown slowly, if at all. In no country has the number of judges kept pace with population increases, much less with the more rapid growth of the legal profession. Wherever we have historical statistics (Belgium, the Netherlands, Germany, Brazil, and Japan), the ratio of judges to private practitioners has declined (see table 1.1). The fiscal crisis of the state has frozen or reduced the number of lawyers in the civil service, which had risen dramatically until the 1970s (in Belgium and the Netherlands, for example, see table 1.1). Even though the state cannot employ more lawyers it may not want to decrease their production because the oversupply allows it to attract better graduates at lower salaries. Although large private enterprises have hired many law graduates since World War II (see table 1.1), further growth in this sector is unlikely. The disproportion between the number of law students (even allowing for attrition) and the number of private practitioners in Scandinavian countries in 1980—4,000 to 2,500 in Denmark, 3,600 to 2,000 in Norway, 10,000 to 1,400 in Sweden (Katz, 1986e: 280–281)—strongly suggests that private practice will continue to expand rapidly. In Germany, judges actually outnumbered private practitioners at the end of the nineteenth century and again following the expulsion of Jewish lawyers in the 1930s; yet by 1984 there were five private practitioners for every three judges. That year there were equal numbers of private practitioners and lawyers in the civil service; however, whereas 30 percent to 35 percent of law graduates entered the civil service in the 1960s and early 1970s, only 10 percent can do so today. Half of all law graduates now become advocates. Although the common and civil law worlds retain different distributions of law graduates among the magistracy, civil service, private practice, and private employment, continuing expansion in the total number of law graduates over the next two decades inevitably will cause the resemblance to increase.

We saw above that law firms had become the dominant mode of private practice in the common law world and were growing in size. In the United States, solo practitioners declined from more than two-thirds of all private practitioners in 1948 to less than half in 1980. By the latter year, 29 percent of private practitioners were found in firms with more than five lawyers. In England, solo practitioners declined from a fifth of all private practitioners in 1957 to a tenth in 1984. In Australia, barristers (who still practice individually) were losing business to large solicitors' firms. Yet this trend clearly has slowed: solo practitioners as a proportion of private practitioners in the United States declined only 1 percent between 1970 and 1980 (from 50 percent to 49 percent). It may even be reversing: the number of solo practitioners in England grew by 57 percent between 1978 and 1983, far faster than the profession as a whole. It seems likely that the proliferation of private practitioners may force graduates unable to find law firm employment into practice on their own.

The civil law world retains its strong ideological attachment to independent practice. Yet here, too, change may be occurring. Partnerships no longer are prohibited. Because the demand for advocacy appears fairly inelastic (except as it is fueled by legal aid programs or legal expense insurance), private practitioners will have to expand their counseling services. This will put them in competition with house counsel, other occupations (such as conseils juridiques in France, or judicial and administrative scriveners and tax attorneys in Japan), and multinational law firms, forcing law firms to expand in order to achieve economies of scale. The outpouring of law graduates encourages such expansion by assuring inexpensive labor. Firms have grown as large as fifty lawyers in Europe and Latin America. Apparently, environmental changes can overcome inherited traditions, as suggested by the fact that private practice in Quebec resembles that in English-speaking Canada more than that in France, in terms of the proportion of law graduates in private practice, the size of law firms, and the amount of time devoted to advice rather than advocacy (compare Mackaay [1982: tables II, VII, XIII] with Arthurs et al. [1971: table 14] and Colvin et al. [1978: tables VI.1, VI.2, VI.6]). An even more dramatic illustration of the influence of the world economy is the emergence of private law firms in the major trading centers of the People's Republic of China— some of which are billing as much as $200 per hour (Stille, 1985). We can expect further convergence in the structure of private practice, although solo practice may remain more dominant and law firms smaller in the civil than in the common law world.

## LAWYERS AS A POLITICAL FORCE

Lawyers exercise political influence in two ways: collectively through their professional associations and individually as elected and appointed officials. We saw above that civil law professions did not create the powerful, private, voluntary, self-interested, self-regulating associations characteristic of the common law world. Instead, associations of private practitioners were created and dominated by the state, were compulsory, and were limited in their competence and interests. In the last two decades, this began to change dramatically in several ways. First, local organizations have sought to form national coalitions or to take concerted action. Second, some associations of law graduates have adopted a syndicalist form. This began in Italy and France in the 1960s, initially among the younger and more radical magistrates, but it gradually extended to private practitioners (67 percent of Lombard lawyers in 1978 expressed a preference for trade unionism) (Prandstraller, 1981). In 1986, the centrist Union syndicale des magistrats claimed 52 percent of all French magistrates, the leftist Syndicat de la magistrature claimed 30 percent, and the rightist Association professionelle des magistrats claimed 14 percent (Soulez Larivière, 1987: 48). The change reflected a profession that rapidly was growing more youthful (as mentioned earlier, 44 percent of French judges were less than thirty-five years old in 1982), the political radicalization of the period (the proportion of Italian private practitioners describing themselves as left-wing increased from 9 percent to 22 percent between 1966 and 1978, while the proportion describing themselves as right-wing declined from 24 percent to 10 percent) (Prandstraller, 1967; 1981), and disenchantment with local bar associations (63 percent of the Paris Bar in 1973/74 felt that its governing body was unrepresentative, and 39 percent did not participate in bar activities) (Karpik, 1986: 505). If younger lawyers are politically more radical, they may be economically just as conservative as their elders when confronted by growing competition from each other, new entrants, and other occupations. In fall 1985, the 12,000-member Athens Lawyers' Association struck for more than three months, totally paralyzing legal proceedings, to protest a law allowing nonlawyers to assess damage in automobile accidents; the strike ended only when the government assured the Athens Lawyers' Association that these nonlawyers would not be able to evaluate legal liability (*New York Times*, 11 January 1986, p. 4). Third, these outside competitors also are organizing to advance their economic interests and enhance their social status: judicial scriveners in Japan (Brown, 1983: 356), conseils juridiques in France (Le, 1982: 91–92), and house counsel in Japan, Belgium, and Norway. Finally, private practitioners are forming coalitions with the other categories of law graduate and other free professionals to promote their common concerns, particularly in negotiations with the state.

The common law world also displays tensions (although the substance is different) between established professional associations claiming to represent the public interest and newer organizations openly championing the parochial concerns of lawyers: between the American Bar Association and the American Trial Lawyers' Association in the United States; between the General Council of the Bar and the Campaign for the Bar, or the Law Society and the British Legal Association in England and Wales; and between the Law Society of Upper Canada and the Ontario Lawyers' Association in Canada. At the same time, common law professional associations, which jealously defend their powers of self-regulation, increasingly are subject to external demands that they become more accountable to either the state or the public (through the addition of lay officers) or be divested of regulatory power. Although major differences still separate professional associations in the two worlds, political and economic pressures may be producing some convergence.

A partial explanation for the historical weakness of civil law professional associations may have been the prominence of law graduates in legislatures, where they were able to influence state action. At the end of the nineteenth and the beginning of the twentieth centuries, law graduates (some of whom were private practitioners) represented nearly three-fourths of the Italian legislature, three-fifths of the French, half of two-thirds of the Dutch, a third of the German, and a fourth of the Norwegian. They were equally dominant in Brazil and Venezuela. In most of Europe, their representation has declined markedly: to a fifth of the German and Italian legislatures, a fifth or less of the Dutch, and a tenth of the French and Norwegian. (In evaluating this trend it is important to remember that law graduates continue to dominate the civil service in most of northern Europe [Rusechemeyer, 1973: 188; Schreuer, 1981: 27].) This decline may have contributed to the increased interest in professional, and particularly syndicalist, associations.

Several hypotheses have been offered to explain the reduction: the growing demands of private practice, the displacement of the lawyer's generalized expertise by that of the technical specialist, and the rise of labor parties (Aubert, 1970; Rueschemeyer, 1973: 71 n. 17, 74 n. 24). Yet no decrease in the historically high proportion of lawyer-legislators is found in the common law world, although the first two explanations apply everywhere and the third everywhere except the United States. Perhaps the continued prominence of lawyer-legislators in the common law world reflects the more explicit politicization of law in those countries.


## CONCLUSION

I believe that the following chapters justify our decision to divide legal professions into common and civil law worlds. There are strong family re- semblances within each and major divisions between them. These begin with the self-conception of law graduates: as members of a single profes- sion in the common law world and as members of distinct categories (magistrate, civil servant, private employee, and private practitioner) in the civil law world. Those categories differ in historical priority, prestige, and income, as well as in the degree of lateral mobility between them. The two worlds display different means of controlling entry (a defining characteristic in any concept of professions), especially with respect to the role of the state and the university. They differ in the content and style of pedagogy, the structure and significance of apprenticeship, and the nature of legal careers. Even within the category of private practice (dominant in the common law world; subordinate to the magistracy and civil service in the civil law world) there are major differences in the relative emphasis on advocacy and counseling, the prominence of individual practice, the size and structure of law firms, relations with clients, and the degree of internal stratification. Although all private practitioners seek to control competi- tion, those in common and civil law worlds differ in the definition of their monopolies, relations with external rivals, concepts of incompatibility, geographic limitations on practice, and eagerness to expand their markets and stimulate demand. The voluntary associations that are central to the professional project of private practitioners in the common law world are not only irrelevant to the majority of law graduates employed in the pub- lic or private sectors in the civil law world but also differ significantly from the local, official, compulsory associations of civil law private practitioners.

Despite these historical differences, lawyers in both worlds have been exposed to similar influences in the postwar years. After a long period of stasis, each has experienced rapid growth in the number of law graduates.

Universities play a central role in this process—displacing apprenticeship in many common law countries, opening their doors to a larger proportion of secondary-school graduates everywhere. In the process they have become the primary gatekeepers to the profession. One consequence of the rapid rate of growth is that civil law jurists, and especially private practitioners, have become interested in controlling supply. Much of the increase in numbers is attributable to the entry of women, which explains why the rate of growth has stabilized now that women represent a third to a half of all law students. In both worlds, women have gravitated toward employment, particularly in the public sector, but remain underrepresented in the most prestigious forms of private practice. In both, the profession has grown more youthful but not significantly more open to lower class entrants. Rapid growth has tended to increase the number of lawyers employed in the public and private sectors in the common law world and the number of private practitioners in the civil law world. It also may be contributing to a revival of solo practice in the common law world while forcing civil law private practitioners to engage in counseling and to enlarge their law firms. In both worlds, private practitioners have become more vigorous defenders of their economic interests and social status, while professional associations in the common law world have suffered challenges to their self-regulatory powers.

I do not want to exaggerate the extent to which these influences have obliterated historical differences. No one entering a law faculty today would have any difficulty identifying the world in which it was located, even before a word had been spoken. The magistracy and the civil service play very different roles and attract different recruits in the two systems. Private practice still is structured differently and relates differently to large corporate clients—and professional associations are viewed differently by their members and interact with the state in different ways. Yet legal professions in both systems are being transformed by similar forces that operate across national boundaries. Some of these forces are social: the expansion of higher education (a response to the need for skilled personnel, the drive for mobility within the middle class, and the progressive inflation of credentials) and the entry of women into the labor force. Some are economic: progressive concentration within industry and commerce, the expansion of the service sector, and the internationalization of business (accelerated by the EEC). Some are political: the increased role of the state in all economies, the growth of welfare programs, and the emergence of movements to oppose the growing dominance of the state and to equalize access to law. Some are cultural: the availability of divorce, the demand by racial and ethnic minorities for equal opportunity. Just as national cultures, languages, polities, and economies have been losing their distinctiveness, so national legal professions necessarily will converge, even if they never will become identical.

# TABLES

1.1. Ratio of Judges, Prosecutors, House Counsel, and Jurist Civil Servants to Private Practitioners

| Country | Year | Private practitioners | Judges No. | Judges Ratio[a] | Prosecutors No. | Prosecutors Ratio[a] | House counsel No. | House counsel Ratio[a] | Civil servants No. | Civil servants Ratio[a] |
|---|---|---|---|---|---|---|---|---|---|---|
| England | 1982 | 40,580[b] | | | | | 3,598[c] | 9 | 5,992[c] | 15 |
| | 1957 | 15,737[b] | | | | | 853[c] | 5 | 3,115[c] | 20 |
| United States | 1980 | 369,242 | 19,160 | 5 | | | 59,017 | 16 | 50,490 | 14 |
| | 1951 | 192,353 | 7,978 | 4 | | | 12,631 | 7 | 21,718 | 11 |
| Scotland | 1982 | 4,502[d] | 1,100 | 2 | | | 89 | 2 | 911 | 20 |
| India | 1970 | 90,906 | 5,943 | 7 | | | | | | |
| New Zealand | 1981 | 3,915 | 108 | 3 | | | 126 | 3 | | |
| | 1971 | 2,634 | 73 | 3 | | | 26 | 1 | | |
| Australia | 1985 | 22,000 | 1,000 | 5 | | | | | | |
| France | 1983 | 15,757 | 5,640[e] | 36 | | | 4,264[f] | 27 | | |
| Belgium | 1984 | 7,504 | 1,669 | 22 | | | 13,600[g] | 181 | | |
| | 1970 | 3,827 | 1,586 | 41 | | | 4,458 | 116 | 2,390 | 62 |
| | 1947 | 3,309 | 1,116 | 34 | | | 1,540 | 47 | 1,052 | 32 |
| Netherlands | 1986 | 5,124 | 696 | 14 | | | | | | |
| | 1970 | 3,823 | 503 | 13 | | | 4,736 | 124 | 4,063 | 106 |
| | 1930 | 1,796 | 372 | 21 | | | 1,247 | 69 | 649 | 36 |
| Norway | 1970 | 1,225 | 408 | 33 | 255[i] | 21 | 1,379[h] | 113 | 1,583 | 129 |
| Spain | 1985 | 32,000 | 1,694 | 5 | 540 | 2 | | | | |
| Germany | 1984 | 33,750[j] | 20,000[l] | 59 | | | 37,500[k] | 111 | 33,750 | 100 |
| | 1962 | 13,020[j] | 11,780[l] | 90 | | | 18,600[k] | 143 | 18,600 | 143 |
| | 1883 | | | 157[l] | | | | | | 77 |

| Country | Year | | | | | | | | | |
|---|---|---|---|---|---|---|---|---|---|---|
| Brazil | 1980 | 85,716 | 4,624 | 5 | 8,130 | 9 | | | | 100 |
| | 1950 | 15,912 | 2,265 | 14 | 1,346 | 8 | | | | |
| Venezuela | 1985 | 5,000 | 2,500[m] | 50 | | | 1,500 | 30 | 5,000 | 157 |
| Chile | 1968 | | | 65 | | | | 109 | | 12 |
| Colombia | 1967 | | | 14 | | | | 35 | | |
| Japan | 1976 | 10,792 | 2,703[n] | 25 | 2,089 | 19 | | | | |
| | 1956 | 6,040 | 2,327[o] | 39 | 1,717 | 28 | | | | |
| Italy | 1980 | 25,000 | 7,692[p] | 31 | | | | | | |
| Finland | 1983 | 3,353 | 1,300 | 39 | | | 2,189 | 65 | 3,772 | 106 |
| Sweden | 1962 | 1,064 | | | | | 1,000[c] | 100[c] | | |

[a] Ratio to 100 private practitioners.

[b] Solicitors and barristers.

[c] Assumes that number of employed barristers equals number in private practice and that former are distributed between public and private employment in same ratio as employed solicitors.

[d] Solicitors and advocates.

[e] Magistrates (includes prosecutors).

[f] Conseils juridiques.

[g] Combines house counsel and civil servants.

[h] Includes house counsel and management.

[i] Includes police.

[j] Excludes Syndici.

[k] Includes Syndici.

[l] Includes prosecutors.

[m] Include court clerks, registrars, notaries, public defenders, and prosecutors.

[n] Includes 791 summary court judges.

[o] Includes 730 summary court judges.

[p] Magistrati.

Sources: Sweden—Ginsburg & Bruzelius (1965: 52 n. 7; 67 n. 81); Italy—de Francisis (1986: 158, 160); Finland—(Katz, 1986e: 282); Chile—Lowenstein (1970: 39–40); Colombia—Lynch (1981: 53); all others: chapters in this volume and Abel & Lewis (1988).

## 1.2. Increase in Law Student Enrollment: Absolute and Annualized Percent

| Year | France[a] | Brazil | Spain | Italy | Venezuela | Belgium | Norway | Netherlands | Germany | Japan | United States | England and Wales | Scotland | Canada | Australia | New Zealand |
|---|---|---|---|---|---|---|---|---|---|---|---|---|---|---|---|---|
| 1985 | | | | | | 4,394 / 1,205[b] | 4,400 | | | | | | | | | 1,029 |
| 1984 | | | | | | | | | | | 128,742 | | | | 8,762 | |
| 1983 | | | | | | | | | | | | 14,362 | | | | |
| 1982 | | | | | | | 4% | | | | | 6% | | | −0.6% | 4% |
| 1981 | | | | | | | | | | | | | 1,850 | | | |
| 1980 | | 135,026 | | | | 1% / 0.6%[b] | | 18,588 | | 149,453 | 0.3% | 12,105 | −0.3% | 9,590 | 8,981 | 853 |
| 1979 | | | 74,117 / 4,550[b] | | | | 3,500 | 19,744 | | | | | 1,864 | | | |
| 1978 | | | | | | | | | | | | | | | | |
| 1977 | | | | 128,604 | 13,900 / 1,060[b] | | | | 46,000 | | 125,010 | | 5% | | 3% | 2% |
| 1976 | | | | | | | 6% | 5% | | | | 10% | 1,700 | 5% | | |
| 1975 | | 17% | 28% / 24%[b] | | | | | | 7% | | | | | | 7,917 | |
| 1974 | | | | | | 3,907 / 1,144[b] | | | | | 8% | | | | | 777 |
| 1973 | | | | | 14% / 26%[b] | | 2,700 | | 36,000 | | | | 7% | | | |
| 1972 | 8,710 | 53,000 | 24,824 / 1,678[b] | 18% / 104% | | | | | | | | | | | | −0.6% |
| 1971 | | | | | | | 17% | 12,763 | | | 86,028 | 5,998 | 1,260 | 6,443 | | 799 |
| 1970 | | | | | 6,900 / 380[b] | 24% / 27%[b] | | | | 8% | | | | | 16% | |
| 1969 | 49% | | 18,973 | 52,718[d] / 13,839 | | | | | 9% | | | | 4% | | | |
| 1968 | | | | | | 360[b] | 1,500 | | | | | 9% | | | | |
| 1967 | | | | | | | | | | | | | 1,034 | | | |
| 1966 | | | | | 3%[b] | | 10% | | | | | | | | | 4% |
| 1965 | 1,766 | 13% | | | | 1,221 | 1,000 | | 19,000 | | 10% | 3,838 | | 14% | 3,039 | |
| 1964 | | | | 0.5% | 7% | | | | | | | | | | | |
| 1963 | | | 5% | | | −2%[b] | | | | | | | | | | |
| 1962 | | | | | | −1% | | | | | | 6% | | | 7% | |
| 1961 | | 23,519 | | | | | | | | | | | | | | |
| 1960 | | | 13,673 | 50,499[d] | 4,000 / 300[b] | 1,294 / 4.5[b] | | 3,014 | | 57,142 | 43,695 | 3,070 | | 2,710 | 2,257 | 465 |

[a] Four-year university law degree.
[b] Law graduates.
[c] Auckland University.
[d] Merryman et al. (1979: 426).

Sources: This volume and Abel and Lewis (1988), except Germany—Geck (1977: 93); Japan—Brown (1983: 231); Italy 1969 (lower figure) and 1960—Merryman et al. (1979: 426); Spain 1968 and 1960: Merryman et al. (1979: 433).

1.3. Increase in Number of Private Practitioners: Absolute and Annualized Percent

| Year | France[a] | Brazil | Germany | Japan | Italy | Belgium | Norway | Netherlands | United States | England and Wales | Scotland | Canada | New Zealand |
|---|---|---|---|---|---|---|---|---|---|---|---|---|---|
| 1986 | | | 48,658 | | | | | | | | | | |
| 1985 | | | | | | | 2,500 | 5,124 | | 51,857 | 6,377 | | |
| 1984 | | | | | | 7,504 | | | 649,000 | | | | |
| 1983 | | | | | | | | 7% | | | 5% | | |
| 1982 | | | 6% | | 46,401 | | 5% | | 5% | 4% | | | |
| 1981 | | | | | | | | 3,989 | | | 5,502 | | 4,149 |
| 1980 | 15,170 | 85,716 | 36,077 | | | | 2,000 | 5% / 3,600 | 542,205 | 42,421 | 6% | 34,205 | |
| 1979 | | | | | | | | | | | 4,722 | | |
| 1978 | | | | | | | | | | | | | |
| 1977 | | | | | | | | | | | | | |
| 1976 | | | | 10,792 | 1% | 7% | 4% | 7% | | | 6% | | 5% |
| 1975 | 12% | 13% | | | | | | | | | | 11% | |
| 1974 | | | 6% | | | | | | | | | | |
| 1973 | 8,307 | | | | | | | | | | 3,794 | | |
| 1972 | | | | | | | | | 5% | 6% | | | |
| 1971 | | | | | | | | | | | | | |
| 1970 | | 37,719 | 22,882 | | 41,639 | 3,827 | 1,400 | | | | | | |

1.3. (continued)

| | France[a] | Brazil | Germany | Japan | Italy | Belgium | Norway | Netherlands | United States | England and Wales | Scotland | Canada | New Zealand |
|---|---|---|---|---|---|---|---|---|---|---|---|---|---|
| 1969 | | | | | | | | | | | | | |
| 1968 | | | | 4% | | | | | | | | 16,315 | 2,733 |
| 1967 | | | | | 1% | | | 2,063 | 355,242 | 26,991 | | | |
| 1966 | | | | | | | | | | | | | |
| 1965 | | 3% | 2% | | 39,415 | 0.7% | -0.7% | | | | | | |
| 1964 | | | | | | | | | | | 0.7% | | 4% |
| 1963 | | | | | | | | | | | | | |
| 1962 | | | | | 3% | | | 1% | 2% | 3% | | | |
| 1961 | | | | | | | | | | | | | |
| 1960 | | 30,066 | 18,347 | 6,040[b] | 33,059[c] | 3,579 | 1,500 | 1,851 | 285,933 | 20,988 | 3,412[d] | | 12,068 |

[a] Avocats (excludes avocats at Conseil d'Etat and Cour de Cassation and avoués).

[b] 1956.

[c] 1958.

[d] 1954 figure for solicitors, 1962 for barristers.

Source: This volume and Abel & Lewis (1988), except Italy 1970—Merryman et al. (1979: 470).

# NOTE

All factual statements unsupported by citations are taken from the chapters in this volume or in volume one (Abel & Lewis, 1988). I am grateful to Philip Lewis for his close reading of this chapter and his useful suggestions.

# REFERENCES

Abel, Richard L. 1985. "Law Without Politics: Legal Aid Under Advanced Capitalism," 32 *UCLA Law Review* 474.

————. 1988. *The Legal Profession in England and Wales*. Oxford: Basil Blackwell.

Abel, Richard L., and Philip S. C. Lewis, eds. 1988. *Lawyers in Society*, vol. 1: *The Common Law World*. Berkeley, Los Angeles, London: University of California Press.

Arthurs, Harry W., J. Willms, and Larry Taman. 1971. "The Toronto Legal Profession: An Exploratory Study," 21 *University of Toronto Law Journal* 498.

Aubert, Vilhelm. 1970. "Law as a Way of Resolving Conflict: The Case of a Small Industrial Country," in Laura Nader, ed., *Law in Culture and Society*. Chicago: Aldine.

Barton, John, James Lowell Gibbs, Jr., Victor Hao Li, and John Henry Merryman. 1983. *Law in Radically Different Cultures*. St. Paul, Minn.: West Publishing Company.

Bedford, Sybille. 1961. *The Faces of Justice: A Traveller's Report*. New York: Simon & Schuster.

Bogdan, Michael. 1981. "Sweden," 5 *Comparative Law Yearbook* 137–144.

Braun, Manfred, and Ralf Birk. 1981. "Germany, Federal Republic," 5 *Comparative Law Yearbook* 69–81.

Brown, Robert. 1983. "A Lawyer By Any Other Name: Legal Advisors in Japan," in Edward J. Lincoln and Douglas E. Rosenthal, eds., *Legal Aspects of Doing Business in Japan*, pp. 201–502. New York: Practicing Law Institute (Commercial Law and Practice Course Handbook Series, No. 295).

Burdick, William L. 1939. *The Bench and Bar of Other Lands*. Brooklyn: Metropolitan Law Book Company.

Cappelletti, Mauro, John Henry Merryman, and Joseph M. Perillo. 1967. *The Italian Legal System: An Introduction*. Stanford, Calif.: Stanford University Press.

Certoma, G. Leroy. 1985. *The Italian Legal System*. London: Butterworths.

Clark, David S. 1981. "The Legal Profession in Comparative Perspective: Growth and Specialization," 30 *American Journal of Comparative Law* 163–175 (Supplement).

Clark, David S. 1987. "The Medieval Origins of Modern Legal Education: Between Church and State," 35 *American Journal of Comparative Law* 653–719.

Cohn, E. J. 1960. "The German Attorney—Experiences with a Unified Profession (I)," 9 *International and Comparative Law Quarterly* 580–599.

———. 1961. "The Germany Attorney—Experiences with a Unified Profession (II)," 10 *International and Comparative Law Quarterly* 103–122.

Colvin, Selma, David Stager, Larry Taman, Janet Yale, and Frederick H. Zemans. 1978. *The Market for Legal Services: Paraprofessionals and Specialists.* Toronto: Professional Organizations Committee, Ministry of the Attorney General, Province of Ontario.

Conze, Werner, and Jürgen Kocka, eds. 1985. *Bildungsbürgertum im 19. Jahrhundert, vol. 1: Bildungssystem und Professionalisierung internationalen Vergleichen.* Stuttgart: Klett-Cotta.

Curran, Barbara A. 1977. *The Legal Needs of the Public: The Final Report of a National Survey.* Chicago: American Bar Foundation.

Dahrendorf, Ralf. 1967. *Society and Democracy in Germany.* New York: Doubleday.

Damaska, Mirjan. 1986. *The Faces of Justice and State Authority: A Comparative Approach to the Legal Process.* New Haven: Yale University Press.

David, René, and John E. C. Brierly. 1968. *Major Legal Systems in the World Today: An Introduction to the Comparative Study of Law.* London: Stevens & Sons.

———. 1978. *Major Legal Systems in the World Today: An Introduction to the Comparative Study of Law,* 2d ed. New York: Free Press.

———. 1985. *Major Legal Systems in the World Today: An Introduction to the Comparative Study of Law,* 3d ed. London: Stevens & Sons.

David, René, and Henry P. de Vries. 1958. *The French Legal System: An Introduction to Civil Law Systems.* New York: Oceana.

de Francisis, Maria Elisabetta. 1986. "Italy," in Alan N. Katz, ed., *Legal Traditions and Systems,* chap. 8. Westport, Conn.: Greenwood Press.

Dias, C. J., R. Luckham, D. O. Lynch, and J. C. N. Paul, eds. 1981. *Lawyers in the Third World: Comparative and Developmental Perspectives.* Uppsala: Scandinavian Institute of African Studies; New York: International Center for Law in Development.

Ehrmann, Henry W. 1983. *Politics in France.* Boston: Little, Brown.

Evan, William. 1968. "A Data Archive of Legal Systems: A Cross-National Analysis of Sample of Data," 9 *European Journal of Sociology* 113, reprinted in *The Sociology of Law,* chap. 35. New York: Free Press, 1980.

Farnsworth, Clyde H. 1987. "Japan to Open Its Doors to American Lawyers," *New York Times,* February 27, p. 38.

Freidson, Eliot. 1970. *Profession of Medicine.* New York: Dodd & Mead.

Geck, Wilhelm Karl. 1977. "The Reform of Legal Education in the Federal Republic of Germany," 25 *American Journal of Comparative Law* 86.

Ginsburg, Ruth Bader, and Anders Bruzelius. 1965. *Civil Procedure in Sweden.* The Hague: Martinus Nijhoff.

Glendon, Mary Ann, Michael Wallace Gordon, and Christopher Osakwe. 1982. *Comparative Legal Traditions in a Nutshell.* St. Paul, Minn.: West Publishing Company.

————. 1985. *Comparative Legal Traditions.* St. Paul, Minn.: West Publishing Company.

Gutteridge, H. C. 1949. *Comparative Law: An Introduction to the Comparative Method of Legal Study and Research,* 2d ed. Cambridge: Cambridge University Press.

Heinz, John P., and Edward O. Laumann. 1982. *Chicago Lawyers.* Chicago: American Bar Foundation; New York: Russell Sage Foundation.

Herzog, Peter. 1967. *Civil Procedure in France.* The Hague: Martinus Nijhoff.

Herzog, Peter, and Brigitte Ecolivet Herzog. 1973. "The Reform of the Legal Professions and of Legal Aid in France," 22 *International and Comparative Law Quarterly* 462–491.

Holdsworth, W. S. 1926. *A History of English Law,* vol. 9. London: Methuen.

Johnson, Earl, Jr., Steven A. Bloch, Ann Drew, William L. F. Felstiner, E. Wayne Hansen, and George Sabagh. 1977. *A Comparative Analysis of Statistical Dimensions of the Justice Systems of Seven Industrial Democracies.* Los Angeles: Social Science Research Institute, University of Southern California.

Karpik, Lucien, 1985. "Avocat: une nouvelle Profession?" 26 *Revue française de sociologie* 571–600.

————. 1986. "Democratie et Pouvoir au Barreau de Paris: La question du gouvernement privé," 36 *Revue française de science politique* 496–518.

Katz, Alan N., ed. 1986a. *Legal Traditions and Systems: An International Handbook.* Westport, Conn.: Greenwood Press.

————. 1986b. "France," in Alan N. Katz, ed., *Legal Traditions and Systems,* chap. 6. Westport, Conn.: Greenwood Press.

————. 1986c. "Federal Republic of Germany," in Alan N. Katz, ed., *Legal Traditions and Systems,* chap. 5. Westport, Conn.: Greenwood Press.

————. 1986d. "Japan," in Alan N. Katz, ed., *Legal Traditions and Systems,* chap. 9. Westport, Conn.: Greenwood Press.

————. 1986e. "Scandinavia," in Alan N. Katz, ed., *Legal Traditions and Systems,* chap. 13. Westport, Conn.: Greenwood Press.

Kötz, Hein, Wolf Paul, Michel Pédamon, and Michael Zander. 1982. *Anwaltsberuf im Wandel: Rechtspflegeorgan oder Dienstleitungsgewerbe.* Frankfurt: Metzner.

Lancaster, Thomas D., and Michael W. Giles. 1986. "Spain," in Alan N. Katz, ed., *Legal Traditions and Systems,* chap. 16. Westport, Conn.: Greenwood Press.

Langbein, John H. 1985. "The German Advantage in Civil Procedure," 52 *University of Chicago Law Review* 823–866.

Larson, Magali Sarfatti. 1977. *The Rise of Professionalism: A Sociological Analysis.* Berkeley: University of California Press.

Le, Tan Thi Thanh Trai. 1981. "Professional Independence and the Associate in a

Law Firm: A French Case Study," 29 *American Journal of Comparative Law* 647–670.

————. 1982. "The French Legal Profession: A Prisoner of Its Glorious Past?" 15 *Cornell International Law Journal* 63–104.

Lewin, Tamar. 1987. "Increasingly, Pro Cash Beats Pro Bono," *New York Times*, March 22, 1987, sec. 4, p. 28.

Lewis, Philip S. C. 1988. "Introduction," in Richard L. Abel and Philip S. C. Lewis, eds., *Lawyers in Society*, vol. 1: *The Common Law World*, chap. 1. Berkeley, Los Angeles, London: University of California Press.

Lowenstein, Steven. 1970. *Lawyers, Legal Education and Development: An Examination of the Process of Reform in Chile*. New York: International Legal Center.

Luban, David. 1984. "The Sources of Legal Ethics: A German-American Comparison of Lawyers' Professional Duties," 48(2) *Rabels Zeitschrift* 245–288.

Lynch, Dennis O. 1981. *Legal Roles in Colombia*. Uppsala: Scandinavian Institute of African Studies; New York: International Center for Law in Development.

MacDonald, Scott B. 1986. "Latin America," in Alan N. Katz, ed., *Legal Traditions and Systems*, chap. 10. Westport, Conn.: Greenwood Press.

Mackaay, Ejan. 1982. *Le Sondage 1981 Auprès des Avocats du Québec: Premiers Résultats*. Montreal: Faculté de droit, Université de Montréal.

Magnus, Julius, ed. 1929. *Die Rechtsanwaltschaft*. Leipzig: Moeser.

Merryman, John Henry. 1969. *The Civil Law Tradition*. Stanford, Calif.: Stanford University Press.

————. 1975. "Legal Education There and Here: A Comparison," 27 *Stanford Law Journal* 859–878.

Merryman, John Henry, David S. Clark, and Lawrence M. Friedman. 1979. *Law and Social Change in Mediterranean Europe and Latin America: A Handbook of Legal and Social Indicators for Comparative Study*. Dobbs Ferry, N.Y.: Oceana.

Nagourney, Janice Y. 1981. "France," 5 *Comparative Law Yearbook* 45–68.

Organisation for Economic Cooperation and Development (OECD), Committee of Experts on Restrictive Business Practices. 1984. *Report on Competition Policy and the Professions*. Paris: OECD.

Prandstraller, Gian Paolo. 1967. *Gli Avvocati Italiani; Inchiesta sociológica*. Milan: Editore di Communità.

————. 1981. *Avvocati e Metropoli: Inchiesta sulla professione di avvocato nell'area Lombarda*. Milan: Franco Angeli.

Ramseyer, Mark. 1986. "Lawyers, Foreign Lawyers, and Lawyer-Substitutes: The Market for Regulation in Japan," 27 *Harvard International Law Journal* 499–539.

Ranieri, Filippo. 1985. "Vom Stand zum Beruf: Die Professionalisierung des Juristenstandes als Forschungsausgabe der europäischen Rechtsgeschichte der Neuzeit," 13 *Jus Commune* 83.

Redden, Kenneth Robert, gen. ed. 1984. *Modern Legal Systems Cyclopedia* (10 vols.). Buffalo: William S. Hein & Co.

Reifner, Udo. 1986. "The Bar in the Third Reich: Anti-Semitism and the Decline of Liberal Advocacy," 32 *McGill Law Review* 96–124.

Royal Commission on Legal Services. 1979. *Final Report* (2 vols.) London: Her Majesty's Stationery Office (HMSO) (Cmnd. 7648).

Royal Commission on Legal Services in Scotland. 1980. *Report* (2 vols.). Edinburgh: HMSO (Cmnd. 7846).

Rueschemeyer, Dietrich, 1973. *Lawyers and Their Society: A Comparative Study of the Legal Profession in Germany and the United States.* Cambridge, Mass.: Harvard University Press.

———. 1978. "The Legal Profession in Comparative Perspective," in Harry M. Johnson, ed., *Social System and Legal Process*, chap. 3. San Francisco: Jossey-Bass.

Schlesinger, Rudolf B. 1960. *Comparative Law: Cases—Text—Materials* (2d ed.). London: Stevens & Sons.

Schreuer, Christoph. 1981. "Austria," 5 *Comparative Law Yearbook* 17–28.

Sereni, Angelo Piero. 1950. "The Legal Profession in Italy," 63 *Harvard Law Review* 1000–1008.

Soulez Larivière, Daniel. 1987. "Faut-il faire le procès des juges?" *L'Express*, April 10, 1987, p. 46.

Stille, Alexander. 1985. "Chinese Lawyers Form Firms There," 8(1) *National Law Journal*, September 23, 1985, p. 3.

Union Internationale des Avocats. 1959. *Les Barreaux dans le monde* (2 vols.). Paris: Dalloz et Sirey.

von Mehren, Arthur T. 1957. *The Civil Law System: Cases and Materials for the Comparative Study of Law.* Englewood Cliffs, N.J.: Prentice-Hall.

von Mehren, Arthur Taylor, and James Russell Gordley. 1977. *The Civil Law System*, 2d ed. Boston: Little, Brown.

Wagner, W. J. 1985. "The Role and Function of Legal Professions: A Comparative Study," 16 *University of Miami Inter-American Law Review* 661–693.

Watson, Alan. 1981. *The Making of the Civil Law.* Cambridge, Mass.: Harvard University Press.

Weber, Max. 1954. *Law in Economy and Society* (Max Rheinstein, ed.). Cambridge, Mass.: Harvard University Press.

Weyrauch, Walter. 1964. *The Personality of Lawyers: A Comparative Study of Subjective Factors in Law, Based on Interviews with German Lawyers.* New Haven, Conn.: Yale University Press.

Wigmore, John Henry. 1928. *A Panorama of the World's Legal Systems* (3 vols.). Washington, D.C.: Washington Law Book Company.

# 2

# The Professionalization of Legal Counseling in Norway

## JON T. JOHNSEN

## INTRODUCTION

"Professions" are not a kind of occupation but a relationship between an occupation and a specific education. The archetypical profession is characterized by the prerequisite of a definite, lengthy, formal education (Torgersen, 1972: 10–12). From this perspective, it seems to me that the central concept of comparative study—"legal professions"—applies to different phenomena in different countries. Therefore, I will use a functional definition. *Legal counseling* will be the main criterion of "lawyering." My definition of legal counseling is the use of legal expertise to assist clients in clarifying, avoiding, achieving, or exploiting their legal positions.

Legal expertise can be divided into three main parts: *dogmatics*—knowledge of the normative content of legal rules and how to locate and interpret them; *application*—legally relevant factual analysis ascertaining actual legal positions; and *strategy*—familiarity with the structure and behavior of the legal and administrative machinery and the ability to advance cases within, and initiate reactions from, the system. Legal counseling typically consists of one or more of the following elements: (1) mapping the legal positions of the client and informing the client about the likely consequences; (2) outlining alternative strategies to eliminate or reduce the problem; (3) implementing the chosen strategies in cooperation with, or on behalf of, the client.

Most legal counseling in Norway is performed by legally educated professionals called *jurists*. However, legal counseling is not a professional skill instilled through specialized study; rather, it is just one of the skills one can acquire at law school

Professional legal counseling can be organized in different ways. The counselor can be employed or self-employed; counsel one or a few clients in a permanent, lasting relationship; or serve a larger number of clients on a case-by-case basis. Legal counseling can be the sole professional activity of the jurist, or counseling can be combined with management and decision-making or other profit-making activities. This means that legal counseling is one of the professional skills performed by jurists in a variety of occupational rules.

In the first part of this chapter, I will describe the historical development of jurists as professionals in Norway, focusing on legal science and university education. I also will consider how the larger occupational structure influences legal counseling by jurists and how legal science and education prepare jurists to engage in counseling. In the second part, I will concentrate on self-employed professional legal counseling performed by jurists who hold an advocate's license, in order to describe legal counseling as a professional trade.

## THE PROFESSIONALIZATION OF JURISTS

### THE HISTORY OF JURISTS

#### Main Developmental Trends

Law emerged as a practical discipline. It was established as an occupation long before any theoretical education was demanded. The University of Copenhagen began teaching Roman law in the sixteenth century, but few obtained doctorates in Roman law, and their knowledge of Danish–Norwegian laws and customs was limited. In addition to these scholars, a more popular type of lawyer existed, usually named *procurator* (Latin for "attorney"), who stressed artisanship and practiced privately.

In the Kingdom of Denmark and Norway, a university degree was required of both judges and procurators in 1736. Two different courses were offered: a traditional one in Roman law and a shorter one in Danish law. The latter allowed government clerks, who had gained legal knowledge in the course of their work, to seek appointment to legal posts. In the eighteenth century, only a few months of study in Copenhagen were needed to pass the Danish law examination. Those aspiring to minor, poorly paid jobs, especially in Norway, could be examined by a competent jurist at home so as to avoid the long and difficult trip to Copenhagen.

The educational standards and social status of jurists were rising throughout the eighteenth century. When the Danish–Norwegian union was dissolved after the Napoleonic wars, and the modern Norwegian state began to assume its present shape, most legal office-holders had studied law for some years. District judges were especially well regarded (Aubert, 1964a: 301–302; 1976: 255–261). They constituted an important part of the assembly that produced the Norwegian constitution of 1814, which still is in force.

At the beginning of the nineteenth century, jurists could be divided into three occupational groups approximately equal in size: judges, procurators, and senior officials in local governments. Few jurists were employed in central government. Almost all jurists, including procurators, were public servants. They were appointed by the king, even though private clients paid for their services according to tariffs set by the king:

> Before 1814 and for some time afterwards, lawyers were predominantly decision-makers in the service of the state.... The diffuseness of professional roles at the beginning of the last century was not solely dependent on the concentration of many specialities in the profession. It was also the lack of clear distinction between public and private interests.... Thus the incumbency of a government post in no small measure took the character of a private business, with much scope for the commercial abilities and motives of the officials. (Aubert, 1964b: 243).

In 1815, Norway had 329 university-educated jurists, or 1 for every 2,500 inhabitants. Jurists were the third largest profession, after the military and the clergy. The first Norwegian university—and for one and a half centuries the only one—was founded in Oslo in 1811. To a large extent it became a law school. Throughout much of the nineteenth century, more degrees were taken in law than in all other subjects combined (see fig. 2.1). This expansion in the number of law degrees also meant a continuous rise in the number of new jurists (see fig. 2.2).

From 1830 to 1870, an average of about 50 new jurists qualified each year, increasing to 75 around the turn of the century and to approximately 150 in 1920. From 1945 to 1955 the number of entrants was more than 250 a year, compensating for the effects of war; it dropped to 100 per year before returning to 250 in the 1970s.

The effect on the profession as a whole is shown in fig. 2.3. According to the 1980 census, the legal profession consisted of 6,572 active jurists. The ratio of 625 people per lawyer that year was one-fourth of what it had been in 1818.

Jurists experienced a sharp growth within the private sector throughout the nineteenth century. In 1848 procurators were made a private profession. Later on, jurists became involved in the management of industry and trade, both as private practitioners and as employees and managers. In the present century the growth of central government is pronounced, creating a rising demand for legal expertise. However, judges are a declining proportion of the profession because their numbers only doubled during the last 150 years (Aubert, 1964a: 305–306).

The last census to contain detailed information about jurists was completed in 1970. At that time, the profession was extremely male dominated; only 5 percent of jurists were women. Jurists were fairly evenly distributed across age cohorts (Albrechtsen, 1976). However, the sharp rise in the number of law students in the 1970s changed this picture. The profession grew more than 25 percent between 1970 and 1980. The proportion of women was 8 percent in 1977 and now probably is more than 10 percent, and the average age has fallen.

In 1970 the average income of jurists was two and a half times that of all income earners and five times the per capita income. Half the profession earned between four and eight times the per capita income, and a tenth earned even more. Jurists thus constitute a typical high-income group within Norwegian society.

The density of jurists is highest in southeastern Norway, the most urbanized and industrialized part of the country (see fig. 2.4). It contains Oslo, which is the political, economic, and cultural center. Approximately 60 percent of all jurists lived and worked in the Oslo region. In northern Norway, the least industrialized, most remote, and most sparsely populated part of the country, the density of jurists is significantly lower. The jurists' connections to urbanized parts of the Norwegian society are very strong, probably more so than for other major professions.

A little less than half of all jurists work in the public sector (see table 2.1). More than four-fifths of these work for the national government, while the rest are engaged in local administration in municipalities and counties. More than two-thirds of the lawyers employed by the national government work in central government; the remainder are found in directorates and regional offices. One-third of central government jurists occupy leading positions. Nearly half of the governmental positions involving the exercise of significant discretion are occupied by jurists, while economists hold a tenth and functionaries without an academic degree, a fourth (Aubert, 1976: 281–282). Most of the lawyers in local administration occupy leading positions. The private sector is evenly divided between private practice and employment in commerce or industry.

Jurists prospered between 1890–1900, 1910–1920, and 1950–1975; they suffered economic hardship between 1900–1910 and 1930–1950 and since 1975. There is some connection with general business cycles. The private sector is more attractive during economic expansions, whereas the public sector has the advantage during periods of contraction. This is especially true for the best qualified jurists and strongly influences the ability of government and trade to recruit skilled lawyers.

The government encountered difficulty between 1920 and 1950 (Torgersen, 1967) and now is finding increasing interest among law graduates. Between 1970 and 1980 the number of jurists employed in the public sector grew by 44 percent, compared with an increase of 15 percent in the private sector.

Economic cycles also may influence the geographic distribution of jurists. When there are many jobs, the market mechanism will dominate allocation, and university graduates will concentrate in urban areas, since the market is the main instrument of the center. This implies a "braindrain" away from the rural districts as part of the urbanization process. When the economy contracts, politics will dominate, and this means more growth in the rural districts, since politics is their main instrument—at least in Norway (Torgersen, 1967: 9).


### Recruitment and Motivation

The jurists' ties to the upper classes always have been strong (see fig. 2.5). Less than a tenth of all jurists originated from working-class backgrounds until after World War II, although the proportion doubled between 1920 and 1980. About a fifth of all jurists consistently have had fathers who themselves were jurists or were engaged in trade. According to Aubert, ever since the nineteenth century there has been strong social cohesion between academics and merchants and between government employees and those engaged in trade, despite differences in technical skills and professional ideologies (Aubert, 1964a: 315–316). There have been marked historical changes in the social recruitment of lawyers, however: the proportion whose fathers were clergymen and senior public officials has diminished, while the proportion whose fathers were civil servants or teachers has risen steadily since 1850, and the proportion whose fathers were advocates has risen since 1900.

A monolithic professional hierarchy does not exist, although jurists do participate in a variety of partial hierarchies. Nevertheless, a ranking can be perceived, the top of which is occupied by Supreme Court justices, law professors, ministerial deputy secretaries, chief administrative officers of the counties, Supreme Court advocates, and some high executives in industry and trade. The first two categories enjoy the greatest respect, the next two wield the most power, and the last two earn the highest incomes.

The main career alternatives for jurists are state administration and the judiciary, regional and local government, police and public prosecution, private practice as an advocate, and employment in commerce or industry. Individual careers often move between these paths. Judges may have begun in central government, in police and prosecution services, or as advocates. Advocates may have worked in central and local government, and more than half of them have been deputy judges. The most "closed" career is in central government. These jurists usually start there and remain their entire careers, unless they become judges (Aubert, 1963: 189–214).

Women and men have not been proportionally distributed in the various careers. Women have been overrepresented in the lower positions in central government and underrepresented in the judiciary, as advocates, and in higher administrative posts. According to Aubert, advocacy might be expected to attract women because it is a service occupation. Advocacy also demands aggressive partisanship, however, which may be inconsistent with traditional female roles. Advocates also tend to depend on connections to trade and other networks that traditionally have excluded women. Employment in a government bureaucracy, by contrast, offers safety and protection against clients and reduces the need to exercise power and authority directly (Aubert, 1961:238–263).

## General Viewpoints

The rise of the jurists was related to a specific historic situation—the development of a secular centralized state. Jurists always have been connected to the centers of social and political power in the Scandinavian countries and have been recruited from the upper social strata. The changes in the distribution of jurists among different occupational roles mirror important social developments. The rise of private practitioners and the growth in the number of jurists in commerce and industry are important factors in the political aggrandizement of the middle class. The Liberal party, which was a dominant political force in the second half of the nineteenth century, sometimes was called the "Advocates' party." Between 1814 and 1884 a fifth of the parliament and half of the ministers were jurists. The former proportion declined to a tenth between 1910 and 1940 and to a twentieth in the 1960s (Aubert, 1964a: 313).

The growth in the number of jurists in central government after 1930 was closely connected to the emergence of a new political climate, emphasizing planning and extending public responsibility to new areas, mainly as a consequence of the rise of the working class (Torgersen, 1972: 29).

The stagnation of the court system probably is primarily attributable to finding new ways of solving conflicts. The proliferation of statutes and administrative regulations and the standardization of contracts have anticipated possible conflicts. The public administration resolves many others.

The growth of private practitioners also has entailed devotion of additional energies to solving conflicts outside court through informal negotiations. Important functions have been transferred from the public to the private sector. The intermediation of advocates has replaced judicial decisions. Advocates also fulfill an important function in implementing public policies by persuading clients to accept the norms of the state (Aubert, 1964a: 310–311; Aubert et al., 1960: 185–205).

During the nineteenth century, Norwegian jurists permeated most of the important sectors of society and became the main "entrepreneurs" in the intense efforts at nation-building. According to Aubert, this spread of legal techniques was an important condition for developing a complex industrial economy. Lawyers formed a strong, homogeneous culture throughout Norwegian society because they shared an upper-class background, experienced a uniform education, and generally were nationalistic and uncorrupt. Jurists stressed predictability and the resolution of conflict by peaceful means. Therefore, they could create the confidence necessary to build an industrialized society (Aubert, 1964a: 307; 1976: 257).

During the twentieth century, the dominance of lawyers has decreased. Because of their upper-class background, lawyers had few connections to the organized working class, which became the main power in Norwegian politics between 1935 and 1965. However, the most important factor probably is the increase in functional specialization throughout society as a result of industrialization. Economists, engineers, and other professionals gained entry to both the public and the private sectors. The jurists' hegemony as generalist leaders was broken. In contrast, the steady growth of the complex organizational structures and tasks of the modern welfare state generated a rising demand for rule-oriented counseling, decision-making, and management. In an industrialized society, most of the needs of the individual must be met through either the market system or public welfare. The apparatus for planning and regulating the market and for distributing welfare requires legal expertise. The need for bureaucratic management and decision-making is just as great in large companies as it is in public administration. While the demand for jurists as generalist leaders has decreased, the demand for the unique expertise of the legal profession—the manipulation of rules—has risen sharply during recent decades.

Norwegian jurists, beyond doubt, still are a powerful social group. It is mainly the privileged who consume their services, and these consumers pay well, maintaining the high incomes jurists enjoy. There are four main power centers in Norwegian society: elected bodies, public administration, interest organizations, and big-business firms. Most of the activity of jurists is located within the last three. In the first, their power has diminished. The increase in specialization, which reduced the importance of jurists as general-purpose social entrepreneurs, has not led to a renaissance of the judicial machinery. Instead, legal techniques have been developed and adjusted for service in other parts of society.

## UNIVERSITY AND PROFESSION

### Legal Science

Western civilization has been characterized by the rapid development of natural science during the last two centuries. Science is an integrated and important element in economic and technological development in industrialized countries, and a significant part of the gross national product is reinvested in science to create new development. Norwegian legal science has lagged behind natural science. As shown in table 2.1, only 1 percent of jurists were occupied with research and education at the university level in 1970. Law also has been massively outstripped by the social sciences, which gained prominence in Norway only after World War II. Today economies, sociology, political science, social anthropology, and psychology together employ at least ten times as many researchers as law. The number of doctoral dissertations in law always has been very small compared to the other sciences. Between 1930 and 1960, 12 new doctorates in law were awarded, compared to 210 in medicine, 128 in philology, 95 in natural science, and 32 in theology. In 1983 only 40 people held doctorates in law, or less than 2 percent of the total, compared to 669 in medicine, 487 in the natural sciences, and 394 in engineering. Although the number of legal scientists at the law faculties of Oslo and Bergen tripled during the last twenty years, there still were only 75 in 1983. As a profession, therefore, jurists place much less emphasis on research as an innovative force than do physicians, engineers, economists, and social scientists. Because law is a national science, research results from abroad are of limited importance, and law also is weakly integrated in international scientific networks.

Nevertheless, university teachers generally are well respected within the profession. They are recruited from the graduates with the best academic marks. In 1970 their income was among the highest—approximately the same as that of advocate—since then, however, salaries in the public sector, and especially in the university, have been lagging behind those in the private sector.

There are three main trends in the relationship between research and the legal profession:

1. Traditionally, experience as a professional jurist—especially as deputy judge—is regarded as an advantage for someone aspiring to a scien-

tific career. Conversely, experience as a researcher is regarded as valuable for many professional jobs. For example, university research and teaching are given full credit as practical experience in qualifying for an advocate's license. However, movement between scientific and practical work is not peculiar to *young* researchers. Of the twenty-two Norwegian law professors who died before 1970, only eight held no other important professional post during their careers. Among the fourteen who did hold such a post, there were three prime ministers, five cabinet ministers, four members of parliament, three advocates, four Supreme Court judges, one general attorney, and one national archivist. Movement occurred in both directions: some jurists became law professors after a professional career, while others left law school for important posts (Robberstad, 1971: 245–275). The university career has a greater hold over law professors today, but movement still occurs.

2. Law professors are engaged in important practical work because of their scientific competence. Participation in committees to prepare legislation and to conduct other public inquiries is common. University lawyers also draft expert legal opinions (*responsa*) at the request of judges, administrators, advocates, commerce and industry, and organizations, as well as individuals. Written opinions are a lucrative and important part of the work of the better-known professors, especially in the field of private law.

3. The scientific publications of university lawyers normally are designed for practical purposes. Much weight is placed on advising practitioners and educating students in problems of practical importance. The primary goal is normative—to indicate the correct legal decision. Cumulative research and the construction of general theory are less important. Even doctoral dissertations, which primarily serve to demonstrate the authors' scientific qualifications, usually are intended for use by practitioners. The main material for legal science is court decisions (primarily those of the Supreme Court) and legislation.

These three factors introduce a strong social bias into legal science. The practical experience of the university lawyer tends to be limited to elite positions. The production of expert opinions occurs mainly on the instructions of the leading jurists. The principal research material is Supreme Court decisions, which are a socially biased selection from the totality of legal problems in society. Legal science, therefore, concentrates on analyzing the problems handled by leading practitioners and uses the techniques and knowledge they apply in solving them. Since legal science lacks objective criteria for determining whether a result is correct, acceptance among leading practitioners is the main criterion of success. The professional status of legal scholars is largely a function of their ability to serve the leading practitioners.

The most influential innovation in Norwegian legal science after World War II was Scandinavian legal realism, whose principal spokesman was the Danish scholar Alf Ross (1958). To oversimplify, its effect was to emphasize the study of law in action and to downplay free normative statements by legal scientists in the course of interpreting legal rules. Legal realism has made legal science more open to considering the problems of legal counseling; insisted on empirical research concerning the actual operation of doctrine and legal theory in judicial decision-making; and initiated the analysis of legal ideology in other important institutions applying law, including administrative agencies. Legal realism may also be said to have furthered an orientation toward social science and empirical research in general. The empirical methods of social science have been used to map and describe the law in force (Boe, 1979). However, legal realism has been criticized for failing to supply practitioners with normative arguments that they can use to further the interests of their clients.

While these impulses derive mainly from developments in philosophy and epistemology and may be labeled the scientific critique, there also has been a reorientation based on social criticism inspired by Marxist and other socialist ideologies and by feminist analyses of law as a political instrument of patriarchy. Much of this critique is rooted in the "student revolution" and the "women's movement" of the late 1960s and early 1970s. The social critique has redirected legal science toward areas of interest to both the working class (e.g., housing law, social security, social insurance, and labor law) and women (e.g., unpaid care-taking, housewives and social security, children's law, rape, pornography, prostitution, divorce, and job discrimination). Legal scholars also have studied the legal aid and assistance program for the working class, women, the poor, and other deprived groups. However, it would be erroneous to classify these changes as revolutionary. Legal science concentrates mainly on doctrinal issues, the first of the three elements that constitute legal expertise. Factual analysis and strategic planning are neglected by scholars and left to practitioners.

## Law Study

University legal education in Norway seems to have fulfilled many of the same functions as the "public" (i.e., elite private) secondary-school system in England. Law study offered a general education in leadership, which qualified graduates for participation in most important areas of society. The law school in Oslo adopted two parallel curricula from the University of Copenhagen, one in Roman law and the other in Danish-Norwegian law. A Norwegian law examination could be taken by students who had not completed high school (*artium*) and knew no Latin. However, the Norwegian law degree qualified only for lower legal posts and had lost its importance by the 1850s. Since the end of the nineteenth century law study has been characterized by a high degree of uniformity, which has allowed jurists to play an integrative function.

The law course was shorter than that in other subjects, and there were fewer teachers. Throughout most of the nineteenth century there were six times as many students per teacher in law as in philology. The education was purely theoretical and presented through lectures to large audiences. The study was meant to confer competence in law in *general*. No set syllabus was issued, and lectures were not obligatory. Attendance depended on the extent to which the subject was covered by textbooks. Much of the education took place outside law school, especially with the help of tutors who prepared students for the law examination.

As a consequence of the unstructured character of law study, there was great concern to ensure that students had attained an acceptable level of knowledge. The vehicle was an extensive and harsh examination system, set and marked by the most skilled jurists. A law student was unlikely to be able to talk directly with a law professor, but Supreme Court justices frequently served as law examiners. The examination was taken at the end of the course of study and lasted two weeks.

Although "dependence on science" is a main criterion of professionalization, its importance should not be exaggerated. Law study today teaches students little about the scientific method. The characteristics of nineteenth-century educations still prevail. There are few teachers; thus the present student:teacher ratio is approximately 80. The education provided by academics, therefore, is supplemented by part-time teaching by practitioners from both the public and the private sectors. Private tutoring has been taken over by the university. Law study still is purely theoretical, although its main goal is educating practitioners. The syllabus allows very little freedom of choice. Today all obligatory subjects are covered by textbooks. The main effort of the students is invested in learning the content of these books. Lectures still are addressed to large audiences, but attendance is not compulsory. It is entirely possible to pass the law examinations without participating in the education offered by the university. Reading by oneself is the main technique for learning law; even the law schools emphasize independent study by students. From the moment they enter they are organized into small groups, which meet regularly to educate each other, initially with the leadership of a graduate. The length of the formal course is six years, but the average student takes longer, mainly because of the demands of part-time work.

The emphasis on theory in legal education mirrors the orientation of legal science. Neither is concerned with factual analysis or legal strategy.

Legal needs research shows that authoritative decisions based on unsatisfactory factual analysis represent a greater threat to the rule of law than does wrong or dubious interpretation of legislation. The danger is especially great for the weak and unorganized groups in society (Johnsen, 1982: 842–843). Since jurists are important participants in the legislative process, their lack of familiarity with modern social science also means that the process of incorporating its findings into political decision-making is retarded.

Interaction with clients also is neglected in legal education. Modern theories regarding the relationship between clients and professionals are unknown to most legal scientists and omitted in their teaching. Moreover, legal clinics or other forms of practical training are not included in law school courses. Voluntary student legal aid projects exist in both Oslo and Bergen, however, and approximately fifty students participate yearly. Much of the socially grounded criticism of legal science has been initiated by participants in these projects.

The Oslo law faculty has allocated one position to the Juss-Buss project. This was established in 1971 by young jurists and law students who sought to deliver legal aid to poor people in the Oslo region, conduct research for such groups, reform the legal aid and assistance system, and offer socially conscious law students an opportunity to develop their understanding of the class biases inherent in law. Today, the project specializes in immigrants from third world countries, tenants' problems, and prisoners—in addition to promoting the reform of legal aid. Ten new students are accepted each semester after they have completed between two and four years of law study. They spend a year and a half in the program, working twenty to thirty hours per week the first year and five to ten hours per week the last semester (excluding the summer months). They are paid for only ten to fifteen hours per week the first year and three to five hours per week the last semester, as a result of insufficient financial resources. New students receive fifty to seventy hours of training in dealing with clients, handling cases, the relevant law and practice, legal aid schemes and research, and impact or law reform work for the poor. The project is run collectively: the main administrative decisions are made in meetings where all participants can vote, and cases are handled in specialized groups containing five to ten members. The yearly caseload is approximately 1,500 matters.

While the universities devote fewer resources to educating lawyers than they do to students in any other subject, they clearly spend more per capita in testing law students. Until 1946, the entire examination was taken at the end of the course of study. Then permission was given to take the first half of the examination (in private law) halfway through the course. In 1968 this first examination was divided into two: an introductory examination taken after one and a half years and a major examination usually taken after four years. Starting in 1985 the examination was divided into five yearly examinations, and the official period of study now is five years of full-time work (excluding preliminary examinations in philosophy).

Much weight is placed on ranking the students. The aggregate results are expressed in an average mark on a twenty-three-point scale, where the first fifteen marks are *laudabilis* and the last eight *haud illaudabilis*. The average secondary-school grades of law students always have been significantly lower than those of other students. There also has been a rather close connection between those grades and performance in law school. If we control for high-school grades, the children of jurists do best at law school. (Differences among the other social groups are insignificant.) A plausible explanation is that legal reasoning is difficult to impart theoretically, and jurists' children have had experience in analyzing concrete legal problems, which other law students lack. The average mark is very important to the lawyer's career for both obtaining a first job that provides valuable practice and competing for the top jobs in the public sector later on. Most jobs are open to a jurist with a degree laudabilis. A few high-ranking positions, such as public prosecutor and Supreme Court judge, require that distinction by law, and others do so in practice (university law teaching posts and jobs in the legislation division in the Ministry of Justice). The honor also has been important for careers in trade and private practice, although here social connections and inheritance have been influential as well (Aubert, 1963: 204–208). Jurists with laudabilis therefore constitute an elite within the profession, and considerable social prestige is conferred by this mark. Figure 2.6 shows the proportion of candidates with laudabilis.

Unlike nineteenth-century law students, law students today have little experience with the work of jurists, and prior education no longer provides much opportunity to learn law. Law study thus is perceived as theoretical, with few ties to the experience of the students. Since the main criterion of legal expertise is the techniques and reasoning of leading private practitioners, and the examination system still is dominated by them, the underlying ideal for the students is a professional role they can imagine only vaguely. This inspires much uncertainty and doubt concerning the professional skills that they are acquiring and transforms law study into a "rite de passage" to the profession. The ability to learn quickly and regurgitate great amounts of knowledge still is the key to success. An ability to engage in independent critical analysis is of less importance. There is no obligatory dissertation, where students must gather materials and analyze them independently. The single greatest motivation for studying is fear of the examinations.

Legal education in Norway traditionally has been open to anyone who has completed high school. Law school is an institution for students with uncertain goals, who want to keep open a wide spectrum of occupational possibilities. It also represents "a second choice" for students who lack the necessary qualifications to enter subjects whose enrollment is limited, such as medicine, dentistry, engineering, and business administration.

The educational explosion in Norway has sharply increased the demand for university education (see fig. 2.7). Between 1950 and 1980, the number of students increased fivefold. The growth in the 1960s is especially striking; however, since 1975 the number of university students has remained at about 40,000. The rising demand for higher education in the last decade has been channeled to district colleges, established during the 1970s. The "educational explosion" also implies a rise in the proportion of the population holding a university or college degree (see fig. 2.8). Women were lagging behind in the 1950s, but since 1960 they have increased their share of university and college graduates at approximately the same rate as men.

The policy of limiting further growth in higher education to the district colleges led most university faculties to impose entrance restrictions during the 1970s. Because the law schools retained an "open-door" policy, they experienced a great increase in numbers during the last twenty years (see fig. 2.9).

The number of law students has quadrupled since the beginning of the 1960s. Women, who accounted for only a few percent in 1958, constituted 10 percent in 1964, 32 percent in 1978, and 40 percent in 1981. In 1983, 54 percent of entering law students were women. The changes in the gender composition of the student body have been revolutionary, although a significantly smaller proportion of women complete the course.

Another consequence of the high numbers of entrants is that both the motivation and the ability of law students have deteriorated. Overcrowding also reduces the quality of education and the intensity of student relations, which always have strongly affected success. These factors have led to a decrease in the completion rate (see fig. 2.10). Between 20 and 30 percent of the examination candidates fail the first major examination, and 10 to 20 percent fail the last one. About a third of entering law students quit without trying to pass any of the main examinations. The academic skills of new jurists also have dropped steadily (see fig. 2.11). While the number of new law candidates has increased three to four times since the beginning of the 1960s, the number of candidates with laudabilis has only doubled. The growth in the number of jurists also means that the elite jobs are open to a smaller portion of the profession.

The consequent overcrowding led the Oslo law faculty to seek restrictions on admissions, which the government imposed in fall 1985. The number of new law students probably will be limited to 500 a year, or less than half the number who enrolled in 1983/84.

Law students still are recruited from the upper-class families. Figure 2.12 shows the background of the entering law students in 1958/59, compared with those entering in fall 1983. The former now are in their forties and at the height of their careers. Two-thirds of all law students had fathers in white-collar occupations; by contrast, only one-fourth of all employed men were found in such occupations in 1981, and more than half were manual workers. There are two significant historical trends: the proportion of students whose fathers had jobs requiring a university degree has risen by a fourth, and the proportion from working-class backgrounds has increased by nearly three-fourths. The first trend probably is a consequence of the rising educational level throughout society—especially the rising proportion of women law students, who are more likely than men to come from upper-class families. The second is a continuation of the historical trend shown in figure 2.2 and reveals that the upward mobility of working-class people has accelerated within the last twenty-five years.

The average age of entering law students today is high—nearly half are over twenty-five—and a third are married. More than a fourth already had taken another academic degree. Three-fifths intended to take the full law school examination, while a fourth intended to take only the first examination—probably as part of an interdisciplinary program (15 percent had not decided). Nearly half regarded themselves as part-time students. Law students, especially part-time students, are fairly affluent. Nearly half own their homes. More than two-thirds of the part-time students finance their studies without any public loans, compared to 12 percent of the full-time students. Half of the full-time students rely mainly on public loans. Four out of five students came from southeastern Norway, mostly from urbanized areas. More than half the students do their reading at home and not at the university (Rekve, 1983). The high number of part-time students, the high average age, and the high proportion who own their dwellings, together with the high proportion of women students, probably indicate that law is particularly attractive to married or divorced women, who want to combine studying with housekeeping and who already have completed a shorter course in a subject traditionally studied by women.

CONCLUSIONS

Professionalization implies monopolization of a vast amount of knowledge. Professions often claim that their knowledge constitutes a natural whole, which must be learned systematically and in its entirety. Mastery of only part may be worse than nothing at all: "a little knowledge is a dangerous thing." Jurists explicitly embrace this ideology., stressing that the various branches of law are closely interconnected. Law is a single entity—and legal education and knowledge have been strongly centralized. Law never has been taught in the secondary schools. Until 1965, the law school in Oslo was the only one in Norway. Legal education for other professionals was limited to economists and agronomists. With the expansion of district colleges in the 1970s, however, legal training has been incorporated into many new forms of education. Ease of transfer between different programs and institutions has been an important part of Norwegian educational policy for the last decade. The dissemination of such semiprofessional knowledge is likely to increase as a consequence of the rise in the general level of education in society (Torgersen, 1972: 19).

The historical development of professional knowledge and education can be divided into four stages: (1) a prescientific period, when knowledge developed through practice is dominant; (2) a mixed period, when science is one authoritative source among others; (3) a period characterized by great confidence in science and an uncritical attitude toward established knowledge; and (4) a critical scientific stage, in which the importance of research and innovation is unquestioned but a critical attitude toward empirical findings and theories is common (Torgersen, 1972: 20). As a profession, jurists still seem to be at the second stage, while legal education always has been one of the most scholastic of academic subjects.

Science gives a profession the premises for making decisions, both factual and normative. It provides professionals with a number of routinized techniques for solving problems and relieves them of the burden of considering alternatives (Eckhoff, 1967: 304–316). Jurists generally regard their education and science as fully satisfactory for their professional work. Formal evaluation and criticism of established professional practices is not common among jurists in Norway.

In contrast, the existence and activities of a profession are the strongest evidence of the utility of its science, especially for the lay public. Professional activities also persuade public authorities to allocate resources to the science and help to recruit students. However, an undue amount of growth by a profession also may impose strain on the science. Too many resources must be allocated to educating students and advising practitioners at the expense of innovative research, resulting in the stagnation of scientific development and reduced prestige within the scientific community (Eckhoff, 1967). This clearly is the case for law, but the limited achievements of legal science are more a consequence of attitudes toward research among jurists than of the unwillingness of society to allocate more resources to scientific work. The recruitment of lawyers has varied, but it always has been sufficient to maintain jurists as one of the larger professions. If the entry of law students continues at the present rate, jurists once again will become the largest profession in Norway, as they were at the turn of the century.


## THE LEGAL COUNSELING MARKET

### THE LEGAL COUNSELING MONOPOLY

#### Counseling As a Professional Trade

Counseling and representing people in court became an economic activity in Norwegian towns during the seventeenth century. For a time the king tried to restrict the use of procurators (private practitioners), but professional representation was accepted in the towns in 1638 and in the countryside a century later, when success in the law examination became a prerequisite for procurators. Permission to work as a procurator was granted by the town magistrates, later by the chief administrative officer of the county (NL 1-9-4, Ordinance of 19 August 1735).

In 1809 procurators were made government officials, although clients still had to pay for their services according to a tariff. The title "procurator" gradually was replaced by "advocate" (*advokat*) of a particular court, for instance, "Supreme Court advocate" or "district court advocate."

Toward the end of the eighteenth century a campaign emerged to make justice free, as a return for the taxes paid by all citizens. Its proponents urged that all legal personnel, including procurators, be salaried state officials. Naturally this proposal was attacked by leading jurists. They argued that, although the government was responsible for ensuring justice to everyone, free legal services would have too many negative consequences. The requirement that clients pay for services helped to reduce the number of conflicts. People became involved in legal quarrels because they had been thoughtless or careless, especially in the conduct of their trade or business. When they had to pay the costs of legal counseling themselves, they had an incentive to be more careful. It also was unjust to spend the money of taxpayers who may have done their utmost to avoid becoming involved in legal quarrels (Ørsted, 1819: 432–461). Public salaries for procurators would lower the quality of the service offered. A party would not be free to choose the preferred advocate. Only cases deemed worthy of public support could be taken to court, and everyone would want the most skilled advocate. This would result in an unbearable work load for the best and nothing for the unskilled or incompetent. The probable result would be the erosion of competence and ethics among advocates. Paradoxically, the advocate would have to avoid public confidence. Freedom of choice had to be limited to advocates situated nearby, to avoid additional travel costs. Fees should not be fixed by the state because it was impossible to calculate the value of the service to the individual client by objective measures. The fees had to be negotiated by client and advocate on a case-by-case basis (Ørsted, 1819).

This market ideology soon prevailed. In 1848 court counseling and representation in all except the Supreme Court was turned back into a private trade requiring an advocate's license. In 1861 the same system was introduced in the Supreme Court. A governmental appointment no longer was necessary to become an advocate; all qualified jurists could obtain a license. To practice in the lower courts, nothing was required except passage of the law examination. Jurists with haud illaudabilis needed to practice for a year in the lower courts before appearing in the high courts, whereas jurists with laudabilis were entitled to a license immediately. To practice in the Supreme Court, laudabilis was required, and the advocate had to conduct three cases to the satisfaction of the justices. This system still is in force and has led to a great expansion in the number of advocates (see fig. 2.13).

## The Advocates' Association

The Advocates' Association (*Den Norske Advokatforening*), which today contains 90 percent of Norwegian advocates, was founded in 1908. Its precursor, founded in 1860, when Supreme Court procurators became private practitioners, was of little importance. A new national organization, established in 1894, lacked local chapters and was dominated by Oslo advocates. Local advocates' organizations were established through the country at the turn of the century.

When civil procedure was changed from written to oral at the beginning of the twentieth century, the proposed reforms also contained regulations for advocates. In response to this threat of state control, advocates created a national association in 1908, by electing representatives from the existing district associations to a national governing body. As a result, the state abandoned any attempt to regulate the professional association.

The highest organ is a national assembly to which the local associations send representatives. Originally, this assembly was combined with a meeting of the general membership, in which all advocates could participate. Because of travel costs, most individual participants came from the local association that hosted the assembly, and since 1950 no general membership meeting has been held. The assembly decides on the main policies of the Advocates' Association and elects the General Board, which governs the work of the association. In 1936 a secretary general was employed, and the secretariat runs the daily activities.

Today the Advocates' Association has divided the country into nineteen local associations, most of which follow county lines. Membership in the local associations varied between 10 (Finmark) and 1,120 (Oslo) in 1985. Each local association has a governing board of at least 3 members, with a maximum of 5 for associations containing fewer than 100 members and 7 for those with more. The chairperson and half the board are elected each year by the local members.

The general assembly consists of the members of the Governing Board, the chairpersons of the local boards, and additional representatives from local associations with more than 40 members (one for each 100 members, with a maximum of 6). The General Board has 9 members, normally 3 from Oslo, 2 from the rest of southeastern Norway, 1 from southern Norway, 1 from middle Norway, and 1 from northern Norway— an allocation that mirrors the geographic distribution of advocates. The secretariat had 17 employees in 1983, three of whom were advocates. Membership in the Association climbed from 650 in 1908 to 2,893 in 1985 (see table 2.2).

The most important functions of the Advocates' Association have been as follows: editing practical handbooks for advocates, organizing educational courses, promulgating rules concerning advertising, dealing with the mass media, deciding who can use the titles of advocate and Supreme Court advocate, regulating client trust accounts, and defending the economic interests of advocates. The association also has established committees to produce opinions on proposed legislation. In the legislative year 1984/85 it issued almost fifty opinions. To avoid political controversy among members, the guidelines direct these committees to concentrate on problems of compliance with the rule of law, the practicability of existing or proposed rules, and what is missing or misconceived in the proposed legislation.

## Monopoly Regulations

The monopoly enjoyed by advocates has its roots in the seventeenth century. When procurators first were allowed to charge fees for advocacy in 1638, the king also restricted entry to the profession. Procurators had to be appointed by the magistrate, possess high moral character, and swear not to promote unjust causes or incite people against the public authorities. The main goals were to ensure that the problems of unskilled workers were treated fairly and the courts were not misused to enforce unjust claims, protect the poor against unreasonable fees, and avert any litigation that might lead to social unrest (Procuratorforordningen, 1638). At the same time, procurators were given a monopoly of legal advice and representation in town courts (which was extended to rural courts half a century later). The monopoly was limited to civil cases and did not include arrests, the execution of judgments, inheritance, or bankruptcy (NL 1-9-14; Ordinance of 19 August 1735, art. 14). People still were free to handle cases on their own, however, and relatives and servants also could act as representatives. Other reliable persons were allowed to handle individual cases, with the permission of the magistrate. The impact of these regulations was that *professional* civil legal representation in courts became a monopoly of procurators.

In the second half of the nineteenth century there was a populist movement for demonopolizing legal counseling in court. Improved public education and greater participation by the public in legal institutions led the Ministry of Justice to propose that the advocates' monopoly should be restricted to the Supreme Court, as part of a policy to make legal counseling freely competitive (Odelstingsproposisjon no. 3, 1913: 119–120). However, the outcome was only a limited acceptance of laypersons as legal counselors in the lower courts.

In criminal cases the defendant still can be represented by a layperson. Until 1986, in principle, lay advocates also could be appointed everywhere except the Supreme Court as "permanent defenders"—representatives who agreed to handle criminal defense at fees set and paid by the state and who were appointed for any accused who did not exercise the right to choose another lawyer. Today, all permanent defenders are advocates in private practice.

Legal counseling outside court (hereafter referred to as "legal advice") was free from state regulation until the twentieth century. Proposals to make legal advice a monopoly for procurators were discussed during the middle of the eighteenth century but rejected. The Procurator General (the equivalent of the English Lord Chancellor) declared that the laws of the land were simple and that citizens either knew them or could learn what they needed in an hour (Pedersen, 1962: 16).

The first step in the monopolization of legal advice was taken in 1913, when this function was made a licensed trade. Municipal councils could authorize any honest and able person to give legal advice on a commercial basis within the municipality, in addition to the advocates who already performed this function. Public legal aid and advice offices and sheriffs also were excepted from the licensing system. The main reason for the reform was to protect clients against exploitation. The public had a limited ability to judge the competence and ethics of the various categories of legal counselors. However, a subsidiary aim was to eliminate unfair competition by the incompetent or the dishonest. Therefore, there was no need to license the legal aid offices established, funded, and controlled by local government in Oslo, Bergen, and Stavanger to serve the working class. In addition, sheriffs, who performed police functions, conducted auctions, and executed judgments in the countryside, already were appointed by the government.

The licensing system also could be used to control the number of legal advisers in different parts of the country. Since the law did not regulate counseling by advocates, it worked to their advantage by eliminating some of their competition (Odelstingsproposisjon no. 3, 1913).

The second, and more important, step was taken in 1936, when the licensing of nonjurists was terminated. The Great Depression in the 1930s led to an overproduction of jurists, and the Advocates' Association sought restrictions. The Ministry of Justice agreed that the number of private practitioners was much too high. While there had been 4,500 inhabitants per advocate in 1880, there were only 2,000 in 1935. The need for advocates also was diminishing, as many of the tasks that they previously had handled were taken over by collection agencies, banks, and licensed agents of various sorts. Despite the poor economic prospects for advocates, more than 100 new licenses were issued each year, as a result of the overproduction of jurists. The situation was unsatisfactory not only to the advocates but also to their clients. An advocate with insufficient income could be tempted to advise clients to undertake unnecessary actions and to misuse clients' trust accounts. The frequency of advocate misconduct had risen sharply (Odelstingsproposisjon no. 29, 1935). A reasonable income for advocates was said to be a condition for due process of law.

Two responses were discussed: further restrictions on the admission of advocates and an extension of the legal counseling monopoly. The Ministry was skeptical about tightening entry control, although this was strongly urged by the Advocates' Association. However, the Ministry favored extending the monopoly at the expense of licensed lay counselors. The Advocates' Association emphasized that there were enough advocates to meet the need for legal advice everywhere in the country, and the Ministry of Justice affirmed the principle that professional legal counseling should be performed by those best qualified. It was appropriate to authorize laypersons only where there were too few advocates (Odelstingsproposisjon no. 29, 1935). The result was virtually a commercial monopoly for advocates, although some new exceptions were introduced for accountants and bachelors of commerce, who were allowed to give legal advice in cases before the tax authorities.

The Advocates' Association has promoted this view ever since and has been hostile to counseling by economists, sheriffs, law students, banks, and estate agents, even when the latter limit activities to their special fields. In the 1950s the Ministry of Justice modified its earlier stance, stating that monopolization of professional legal counseling had to be justified by the needs of the public. Professions with the necessary qualifications in a particular field should not be excluded in order to protect the market for advocates (Odelstingsproposisjon no. 22, 1954). Nevertheless, the last step was taken in 1980, when publicly organized and financed legal advice agencies also were required to obtain a license from the Ministry of Justice.

The main features of the advocates' monopoly today are as follows. The defendant still is free to choose any representative in criminal cases (except in the Supreme Court, where an advocate must be used), but almost all choose advocates (Straffeprosessloven arts. 74, 77). In civil cases, commercial legal counseling remains the monopoly of advocates. But lay persons can appear in individual cases (except in the Supreme Court) (Tvistemålslovens art. 44). The use of legal counsel is not obligatory (except in criminal cases in the Supreme Court), but most parties are represented by advocates in all but minor offenses.

The monopoly is not complete. Legal advice may be given for idealistic motives, without payment of a fee. Other professions, such as estate agents, architects, and physicians, may render legal advice as part of their services. Employees may offer legal advice to their employers—an important exception for big firms, organizations, and governmental and other public institutions able to employ their own legal expertise. The monopoly primarily covers legal assistance on a case-by-case basis, paid for by either the client or a third party, such as an insurance company or a public agency.

## Advocates' Regulations

An advocate's license today is the principal qualification for engaging in professional legal counseling. This requires a law degree and two years of practice as either a deputy judge, a police officer, an advocate's deputy, a university professor, or a research scholar.

Deputy judgeships in Norway are filled by recent law graduates, appointed mainly on the basis of grades. They work for one to three years, and this experience is regarded as the basic training for a career as a jurist. After a probationary period of three to six months, a deputy judge is empowered to hear all sorts of cases at the district court. In 1972 nearly 60 percent of all cases at these courts were handled by deputy judges (Aubert, 1976: 228–231).

By law, senior police officers "usually" should have a law degree. The lowest of these senior posts—"police deputies"—tend to be filled by young jurists who want experience in order to become advocates or embark on careers in police and prosecution.

The third main alternative is to work as a deputy advocate. Under the supervision of a senior advocate, the deputy can perform all types of legal assistance except for litigation in the high courts and the Supreme Court.

There are no statistics available showing the actual distribution of graduates among these alternatives, but practice as a deputy judge generally is regarded as the most valuable. The large number of law graduates may increase the competition for these positions, but so far this has not created serious problems. The salary is approximately the same in all three categories—about half of the average income of senior advocates (Norges Juristforbund, 1984: 478, 486).

In order to appear before the Supreme Court, an advocate must have one year of experience and satisfactorily conduct three practice cases before the court. An important restriction on the number who qualify is the paucity of high court cases. Those who aspire to such a practice may handle such cases free and seek referrals from other advocates (advertising their availability and even paying for the referral) in order to obtain the license, before establishing their own firms. The requirement of laudabilis was abolished in 1978, when the title "Supreme Court advocate" also was dropped, but those who held the title at that time still are allowed to use it.

Licenses are issued by the Ministry of Justice. Membership in the Advocates' Association is not required, but an advocate must pay an annual contribution to the Advocates' Damage Fund for clients before starting to practice (500 Norwegian kroner [NKr] or U.S. $75 in 1985). Licenses may be withdrawn by the Ministry of Justice if an advocate (1) engages in inappropriate behavior or behavior inconsistent with the public confidence essential to the work of an advocate, (2) fails to pay the contributions to the Damage Fund, (3) violates professional regulations and fails to respond to inquiries by the Damage Fund or provide documents and books requested by the fund, or (4) fails to give a satisfactory account of personal operations when being investigated by the Ministry of Justice (Domstolslovens art. 229). A license also may be withdrawn if the advocate suffers severe mental illness, but only by the courts at the petition of Ministry, and it must be restored if the advocate recovers (Domstolslovens art. 229[a]).

These regulations give the Ministry of Justice great discretion. Economic misbehavior is the most frequent cause for suspension under the first heading. The Ministry normally acts only when the behavior also is a crime. Other forms of misbehavior, such as drunken driving or assaults, generally are not regarded as sufficient reasons for withdrawal unless they are closely connected to the advocate's work. The withdrawal of a license may be appealed to the appellate board of the Supreme Court, but such appeals are rare (Røkkum, 1982: 175).

Besides the right to engage in legal counseling for a fee, an advocate's license also allows the holder to enter other regulated trades, such as conveyancing and property trading, debt collection, and auctioneering. Also, the license places no restrictions on such unregulated activities as managing property for landlords or rendering financial advice.

## Professional Restrictions

Although competition among advocates is not regulated by law, the rules of the Advocates' Association place heavy restrictions on market behavior. The 1939 rules of conduct of the Advocates' Association directed that advertising (which always has been permitted) must avoid statements that are untrue, misleading, or disloyal toward colleagues (Halvorsen, 1983:64–65). Advertisements must not suggest that the advocate is cheaper, more competent, or faster than others. Advertisements must be dignified in form (art. 27). Consequently, advertising is rare, largely limited to young advocates beginning their practices and to a few older divorce advocates dependent on an anonymous clientele, and generally restricted to a small notice in a newspaper, giving the name and address of the advocate and listing the types of problem handled. Personal communication for the purpose of securing clients is forbidden (art. 30). An advocate should not try to secure additional business as a real estate agent through contacts with existing clients (art. 14).

Although the advocate is free to charge any fee, the Advocates' Association has issued detailed guidelines. The fees can be calculated in two ways: by averaging the usual fee for the case in question (normally a percentage of the amount involved) or by setting an hourly fee based on the amount and difficulty of the work. The first method is used in real property transactions and apartment leases, construction and housing management, debt collection, and trusteeship work. The second is used in all other cases. For calculating hourly fees, the guidelines recommend comparability with the income level and normal working hours of employees in leading positions in industry and trade. On the basis of surveys of its members, the Advocates' Association has found that a normal working year of 1,800 hours will produce approximately 1,200 billable hours. For a while the association recommended that the hourly fee be fixed so that 1,200 hours would give the advocate a net yearly income 20 percent higher than that of a civil servant.

Fees also should compensate for the size, importance, difficulty, and outcome of the case, for work that is "less pleasant," and for the nature of the advocate's practice and any special know-how or reputation. The client's ability to pay also may be considered (Christophersen, 1967). In these cases the fee should not be set before the amount of work is clear. Permanent clients can be charged a minimum retainer for the year. Contingent fees are forbidden, except for foreign clients from countries where they are common (only the United States and some Canadian provinces) (art. 13).

## ADVOCATES IN NORWAY

### Demography

There are no statistics showing how many jurists hold an advocate's license in Norway. The Ministry of Justice estimated the number at 4,000 to 5,000 in 1983, or 60 to 85 percent of all jurists. The number of advocates who paid their contribution to the Advocates' Damage Fund (a condition of practice) was 2,200 in 1982, or less than half of the ministry's estimate. Most practicing advocates are either active or passive members of the Advocates' Association. In order to be an active member, an advocate must contribute to the damage fund. Deputy advocates also may become active members. Passive membership is for pensioners and for advocates who are employed by private or public institutions and hence do not pay this contribution but still want to maintain contact with private practitioners. Employed advocates also are a significant proportion of active members, however, probably because they handle some litigation for their employers. Figure 2.14 shows the growth in the number of advocates entitled to practice.

The active membership of the Advocates' Association has increased by 80 percent during this period. The number of advocates who contributed to the damage fund has increased by 50 percent since 1950 and was 2,506 in 1985. This means that membership in the Advocates' Association has increased from 84 percent of the advocates entitled to practice in 1970 to 90 percent of that category in 1985.

Figure 2.15 shows the proportions of active members of the Advocates' Association who are private practitioners, deputy advocates, and employed advocates. The number of private practitioners has increased by 40 percent during this period, all of the increase taking place after 1975. The number of deputy advocates also has risen steadily, tripling during the period. The number of employed advocates nearly doubled; now they constitute one out of five active members of the Advocates' Association. Furthermore, the difference between private practitioners and employed advocates should not be exaggerated. More than a fourth of the private practitioners had incomes from outside their firms in 1976.

Although men continue to dominate the Association, the proportion of active members who are women has more than doubled since 1970, reaching 5 percent in 1982. Nearly 10 percent of deputy advocates are women. The steep rise in the number of deputy advocates and the proportion of women among them—consequences of the greater number of women law students in the 1970s—indicate continued growth in the number of private practitioners and in the proportion of advocates who are women, since deputy advocates normally become practicing advocates when they qualify for the license. The average age is about forty and has fallen as a result of the rapid expansion of the last decade (see fig. 2.16). In 1970, three-fourths of the advocates in private practice were over fifty (Albrechtsen, 1976: 25).

In southeastern Norway, the density of advocates is two to three times as high as it is in the rest of the country (see fig. 2.17). This means that advocates are an urbanized profession (see table 2.3). Nine out of ten advocates are located in towns, more than half in Oslo or its suburbs, the dominant urban center in Norway. The density of advocates in greater Oslo is two and a half times as high as in other Norwegian towns and populated areas and fifteen times as high as in the countryside. In 1970 more than 40 percent of the active members of the Advocates' Association had their offices within an area of less than one square kilometer in the center of Oslo (Albrechtsen, 1975).

The age distribution is geographically uneven (see fig. 2.18). The proportion of (relatively) young advocates is greatest in the most and the least urbanized parts of the country, which suggests that these locations offer the greatest opportunities for new advocates. The proportion of women advocates also differs by region (see fig. 2.19). The greatest opportunities for women seem to be located in the northern part of the country. The relatively high proportion of women advocates in southeastern Norway may be attributable partly to the location of their husbands' jobs.

## Economy

As mentioned earlier, private practitioners do more than just legal counseling and representation. Figure 2.20 shows the proportion of income that private practitioners earn from different areas of work.

What once was the main task of the advocate and the stimulus for the emergence of the profession—litigation—accounts for only a fourth of advocate income today. Legal advice outside of court produces a higher proportion. However, an entire third is derived from work other than legal counseling, most of it from business work, such as debt collection, property transactions, housing management, and investments. This departure from the traditional work of the advocate is most pronounced among Oslo advocates: while advocates outside Oslo earned two-thirds of their gross income from traditional legal counseling, less than half the income of Oslo advocates was generated in this fashion.

There is ample work for advocates. In 1976 only 3 percent of private practitioners who earned all their income from law practice reported that they had too little work; 71 percent found the amount of business sufficient; while 26 percent had too much to do. Twenty-eight percent worked more than 2,000 hours per year, and even among the 17 percent working less than 1,500 hours a year, only 10 percent reported that they lacked work. Among advocates who earned income outside their practice the picture was the same: 6 percent said their practice provided too little work, 73 percent had enough, and 21 percent had too much. Even within this group, 18 percent devoted more than 2,000 hours per year to their practice. Since the average gross income for this group was higher than that for the practitioners who earned all their income from practice, the main reason for taking work outside private practice probably is better payment (Den Norske Advokatforening, 1976).

Overhead rose from 41 percent of gross income in 1964 to 45 percent in 1976. Nevertheless, advocates in private practice remain a typical high-income group. In 1970 the average income was three times the average income for all full-time wage earners, 10 percent higher than that for employed advocates, and somewhere between permanent secretaries and deputy secretaries in the public sector (well above the salaries of law professors). The income distribution is uneven, however: solo practitioners earned less than two-thirds as much as advocates in bigger firms; Supreme Court advocates earned half again as much as other advocates; and advocates in Oslo earned 20 percent above the national average (see fig. 2.21).

## Use of Advocates

In a 1966 survey, 14 percent of respondents stated that they had received advice from (been a client of) an advocate at least once (Albrechtsen, 1969). A second survey the following year revealed that 20 percent had contacted an advocate after 1945, on their own or on behalf of somebody else (Albrechtsen, 1975). The following analysis is based on the latter survey. Every year approximately 1 percent of the population are the clients of advocates. This also means that only about a fifth of the efforts of private practitioners are devoted to individual clients. Men consulted lawyers nearly twice as often as women (22 percent vs. 13 percent). Lawyer utilization in the three biggest towns is 80 percent higher than in the rest of the country, but there are no differences between other towns and the countryside comparable to the differences in lawyer distribution (see table 2.3). Therefore, there is no clear correlation between the frequency of lawyer use among individuals and the density of advocates (Albrechtsen, 1971).

The use of advocates is clearly related to income and education, however (see figs. 2.22 and 2.23). Those with the best education and highest income use lawyers 2.5 times as often as those with the lowest. Thus, the use of advocates is a typical high status phenomenon (see Albrechtsen [1975] and fig. 2.24). The Oslo elite, who consist of financiers, the owners of commercial and industrial firms, academics, and other upper-class groups, used advocates seven times as frequently as small farmers and farm workers and four times as frequently as industrial workers.

Figure 2.25 shows the use of advocates by the type of case. More than half of the cases concerned the maintenance and management of property and capital. Advocates were used to sell, buy, or mortgage real property and to assist with business or tax problems. However, dispute resolution outside court—especially the arbitration of business conflicts and divorces—also constituted an important part of the caseload. The cases concerning personal problems mainly involved inheritance, marriage settlements, and adoptions. Three-fourths of the clients in cases concerning property, capital, and civil litigation were men, while two-thirds of the clients in personal matters were women.

Attitudes toward the use of advocates also were socially biased (see figs. 2.26 and 2.27). More than two-thirds of the population said that they *never* had considered using an advocate. Only a third believed that they could profit significantly from an advocate's services. These negative attitudes were most common among the least educated and poorest (see fig. 2.28).

These figures show that satisfaction with the lawyer's work varies widely with class. While three-fourths of the elite who had previous experience with an advocate expressed great confidence in advocates, this was true of less than half of the workers and little more than a third of the farmers with similar experience. These figures also suggest that actual experience with advocates promotes a positive attitude and that this tendency is strongest among those with the least experience—specifically, the lower classes. Table 2.4 presents additional information about public attitudes toward advocates.

## Public Legal Aid and Advice Schemes

Public legal aid and advice in Norway always has been delivered through "judicare" schemes using private practitioners. In the seventeenth century, when the system of procurators appeared, the king introduced a legal aid system for civil litigation. The public authorities could appoint procurators to handle the cases of the deserving poor (who were thought not to be responsible for their poverty). These procurators depended for compensation on what they could collect from their clients' adversaries. Soon a practice developed of issuing *beneficium paupertatis* (poverty licenses). Poor people applied to the king—and later to the Ministry of Justice—for free legal aid. A poverty license provided for waiver of court costs and payment of the procurator's fee by the public purse (originally at a fixed price and later at a level set by the court).

The Criminal Procedure Act of 1887 introduced a scheme of free defense in criminal cases, which was preserved by the Criminal Procedure Act of 1981. Defenders are appointed for the trial of all criminal cases (except in minor offenses) and also for bail hearings. The accused is entitled to choose an advocate or another fit person within the court district as a defender. If the accused has no one to propose, the court will appoint someone, usually a private practitioner who has been appointed permanent defender at that court. This scheme is not limited to the poor; a defender is appointed regardless of the defendant's income. The fee is paid by the court, but a convicted defendant who has the means will be ordered to repay some or all of the costs of the case, depending on the gravity of the crime and the certainty of guilt (Straffeprosessloven of 1887, art. 452[2]).

A general legal advice scheme for the poor outside court first was established around 1960. During the 1970s, the international legal assistance reform movement stimulated efforts to change the Norwegian system. However, the first Legal Aid and Advice Act, passed by Parliament in 1980 without significant political controversy, mainly codified the existing administrative scheme. It authorizes public financing for low income clients who wish to hire private practitioners, but it creates no special legal services programs for the poor nor any procedures for ensuring that those who seek legal aid are well served by their lawyers. All advocates who have paid their contributions to the Damage Fund are entitled to give legal aid, although they have no obligation to do so. Legal aid and advice work is paid at an hourly fee set by the Ministry of Justice, usually after informal negotiations with the Advocates' Association.

The proportion of the population eligible for civil legal aid and advice under the 1980 act varies with changes in the means test and the income distribution. Because inflation has been high in Norway recently and the income limits have not been changed since the act was passed, eligibility has contracted. Exact figures are not available, but when the 1980 act went into effect, approximately half the households in the country were covered by the civil schemes. Today, the figure is approximately a third.

Use of the legal advice scheme has grown steadily since it was introduced, more steeply in the last ten years (see fig. 2.29). The main cause probably is the growth in the number of private practitioners. In 1983 free legal advice outside court was given to 17,514 people—one out of every 83 people eligible. Table 2.5 shows the distribution by subject matter. No reliable statistics are available for legal aid in civil litigation, although a fair estimate would be 3,000 to 4,000 cases per year, mostly in family matters. No estimate can be made for legal aid in criminal cases.

Public legal aid in civil and criminal cases and free legal advice outside court together accounted for only 5 percent of aggregate lawyer income in 1976. The fees paid by the government for legal aid and advice always have been significantly lower than those paid by private clients. In 1985 the fee paid for legal aid and assistance was 300 NKr per hour (about $40 at U.S. $1 = 7 NKr.); in 1984, the secretary general of the Advocates' Association estimated that the average fee paid by private clients was 400 to 600 NKr (about $50 to $80) per hour.

In 1982 the Advocates' Association distributed a questionnaire to its members to ascertain the extent of participation by advocates in the civil legal aid and advice schemes. Only 570 advocates replied (the remainder probably had very little experience with legal aid and assistance). Twenty advocates (3.5 percent of respondents) reported that more than half of their income came from the public legal assistance schemes; 60 (10.5 percent) earned a fourth to a half from this source, 185 (32.5 percent) earned 5 percent to 25 percent, 145 (25.4 percent) earned less than 5 percent, and 160 (28.1 percent) earned little or nothing (Villum, 1982: 230–237)

A study of the use of the legal advice scheme in Troms county between 1971 and 1980 revealed that only 13 percent of the advocates earned a regular part of their income over a five-year period from the legal advice scheme. In 1976 such cases accounted for 15 percent of the income of this group. Another 42 percent of the advocates handled public legal advice cases occasionally and earned 4 percent of their 1976 income from this source, while 45 percent never used the scheme. Most newly established advocates rendered decreasing amounts of legal assistance after the first few years. Eligible clients were turned away in large numbers. Nevertheless, one out of five new advocates seemed interested in making legal advice cases a permanent part of their practice (Johnsen, 1981: 91–98).

Unsolved legal problems, therefore, are common among most strata of the population. While the use of lawyers increases with income and social status, unmet legal need varies inversely with social status. The most important areas of unmet legal need are social security and insurance, housing, tax, and family matters. The civil legal aid and advice schemes satisfy only a fraction of the needs revealed by legal services research, although they cover a third of the population. At the level at which the free legal advice scheme was operating in 1983, each eligible person could be seen only once in a lifetime. The lack of legal counseling represents an important welfare problem for the working class. These "markets" are regarded as less profitable by the advocates and have not been exploited because of insufficient personnel.


## General Conclusions


Advocates emerged as a profession by selling their advice in court on a case-by-case basis. Private practitioners then found new functions more rewarding than litigation. One of these was legal advice, often given to permanent clients such as business firms and municipalities. Advocates also turned to different activities, both those performed by other professions and those open to everybody regardless of training, such as financial transactions, investments, transferring realty, property development and management, organization, and public commissions. Yet, this evolution has not been able to satisfy the need for legal counseling in industry and commerce or in public administration. These institutions increasingly employ their own expertise in order to create a stable relationship with an adviser, enhance specialization and competence, ensure loyalty and availability, combine legal counseling with management and decision-making, and reduce costs. Today, even private practitioners participate in decision-making in both public and private organizations.

Self-employed professional legal counseling in Norway can be characterized as a monopoly dependent on the market. Jurists with an advocate's license are free to engage in private practice whenever they wish. They can choose the clients they want to serve and the prices they want to charge. Within this monopoly competition is unrestricted by law, although the ethical rules of the Advocates' Association severely limit marketing practices.

The production apparatus of advocates is simple. The main element is the advocate, together with some books and office facilities. The constraints on location are the client market and the distance to courts, administrative agencies, business centers, and similar institutions.

Advocates seek the most rewarding work. The most profitable commissions are derived from public institutions, industry and commerce, organizations, and wealthy individuals. Since advocates are free to engage in other trades, they also must consider real property sales, housing management, property and financial management, and board membership in corporations. Individual clients from the lower classes are less remunerative. This part of the market will be served only when the remainder is saturated.

These two factors exert very strong pressures on advocates to locate their offices in urban areas. Table 2.6 shows the covariation between population density, median individual income, number of firms, value of trade, number of low income households (with income under $7,000), proportion of low income households, and density of advocates in the nineteen Norwegian counties. There is a strong correlation between the location of advocates and population density, level of personal income, and trade activity. The location of advocates is unrelated to the *number* of low-income households, but it is inversely related to their proportion of all households.

Competition for the most profitable sectors of the market will be influenced by the number of private practitioners. The latter depends on two main factors: the production of jurists and the demand for their services in other parts of the professional market. The recruitment of new advocates increases when the job market elsewhere is contracting and decreases when there is greater demand for jurists in public administration and business. Advocates equilibrate the market for jurists.

The number of advocates has risen sharply during the last ten years. This may explain the steep rise in the use of the legal advice scheme. However, growth has not changed the geographical distribution of advocates (see table 2.7).

The existing supply of advocates is insufficient to satisfy the demand for legal counseling among people eligible under the legal aid and assistance schemes. For private practitioners, legal aid clients function as a reserve market, which is exploited to compensate for temporary shortages in the stream of paying clients. When competition increases, because of the overproduction of jurists or lack of other opportunities in the professional market, more legal aid work will be performed. Legal aid and advice schemes also are exploited by new advocates until they are able to establish more profitable relationships with paying clients in industry and commerce (Johnsen, 1981).

This means that the distribution of legal counseling in society is class-biased. The problems of the upper classes represent a continuous stream of profitable work that is professionally and socially rewarding and can offer a stable source of income. The problems of the lower classes are nonrecurring and promise only small fees. They also provide fewer professional and social rewards. The lower classes receive what is left on the market—those advocates with the least competence and the lowest ethical principles. These clients probably receive the most expensive and least effective counseling, if they receive any professional service at all. These class biases mean uneven distribution of legal talent: at the expense of the majority of the population, the poor, and inhabitants of the rural areas; and to the advantage of large corporations and organizations, public agencies, the wealthy, and city dwellers (Blom, 1974: 12–3).

DISCIPLINE

Professions generally prefer to regulate themselves; extensive regulation
by law is perceived as a lack of public confidence. This is reflected in the
standard for the professional conduct of procurators, established by the
king in 1685: "They shall not incite people nor try to obstruct lawful settlements nor impoverish the poor nor others through unreasonable fees"
(NL 1-9-10). Today, the penal code applies the same rules to lawyers that
it does to civil servants. The punishment is fines and loss of license for repeated violations (Straffelovens arts. 324, 325; Domstolslovens art. 230).

The rules of conduct of the Advocates' Association regulate the relationship between the advocate and society, the client, and other members
of the profession. The first category of norms is aspirational, proclaiming
a general, vague standard establishing ideal, superhuman goals for professional conduct: Advocates must do their best to further the interests of
their clients within the limits of law and without regard to personal gain
or risk, political sympathy, race, religion, or other irrelevant circumstances
(art. 1). The function of such norms may be as much to legitimize the profession in the eyes of the public as to influence professional behavior. The
second category seeks to regulate the advocate's obligations and to protect the advocate against excessive demands by clients. Since these norms
are intended to resolve important and concrete conflicts between advocate and client, they are more detailed. Here we find regulations concerning the independence of the advocate, conflicts of interest with clients,
settlements, costs, the freedom to terminate the relationship before the
matter is completed, and so on (arts. 6–15). Advocates, like other professionals, also have rules limiting conflict among colleagues: other advocates always should be treated with respect and consideration, and criticism
of their work must be impartial and sober (art. 19). The public is unable to
evaluate the skill of the advocates, although the client's freedom of choice
is an important part of the ideology of the Advocates' Association.
Official evaluations must be left to the profession, through its disciplinary
organs.

There is little research on the quality of legal services. However, a
survey of custody cases in the city court of Oslo in 1973 revealed that the
service delivered by the permanently appointed defenders varied widely
and that a significant proportion of the clients did not receive assistance in
accordance with the standards established by the trial law (Bjerke, 1976:
70–86).

The ethical code is written in vague, general language. This allows
flexibility in responding to professional development and the demands of
society. However, vagueness also permits different interpretations by
lawyers and leads to a narrow definition of the conduct that is deemed

"unprofessional." The Disciplinary Board decided in 1975 that complaints that could lead to liability for malpractice should be left to the ordinary courts, except in cases of obvious neglect of professional standards. It was not unethical to fail to be clever or to commit documented and uncontested mistakes. The board concluded that disciplinary sanctions were of very limited value in improving the professional standards of advocates (Den Norske Advokatforening, 1975: 434).

The principal sanction is expulsion. In some professions this means loss of the license to practice. For advocates it has little formal effect, since licenses are issued by the Ministry of Justice. However, expulsion by the Advocates' Association will be reported to the ministry and often lead to loss of license. This is not automatic, since the disciplinary code and statutory regulations are not coterminous; consequently, the ministry will make its own judgment (Røkkum, 1982: 175).

Discipline within professions generally is ineffective. Unreported deviance probably is high, because professional organizations must give their members considerable freedom and because nonbureaucratic environments allow greater latitude for deviance than do bureaucratic work settings (Torgersen, 1972: 62–64). This clearly is true for Norwegian advocates, most of whom are solo practitioners.

Disciplinary cases are heard by the local boards of the Advocates' Association, whose decisions can be appealed to the Central Disciplinary Board, composed exclusively of advocates. Between July 1982 and June 1985 there was an average of 116 complaints per year to the local boards and fifty appeals, suggesting a rather high degree of dissatisfaction with the decisions of the former. More than a fourth of the complaints were dismissed or withdrawn. Ethical misconduct was the reason for half the complaints and appeals, fee disputes generated a fourth, and both issues were raised in the remainder.

More than three-fourths of the complaints ended with an acquittal or warning (see fig. 2.30). More severe sanctions, such as fines and expulsions, are uncommon and rarely have been imposed in recent years. These figures indicate that the disciplinary system is rather ineffective in regulating professional conduct. The main function is to legitimize established behavior. Professional associations often negotiate with governmental authorities to improve professional salaries or strengthen the profession's monopoly. In such negotiations the "rotten apples" within the profession are a source of embarrassment and may generate demands for more effective discipline (Torgerson, 1972: 56–57). As members of a self-employed profession working mainly for private clients, advocates feel little need to improve their bargaining position with respect to the government. Consequently, the Advocates' Association has resisted proposals to add laypersons to the disciplinary bodies.

POLICY QUESTIONS

## Advocates as a Private Profession

The principal policy question of the 1970s has been whether the system of self-employed advocates selling their professional services on the market on a case-by-case basis is a satisfactory solution to the legal needs of the lower social strata. Opposition to the market model has come mainly from the organized labor movement. The huge amount of unmet legal need among lower- and middle-class people, documented by research and student legal advice projects for the poor, stimulated leading Labor politicians to advocate new ways of delivering legal services to the working class. Legal counseling could be an instrument for reducing class differences and improving the effectiveness of the welfare system. If socialist politics were to function fairly, it was necessary that *all* citizens have effective remedies to enforce their rights. This model also implied the need for new professional techniques. Enforcing the rights of broad segments of the population required the abandonment of the traditional emphasis on individual cases, which has dominated both judicare and salaried legal aid and advice schemes in Scandinavia. Such a legal assistance system also could promote socialist governance, for legal services would produce valuable information about defects in the welfare system, which could influence the ongoing reform process (Valle, 1975: 6–7; Ekanger, 1975: 201–209).

Two strategies were advocated to promote these goals: a liberal judicare scheme and salaried offices. The latter was perceived as a threat by the private profession and therefore opposed by the Advocates' Association. During the first half of the 1970s the Association advocated a modernized judicare scheme, supplemented by small salaried offices outside the central cities. At the time the profession had problems recruiting new entrants, and small public offices could encourage jurists to enter private practice and give them valuable experience. Concern for the legal needs of the underprivileged also was a way to attract the radicals among law students and young lawyers and channel them into the profession. A liberal judicare scheme could expand the client market and reduce the economic insecurities of the early years of practice.

In the second half of the 1970s the profession's attitude changed. Whereas leading advocates with few economic interests at stake had influenced the policies of the Advocates' Association during the first half of the decade, now local practitioners had a greater say. Less altruistic attitudes prevailed. Salaried offices in the outskirts might attract part of the client market from the most vulnerable private practitioners. Raising the income ceiling could force advocates to accept the low fees stipulated by the Ministry of Justice for a considerable proportion of their individual clients. Recruitment into private practice also had improved significantly, as a result of the high influx of law students. When arguments of the Advocates' Association were adopted by the nonsocialist parties, the Labor party abandoned the proposal of salaried offices before it became a political controversy.

MARKET CONTROL

Professions try to avoid unregulated market competition in several ways. They may seek to control supply by lowering the age of retirement or regulating entrance to professional studies, either by quotas or by raising the cost. They may seek to stimulate demand, but this is much more difficult and requires close cooperation with public authorities. They may try to expand the professional monopoly, usually by incorporating tasks that offer fewer rewards. Professionals may emigrate to countries experiencing a scarcity of trained personnel, but since law is a national profession this is not an option (Torgersen, 1972: 80–89). Let us consider the extent to which these strategies have been pursued by Norwegian advocates.

Professions always fear overproduction. Open admission to professional study restricts their control over supply. One response is to give potential recruits information about the market for professional services. But estimates of future demand often are short-sighted extrapolations of the present situation.

As we have seen, overproduction of jurists has been a growing problem in Norway for the last fifteen years, mainly as a result of entrance restrictions in other university subjects. The effect also is a rise in the number of advocates. Limitations on entry now have been introduced at the Law Faculty of Oslo University. Yet the impetus for this reform was not advocates but rather university teachers and students, who complained about the steadily deteriorating educational conditions. The scarcity of resources for legal education is more an unintended consequence of social democratic policies concerning education and social mobility than a conscious project of market control among advocates. The funding crisis also is connected to the principles governing the allocation of resources within the university. Other faculties opposed the request for an increase in the per capita expenditure for law students unless admission was restricted. So far, there has been no attempt to limit the number of law graduates who become advocates. The possibility of lowering the retirement age is limited within a self-employed profession. The capacity of the Advocates' Association to influence the influx of law students also is limited, since advocates represent only one of the occupations that recruit jurists, and public employers may regard overproduction as a good way to ensure that competent jurists seek central and local government posts.

The Advocates' Association did seek to raise the requirements for an advocate's license in the 1930s, when there also was overproduction. Since the Ministry of Justice issues the license, however, this, too, is difficult. Recently, however, the Advocates' Association recommended to the ministry that law graduates be required to gain three years of experience (rather than the present two) before being licensed, during which period they would have to engage in certain kinds of work and complete further education.

Competition among advocates may be viewed as serving the public interest, although excessive competition also may lead to unprofessional conduct. Restricting the number of advocates' licenses during a period of overproduction also may increase unemployment among jurists, creating political problems for the government, which has a constitutional obligation to provide work for everyone who is physically fit (Grunnlovens art. 110). Such proposals also may elicit opposition among other jurists, most of whom have an advocate's license and want to retain the option of entering private practice.

Capturing new areas for professional work historically has been, and still is, an important strategy for advocates. Broadening the scope of private practice also increases the possibility of leaving practice and becoming a company or organization lawyer or manager. However, advocates have been reluctant to seek new markets by expanding government support for legal aid and advice to the poor for two reasons: (1) the low level of recruitment during the first half of the 1970s created little pressure to generate demand, and (2) full recognition of the extent of unmet legal need would highlight the inability of the profession to satisfy it and raise the question of delivering legal services through means other than private practitioners.

The fight against paralegals has been won. The advocates could extend their monopoly only by ousting other professions who perform legal counseling as part of their ordinary services. This would evoke heavy opposition, and thus far the Advocates' Association has been unsuccessful.

## CONCLUSION

In a broad historical perspective we can distinguish four stages in the professional development of advocates. In the middle ages, free men represented themselves in legal matters. Although the Vikings were warriors who brutally plundered and destroyed other peoples, at home they were highly legalistic. Representatives of the king handled the legal affairs of powerless categories, such as women, children, the physically handicapped, and the mentally ill. However, the expansion of the king's power during the sixteenth and seventeenth centuries and the emergence of a centralized bureaucracy generated the demand for experts who could advise those subjected to this authority. Legal counseling now could become a commercial activity. As the legal services market developed, wealth began to influence the distribution of legal services, and the social status of procurators depended on their ability to sell their services to those who commanded economic and political resources. The third stage is closely connected to the intense nation-building, industrialization, and growth of the market economy that occurred during the nineteenth century. Jurists were the principal entrepreneurs and managers. When advocates' licenses were made available to all jurists around 1850, there was an enormous increase in their numbers. Finally, in the twentieth century, the increasing complexity of the industrial economy and the growth of welfare and planning generated a demand for more specialized functionaries. Jurists lost their hegemony as generalized leaders, but new demands for rule-oriented management and decision-making led to continued numerical growth.

Norwegian advocates do not constitute a distinct, independent profession as they do in the common law world. Rather, they are part of a wider entity—the professional culture of jurists—which allows considerable lateral mobility. Jurists may switch occupational roles and move between the public and private sectors. The availability of these other roles helps to equilibrate the market for advocates. Consequently, advocates feel less pressure to seek to control the market. If demand within the private sector declines, advocates find other professional work as jurists.

Today, the needs of capital dominate the legal services market, and the activities of advocates are organized to satisfy those needs. This dominance, together with the high fees that capital pays, creates considerable loyalty to the interests of capital (Albrechtsen, 1974b: 102–104). The distribution of legal services therefore reinforces class differences. Elites in commerce and industry use advocates' services to develop more profitable ways of organizing and operating their businesses and influence the evolution of the legal system to their own advantage, especially within the realm of private law (Albrechtsen, 1974a). As a result, the legal system gradually becomes increasingly biased in favor of the interests of capital (Albrechtsen, 1974b: 104).

# TABLES

2.1. Distribution of Jurists by Occupation, 1970 ($N = 5,106$)

| Occupation | Percent | |
|---|---|---|
| Public sector | | |
|   Courts | 8 | |
|   Police and prosecution | 5 | |
|   Public administration | 31 | |
|   University | 1 | |
|   Research and education outside university | 2 | |
|     Total public sector | | 47 |
| Private sector | | |
|   Advocate in private practice | 24 | |
|   Company advocate | 6 | |
|   Management of business or organization | 20 | |
|   Press | 2 | |
|   Farmer | 1 | |
|     Total private sector | | 53 |

*Source:* Albrechtsen (1976).

2.2. Membership in Advocates'
Association, 1985

| Type of membership | | |
|---|---|---|
| Active members | | |
| Advocates | 2,257 | |
| Deputy advocates | 283 | |
| Total | | 2,540 |
| Passive | | 353 |
| | | |
| Total | | 2,893 |

*Source:* Unpublished statistics from Den
Norske Advokatforening.


2.3. Density of Advocates by Degree of Urbanization, 1980[a]

| | Percent of population | Percent of advocates | Advocates per 10,000 inhabitants |
|---|---|---|---|
| Oslo and suburbs | 16 | 51 | 15 |
| Other cities and towns with more than 6,000 inhabitants | 31 | 39 | 6 |
| Rest of the country | 53 | 10 | 1 |
| | | | |
| Whole country | 100 | 100 | 5 |

[a] Active members of Advocates' Association.
*Source:* Den Norske Advokatforening (1980); Central Bureau of Statistics of Norway (1981).

### 2.4. Public Attitudes toward Advocates

Percentage who answered affirmatively to the question:
"Do you think advocates generally are"

| | |
|---|---|
| Well suited to defend the interests of the common man and woman? | 34 |
| Well suited in some areas but not others? | 25 |
| Too busy earning money? | 14 |
| Too eager to go to court? | 3 |
| Too eager to make settlements? | 2 |
| Too weak in conflicts with the authorities? | 4 |
| Too much involved with the wealthy? | 7 |
| Lacking in legal knowledge? | 1 |
| Lacking in understanding of real life? | 6 |
| Other | 2 |

*Source:* Albrechtsen (1971).

### 2.5. Distribution of Free Legal Advice by Subject, 1983 ($N = 17,514$)

| Subject | % |
|---|---|
| Family | 41 |
| Inheritance | 18 |
| Housing, property | 11 |
| Debts | 6 |
| Damages | 4 |
| Labor | 3 |
| Social insurance, pensions | 3 |
| Miscellaneous | 14 |
| Total | 100 |

*Source:* Odelstingproposisjon no. 57 (1983/84: 3).

2.6. Relationship between Distribution of Advocates and Other Socioeconomic Variables (Pearson's r)[a]

| | Number of advocates by county, 1985 | Advocates per 10,000 inhabitants by county, 1985 |
|---|---|---|
| Inhabitants per square kilometer, 1985 | 0.87 | 0.88 |
| Average personal income per taxpayer, 1983 | 0.68 | 0.65 |
| Number of firms, 1985 | 0.98 | — |
| Value of trade, 1982 | 1.00 | 0.95 |
| Number of households with income below NKr 50,000 in 1979 | 0.05 | 0.05 |
| Percentage of households with income below NKr 50,000 in 1979 | −0.64 | −0.66 |

[a] See Hellevik (1977: 229–240).
Source: Central Bureau of Statistics of Norway (1983; 1984); unpublished statistics from Den Norske Advokatforening.

2.7. Relationship between Distribution of Growth of Advocates and Other Socioeconomic Variables (Pearson's r)[a]

| | Growth in the number of advocates by county, 1975–1985 | Growth in the number of advocates per 10,000 inhabitants by county, 1975–1985 |
|---|---|---|
| Inhabitants per square kilometer, 1985 | 0.75 | 0.77 |
| Average personal income per taxpaper, 1983 | 0.72 | 0.69 |
| Number of firms, 1985 | 0.98 | — |
| Value of trade, 1982 | 0.99 | 0.89 |
| Number of households with income below NKr 50,000 in 1979 | 0.00 | 0.14 |
| Percentage of households with income below NKr 50,000 in 1979 | −0.67 | −0.66 |

[a] See Hellevik (1977: 229–240).
Source: Central Bureau of Statistics of Norway (1983; 1984); unpublished statistics from Den Norske Advokatforening.

# FIGURES

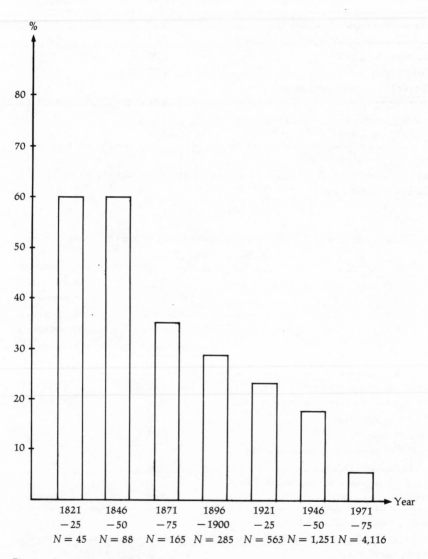

Fig. 2.1. Jurists as a proportion of all university graduates, 1820–1975. (*Source*: Central Bureau of Statistics of Norway [1978: 628–631].)

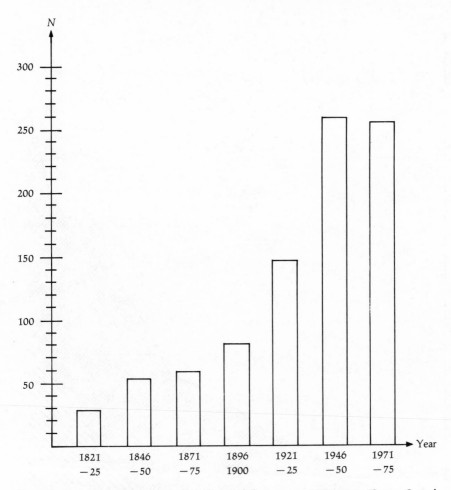

Fig. 2.2. Average number of law degrees awarded per year, 1820–1975. (*Source*: Central Bureau of Statistics of Norway [1978: 627–631].)

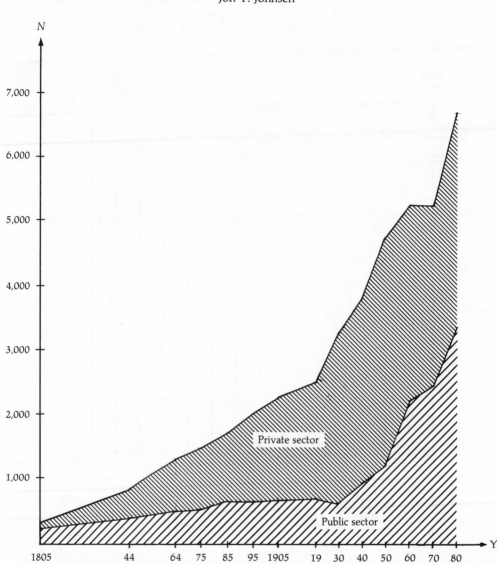

Fig. 2.3. Growth in the number of jurists in the private and public sectors, 1815–1980. (*Source*: Aubert [1964*a*: 305–306].)

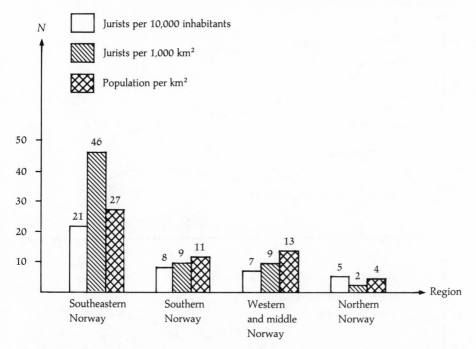

Fig. 2.4. Geographic distribution of jurists, 1970. (*Sources*: Albrechtsen [1976]; Central Bureau of Statistics of Norway [1973].)

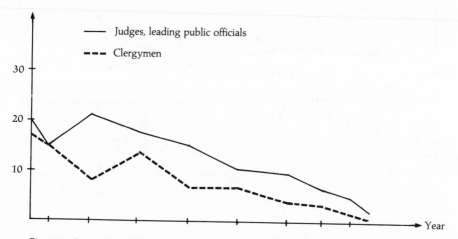

Fig. 2.5. Occupation of jurists' fathers, 1815–1950. (*Source*: Aubert et al. [1960: 185–204].)

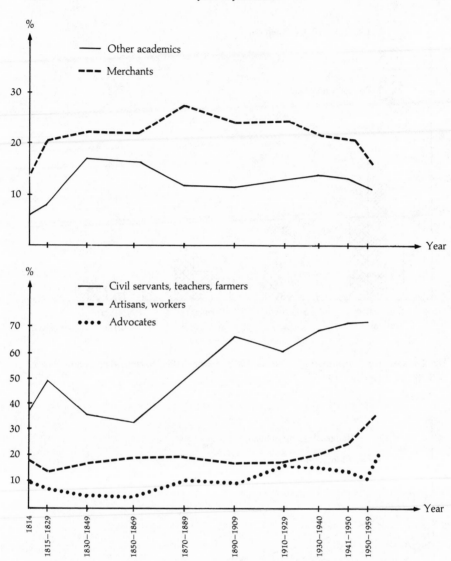

Fig. 2.5. (*continued*)

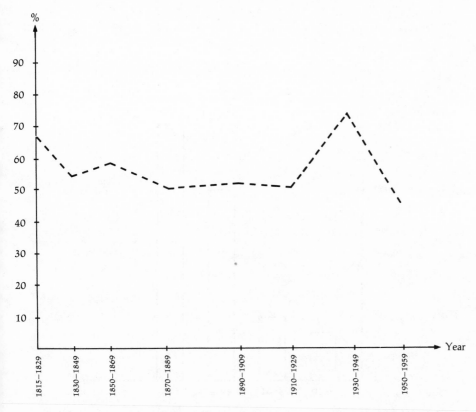

Fig. 2.6. Proportion of law graduates receiving degree laudabilis, 1815–1959. (*Sources*: Aubert [1960: 123]; Norsk Rettstidend [1950–1959].)

Jon T. Johnsen

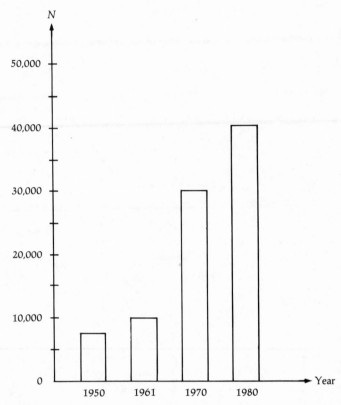

Fig. 2.7. Number of university students, 1950–1980. (*Source*: Central Bureau of Statistics of Norway [1978: 357; 1984: 386].)

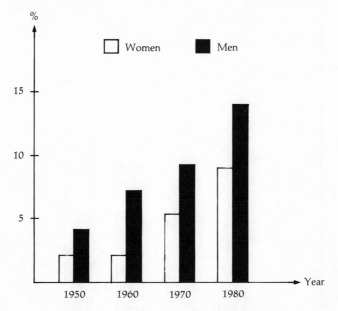

Fig. 2.8. Proportion of population aged sixteen and older with a university or college degree, 1950–1980. (*Source*: Central Bureau of Statistics of Norway [1983: 185].)

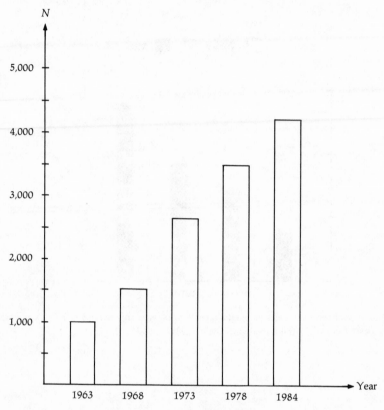

Fig. 2.9. Number of law students, 1963–1984. (*Source*: Law Faculty of Oslo University [1984*b*].)

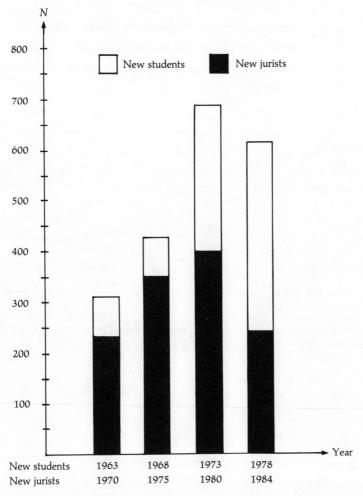

Fig. 2.10. Oslo University law graduates as a proportion of entering law students seven years earlier, 1970–1984. (*Source*: Law Faculty of Oslo University [1984*a*].)

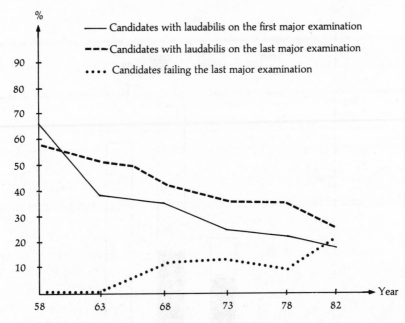

Fig. 2.11. Number receiving laudabilis and number failing as proportions of those taking law examinations, 1958–1982. (*Source*: Law Faculty of Oslo University [1983].)

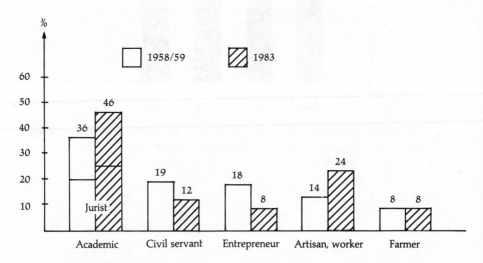

Fig. 2.12. Occupations of fathers of Oslo University law students, 1958/59 and 1983. (*Sources*: Aubert [1976: 259]; Rekve [1983].)

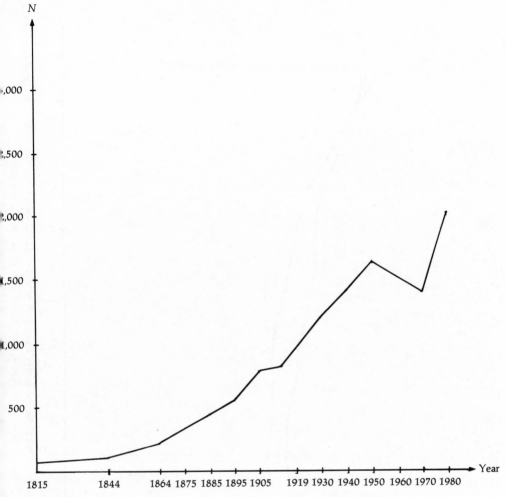

Fig. 2.13. Number of advocates, 1815–1980. (*Sources*: Aubert et al. [1960: 2]; Aubert [1976: 263]; Albrechtsen [1976].)

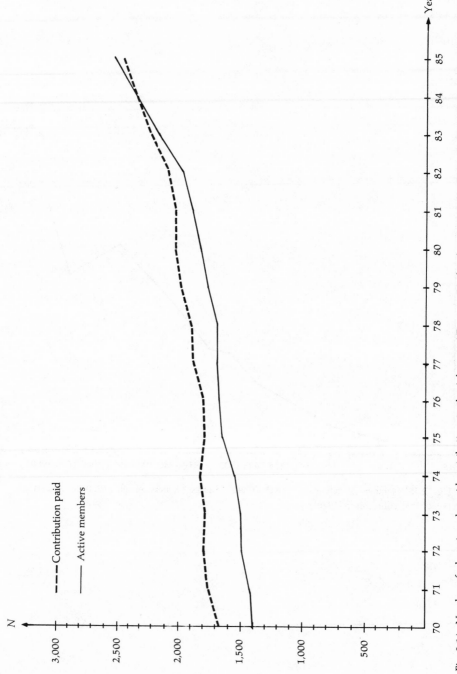

Fig. 2.14. Number of advocates who paid contributions to the Advocates' Damage Fund and active members of the Norwegian Advocates' Association, 1970–1985. (*Source:* Unpublished statistics from Den Norske Advokatforening [Norwegian Advocates' Association].)

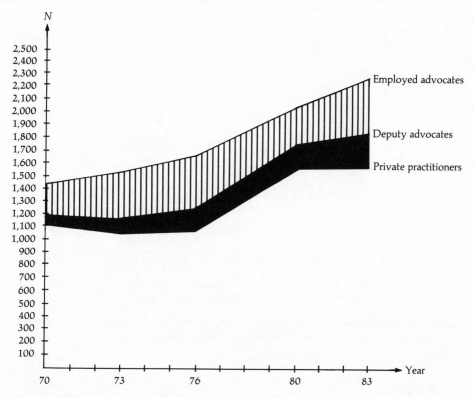

Fig. 2.15. Private practitioners, deputy advocates, and employed advocates who were active members of the Advocates' Association. (*Source*: Den Norske Advokatforening [1970, 1973*a*, 1980, 1982].)

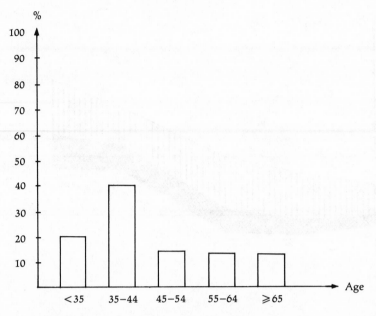

Fig. 2.16. Age distribution of active members of the Norwegian Advocates' Association, 1985. (*Source*: Unpublished statistics from Den Norske Advokatforening.)

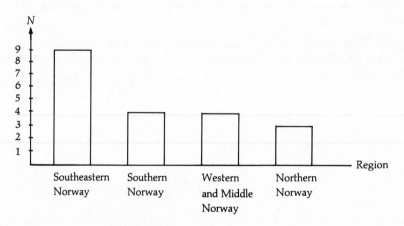

Fig. 2.17. Active members of Advocates' Association per 10,000 inhabitants, by region, 1985. (*Source*: Unpublished statistics from Den Norske Advokatforening.)

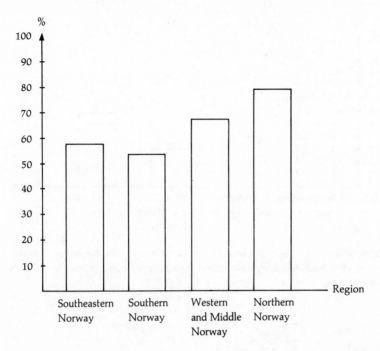

Fig. 2.18. Active members of the Advocates' Association under age forty-five as a proportion of all active members, by region, 1985. (*Source*: Unpublished statistics from Den Norske Advokatforening.)

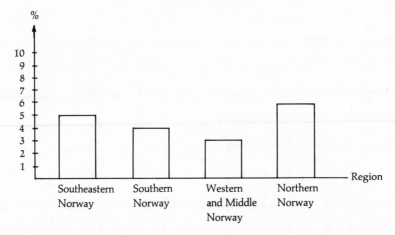

Fig. 2.19. Women as a proportion of advocates contributing to the Advocates' Damage Fund, by region, 1985 (excluding deputy advocates). (*Source*: Unpublished statistics from Den Norske Advokatforening.)

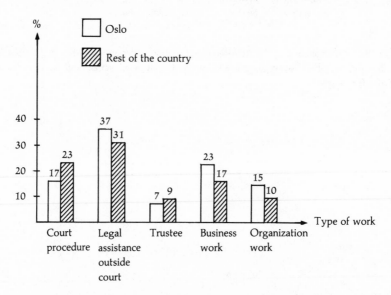

Fig. 2.20. Proportion of advocates' gross income earned, by type of work, Oslo and rest of Norway, 1966. (*Sources*: Den Norske Advokatforening [1966]; Aubert [1976: 266].)

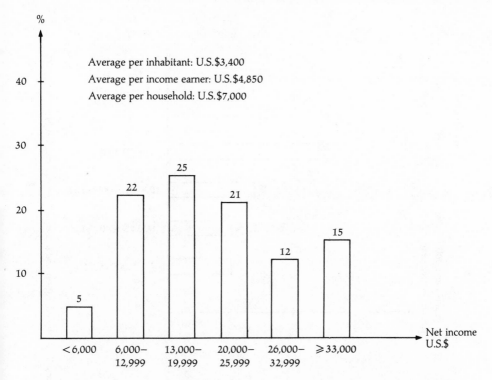

Fig. 2.21. Distribution of active members of the Advocates' Association in private practice by net income, 1976. (*Source*: Den Norske Advokatforening [1976: 5].)

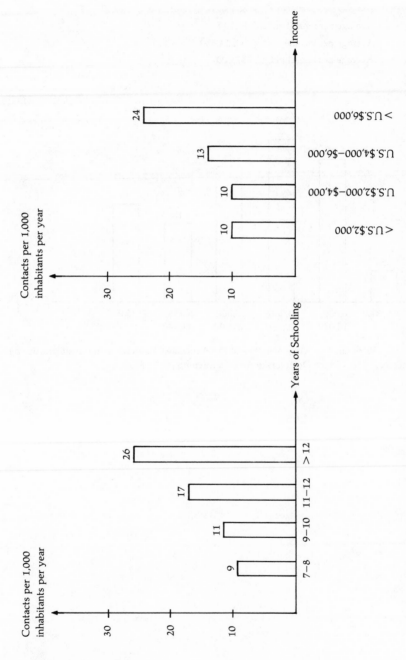

Figs. 2.22 and 2.23. Contacts with lawyer per year per 1,000 inhabitants, by education and income of client. (*Source*: Albrechtsen [1975].)

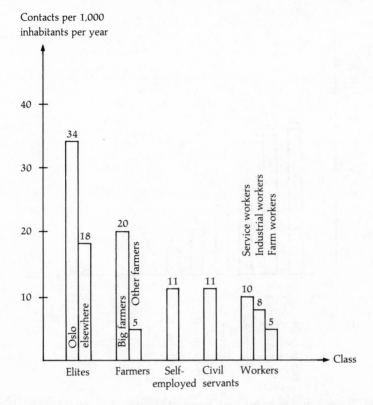

Fig. 2.24. Contacts with lawyer per 1,000 inhabitants, by class. (*Source*: Albrechtsen [1975].)

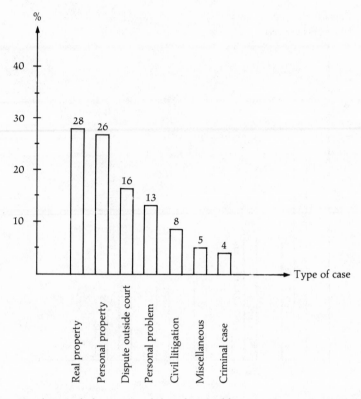

Fig. 2.25. Distribution of advocates' work, by subject and function. (*Source*: Albrechtsen [1975].)

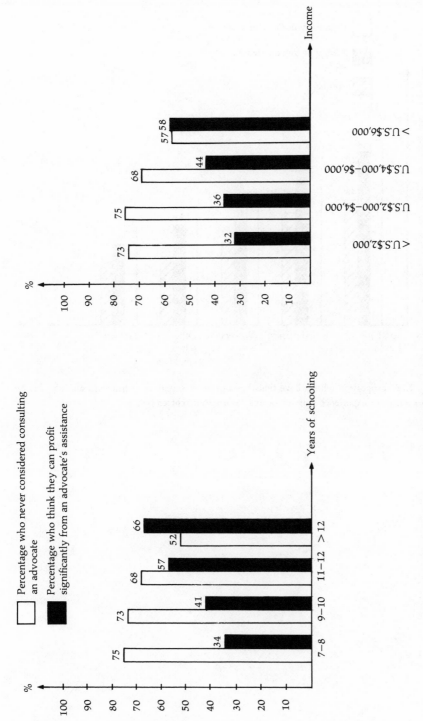

Figs. 2.26 and 2.27. Public attitudes toward lawyer use, by education and income. (*Source:* Albrechtsen [1975].)

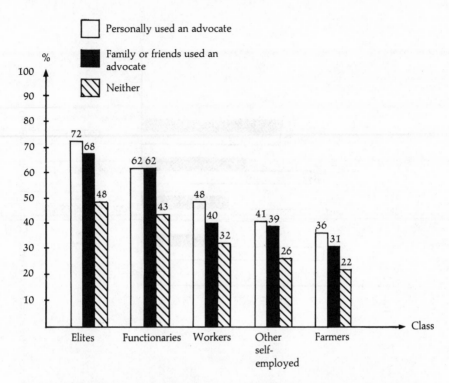

Fig. 2.28. Proportion who believe that they can profit significantly from using advocates, by class and prior experience with advocates. (*Source*: Albrechtsen [1975].)

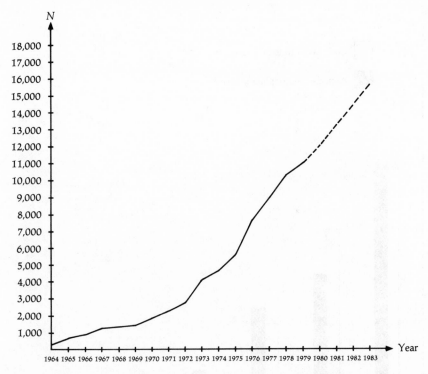

Fig. 2.29. Instances of free legal advice, 1964–1983 (figures for 1979–1982 missing). (*Source*: Unpublished statistics from the Ministry of Justice.)

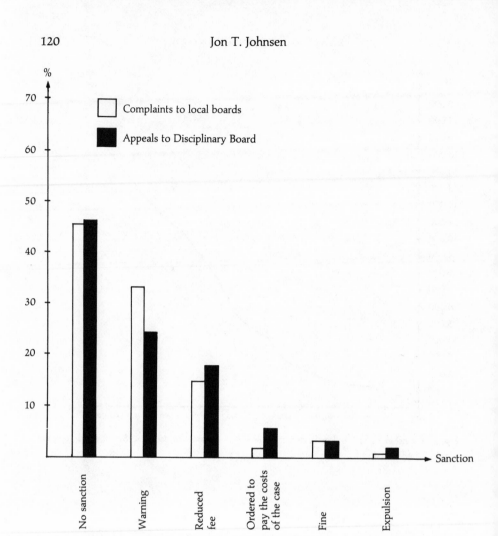

Fig. 2.30. Outcome of disciplinary cases in the Advocates' Association, July 1982 to June 1985. (*Source*: Den Norske Advokatforening [1985: 163].)

# REFERENCES

Albrechtsen, Erling H. 1969. *Norske advokater og deres klienter.* Oslo: Institute for Sociology of Law, University of Oslo.

———. 1971. "Advokatene i norsk rettsorden." Master's thesis, Institute for Sociology of Law, University of Oslo.

———. 1974a. "Kritikk av den rene jus I: Jus og politikk," 15 *Tidsskrift for samfunnsforskning* 1.

———. 1974b. "Kritikk av den rene jus II: Jurister og kapitalinteresser," 15 *Tidsskrift for samfunnsforskning* 87.

———. 1975. "Om advokater og advokatsøking," in Arild Eidesen, Ståle Eskeland, and Thomas Mathiesen, eds., *Rettshjelp og samfunnsstruktur* 23. Oslo: Pax.

———. 1976. "Tabellsamling. Jurister etter folketellingen 1970." Oslo: Institute for Sociology of Law, University of Oslo.

Aubert, Vilhelm. 1960. "Norske jurister fra 1814 til den annen verdenskrig." Oslo: Institute for Social Science, University of Oslo.

———. 1961. "Kvinner i adademiske yrker," 2 *Tidsskrift for samfunnsforskning* 238.

———. 1963. "Eksamenskarakterer, sosial bakgrunn og karriere," 4 *Tidsskrift for samfunnsforskning* 189.

———. 1964a. "Norske jurister: En yrkesgruppe gjennom 150 år," 71 *Tidsskrift for rettsvitenskap* 301.

———. 1964b. "The Professions in Norwegian Social Structure," III *Transactions of the Fifth World Congress of Sociology* 243.

———. 1976. *Rettens sosiale funksjon.* Oslo-Bergen-Tromsø: Universitetsforlaget.

Aubert, Vilhelm, Ulf Torgersen, Karl Tangen, Tore Lindbekk, and Sonja Pollan. 1960. "Adademikere i norsk samfunnsstruktur 1800–1950," 1 *Tidsskrift for samfunnsforskning* 185.

Bjerke, Hans Kristian. 1976. *Fengsling.* Oslo: Universitetsforlaget.

Blom, Raimo. 1974. "The Satisfaction of Legal Needs: Some Theoretical Ideas." Institutes of Sociology and Social Psychology, University of Tampere, Finland (Research Report no. 6).

Boe, Erik. 1979. *Distriktenes utbyggingsfond.* Oslo: Tanum-Norli.

Brunsvig, Per. 1973. "Advokatens rådgivende virksomhet," in Den Norske Advokatforening, ed., *Forelesninger om advokatgjerningen.* 21 Oslo: Universitetsforlaget.

Central Bureau of Statistics. 1973. *Statistical Yearbook 1973.* Oslo: Central Bureau of Statistics of Norway.

———. 1978. *Historical Statistics 1978.* Oslo: Central Bureau of Statistics of Norway.

———. 1981. *Statistical Yearbook 1981.* Oslo: Central Bureau of Statistics of Norway.

———. 1983. *Social Survey 1983.* Oslo: Central Bureau of Statistics of Norway.

———. 1984. *Statistical Yearbook 1984.* Oslo: Central Bureau of Statistics of Norway.

Christophersen, Rolf, 1967. *Advokaters salærberegning. Den Norske Advokatforenings Håndbok del IV.* Oslo: Den Norske Advokatforening.

Den Norske Advokatforening. 1966. *Inntektsundersøkelsen 1966.* Oslo: Den Norske Advokatforening.

———. 1970. *Inntektsundersøkelsen 1970.* Oslo: Den Norske Advokatforening.

———. 1973a. *Inntektsundersøkelsen 1973.* Oslo: Den Norske Advokatforening.

———. 1973b. *Forelesninger om advokatgjerningen.* Oslo: Universitetsforlaget.

———. 1975. *Uttalelser om god advokatskikk og salærberegning I.* Oslo: Den Norske Advokatforening.

———. 1976. *Inntektsundersøkelsen 1976.* Oslo: Den Norske Advokatforening.

———. 1980. *Medlemslister 1980.* Oslo: Den Norske Advokatforening.

———. 1983. *Håndbok del II: Medlemsliste.* Oslo: Den Norske Advokatforening.

———. 1985. "Disiplinærnemdens årsberetning 1984/85," 52 *Norsk advokatblad* 163.

Eckhoff, Torstein. 1967. "Vitenskaper, profesjoner og klienter," 2 *Nordisk Forum* 304.

Ekanger, Kai. 1975. "Hvilke ressurser bør samfunnet som helhet satse på retts-hjelpssektoren, og hvordan skal ressursene settes inn?" in Justisdepartementet, *Justisdepartementets rettshjelpskonferanse 2. desember 1974 og 5.–6. mai 1975.* Oslo: Justisdepartementet.

Halvorsen, Harald. 1983. "Den Norske Advokatforening. 75 år i fugleper-spektiv," in Harald Halvorsen, ed., *Advokat—rettens og samfunnets tjener,* p. 11. Oslo: Den Norske Advokatforening.

Hellevik, Ottar. 1977. *Forskningsmetode i sosiologi og statsvitenskap,* 4th ed. Oslo: Universitetsforlaget.

Johnsen, Jon T. 1981. "Rettshjelp i utkantstrøk: Delrapport III: Avsilings-mekanismer." Oslo: Institute for Sociology of Law, University of Oslo.

———. 1982. "Ytringsfriheten i forvaltningsstaten," 95 *Tidsskrift for rettsviten-skap* 785.

Law Faculty of Oslo University. 1983. "Ressurssituasjonen ved Det juridiske fakultet." Faculty paper (December 8).

———. 1984a. Faculty paper (September 4).

———. 1984b. Faculty paper (September 4).

Norges Juristforbund. 1982. "Antallet juridiske studenter holder seg stabilt," 16 *Juristkontakt* 304.

———. 1984. "Lønnsstatistikk 1984," 18 *Juristkontakt* 478, 486.

Norsk Rettstidende. 1950–1959. Oslo: Den Norske Sakførerforening.

Odelstingsproposisjon no. 1. 1910. *Om utferdigelse av Love om Domstolene og om Rettergangsmaaden i Tvistemaal.*

Odelstingsproposisjon no. 3. 1913. *Om utferdigelse av en lov om inkasso-, auktions-retshjælp-og oplysningsvirksomhet.*

Odelstingsproposisjon no. 29. 1935. *Om forandringer i domstolsloven og lov om inkasso-, auksjons'-og rettshjelpsvirksomhet.*

Odelstingsproposisjon no. 22. 1954. *Lov om endringer i rettergangslovgivningen m. v.*

Odelstingsproposisjon no. 57. 1983/84. *Om lov om endringer i lov av 13. juni 1980 nr. 35 om fri rettshjelp.*

Pedersen, Axel H. 1962. *Innledning til Advokatgiærningen I.* Copenhagen: Arnold Busck.

Rekve, Liz. 1983. "Studentrapport om 1. avdelingsstudenten. Mulige konsekvenser ved lukking av Det juridiske fakultet." Oslo: Olso University Law Faculty (Faculty Paper, December 8).

Robberstad, Knut. 1971. *Rettssoga I.* Oslo-Bergen-Tromsø: Universitetsforlaget.

Røkkum, Kare, 1982. "Om tilbakekalling av advokatbevillinger," 49 *Norsk Advokatblad* 174.

Ross, Alf. 1958. *On Law and Justice.* London: Stevens & Sons.

Torgersen, Ulf. 1967. "Adademisk forsiktighet og frodighet—og arbeidsmarkedet." Paper presented to Rettssosiologisk seminar (March 1).

———. 1972. *Profesjonssosiologi.* Oslo: Universitetsforlaget.

Valle, Inger Louise. 1975. "Rettshjelpproblemet i samfunnet," in Justisdepartementet, *Justisdepartementets rettshjelpkonferanse 2. desember 1974 og 5.–6. mai 1975.* Oslo: Justisdepartementet.

Villum, Jan. 1982. "Erfaringene med praktiseringen av den nye rettshjelploven med resultatene fra spørreundersøkelsen." *Norsk Advokatblad* 230.

Ørsted, Anders Sandøe. 1819. *Eunomia III* 432. Copenhagen.

# 3

# German Advocates: A Highly Regulated Profession

ERHARD BLANKENBURG AND ULRIKE
SCHULTZ

## WHY THE CONCEPT OF A "LEGAL PROFESSION" IS MISLEADING IN THE GERMAN CONTEXT

### THE ROLE OF ADVOCACY IN THE GERMAN LEGAL PROFESSION

If Germans talk about the "legal profession," they do not think first of practicing lawyers but rather of all those who have passed two state examinations to become "full-fledged jurists" (*Volljuristen*). Less than a third of those with law degrees actually practice as "Anwälte" (hereafter translated as "advocates"). Legal education in the Federal Republic of Germany is controlled by examination boards at the Ministries of Justice of the eleven Länder (states). University law faculties generally write the first of the two state examinations and, aided by practitioners, mark them; the second is set and marked by practitioners. During the compulsory in-practice training, which leads to the second state examination, future lawyers spend two and a half years in courts and government offices but no more than five months in an advocate's office.[1] It is not "admission to the bar" that marks entry into the "legal profession," therefore, but passing the two state examinations. A "jurist" is someone who has completed the prescribed legal education, which qualifies one for a career as a judge, civil servant, company employee, or advocate. Mobility between these careers is exceptional. Furthermore, law school teaching is oriented not to the practice of law by advocates who represent parties but almost entirely to the role of a judge who is above the parties. This emphasis corresponds to the numerical dominance of judges and civil servants in the legal profession, where advocates traditionally have been a minority. Advocates have increased their share in the profession only very recently, as a result of the growing numbers of graduates from higher education in general and legal education in particular. This increase in the number of advocates is a result of overproduction by the educational system for a job market that is only partly regulated, not a greater demand for legal services. However, the enlarged supply may well force advocates to try to create new markets for their services. This would require considerable relaxation of the statutory fee scheme and the restrictions on advertising and specialization; and cooperation with present competitors, such as estate agents, might require the bar to relinquish its monopoly over legal advice. We predict that the increase in the number of practicing lawyers as a result of the growing output of law school graduates will not only change the composition of the legal profession but also overturn the current system of regulation, thereby transforming the profession's traditional legal functions.

This market perspective will surprise readers familiar with the literature on the German legal profession. Interest in lawyers in Germany traditionally had concentrated on their roles as judges and civil servants and on their orientation toward authority rather than advocacy. This emphasis on law as government regulation rather than the assertion of individual rights corresponds exactly to the occupational structure of the legal profession and the relatively minor position of advocates within it. The role of jurists in the ideology and institutions of the German state shapes and is shaped by the regulation of legal education and the legal profession. The changes we are seeing today may lead to a convergence with the more adversarial cultures of common law countries, a daring prospect, which must be seen in the context of an overall convergence of Western legal cultures. To develop this thesis we must briefly outline the history of the German legal profession and its present composition.

## THE HISTORICAL WEAKNESS OF ADVOCACY WITHIN THE LEGAL PROFESSION

Legal training in Germany traditionally was education for the judiciary and civil service. Lawyers were expected to serve "the state" rather than represent citizens. The training of future lawyers was strictly regulated by government, admission to the profession was dependent on passing two state examinations, and the choice among careers available to jurists was regulated by admission quotas. The influx of law graduates could be adjusted to the perceived needs of the judiciary and civil service. In 1839, for instance, the Prussian Minister of Justice Mühler published the following warning:

> According to our survey of the yearly influx of graduates from the 1st and 2nd state examinations there are only very distant prospects for anyone aspiring to join the judiciary and to find admission therein; parents and foster

parents of such young men [sic] can only be advised to deter them from study-ing law, unless they show extraordinary qualifications and are able to provide themselves with the necessary means of subsistence for at least ten years.[2]

In those days there were 4,300 positions in the Prussian civil service, including advocates and procurators. (Both of these belonged to the judi-cial services until entry to advocacy was deregulated in 1879.) How much the Prussian authorities considered judicial services to be part of the ma-chinery of government and how they valued adversarial advocacy can be seen from the fact that 75 percent of the law graduates who entered the judicial services chose a career as a judge, whereas only 25 percent be-came advocates (Weissler, 1905: 236–300).

There is ample historical evidence of the deep distrust that sovereigns felt toward advocates. The Prussian King Friedrich Wilhelm I, enthroned in 1713, personally determined the number of lawyers admitted as advo-cates and prescribed the clothes they were to wear. There could not have been a more explicit expression of his disdain for lawyers than the title he gave his 1739 edict:

> Edict that those advocates, procurators and draftsmen [Konzipienten] who dare make people rebellious by having soldiers hand over to His Royal Majesty petitions on the most negligible matters or any other documents on justice, such as those asking for pardon, shall be hanged with a dog hanged at their side, granting neither mercy nor pardon.[3]

In 1713 examination requirements were introduced by the courts to which lawyers sought to be admitted as advocates; incompetence, mal-practice, and an uncontrolled increase in their numbers were given as reasons. In 1780 a Prussian Royal Order went so far as to abolish the pro-fession of advocate. Representation in court was prohibited, and advo-cates were replaced by judgelike civil servants (Assistenzräte), who were both to assist the parties and to help the judges in investigating the facts. The former practicing lawyers were granted the right to work as Com-missioners of Justice (Justizkommissare). Their functions were restricted to advice and representation in noncontentious legal matters, such as land registration, probate, guardianship, bankruptcy, drafting contracts, and notarial work.

However, this attempt to do away with advocacy was bound to fail. Pressure from lawyers brought advocates back into judicial proceedings in 1783. The Corpus Juris Fridericianum (1793) permitted Commissioners of Justice to combine advocacy and notarial functions. However, the local courts still exercised strict control over admissions because lawyers re-mained civil servants appointed by the state, even though private clients paid their fees.

After 1871, when unification of the Reich demanded uniform regulation, there were attempts to establish a true "free advocacy" with unrestricted admission and rights to practice, separating advocates from notaries and abolishing apprenticeship for the former.[4] These reforms were only partly successful. In 1877, the "Act on the Constitution of the Judiciary" (Gerichtsverfassungsgesetz) made the judiciary autonomous, although it continued to regulate university education and apprenticeship and strictly controlled access to the legal professions. In 1879 the Statute on Advocacy granted admission to the bar to all those who had passed both state examinations, without numerical limits. The continuation of ministerial supervision over the uniform legal education, and both state examinations, however, denied advocates any opportunity under the German Kaiserreich to gain control over entry to the profession.

Soon after the deregulation of entry into the profession in 1879 there were complaints about an oversupply of advocates, which reached a peak at the beginning of this century. Numerous articles were written about the alleged "misery" of the advocates. Although there were no formal quotas, and advocates still had no control over supply, state examinations remained an excellent means of regulating access. Just as the Prussian Ministry of Justice had responded to complaints about "a threatening supply of lawyers" in the 1840s and 1858 by successfully persuading examination boards (despite some resistance) to make examinations more selective, raising drop-out rates and curtailing the influx of new students, so the Reich Ministry of Justice did the same thing in the 1910s (Kolbeck, 1978: 41, 55).

The reasons for the periodic increase in the numbers of law graduates in the nineteenth century are similar to those underlying the present increases. A prosperous economy, which allowed more students to attend university, caused an increase in the number of law students in the 1820s, 1840s, and 1860s. Reduced quotas for entry to the civil service and judiciary during economic contractions compelled graduates to resort to other careers—advocacy clearly remaining the second choice for many.


THE RECENT GROWTH OF ADVOCACY

The number of advocates has been increasing relative to those of civil service lawyers and judges ever since the turn of the century. In the last twenty years, in particular, the number of advocates has more than doubled (from 18,347 in 1960 to 46,927 in 1985). The advocates' journal, Anwaltsblatt, has commented: "No profession shows a comparable development. The figures have never been more alarming" (1984/5 Anwaltsblatt 254; see also 1985/5 Anwaltsblatt 249). Yet other professions do share the problem to some extent. The 1982 annual report of the Federal Association of Professions (Bundesverband der Freien Berufe, 1984: 247) states that all professions of independent practitioners have increased by 50 percent since 1970; in 1982 they numbered 330,000 (0.8 percent of the labor force). It points out that the professions of pharmacy and architecture are just as overcrowded as advocacy. Similar fears have been expressed by tax consultants and, recently, by physicians.

However, the growth rates of the legal profession, and especially those of advocates, have been more closely related to political changes than those of other professions. Because legal education provides the backbone of civil service training, all legal occupations are highly vulnerable to changes in political power. Advocates had to fight for emancipation within the legal profession throughout the Kaiserreich. Since the bar never gained control over entry, its membership remained a function of access to law schools and to the other legal occupations within the judiciary and the government. The distinction between practicing advocates and salaried lawyers in business remains nebulous.

Table 3.1 shows that there has been a trend toward long-term growth in the number of advocates in Germany, once we have discounted the historical political upheavals. Until the turn of the century, newcomers clearly were discouraged from becoming advocates rather than joining the civil service and judiciary. Examination standards were used to keep the expansion of the legal profession below population increases resulting from both natural growth and territorial occupation. In light of nineteenth-century industrialization and the expansion of trade (even though Germany was an economic latecomer), these limitations led to uncontrolled expansion of the number of scriveners, law clerks, and unregistered paralegals (Gneist, 1867). Overcontrol of entry into advocacy thus led to a black market of unlicensed practitioners, who worked both clandestinely and as employees of and in the name of the few registered advocates. At the same time, the Prussian Minister of Justice was able to employ law graduates for a number of years without pay by holding out the hope that they thereby would gain entry into advocacy. This practice was unique among German states and was sharply criticized in Parliament; nevertheless, it shows the extent to which public administration controlled the careers of lawyers (ibid.; Kolbeck, 1978: 69ff.).

Since the deregulation of entry to advocacy in 1879 the number of registered advocates has been rising steadily—at least if we exclude the Nazi regime, with its suppression of free advocacy and the lower lawyer densities, characteristic of socialist countries, in the German Democratic Republic. The Weimar Republic saw a further deregulation of entry to the profession and a constant rise in the number of advocates. From its inception in 1933, however, the Third Reich expelled Jews and political opponents from advocacy and later women (still insignificant numerically). According to official statistics there were 4,394 Jewish advocates in 1933, 2,550 in 1935, and none in 1938. Nazi ideology stressed the advocate's duty to "guard the law" (*Rechtswahrer*) rather than to represent and defend the interests of clients. Conflicts were regarded as detrimental to the "welfare of the whole nation," and the purpose of advocacy was to persuade the parties to accept the wider interests of the state. In 1935 the "Act Against Misuse of Legal Advice" restricted admission as an advocate to "elements who are loyal to the State." The expulsion of Jews was one element of a general suppression of liberalism, which advocates increasingly had been championing during the Weimar Republic (Reifner, 1984). The Federal Republic of Germany sought to establish an advocacy appropriate to the new political formation. The reconstruction of democratic political and adversarial legal institutions reinstated advocates in public life as well as in legal services. The job market and educational expansion helped. The number of registered advocates rose by 18 percent between 1955 and 1965, 36 percent between 1965 and 1975, and 75 percent between 1975 and 1985.

It was the educational input rather than demand for legal services that stimulated this growth. Between 1973 and 1979 there were about 10,000 entering law students yearly, a level that rose to 14,718 in 1981 and then declined to about 12,000 in 1985. Student numbers are expected to remain at this level in 1986 and then decrease slowly because of the decline in the birth rate since the late 1960s. Given an attrition of about 60 percent, some 5,000 jurists will pass their second qualifying examinations during each of the coming nine to ten years. In the 1960s and early 1970s between 30 and 35 percent of newly qualified lawyers found employment in the civil service. This proportion since has fallen to 10 percent (*Bundestagsdrucksache* 9/1939, p. 4; Senninger, 1983). Considering the youthfulness of most jurists in the civil service today, there is no reason to expect replacement demand to increase significantly in the foreseeable future. An increasing number of graduates thus seek admission to the bar, which alarms lawyers' association about what they call a threatening "flood of advocates" (45 *Der Spiegel* 22 [1983]). The influx into all the professions results from the general educational expansion of the 1960s, which never succeeded in adapting the size of training facilities to job market demand. It coincided with rapid economic growth, which was expected to continue indefinitely. In 1960 only 6 percent of the appropriate age cohort passed the Abitur, rendering them eligible to enter university. By 1982, this had increased to 25 percent. In response, many disciplines with high per capita educational costs (such as medicine, natural sciences, and engineering) restricted student numbers. Law faculties, with their low per capita educational costs, have not done so. Consequently, many of those not admitted to study their first choice entered law faculties: surveys show that law was the second or third choice of at least 18 percent of all law students. Almost half of these had preferred medicine, dentistry, or pharmacy (Heldrich & Schmidtchen, 1982: 15–16; Portele & Schütte, 1983: 98ff.); thus, it is restrictions on entry to other faculties that have increased the proportion of law students. In 1977, 5.3 percent of all secondary school graduates with university qualifications studied law; in 1980, 6.5 percent did so (*Bundestagsdrucksache*, 1979: 9).

There also is a push factor encouraging graduating jurists to choose advocacy as a career. As job openings for jurists in the public service and the judiciary have become limited because of the fiscal crises in the 1980s, jurists have been forced into advocacy as the one lawyer job without entry limitations.[5] Professional organizations still are pledging to stop the "inflation" of incoming young advocates. Unable to control admissions, they might have sought to widen the scope of legal services by attacking restrictions on combining economic and legal advice, allowing advocates to transfer real estate, or expanding the traditional clientele of advocates with the help of legal aid subsidies. Instead, German advocates have followed the strategy of defending their monopoly over legal advice and representation, although at the price of remaining restricted to the narrow traditional market. This may be a reflection of their historical experience. In the past, advocates had good reason to fear government restrictions if they did not define the scope of the profession very narrowly. The time has come, however, to reconsider this defensive strategy. The supply-induced growth of the legal profession is changing its composition. Never before have German jurists been so close to forming a profession of advocates rather than a source of recruits for the civil service.

## THE JOBS OF GERMAN LAWYERS

Becoming a lawyer in Germany still means choosing a salaried career as often as it means practicing as an advocate. After passing the second state examination, about half of all jurists enter salaried positions in government, the judiciary, or business. Judges and civil servants seldom are recruited from the bar; they have their own lifelong career paths.

A professional qualification, thus, is the gateway to many different occupations; it requires a university education together with in-practice training in judicial and governmental institutions. This "uniform legal education" controlled by examination boards of the state Ministries of Justice is a heritage of the time when legal education was predominately the recruitment reservoir for higher positions in government administration. The state examinations still serve to channel aspirants for legal and management careers. Because the choice of career has to be made soon after the completion of legal education, we describe legal education before surveying the jobs that German lawyers do.

## LEGAL EDUCATION

To become a German jurist, one first must enroll in a university law faculty. People often do so without clear motives: most of those who qualify enter university because of the status it confers. Law students are more uncertain than others about their future careers (Heldrich & Schmidtchen, 1982: 15ff.; Portele & Schütte, 1983: 98ff.). Legal training traditionally has been an all-purpose choice. In 1982 there were 74,756 law students and 14,105 apprentice lawyers (Harms, 1983). German universities are tuition-free, and, until the early 1980s, one-third of all students received grants to help finance their studies (Statistisches Bundesamt Wiesbaden [BAFÖG]). This made university study an attractive low-cost option for anybody who passed their secondary-school examinations. Now, however, loans have replaced grants.

There is widespread dissatisfaction with the quality of university legal studies, however. On average they take almost six years, although only three and a half years formally are required. University teaching consists mostly of lectures and concentrates on imparting knowledge of the legal codes and their application to hypothetical cases. Considerable pressure is exerted by rigid marking of tests and examinations. The drop-out rate is about 50 percent in the first phase of legal education and about 25 percent in the second; for other subjects, the average failure rate in 1980 was 10 percent (*Bundestagdrucksache*, 9/1389, p. 2). Final oral examinations have been described as a "conformity test" to see whether the candidate's thought processes fit the appropriate pattern of "perceiving, thinking and judging" (Portele & Schütte, 1983: 32; Schütte, 1982). To prepare for these examinations, many students attend courses with a private tutor (*Repetitor*). These offer a systematic, limited program oriented toward the examination and concentrate on case-solving techniques. Two types of tutor can be distinguished: the "impresario" who runs a one-person business and the large firms with employed tutors and branch offices in many university towns. Some tutors hand out course notes. About 70 percent of law students take part in these private courses (Heldrich & Schmidtchen, 1982: 91), and almost all students use some of their publications. Two out of three law students in 1980 used those of the largest establishment (*Alpmann* at Münster). Even private tutors cannot guarantee a good result; to be successful, students must construct their own curriculum, and many form private study groups.

Students restrict their reading to legal dogmatics, and traditional legal training omits even a basic exposure to philosophy, sociology, economics, or political science (Wasserman, 1969: 1983). However, there also is no training in the skills needed by an advocate: there are no moot courts, legal clinics, or training in administrative skills in either the universities or the tutorial "crash courses." In the late 1960s both the neglect of social science and the perceived need for some skills training led to demands for reform. In 1971 educational programs were established combining university courses and in-service training.[6] In 1982 approximately 12 percent of all graduating lawyers had completed these programs. In 1985, however, all legal training returned to the earlier model with its well-known deficiencies.

Professional in-service training requires two and a half years and reinforces the judge-centered tendency of German legal education. The trainee has the status of a civil servant without tenure and receives a monthly allowance. Training consists of specified periods in a court of first instance, an appeal court, a public prosecutor's office, and a local government authority, and only five months with an advocate. In addition, the trainee has to attend classes conducted by judges in civil and administrative law, public prosecutors in criminal law, and civil servants in administrative law. This training emphasizes the technical skills needed in the judiciary: giving preparatory opinions and writing judgments. There is hardly any training in advocacy, drafting, negotiation, or legal advice. This orientation to the demands of judicial office is underlined by the fact that the examination panel consists mainly of judges and public prosecutors and government bureaucrats.[7]

## THE ALLOCATION OF GRADUATES TO LEGAL OCCUPATIONS

Those who pass both examinations choose among the different legal occupations largely on the basis of their marks on the second state examination, supplemented by the evaluative report of the training judges. Very good grades on the second examinations (a *Prädikat*, which is achieved by one-sixth of examinees) open the door to a career in the judiciary or civil service. Legal job advertisements generally demand "a young jurist, possibly with professional experience and [two] Prädikat examinations." A Prädikat always was a prerequisite for employment in the judicial service and often was demanded in the civil service, except between 1965 and 1975, when graduates were in short supply. With the present oversupply of graduates and the contraction of all public service labor markets, not even a Prädikat can assure entry to the judicial or public service.

Work as an advocate has become an alternative.[8] It rarely is a deliberate choice, except for those who "inherit" contacts with practicing advocates through family or friends or make contacts as a trainee. Advocates traditionally have been characterized by high self-recruitment and upper-middle-class backgrounds, but advocacy recently has become the occupation for all jurists unable to find government or civil service jobs. It remains to be seen how many manage to leave advocacy after a while for jobs in the civil service or private employment.

As we shall see, solo practice has been declining in recent decades, and young lawyers increasingly start as law firm employees. With the supply of graduates increasing, starting salaries are decreasing, and it takes longer to become a partner. Multilingualism and specialization in economics, tax law, labor law, or commercial law can give the applicant an advantage. There is a reputational ranking among the thirty-two established law faculties in Germany, but the university attended has little influence on one's career. If anything, the state in which examinations are passed is more relevant: Bremen, for instance, has the most thoroughly reformist model and is the scapegoat for some discrimination in the other states.[9]

## Judicial Careers

Germany traditionally has had the highest ratio of judges to population of all countries with a developed formal legal system (Blankenburg, 1986). This is due to a combination of high litigation rates, high appeal rates, and the inquisitorial system. Procedural law gives judges a dominant role in the proceedings, controlling them, directing the inquiry, suggesting settlements, and passing judgment. Procedural law and ideology demand that judges give a detailed reasoned written judgment (Blankenburg, 1985). Thus, German legal culture is thoroughly judge centered.

To be a judge is a lifelong career, starting immediately after the second qualifying examination. The status resembles that of a civil servant, and promotion to a judgeship in the higher courts is the usual expectation. Seniority strongly influences careers, although merit does determine the speed of advancement in the judicial hierarchy and is a prerequisite for achieving such senior positions as president or chairperson. Recruitment to all these posts is vertical; temporary exchanges between ministerial bureaucracies and the judiciary are the only observable type of lateral mobility (Lange & Luhmann, 1974).

## Lawyers in the Civil Service

Most higher civil servants with any sort of administrative responsibility traditionally have been recruited from qualified lawyers. A "judicial qualification" opens the door to higher positions in the civil service and local government (Schmid & Treiber, 1975). Because of their employment status, civil servants cannot represent parties in most judicial proceedings.

Judicial qualification is particularly advantageous for public service careers. Jurists have a very strong position in both the executive and the ministerial bureaucracies. The judicial mode is deeply embedded in German administrative law: every public administrative decision is subject to judicial review on substantive as well as procedural grounds. Because public policy also relies heavily for its legitimation on a belief in legality, jurists play a central role in preparing new legislation (Lange & Luhmann, 1974). Since jurists with a rather homogeneous background dominate the civil service (Brinkmann et al., 1973), training in law has attained a central place in the idea of a "universal education" for public functions (Bleek, 1972).

In spite of the uniform education, each legal occupation has its own career path, and interoccupational mobility is difficult after the early years. The relatively high incomes produced by seniority and promotion practices in both the judiciary and public administration render transfer to private practice after the age of thirty-five a financial sacrifice. Civil servants and judges rarely leave to become advocates. Most mobility is a one-way movement of younger advocates into permanent civil service jobs. Having obtained the status of a permanent civil servant, most lawyers are reluctant to return to advocacy. In contrast to the average advocate, civil servants enjoy extraordinary security: life tenure, health insurance, and generous pension schemes. Many lawyers who have graduated recently have enrolled as advocates simply to wait for a job in the civil service.

## University Teachers

University teachers follow a separate career. Professors have to acquire a long series of academic qualifications. Many are actively involved in other legal functions.

There are slightly more than 500 full professors in the thirty-two German law faculties (Klausa, 1981: chap. 4). Once they are recognized as authorities, professors exercise influence through their publications and their (mostly unpublished) expert opinions on controversial questions in judicial proceedings. The only time most of them ever practiced was during in-service training before the second qualifying examination.[10] Since professors are civil servants they cannot perform all the roles of advocates. They may defend those accused of crimes and represent parties before the Federal Administrative Court and the Federal Supreme Court.

Some also gain prestige by appearing before the Federal Constitutional Court or as experts before any of the Supreme Courts, where they can participate on the "frontiers" of innovative jurisdiction.

## Lawyers in Private Employment (Syndici)

In Germany, larger companies tend to have their own in-house counsel. There are between 30,000 and 40,000 lawyers working in commerce and industry, banks, and insurance companies. Large corporations have legal departments with twenty or more fully qualified lawyers. Lawyers also work in personnel and administrative departments and exercise management functions. Professional associations, trade unions, and other organized interest groups employ lawyers as managers or legal advisers.

That so many lawyers work in salaried positions indicates a particular management style: rather than contracting with lawyers, consultants, or accountants for specific services, German business firms tend to incorporate these services within their permanent organizations. Company lawyers enter business firms at the beginning of their careers and tend to move up internal company ladders.

Some business lawyers are admitted as advocates. Official statistics estimate that 12 percent of all registered advocates are "Syndici," but we believe that the figure is more than twice as high. Income statistics for 1984 show that 30 percent of all registered advocates have no income from their practices. While a few are not practicing because of age or other reasons, the rest probably are employed. However, the dramatic increase in law graduates during the last two decades has not increased the proportion employed in business. Employed lawyers may not represent their employer in court (Bundesrechtsanwaltsordnung [BRAO], art. 46). Many become advocates just to have the privilege of using the title; they see themselves as employees bound by contract to their employer rather than as independent lawyers in private practice. Most are found in the big city bars (A. Braun, 1987; Kolvenbach, 1979).

## What Advocates Do

Advocates traditionally have been regarded as "part of the system of justice." [11] They have a monopoly not only of representation in court but also of legal advice (Legal Advice Act [Rechtsberatungsgesetz]). This "lawyer monopoly" has prevented any other type of advisor from penetrating the "legal market." It also has discouraged the development of any significant legal aid advocacy (Blankenburg, 1980; 1983). Because legal education is oriented toward the judicial service, young advocates will see their role primarily as litigators. This consists mainly of preparing written statements; compared to common lawyers, civil lawyers play an insignificant role in collecting and presenting evidence (Kaplan et al., 1958; Merryman, 1968). Once an action has been filed, the inquiry is in the hands of the court, which directs the proceedings, decides what evidence to take, and hears the witnesses.

Most advocates still work as solo practitioners or in small partnerships. If they are restricted to private clients with nonrepetitive needs, their incomes will derive largely from divorce cases. If they can routinize their litigation to increase volume, they may specialize in automobile accidents and traffic offenses, relying on continuing relations with legal-expense insurance companies. A very few advocates specialize in such administrative law matters as political asylum, admission to university, conscientious objection, and land development. Equally few manage to make a living doing social advocacy reimbursed by legal aid (Blankenburg, 1986). Only those who have acquired additional skills in commercial, tax, and company law and have built up a regular business clientele establish larger more prosperous law firms. However, such specialists often are sought by companies for careers as in-house counsel or in management.

Legal advice outside court is not part of the lawyer's image, but it is lucrative. Solo practitioners generally concentrate on litigation, but in larger law firms the bulk of the work is advice. Here, lawyers face vigorous competition from tax consultants and chartered accountants, who combine advice on business strategies, tax strategies, and management. Tax consultants increasingly form their own partnerships offering comprehensive business advice, including the drafting of contracts and wills. By concentrating on the forensic areas in which they have a monopoly, advocates have lost much of the growing consultancy market.

## Notaries

Advocates are not the only lawyers in private practice; there also are notaries. In most federal states, advocates can be admitted as notaries, a privilege dating back to a Prussian ordinance. In 1985 there were 7,171 advocates who could act as notaries.[12] In the state of Württemberg and in parts of Baden, notaries are civil servants, although they also may collect private fees. In most of the states not previously ruled by Prussia, statute long has provided for a profession of notaries in private practice, with strict entry controls. There now are about 1,000 notaries who are not advocates (nur-Notare).

German law permits notarial certification and attestation in a wide range of matters, but it is required in only a few cases in order to validate legal documents: the purchase, sale, or mortgage of land; the decisions of company meetings; and the sale of shares in a private company. Some legal documents, such as a will (which is executed only if the testator wants to depart from the standard provisions of inheritance law), can be drafted by notaries.

Notaries hold public office and charge fees according to a fixed scale, but they are organized as an independent profession. They do their work under the supervision of their regional court of first instance, which controls admissions. Advocates who also wish to practice as notaries have to wait an average of six to ten years.

## Legal Advisors without University Training in Law

Paralegals are of little importance in Germany. The Legal Advice Act (Rechtsberatungsgesetz) outlaws unauthorized legal practice and requires judicial permission before anyone not qualified as a jurist may practice as legal advisor. A small group of paralegal advisors with a nonuniversity law qualification (Rechtsbeistände) traditionally have enjoyed limited rights to give legal advice. In 1981, however, the Legal Advice Act (formerly the Act Against Misuse of Legal Advice) was amended to terminate the admission of new paralegal advisors. Now only specialist groups of non-lawyers (such as tax advisors) are admitted to practice under the Legal Advice Act.

Of much greater importance, however, are those legal advisors who, while not admitted to the bar, may give legal advice to a specific clientele on specific issues. Trade union secretaries can advise on social and labor law matters and represent workers in court, consumer organizations can advise and represent consumers, tenant or homeowner associations can advise their members about housing disputes, and student advice bureaus can deal with student problems. Many of these organizations provide legal services by contracting with advocates for an annual retainer. They are ideologically oriented toward representing collective interests as well as individual claims. Therefore, they are more capable than traditional advocates of changing the distribution of legal advantage by combining individual representation with the use of litigation and political lobbying (Blankenburg & Reifner, 1982).

## UNIFORM EDUCATION AND DIVERSE OCCUPATIONS

As we have seen, every jurist in the Federal Republic of Germany must complete a uniform legal education; this educational unity of the profession is expressed in the German concept *"Einheitsjurist."* The coherence of the German "legal profession" is perceived as based on a common educational experience rather than a common occupational profile or membership in (predominantly occupational) associations, since subsequent career paths separate judges (including public prosecutors), practicing advocates and/or notaries, civil servants, and salaried company lawyers.

The distribution of jurists among these careers has undergone considerable change since the turn of the century. Until 1909 judges in the German Reich actually outnumbered advocates; the small number of civil servants enjoyed the highest prestige, and other salaried lawyers were rare. Throughout the Weimar and Federal Republics the relative size of the judiciary decreased, while those of advocates, civil servants, and especially salaried lawyers increased. All those shifts took place against the background of the overall growth of the profession. Since 1960 the number of jurists in the labor force has doubled, but the growth rate has been more marked among advocates than in the rest of the profession (see table 3.2).

In 1984 about 45,000 jurists were registered as advocates, 25 to 30 percent of whom derived their incomes from sources other than private practice. About 1,000 jurists work only as notaries, 17,000 as judges, 3,700 as state prosecutors, and about 35,000 as civil servants in federal, state, and local government. An estimated 35,000 jurists work as business lawyers (about 12,000 of whom are registered as advocates).[13]

## REGULATION OF THE PRACTICE OF ADVOCATES

If legal education in Germany seems highly regulated, so is the practice of advocates.[14] While admission as an advocate is a pure formality, the regulation of how advocates must practice law has a distinctly restrictive effect. Advocates may not combine legal practice with other services, form law firms extending beyond the jurisdiction to which they are admitted, advertise their services, or freely announce that they specialize.[15] Regulation not only affects the "product" advocates offer but also fixes the "price" of their forensic representation. Such regulation was justified as necessary to prevent unfair competition and maintain a high standard of professionalism, but it also restrained the innovations in legal services that would have followed the more aggressive marketing strategies of lawyers who could work on contingent fees or form partnerships with other professions. Much of this regulation, even of advocates' fees, is statutory; it is implemented by the "Chambers of Advocates" but under the supervision of the judicial authorities.

## ADMISSION

The application for admission is addressed to the court to which the advocate wants to be admitted and granted by the Court of Appeal of that jurisdiction. The Supreme Federal Court, like the Supreme Court of the Weimar Republic, has interpreted the Statute on Advocacy (BRAO, art. 7) to allow the exclusion of members of the Communist party. The Federal Constitutional Court overruled this decision only recently.[16]

## JURISDICTIONAL AND TERRITORIAL RESTRICTIONS

A practicing lawyer may be admitted either to both first instance and appeal courts in some states (BRAO, arts. 18, 23, 26). Practicing lawyers may represent parties in civil matters only in the courts to which they have been admitted, although they may appear and be heard in another court if the party is represented by an advocate admitted to that court. This territorial restriction does not apply to the local courts that handle small claims, labor cases, and most criminal matters nor to courts of special jurisdiction.

A practicing advocate may maintain only one office and may not hold regular consultation hours outside it. The office must be within the jurisdiction of the court to which the advocate is admitted, and the advocate must reside within the jurisdiction of the regional court of appeal, although EEC law soon may force the repeal of this latter rule and exceptions now are made for advocates with an international practice.

## RESTRICTION AND MONOPOLY OF LEGAL SERVICES

In all family courts, district courts (which handle civil matters of higher status), and appellate courts, parties must be represented by advocates. Advocates also enjoy a monopoly of representation before state Labor Courts, the Federal Labor Court, and the Federal Administrative Court (Civil Procedure Code, art. 78; Criminal Procedure Code, art. 140). In local courts and minor criminal proceedings parties may appear unrepresented.

## DISCIPLINE

Discipline is exercised by the councils of the Chambers of Advocates, which are "autonomous courts under the legal supervision of the state Ministries of Justice" (Statute on Advocacy). Appeal lies to a joint court of judges and lawyers and then to the Federal Supreme Court (BGH), where judges represent a majority. An advocate can be reprimanded by the council for minor offenses, while more serious cases involve judicial proceedings. The disciplinary bodies have very low caseloads, however: in 1983 there were 483 new cases at first instance, most dealing with problems of admission, such as the candidate's desire to combine admission to the bar with work as a salaried employee.[17] Once the advocate is admitted, *any* sanction is extremely rare, let alone disbarment, which is imposed only for serious misconduct, such as a criminal conviction (since 1969 convictions for drunken driving have been irrelevant) (Lehmann, 1984). The few decisions regarding professional misconduct have a good chance of being published: The journal of the Chamber of Advocates (BRAK—Mitteilungen) carries a regular column on such cases. Local chambers, however, prefer to use informal admonitions to express their dissatisfaction with breaches of professional rules, such as those relating to advertising and unfair competitive advantage. Client complaints about service are rare, and advocates' associations and chambers try to deal with them informally. The slight recent increase in formal disciplinary measures only reflects the growing numbers of advocates.

## PROFESSIONAL ASSOCIATIONS

All lawyers practicing within the jurisdiction of each court of appeal must belong to its "Chamber of Advocates" (Anwaltskammer) (BRAO, art. 60). In addition, there are a number of voluntary organizations. In 1986 about 30,000 advocates, or almost 60 percent of all those registered, were members of the Deutsche Anwaltverein (DAV), which protects professional interests, gives practical assistance to its members, and organizes courses of continuing education. It also publishes a journal (*Anwaltsblatt*), organizes a biannual meeting (*Deutscher Anwaltstag*), maintains an institute advising lawyers about office equipment and organizational techniques, establishes committees and working groups on legislation and current problems, and promotes professional interests through publicity and lobbying. It increasingly is involved in continuing education, although a number of private entrepreneurs also offer courses for specialists. The proliferation of special interest groups, such as the leftist "Republican Lawyers" and the "Criminal Defense Lawyers Association," testifies to the increasing differentiation within the bar.

## DIVISIONS AND STRATIFICATION WITHIN THE PROFESSION

Preoccupation with preventing competition among practicing lawyers and defending the monopoly of legal advice has prevented German advocates from extending their services into innovative areas and exploring the possibility of cooperation with neighboring professions. At the same time, it also has avoided the sharp income differences and stratification that typify American lawyers. The social distance between solo practitioners (who still can make a decent living) and members of law firms (those with ten lawyers are among the biggest), although considerable, is far smaller than in the United States. There is not yet much "mega-lawyering" (Galanter, 1983) within the bar, nor are there "street-corner lawyers." German advocates still resemble a guild of craftsmen.

There are differences in the size of practice and the clientele, however. Senior practitioners in larger law firms prefer to serve a clientele of companies and associations and rarely go to court, while juniors in law firms and solo practitioners tend to do more litigation for a clientele of individuals, relying on divorce cases for a larger proportion of their income. Stratification among advocates may increase if the influx of young lawyers continues. We expect that the age, gender, and income distributions of German advocates will experience rapid changes in the late 1980s.

SIZE OF PRACTICE

Advocacy traditionally has been the province of solo practitioners. Small partnerships of two to three advocates began to form in the 1960s. Although some have expanded, few contain more than 10 lawyers (see table 3.3). Nevertheless, the proportion of solo practitioners is declining. Statistics on practicing lawyers do not include salaried lawyers employed by advocates. These have been very rare until recently, however, and only the rapid expansion of the bar in the 1980s has motivated some young lawyers to accept long-term employment.

Advocates employed in business may not be multiplying as rapidly as private practitioners. The recent increase in admissions may be causing a (temporary) increase in the number of solo practitioners with no other source of income. If we exclude all advocates employed as Syndici, the practicing bar appears to be equally divided between solo practitioners and firm lawyers. Even with the recent increase in the number of partnerships, no law firms are as big as those in the United States. In 1985 only forty-two partnerships contained more than ten partners.

INCOME

When Rueschemeyer (1973) compared the income of practicing lawyers with that of other self-employed professionals for 1954, advocates ranked highest. Since then, the incomes of dentists and medical practitioners have been growing faster than those of lawyers, even though the latter have kept pace with the general economic growth. Table 3.4 shows that the average income of advocates now is considerably below that of physicians and dentists, about equal to that of tax advisors, and higher than that of engineers and architects. Notaries rank somewhat above advocates but below the medical professions.

Thus far only the *relative* income of lawyers has been decreasing. With the growing influx of young lawyers in the 1980s their absolute income also may decrease. This will not affect well-established lawyers, but more lawyers will earn low or even very low incomes. Income stratification within the bar thus will increase. This tendency is the long-term effect of what the profession sees as a failure to limit access to legal education or the bar—a failure that also can be seen more positively: despite the comprehensive regulation of legal practice, the profession remains open to newcomers.

## FEES

A compulsory fee scale for advocates is contained in the federal "Statute on Lawyer's Fees" (BRAGO). This regularly is negotiated between the lawyers' association and the Ministry of Justice and the Parliamentary Committee on Legal Affairs. Since any changes require legislation, the lawyers' lobby in each party represented in the committee is very influential. Fees in civil cases vary with the value of the object in dispute; there also are guidelines for fees for criminal defense. For consultation, advocates may charge a proportion of the fee for a litigated case that varies with the kind of work involved. Only in international cases do advocates charge on an hourly basis. Although the statutory fees do not vary linearly with the value at stake, the system still leads to very high fees in large cases. These must compensate for the time spent on small claims, where the lawyer does not even recover expenses. Undercutting is forbidden and punished by the Chamber of Advocates. Contingent fees are not allowed. There is some clandestine "fee contracting," however, in consultation agreements with long-standing clients. Legal expense insurance payments in litigated matters also must adhere to the fee scheme; bargaining seems possible only in pretrial settlements, especially of traffic tickets.

The rigid fee system has a number of consequences:

1.  A general-litigation practitioner with a predominantly wage-earning clientele can hardly make a living.

2.  Legal aid income is insignificant except in divorce cases. Criminal defense advocates can do well since the inquisitorial system requires them to expend little effort in collecting evidence.

3. Some advocates specialize in routine matters such as automobile accidents and traffic offenses and are paid by legal expense insurance; highly automated mass processing generates a good income.

4. Legal expense insurance is feasible because fees are predictable. Law firms concentrating on business consultation not covered by the fee scheme earn high to very high incomes.

5. Notary-advocates, who often advise companies or land developers, earn the most.

6. The highest incomes are found in partnerships of four or more, characterized by internal specialization, consultation, a clientele composed almost entirely of businesses, and no debt collection (Oellers, 1982; A. Braun, 1986a).

## LEGAL EXPENSE INSURANCE

The predictability of fees has allowed legal expense insurance to develop more extensively in Germany than in any other country. Because insurance companies may not give legal advice themselves but only reimburse the costs of legal advice and representation by advocates, this kind of insurance has become an important element in lawyer incomes. Almost every other German household has a policy. As our own research has shown conclusively, however, legal expense insurance has not increased the likelihood of litigation: about the same proportions of insured and uninsured clients are advised by their lawyers to settle out of court and avoid litigation.[18]

## SPECIALIZATION

Although subject-matter specialization is just beginning, it is growing rapidly.[19] Local advocates' associations generate "lists of specialists" for referrals. Although many advocates register, not all deal exclusively with these matters. Registration as a "family law specialist," for example, usually indicates only that a general practitioner wants referrals of divorce cases. Since advertising is prohibited, advocates cannot publicize their specializations. Most advocates, including those in smaller partnerships, remain generalists; large firms allow some specialization among the partners but rarely portray the entire firm as specialized.

In light of these remarks, the "specializations" advocates have registered with their local "Advocates' Association" should be seen as an indication of preference rather than as exclusive practices (see table 3.5). The fact that family law, traffic cases, criminal defense, and labor law are the subjects most frequently listed shows that registration serves as a source of referrals for general practitioners rather than for those who specialize by subject matter or clientele.

## THE VIRTUAL ABSENCE OF FREE LEGAL ADVICE

Compared to Anglo-American legal cultures, as well as that of the Netherlands, there is a remarkable lack of "social advocacy" in the Federal Republic of Germany. Few young left lawyers have taken the hard route of representing a welfare clientele for little pay. Until 1981 the government did not subsidize legal advice outside court, which remained the province of pro bono programs organized by lawyer associations. Since 1981 there has been a very modest legal advice scheme (*Beratungshilfe*).

The need to equalize representation *within* court had been recognized by German civil procedure as early as 1879 by the *Armenrecht* or "poor person's law." Criminal defendants also have had a statutory right to a duty solicitor[20] since 1877, though only in the most serious cases. There is no legal aid for the large number of accused in the local criminal courts, nor is there any public defender service for those arrested by the police and detained by the courts. Most legal aid in civil matters (*Prozesskostenhilfe*) concerns divorce for low-income parties. Civil legal aid per capita is slightly higher than in England and Wales or the Netherlands; criminal legal aid is considerably lower, since the duty solicitor scheme only is available in the most serious cases; and in comparison to those other countries, expenditures for out-of-court advice (Beratungshilfe) are insignificant (Blankenburg, 1983; 1986). The defensive attitude of the German bar successfully obstructed the expansion of legal aid beyond fee waivers in divorce proceedings; it also prevented institutional innovations, such as political representation, neighborhood law centers, and university legal clinics. The lawyers' lobby has sought to defend their monopoly over the traditional functions of advocacy rather than expand into new markets. Professions such as tax advisors and accountants, in which the government never had regulated education, entry, or conduct (but that also never enjoyed similar monopoly privileges and price regulation), managed to expand their markets in response to the influx of younger entrants. Advocacy, which is open to any qualified legal graduate, now faces an increasing number of young lawyers demanding a share of the highly regulated market for legal services. The defense of monopoly turns out to be a suitable strategy when supply is stable but an impediment when a growing profession must expand its market. Since continued adherence to that strategy is dysfunctional in terms of the collective economic interests of the legal profession, the explanation must be found in the traditional political functions of German jurists. The change in the background of recent law graduates from elitist to a broader cross section of the population is one reason why the German legal profession is on the verge of a profound change.

## CHANGING THE SOCIAL RECRUITMENT OF PRACTICING LAWYERS

Sociological studies of the recruitment patterns of German jurists generated much controversy in the 1960s. The relationship that they revealed between the class background and the ideologies of the judicial elite could not be ignored. However, sociologists who situated this relationship in the context of the antidemocratic elitism of German political culture aroused public anger. Ralf Dahrendorf, in particular, argued that "the lawyers of the monopoly" were one of the structural factors that explained the blind obedience to authority and avoidance of overt conflict characteristic of traditional German political institutions (Dahrendorf, 1965).

The weak position of advocacy within the German legal profession is an additional reason for relating the respect of German elites for "state and authority" to their antidemocratic sentiments throughout the history of the Reich, as well as to the special dilemmas of an obedient judiciary and civil service during the Third Reich. In the Federal Republic, however, the continuities of German political culture coexisted with substantial changes, and this also was true within the legal profession. The role of German advocates now appears to be converging with that of lawyers in the less authoritarian legal cultures of the "Western victorious powers," which reshaped the Federal Republic after World War II. The schemes of planned ideological and institutional change advanced by "reeducation authors" such as Talcott Parsons (1954) slowly have borne fruit.

### SOCIAL CLASS BACKGROUND

German jurists traditionally came from a rather homogeneous middle-class background in which there was a clear overrepresentation of civil service parents. Advocates deviate somewhat from this pattern, however, by being from more urban backgrounds, Protestant rather than Catholic, and the children of entrepreneurial rather than civil service parents (Kaupen, 1969).

Today, a third of younger advocates and judges (but only 24 percent of law students) are the children of civil servant fathers (although civil servants were only 11 percent of the labor force in that generation), while only 4 to 5 percent of younger advocates and judges (but 11 percent of law students) had worker fathers (although workers were 42 percent of the labor force in that generation) (Heldrich & Schmidtchen, 1982: 252). The fact that 19 percent of advocates come from a professional background, compared to 11 percent of judges, suggests the strength of self-recruitment (see table 3.6), even though the proportion from jurist families is unavailable. The upward social mobility fostered by the overall increase in secondary and tertiary education is more pronounced in other faculties, such as education. Law faculties have been the last to reduce elite recruitment, just as they were the last (except engineering) to admit an increasing proportion of women (see table 3.7).

The ideological climate of the 1970s had some impact on the political and social attitudes of the jurists of that generation, who were more critical of authority and emphasized the importance of social welfare for public policy and the legal profession. The cohort graduating in the 1980s, however, seems politically more conservative and also more instrumental in their attitudes toward their jobs. Changes in the recruitment of jurists, as well as in the political environment, may have been influential. The slight increase in working-class recruitment has amplified welfare-state liberalism, whereas the higher proportion of women students has intensified political conservatism (except on feminist issues, such as employment discrimination and abortion). All cohorts of law students have been more conservative than those of teachers or social scientists, while still participating in the periodic shifts toward or away from liberalism, which we observe in the student population as a whole.[21]

## WOMEN IN THE PROFESSION

In 1922, after long impassioned discussions, advocacy was opened to women (Reichsgesetz über die Zulassung der Frauen zum Richterberuf, 11 July 1922). During the Weimar Republic the number of women advocates was insignificant. As part of their family policy, the National Socialists excluded women from the judiciary (edict of 17 September 1935), and after mid-1936 women no longer were admitted as advocates (Meier-Scherling, 1975). It was not until the abolition of sex discrimination by the Federal Republic that women slowly began to enter this male domain (see table 3.7).

Even in 1966, when women constituted 30 percent of all university students, they were only 7 percent of law students. This changed rapidly in the second half of the 1970s as the total number of students in higher education continued to rise (Statistisches Bundesamt). In the state of Baden-Württemberg, 25 percent of law students were women in 1975/76 and

33 percent in 1981/82, which was about the average representation of women among all students. In 1983 women represented 37 percent of all law students. Today, legal studies are the second choice of women, surpassed only by medicine. The main reason for this dramatic change is declining career opportunities in other fields. Job prospects in teaching, traditionally women's first choice, are very dim at present. The explosion in education graduates in the 1960s created an oversupply of teachers, while the declining birth rate combined with decreased public spending reduced demand. Women traditionally have preferred public sector jobs; for lawyers these were in the judiciary. Women in the public service who are raising children are entitled to work part time and can take maternal leave for several years, with guaranteed reemployment. Although there may have been some reluctance about employing women because of the organizational problems caused by maternal leave, public services have been particularly careful not to discriminate. In 1983 women constituted 28 percent of the young jurists doing their in-practice training and 30 percent of probationary judges (those in their first three years) (see table 3.8).

The proportion of registered advocates who are women rose slowly, reaching 12.5 percent in 1986. Since 1983, however, the number of women qualifying has dropped even more rapidly than the number of men. At the peak in 1983, the 1,201 women who qualified were 36 percent of the total; in 1984, the 857 who qualified were 31 percent of the total; and in 1985, the 482 who qualified were estimated to be 24 percent of the total.[22] Warnings by the advocates' associations that the "flood of young advocates" will not find sufficient work to live on apparently are having a disproportionate impact on women.


RACISM


German lawyers hardly ever discuss racism. However, in 1933 one out of every five advocates in the German Reich and every other lawyer in Berlin was Jewish.[23] As soon as they seized power, the Nazis began expelling Jewish advocates and passed the "Law Against Misuse of Legal Advice" in 1935, which prohibited those expelled from engaging in any kind of practice. The final, official, expulsion of Jews from the legal profession occurred in 1938. Only a few German Jewish lawyers returned to practice after the war.

Today Turkish, Italian, and Yugoslav lawyers are conspicuously absent, despite the high proportion of Mediterranean immigrants in the population and the increasing importance of immigration law. Since university entrance requirements and state examinations present such high barriers to anybody seeking admission to the legal profession, we might ascribe this to "structural" discrimination rather than individual prejudice.

## AGE

Because most of those taking the qualifying examination are between twenty-five and thirty (the average age is twenty-nine) years, few lawyers start practice before they are thirty. However, the boom in admissions during the last fifteen years has made advocacy an extremely youthful profession. Table 3.9 shows the contrast with physicians, who must spend years acquiring specialist training in hospitals before joining the private profession. At the same time, advocates traditionally continue to practice beyond the customary retirement age. This changed slightly when pension insurance started to become compulsory for practicing lawyers in 1982.

## CONCLUSION

The data on the recent growth of the legal profession in Germany are strikingly similar to those in all developed Western countries. Throughout the Western world the numbers of lawyers have been rising rapidly; everywhere, at least since the late 1970s, there has been a considerable influx of women. There has been a general tendency for the largest proportion to enter private practice, partly as a route to other lawyer jobs. Yet, despite the common training, lateral mobility among legal careers is much lower in Germany (and most of continental Europe) than in common law countries. Legal services tend to be provided within public administrative and private corporate institutions rather than purchased from the professional market on a case-by-case basis. Consequently, the job of a practicing lawyer appears to be concentrated much more on traditional, forensic services than it is in the common law world. The bar should be regarded as only a part of the profession of "jurists," therefore, if one that is increasing its share.

The German legal profession traditionally has been oriented toward public service rather than advocacy. Law schools teach judges to decide cases, not advocates to represent parties. Future lawyers serve most of their in-practice training with the judiciary and public administration and little with advocates. Legal training in both university faculties and in-practice settings is highly regulated and controlled by the education boards of the state Ministries of Justice. The fact that legal education generates the recruits for the civil service explains their emphasis on uniformity. The legal profession has been the backbone of the legalistic-authoritarian state. The need for a reliable, uniform elite of civil servants explains the high degree of state regulation of entry and education.

Yet, this has not prevented the numbers of law graduates from rising sharply. Clearly, the growth of the legal profession in the last two decades was not stimulated by greater demand for legal services but by increased supply caused by the expansion of university training. To the degree that traditional careers for lawyers have not multiplied to meet the output of law graduates, more young lawyers have been pushed into advocacy. The composition of the legal profession is slowly changing as a result.

One might expect such quantitative changes to produce a major reorientation of legal education. On the contrary, reforms by newly founded law schools have been terminated by national legislation. The legal profession's reaction to expansion has been to defend established boundaries rather than expand the scope of legal services. It is highly doubtful, however, that such a defensive policy can be pursued for long. It is more likely that advocates will respond to overcrowding by seeking new markets. Reform is more likely to be produced by the self-interested actions of younger advocates than by the efforts of any other political lobby, especially since comparative studies of legal cultures show that the legal services market is influenced more by institutional determinants of supply than by changes in demand or "legal need" (Blankenburg & Verwoerd, n.d.).

# TABLES

3.1. Growth in the Number of Registered Advocates

| Political environment | Year | Number of registered advocates | Population per practicing lawyer |
|---|---|---|---|
| Deregulation of the entry of advocates | 1880 | 4,091 | 11,100 |
| | 1895 | 5,597 | 8,330 |
| | 1905 | 7,835 | 7,140 |
| | 1913 | 12,297 | 5,260 |
| World War I | 1914–1918 | | |
| | 1919 | 12,030 | 5,260 |
| | 1925 | 13,578 | 4,550 |
| Third Reich | 1933 | 19,276 | 3,330 |
| | 1935 | 18,712 | 3,450 |
| | 1939 | 14,800 | 4,760 |
| World War II | 1939–1945 | | |
| Federal Republic of Germany | 1950 | 12,844 | 3,850 |
| | 1955 | 16,824 | 3,120 |
| | 1960 | 18,347 | 3,030 |
| | 1965 | 19,796 | 2,860 |
| | 1970 | 22,882 | 2,630 |
| | 1975 | 26,854 | 2,270 |
| | 1980 | 36,077 | 1,690 |
| | 1985 | 46,927 | 1,300 |
| | 1986 | 48,658 | 1,230 |

*Sources:* 1880–1928—Kneer (1928: 61); Ostler (1971: 60, 207); population 1880–1913—Statistical Yearbooks; 1935–1939—Reifner (1984: 386); 1950–1986—Bundesrechtsanwaltskammer (BRAK).

3.2. Distribution of Jurists in Labor Force[a]

| | Distribution (percent) | |
|---|---|---|
| | 1961 | 1984 |
| Judicial office (including prosecutors) | 19 | 16 |
| Government service | 30 | 27 |
| Private employment (including Syndici) | 51 | 30 |
| Practicing advocates (excluding Syndici) | | 27 |
| N | 62,000 | 125,000 |

[a] The official census of the Statistische Bundesamt found 113,000 persons in the labor force in 1970 who had passed at least one state examination in law, of whom 43.8 percent were advocates, 23.5 percent were in the civil service, 17.1 percent were in the judiciary, 5.3 percent were teachers, and only 3.2 percent were in private business. Such figures misleadingly include all those admitted even if not actually practicing (30 percent of all registered "advocates"). We also have restricted ourselves to "full-fledged lawyers" who have passed both state examinations. Similarly, the Zentrale Forschungsgruppe für Juristenausbildung (1979) treats Syndici as advocates rather than "private employees"; therefore, they estimated a total of 95,000 jurists, 20 percent of whom are in the judiciary, 25 percent in the civil service, 17 percent in private employment, and 37 percent in advocacy. Our estimate that 30 percent of all registered advocates were employed by private companies in 1984 is based on federal income statistics, which show that 30 percent of those who give their occupation as "advocate" derive more than half of their income from salaries.

*Sources:* 1961—Rueschemeyer (1973: 32–33) (recomputed); 1984—Statistisches Bundesamt Wiesbaden, combined with data of the Chamber of Advocates and the Association of Judges and personal estimates.

3.3. Number and Size of Law Firms, 1967–1985

|  |  | 1967 | 1980 | 1985 |
|---|---|---|---|---|
| Total number of advocates | (1) | 20,543 | 36,077 | 46,927 |
| Percent of all lawyers in partnership | (2) | 26.5 | 37.7 | 40.9 |
| Percent estimated not practicing | (3) | 24 | 30 | 30 |
| Estimated percent solo practitioners |  |  |  |  |
| [100% − (2)−(3)] | (4) | 50 | 33 | 29 |
| Solo practitioners as a proportion of all practitioners |  |  |  |  |
| [(4)/(2)] | (5) | $\frac{2}{3}$ | $<\frac{1}{2}$ | $\frac{2}{5}$ |
| Number of law firms with |  |  |  |  |
| 2 or 3 partners |  | 2,185 | 4,440 | 5,680 |
| 4 to 9 partners |  | 149 | 704 | 1,157 |
| ≥ 10 partners |  | — | 14 | 42 |

Sources: Oellers (1982: 4); A. Braun (1987).

3.4. Average Annual Net Pretax Income of Advocates in Comparison to Other Self-Employed Professions, 1954–1980 (1,000 DM)

|  | 1954 | 1961 | 1971 | 1980 |
|---|---|---|---|---|
| Dentists | 12 | 28 | 110 | 240 |
| Physicians | 18 | 40 | 117 | 181 |
| Advocates | 18 | 38 | 79 | 123 |
| Tax advisors/chartered accountants[a] | 16 | 40 | 82 | 139 |
| Engineers | — | — | 72 | 86 |
| Architects | — | — | 60 | 92 |

[a] Only chartered accountants since 1980; this exaggerates the extent to which this profession has surpassed advocates.

Sources: 1954 and 1961—Rueschemeyer (1973: 64); 1971—Oellers (1982: 151); 1980: A. Braun (1986a: 67).

3.5. Percent of Bavarian Advocates Who Registered as Specialists (Multiple Entries)

| | Solo practitioners[a] | Partnerships |
|---|---|---|
| Family law | 55 | 44 |
| Traffic accidents (civil and criminal) | 54 | 50 |
| Criminal defense (excluding tax evasion and traffic offenses) | 40 | 29 |
| Labor law | 29 | 27 |
| Commercial and company law | 28 | 40 |
| Social law | 21 | 8 |
| Tax law | 16 | 19 |
| Administrative law | 9 | 31 |
| Patent and trade mark law | 4 | 19 |
| Others | 9 | 12 |

[a] $N = 265$.

Source: Institut für Freie Berufe (1978: 117).

3.6. Family Background of Advocates Compared to Judges and the General Population (Percent)

| | 1965 | | 1978 | | |
|---|---|---|---|---|---|
| Father's occupation | Advocates | Judges | Younger advocates | Younger judges | General population |
| Self-employed professional | a | a | 19 | 11 | 2 |
| Civil servant | 35 | 52 | 31 | 38 | 11 |
| Worker | a | a | 4 | 5 | 42 |

[a] No comparable data.

Sources: Kaupen (1969: 192); Heldrich & Schmidtchen (1982: 252–254).

3.7. Change in Proportion of Advocates Who Are Women, 1925–1985

|       | Number of advocates | | |
| Year | Women | Total | Percent women |
| --- | --- | --- | --- |
| 1925 | 44 | 13,578 | 0 |
| 1932 | 79 | 19,000 | 0 |
| 1962 | 480 | 19,001 | 2.5 |
| 1972 | 1,035 | 22,882 | 4.5 |
| 1982 | 3,458 | 39,036 | 8.9 |
| 1985 | 5,651 | 46,927 | 12.0 |
| 1986 | 6,133 | 49,087 | 12.5 |

*Source:* Annual statistics of the Bundesrechtsanwaltskammer.

3.8. Representation of Women within Legal Occupations (Percent)

|       | Law students | Probationary judges | Tenured judges | Advocates |
| --- | --- | --- | --- | --- |
| 1973 | 15 | 13 | 9 | 5 |
| 1977 | 25 | 18 | 11 | 6 |
| 1981 | 33 | 24 | 14 | 8 |
| 1983 | 37 | 30 | 14 | 10 |

*Sources:* Students—Statistisches Bundesamt Wiesbaden, Hochschulstatistik, Fachserie 11, Reihe 4, 1; before 1975: Fachserie A, Reihe 10/V; Judges—Bundesjustizministerium; Advocates—Bundesrechtsanwaltskammer.

3.9. Age Distribution of Practicing Advocates (1978, 1986) Compared to Practicing Physicians (1978) (Percent)

|       | Advocates | | |
| Age | 1978 | 1986 | Physicians, 1978 |
| --- | --- | --- | --- |
| <30 | 4 | 8 | 1 |
| 30–39 | 39 | 41 | 22 |
| 40–49 | 23 | 26 | 21 |
| 50–59 | 15 | 12 | 28 |
| 60–69 | 9 | 6 | 23 |
| >69 | 10 | 7 | 5 |

*Sources:* 1978—Bundestagsdrucksache (1979: 17); 1986—A. Braun (1986*b*: 151).

## NOTES

Ulrike Schutz assembled the source materials for this chapter and wrote the more detailed first draft, which was discussed at Bellagio in July 1984; she has continued to supply information on new developments and to check statements of fact and law. Erhard Blankenburg has substantially revised the original, although retaining some of Schultz's language. The authors are not always in agreement in their interpretations; where they differ, the present version represents Blankenburg's views. With respect to the future of advocacy, Schultz is more impressed with the stability of existing structures and Blankenburg, as the text indicates, with the potentialities for change.

1. During the 1970s academic and practical training were amalgamated in some "reformist" law faculties, but these attempts at reform have been terminated by national legislation.

2. Justiz-Ministerialblatt (1839: 415–416), quoted in Kolbeck (1978: 41). All translations are our own.

3. Quoted in Manstetten (1967: 255).

4. See Gneist (1867) for the ideological background and Magnus (1929) and Weissler (1905) for rather eulogistic historical sketches.

5. For an overview of the high degree to which the job market for German lawyers concides with international tendencies, see Abel (1989).

6. There is a flood of literature on the reform of legal education. For the early proposal, see Loccumer Arbeitskreis (1970, 1973). For a proponent of the reform attempts and further literature, see Voegele (1979) and M. Braun (1980) (a useful overview). For the final evaluation of the attempts, see Zentrale Forschungsgruppe für Juristenausbildung (1984).

7. For example, in Northrhine-Westphalia in 1984, only 9 out of 235 examiners were advocates or notaries according to information obtained from the Ministry of Justice at Dusseldorf.

8. For an overview of various legal occupations, see Kaupen and Werle (1974).

9. Klausa (1981) showed that the state of Bremen had the lowest reputation among all German law faculties, even though it would have deserved an above-average rank on objective indicators, such as scholarly merit.

10. According to Klausa (1981: 151ff.), only about 7 percent of the younger professors (thirty to forty-five years old) have practiced as advocates for a significant time. In this age group, 72 percent have served exclusively in university positions. The limited job experience of younger university teachers may, however, be generationally specific. With the fiscal crisis of the 1980s, few positions are available within universities, so that those who wish to become teachers must begin their careers elsewhere.

11. The first article of the Statute on Advocacy (Bundesrechtsanwaltsordnung—BRAO) of 1 August 1959 states that advocates form an "organic part of the

system of justice." For an empirically informed and less ideological analysis of the modern advocate's role, see Volks (1974).

12. Annual statistics provided by the Bundesrechtsanwaltskammer and the Federation of Notaries.

13. No exact figures are available. The sum of these figures is higher than the total shown in table 3.2 because 25 to 30 percent of the admitted Anwälte also are in private employment. Insurance companies alone employed 3,800 lawyer-advocates in 1980 (Ernst et al., 1983).

14. The legal provisions are described in English in Schultz (1982) and Schultz and Koessler (1980). Cohn (1960/61) provides a classic description for an English audience.

15. An attempt to amend the Statute on Advocacy (BRAO) to permit advocates to call themselves specialists in tax, administrative, labor, or social security law did not pass Parliament (Bundesrats-Drucksache 256/85). In response, the 60th Plenary Session of the Chamber of Advocates amended its internal regulations to allow advocates who passed an examination set by their chamber to call themselves "specialists" (76 Richtlinien der Rechtsanwaltschaft).

16. BVerfG, Beschluss v. 8.3.1983-1BvR 1978/80; NJW 83, 1535.

17. Communication from the Bundesrechtsanwaltskammer, subsequently published in 1986/3 *Anwaltsblatt* 148.

18. In 1979, surveys showed that 40 percent of all households were covered by such insurance, about a third of these only for automobile accidents and traffic offenses and the remainder for all legal expenses. Since then insurance sales have increased. See Blankenburg and Fiedler (1981) and Blankenburg (1982*a*).

19. See note 15.

20. "Duty solicitor" is the literal translation of "Pflichtverteidiger," although the functions are less limited than those of the British duty solicitor.

21. For criticism of some of the interpretations of Heldrich and Schmidtchen (1982), see Blankenburg's review (1982*b*).

22. Computed from the membership statistics of the Chamber of Advocates (BRAK—Mitteilungen 88 [1986]), making the reasonable assumption that men constitute all of the older generation containing most of the advocates who leave the profession through death each year (approximately 330).

23. See Weinkauff and Wagner (1968) and Juristische Wochenschrift 2956 (1933). Jews represented 4,394 out of 19,500 lawyers and 60 percent of Berlin advocates.

# REFERENCES

Abel, Richard L. 1989. "Comparative Sociology of Legal Professions," in Richard L. Abel and Philip S. C. Lewis, eds., *Lawyers in Society*, vol. 3: *Comparative Theories*. Berkeley, Los Angeles, London: University of California Press.

Blankenburg, Erhard. 1982a. "Legal Insurance, Litigant Decisions and the Rising Caseloads of Courts," 16 *Law & Society Review* 601–624.

———. 1982b. Review of Heldrich and Schmidtchen (1982), 1982 *Zeitschrift für Rechtssoziologie* 308–311.

———. 1983. "Evaluation des ersten Jahres Beratungshilfe," 1983 *Zeitschrift für Rechtspolitik* 39–45.

———. 1985. "Rechtsmittel im Zivilprozess," in Peter Gilles and Klaus F. Rohl, eds., *Rechtsmittel im Zivilprozess*. Cologne: Bundesanzeiger.

———. 1986. "Subventionen für die Rechtsberatung im Rechtsvergleich," 1986 *Zeitschrift für Rechtspolitik* 108–112.

———, ed. 1980. *Innovations in the Legal Services*. Kronstein and Cambridge: Oelgeschlaeger, Gunn & Hain.

Blankenburg, Erhard, and Jan Fiedler. 1981. *Die Rechtsschutzversicherungen und der steigende Geschaftsanfall der Gerichte*. Tubingen: Mohr.

Blankenburg, Erhard, and Udo Reifner. 1982. *Rechtsberatung*. Neuwied: Luchterhand.

Blankenburg, Erhard, and Jan Verwoerd. n.d. "Comparing Litigation in the Netherlands with that of Northrhine-Westphalia." Unpublished communication.

Bleek, Wilhelm. 1972. *Von der Kameralausbildung zum Juristenprivileg*. Berlin: Colloquium.

Braun, Anton. 1986a. "Einkunfte und Praxiskosten von Rechtsanwalten 1977 bis 1983," 1986/2 *BRAK—Mitteilungen* 67.

———. 1986b. "Altersstruktur der Anwaltschaft," 1986/3 *BRAK—Mitteilungen* 150.

———. 1987. "Sozietäten," 1987/1 *BRAK—Mitteilungen* 4.

Braun, Manfred. 1980. *Juristenausbildung im Deutschland*. Berlin: de Gruyter.

Brinkmann, Gerhard, Wolfgang Pippke, and Wolfgang Rippe. 1973. *Die Tätigkeitsfelder des hoheren Verwaltungsdienstes: Arbeitsanspruche. Ausbildungserfordernisse*. Opladen: Westdeutscher Verlag.

Bundestagsdrucksache. 1979. "Bericht der Bundesregierung über die Lage der freien Berufe," 8/3139 *Bundestagsdrucksache*.

Bundesverband der freien Berufe. 1984. *Der freie Beruf, Jahrbuch 83/84*. Bonn: Bundesverband der freien Berufe.

Cohn, Ernst J. 1960/61. "The German Attorney: Experiences with a Unified Profession," 9 *International and Comparative Law Quarterly* 580–599, 10 *International and Comparative Law Quarterly* 103–122.

Dahrendorf, Ralf. 1965. *Gesellschaft und Demokratie in Deutschland*. Munich: Piper.

Ernst, K., K. Lieser, and V. Mellin 1983. *Als Jurist in der Wirtschaft*. Frankfurt: Zentralstelle für Arbeitsvermittlung (ZAV). In *Frankfurter Allgemeine Zeitung*, no. 13, January 17, 1983, p. 14.

Galanter, Marc. 1983. "Mega-Law and Mega-Lawyering in the Contemporary United States," in Robert Dingwall and Philip Lewis, eds., *The Sociology of the Professions: Lawyers, Doctors and Others*, pp. 152–176. London: Macmillan.

Gneist, Rudolf von. 1867. *Die Freie Advokatur.* Berlin: Springer.

Harms, Wolfgang. 1983. "Juristenschwemme—Berufsaussichten, Prognosen und Fehlprognosen," 1983 *JuS* 894.

Heldrich, Andreas, and Gerhard Schmidtchen. 1982. *Gerechtigkeit als Beruf.* Munich: Beck.

Institut für Freien Berufe. 1978. *Struktur und Bedeutung der Freien Berufe in der Bayerischen Wirtschaft.* Nurnberg: Erlangen Universität.

Kaplan, Benjamin, Arthur T. von Mehren, and Rudolf Schaefer. 1958. "Phases of German Civil Procedure," 71 *Harvard Law Review* 1461.

Kaupen, Wolfgang, 1969. *Die Hüter von Recht und Ordnung.* Neuwied: Luchterhand.

Kaupen, Wolfgang, and Raymund Werle, eds. 1974. *Soziologische Probleme juristischer Berufe.* Göttingen: Schwartz.

Klausa, Ekkehard. 1981. *Deutsche und amerikanische Rechtslehrer.* Baden-Baden: Nomos.

Kneer, August. 1928. *Der Rechtsanwalt.* München-Gladbach: Volksvereinsverlag.

Kolbeck, Thomas. 1978. *Juristenschwemmen—Untersuchungen über den juristischen Arbeitsmarkt im 19. und 20. Jahrhundert.* Frankfurt am Main: Lang.

Kolvenbach, Walter, 1979. "Die Tätigkeit der Syndikusanwälte im Unternehmen und ihre Zusammenarbeit mit frei praktizierenden Anwalten," 33 *Juristenzeitung* 458–460.

Lange, Elmar, and Niklas Luhmann. 1974. "Juristen, Berufswahl und Karrieren," 65 *Verwaltungsarchiv* 148-152.

Lehmann, Paul. 1984. "25 Jahre Ehrengerichtsbarkeit," in *25 Jahre Bundesrechtsanwaltskammer.* Munich: Beck (Schriften reihe der Bundesrechtsanwaltskammer, no. 6).

Loccumer Arbeitskreis, ed. 1970. *Neue Juristenausbildung.* Neuwied: Luchterhand.

———. 1973. *Der neue Jurist. Ausbildungsreform in Bremen.* Neuwied: Luchterhand.

Magnus, Julius. 1929. *Die Rechtsanwaltschaft.* Leipzig: Moeser.

Manstetten, Fritz. 1967. *Vom Sachsenspiegel zum Code Napoléon.* Cologne: Wienand.

Meier-Scherling, Anne-Gudrun. 1975. "Die Benachteiligung der Juristen zwischen 1933 und 1945," *Deutsche Richterzeitung* (DRiZ) 10–13.

Merryman, John. 1968. *The Civil Law Tradition.* Stanford: Standford University Press.

Oellers, Bernhard. 1982. "Einkunfte und Praxis(un)kosten von Rechtsanwalten, 1971–1979," 1982/4 *BRAK—Mitteilungen* 151.

Ostler, Fritz. 1971. *Die deutschen Rechtsanwälte 1878–1971.* Essen: Ellinghaus.

Parsons, Talcott, 1954. "The Problem of Controlled Institutional Change: Report on the Conference on Germany after the War," in *Essays in Sociological Theory.* Glencoe, Ill.: Free Press.

Paul, Wolf. 1982. "Anwaltsberuf im Wandel: Arbeiten zur Rechtsvergleichung," in Hein Kötz, Wolf Paul, Michel Pédamon, and Michael Zander, eds., *An-*

*waltsberuf im Wandel: Rechtspflegeorgan oder Dienstleitungsgewerbe*. Frankfurt: Metzner.

Portele, Gerhard, and Wolfgang Schütte. 1983. *Juristenausbildung und Beruf*. Hamburg: Interdisziplinares Zentrum für Hochschuldidaktik der Universität Hamburg (IZHD) (Hochschuldidaktische Arbeitspapiere no. 16).

Reifner, Udo. 1984. "Die Zerstörung der freien Advokatur im Nationalsozialismus," 17 *Kritische Justiz* 380–393.

Rueschemeyer, Dietrich. 1973. *Lawyers and Their Society: A Comparative Study of the Legal Profession in Germany and the United States*. Cambridge, Mass.: Harvard University Press.

Schmid, Gunter, and Hubert Treiber. 1975. *Burokratie und Politik. Zür Struktur und Funktion der Ministerialburokratie in der Bundesrepublik Deutschland*. Munich: Fink UTB.

Schultz, Ulrike. 1982. "The German Rechtsanwalt: Images of a Unified Profession," 79 *Law Society's Gazette* 1210.

Schultz, Ulrike, and Paul Koessler. 1980. "The Practicing Lawyer in the Federal Republic of Germany," [1980] *The International Lawyer* 531.

Schütte, Wolfgang. 1982. *Die Einubang des juristischen Denkens. Juristenausbildung als Sozialisationsprozess*. Frankfurt: Campus.

Senninger, Erhard. "Berufsaussichten für jünge Juristen," 1983 *Anwaltsblatt* 394–397.

Statistisches Bundesamt Wiesbaden. *Hochschulstatistik*, Fachserie 11, Reihe 4, 1 (series).

———. *BAFoG-Statistik*, Fachserie 11, Reihe 7 (series).

Voegele, Wolfgang. 1979. *Einphasige Juristenausbildung—zür Pathologie der Reform*. Frankfurt: Campus.

Volks, Holger, 1974. *Anwaltliche Berufsrollen und anwaltliche Berufsarbeit in der Industriegesellschaft*. Cologne: Diss.

Wassermann, Rudolf. 1983. "Zu den Prufungsinhalten der ersten juristischen Staatsprufung," 1983 *JuS* 703.

Wassermann, Rudolf, ed. 1969. *Erziehung zum Establishment*. Karlsruhe: C. F. Muller.

Weinkauff, Hermann, and Albrecht Wagner, 1968. *Die deutsche Justiz und der Nationalsozialismus*. Stuttgart: Deutsche Verlagsanstalt.

Weissler, Adolf. 1905. *Geschichte der Rechtsanwaltschaft*. Leipzig: Pfeffer (reprinted Frankfurt: Sauer und Auvermann, 1967).

Zentrale Forschungsgruppe für Juristenausbildung. 1979. Mannheim: Zentrale Forschungsgruppe für Juristenausbildung.

———. 1984. Mannheim: Zentrale Forschungsgruppe für Juristenausbildung.

# 4

# The Present State of Japanese Practicing Attorneys: On the Way to Full Professionalization?

## KAHEI ROKUMOTO

This chapter attempts to present an overall picture of Japanese lawyers in private practice and the legal services they deliver, drawing on a recent national survey (table 4.1).[1] I shall discuss some of the most salient features of the Japanese bar and its business, primarily on the basis of the survey, focusing on (1) the size of the bar, (2) the recruitment of its members, (3) the forms of their practice, (4) the kind of work they do and the clients they serve, and (5) their income. However, in order to interpret such an overall picture correctly, we must put it in an appropriate framework. So I shall start with a brief summary of the historical and institutional background of the profession.

## HISTORICAL AND INSTITUTIONAL BACKGROUND

Before 1868 there was no distinct occupational group with special expertise in law.[2] Within the government of the central Tokugawa Shogunate, as well as those of the subordinate feudal domains, the judicial function constituted only one of the tasks of generalist administrators. Professional representation before the court was not recognized, although certain innkeepers and their clerks (called *kujishi*) were authorized to offer their knowledge of procedure and of the location of various offices to guests coming to Edo for litigation (Henderson, 1965: 167–169).

The Meiji Government created the entire modern, centralized legal system on the model of the imperial German legal system. This was done during the decades following the Imperial Restoration, through promulgation of a constitution and comprehensive substantive and procedural codes and the establishment of a system of courts distributed throughout the country. In the course of the gradual differentiation of the judicial branch within the governmental structure, the legal profession also emerged. Because it, too, was created by the government, it lacks autonomous authority rooted in tradition. Moreover, in the process of establishing the legal profession, emphasis naturally was placed on securing competent judges and prosecutors—career governmental officers charged with administering the imported systems of laws and courts—to the neglect of private attorneys.

In 1872 judges and prosecutors were recognized as legal officers distinct from ordinary government officials.[3] A certain amount of legal education (based mainly on the European law) was made a prerequisite for their appointment, and a government school was established for the purpose, which later was incorporated into an Imperial University. Beginning in 1890, the positions of both judges and prosecutors were firmly established through the formal examination system, the three-year apprenticeship, and the guarantee of tenure. Private attorneys, however, systematically were treated as the inferiors of judges and prosecutors, although their position gradually improved during the prewar period. Legal representation was recognized in civil cases in 1872 and in criminal cases in 1890, and the professionals who performed those functions officially were recognized in 1876. Their qualifications remained vague until 1893, when the first Practicing Attorneys Act introduced the present title of "bengoshi,"[4] together with a formal qualification based on an examination of legal knowledge. This examination, however, was separate from, and less demanding than, that for judges and prosecutors, and law graduates of Imperial Universities were exempt even from it until 1923. Apprenticeship was not required until 1936 (apprentices were paid by the state). Throughout the prewar period, private attorneys were under the control of the Minister of Justice and the prosecutors subordinate to him, and the activities of their organizations were closely supervised.

The general social and economic patterns determined by the precipitous modernization under the leadership of an authoritarian government also did not constitute a favorable environment for the development of a new profession. The traditional aversion toward "law" still prevailed among the population and was reinforced by the familistic nature of social organizations and governmental indoctrination of Confucian ethics emphasizing "harmony." The rise and growth of modern industry in an agrarian society that had been closed to the outer world for 300 years is attributable less to the workings of an impartial law protecting free entrepreneurial activities and more to active encouragement and protection by the government. Consequently, lawyers' services were not an indispensable element in the making of modern Japanese society and economy. The inquisitorial character of court procedures also narrowed the lawyers' role in civil matters. These circumstances led practicing attorneys to develop a characteristic professional self-image stressing their political role in representing criminal defendants oppressed by the state. They even called themselves the "opposition branch" of the legal profession, in contrast to the judges and prosecutors, who were labeled the "governmental branch."

It is only through the Practicing Attorneys Act of 1949 that Japanese practicing attorneys acquired formal equality with judges and prosecutors, in the sense that all are subjected to the same state legal examination and two-year apprenticeship and that the former were accorded full autonomy in governing their own affairs, including the matters of licensure and discipline.[5] Court procedures for both civil and criminal cases also have undergone substantial reforms to incorporate Anglo-American adversary principles, thus enhancing the role and status of attorneys in the courtroom.

Today, aspirants to the legal profession undergo a unitary state Legal Examination and a common two-year course of practical training at the Institute of Legal Training and Research (ILTR).[6] They decide whether to become judges, prosecutors, or practicing attorneys when they leave this institute.[7] Some efforts were made after the war to unify the legal profession, recruiting judges from among experienced private practitioners, but this effort failed, although a proportion of Supreme Court justices customarily are appointed from among eminent private attorneys.[8] Thus, only a few of those who choose private practice at the time of leaving the ILTR will enter the public sector, although a substantial number of judges and prosecutors resign to become private attorneys even before they reach retirement age.[9]

Within these and other new institutional frameworks, created as part of postwar democratization, the younger lawyers trained in the ILTR grew in number and the general quality and prestige of Japanese private attorneys significantly improved (table 4.2). Against the background of the postwar economic expansion, the importance of lawyers in civil matters gradually was recognized, and the public now accepts them as a major element in the administration of law and justice. Nevertheless, the status of practicing attorneys still reflects the historical handicaps described above. They rank somewhat lower than judges and prosecutors, and, in face-to-face interaction, the latter display their traditional sense of superiority, which is greatly resented by the former.

In analyzing the legal profession, we also have to note some of the distinctive features of the contemporary Japanese legal system. The judicial system resembles that of Germany, with each of the forty-seven prefectures having a district court, the principal court of first instance with general jurisdiction. Above the district courts there are eight high courts and one Supreme Court. Below, there are about 600 summary courts of limited jurisdiction (up to 900,000 yen [¥] in civil matters; about $4,500).

Unlike the German model, however, we also have separate family courts in each prefecture.

Mediation is an integral part of the judicial system. Lay mediators attempt to settle civil cases less formally, less expensively, and more quickly by assisting parties in reaching an agreement.[10] In family matters, a regular lawsuit can be filed only after mediation in the family court has failed. In other civil matters, the plaintiff can choose between mediation and adjudication regardless of the amount in controversy.

Legal representation is *not* compulsory, except in certain kinds of criminal cases (Code of Criminal Procedure, art. 290).[11] In contrast, a non-lawyer can represent a party only in summary courts (Code of Civil Procedure, art. 79). Both lawyers and lay representatives are allowed to participate in mediation.[12] There is no localization of practicing attorneys as in Germany, so that lawyers can represent their clients before any Japanese court. There also is no legal regulation of lawyers' fees. Each association of practicing attorneys establishes a standard fee schedule, in principle proportioned to the amount in dispute, but this has no binding force and is not strictly followed in practice.

## SIZE

It is well known that both the Japanese legal profession as a whole and the practicing bar in particular are very small (see table 4.3). In 1979 there were 1,940 posts for regular judges and assistant judges,[13] 791 posts for summary court judges holding lower qualifications,[14] and 2,092 posts for regular and assistant prosecutors. As of January 1980 there were 11,466 registered practicing attorneys.[15] The ratio of practicing attorneys to the national population (about 116 million) is approximately one to 10,000 persons, only a sixth as high as in England and West Germany.[16]

The distribution of lawyers within the country is far from even. In 1980, 5,361 of the 11,466 lawyers (or 46.8 percent) had their offices in Tokyo and another 2,044 (17.8 percent) were practicing in Osaka or Aichi. Thus, almost two-thirds of all private attorneys are concentrated in the three largest industrial centers. Five other prefectures endowed with a high court contained 918 private attorneys (8.0 percent), and the remaining 39 prefectures with only a district court had a total of 3,143 lawyers (or 27.4 percent). The number of PAs per 10,000 people in each of the four survey areas is as follows: A = 4.58, B = 1.44, C = 0.64, D = 0.43. Therefore, in the peripheral areas there is an extreme shortage of practicing attorneys. Within these peripheral prefectures, lawyers' offices are concentrated in the city where the prefectural government and the district

court are located, so that the nationwide maldistribution of lawyers is re-
produced at the prefectural level.

These gaps are partly filled by the PAs who travel from urban centers
to work on particular cases pending in local courts and by other categories of law-related occupations, each of which has its own examination, registration, and legally prescribed sphere of activities.[17] These
include tax accountants (40,000), patent attorneys (2,500), judical scriveners (approximately 14,500 in 1980), and administrative scriveners
(65,000).

Tax accountants are allowed to draft documents, give advice concerning tax matters, and represent clients in the administrative complaint procedures against tax authorities; however, the number of such cases still is
small in Japan. Patent attorneys may give legal opinions about patents
and similar matters and represent clients in complaint or dispute procedures concerning those matters before the competent authorities (the
Patent Office and the Minister of International Trade and Industry) and, in
certain matters, before the regular courts (Patent Attorneys Act, arts. 1, 9,
9-2). Patent, copyright, and taxation constitute highly specialized fields, in
which only a very few lawyers could work confidently without the collaboration of a patent attorney or a tax accountant. Not surprisingly, the
distribution of patent lawyers and tax accountants resembles that of practicing attorneys.

The activities of judicial scriveners are more general and somewhat
overlap those of PAs.[18] The law authorizes them "to represent the client
in the procedure concerning registration or deposit" and "to draw up documents to be submitted to a court, a prosecutor's office, or a bureau of
judicial affairs," among other functions (Legal Scriveners Act, art. 2).[19]
The registration of real estate transactions and the creation or transformation of commercial corporations makes up the bulk of the work of legal
scriveners. The former includes the registration of many changes in the
rights and duties concerning land and buildings, including transfer and
mortgage. In Japan, these transactions normally are effected with the
assistance of a real estate agent and a judicial scrivener and without the
intervention of a PA. Furthermore, the judicial scrivener lawfully can prepare briefs and all the other documents submitted by the litigant in the
course of a lawsuit. Judicial precedent has recognized that, in drafting such
documents, the judicial scrivener must exercise legal judgment. It is almost
impossible to separate the legal advice necessary to draft a document from
the other advice a judicial scrivener may offer his client. Consequently, it
is widely admitted that in most cases where the litigant is unrepresented a
judicial scrivener is operating behind the scenes, not only drafting documents but also advising the principal on how to conduct the litigation.
They also frequently advise citizens in matters not related to the legiti-

mate work of drafting a document and occasionally are prosecuted for violating the Practicing Attorneys Act.[20] Legal scriveners are much more evenly distributed geographically, partly compensating for the maldistribution of private attorneys.[21]

The work of administrative scriveners concerns the documents submitted to an administrative office (e.g., the application for a driver's license). This does not directly involve a legal transaction or dispute, however, and complaints against an administrative agency still are very rare in Japan. Therefore, administrative scriveners seldom are viewed as lawyer substitutes.

## RECRUITMENT

The principal mode of recruitment to the legal profession is through the state Legal Examination, followed by two years of practical training at the Institute of Legal Training and Research. About 70 percent of attorneys practicing today are those younger, more competent lawyers who entered in this fashion. Within a few decades the others, who qualified under the older system, will completely disappear from the Japanese bar.

Practicing attorneys qualify rather late in life. Among those presently in practice, about 29 percent obtained their qualification before they were twenty-five, about 47 percent between twenty-five and thirty, and 20 percent after thirty. The average age of those who passed the Legal Examination was 27.69 years in 1965, 26.60 in 1970, 26.75 in 1975, and 28.07 in 1980 (Nihon Houritsuka Kyoukai, 1982: 139). (We have to add two more years in order to obtain the average age of qualification for each class.) This undoubtedly is due to the difficulty of the Legal Examination, which is notorious and often severely criticized by law professors. Each year, only 500 out of 29,000 candidates (or 1.7 percent) pass (see table 4.4). Since the normal age of graduation from the university is between twenty-two and twenty-four, those who pass have spent an average of three to five years preparing for the examination.[22] Many candidates attend cram schools, even while they are university students. There is no limit on the age of the candidates or the number of repetitions.

Although lawyers need not have a law degree or even a university degree, we found that only 1.6 percent of practicing attorneys were not university graduates and that 95.3 percent of university graduates had studied law.

Not all graduates aspire to enter the legal profession. Legal education is not offered in a professional school at the graduate level but is a two-year undergraduate course in a law faculty (following two years of general university education) and includes a wide range of subjects, such as political science and economics, as well as law.[23] In fact, those who pass the Legal Examination and go on to the ILTR constitute a small minority of law students (see table 4.5).[24] Others enter the civil service or business. The education in a law faculty, especially at one of the former Imperial Universities (which were founded mainly to recruit and educate civil servants), is considered the entrée to high positions in politics, government, and business. It cannot be said that the best law students become lawyers, either; for one thing, in order to pass the Legal Examination, one must devote two or three years almost exclusively to preparation.

Many law students enter large business corporations and become the "lawpersons" in the firm—employees who have acquired the basic knowledge of and skill in law and legal reasoning in the university and, without possessing the certificate of a lawyer, specialize in handling the legal matters of the firm. These people, of course, represent still another category of competitors with practicing attorneys.[25]

Our study of the social background of practicing attorneys revealed that 13.6 percent of their fathers were professionals, 12.6 percent were managers, 19.0 percent were clerical or technical employees, 28.1 percent were proprietors not in agriculture, 18.9 percent were farmers, 4.7 percent were workers, and 4.2 percent were in other categories. Overrepresentation of the professional and managerial classes on one hand and underrepresentation of workers and farmers on the other hand is clear. In order to ascertain accurately the implication of these data, however, we would need a detailed analysis of the social structure of Japanese society and its change over the past 100 years, particularly because it has undergone a fundamental transformation from a predominantly agrarian, static society into a highly industrialized, mobile society within a very short time (Dore, 1967).

## FORMS OF PRACTICE

All Japanese practicing attorneys have or belong to one (and only one) law office, but their status varies with their relation to that office. Some lawyers are employed by another lawyer or lawyers (principals). Most employed lawyers earn a fixed salary (with annual raises) for the work they do for their principal,[26] and many also receive a percentage of the fee in cases they handle together with their employers or on their own (see table 4.6). A small number work entirely on commission. Most employed lawyers may take their own cases and work for their own clients using the office facilities and clerks of their employers. In this way, they acquire the necessary work experience to launch their own practices. These employed lawyers sometimes are called "*Isoro*-attorneys" ("Isoro" means one who hangs on a master and performs odd tasks). This term is a remnant from the time when practicing attorneys started their careers as personal apprentices of a senior lawyer. Even today, the relationship between principals and their young employees sometimes is colored by the paternalistic attitudes of the former and thus is not altogether free from friction.

Principal lawyers fall into two categories: those who are the only principal within their law office and those who share their office with other principals. The first group divides further into solo practitioners and sole principals who employ other lawyers. We call the latter "masters," in complementarity to the term "Isoro-attorneys." The second group also contains two subdivisions. One is the "office-sharers," who share only the rented office space, telephones, law books, and other equipment, as well as clerks. Sometimes they share employee lawyers, as well. Insofar as the management of the law practice is concerned, however, the members of a *Büro-Gemeinschaft*, as it would be called in Germany, are completely independent of each other. One has personal clients, works independently without consulting office companions, and pays a share of the office expenses out of separate fees. The other subdivision includes those who form a partnership with other lawyers and share not only the office expenses but also the clients, the work, and the fees, as well as responsibility for running the office. Many partnerships also have employee lawyers.

Thus, we can classify practicing attorneys into the following five categories (with the adjusted proportion of the total sample shown in parentheses): (1) "Isoro-attorneys," that is, employed lawyers (18.0 percent); (2) office-sharers (14.0 percent); (3) solo practitioners (50.0 percent); (4) "masters," that is, solo principals with employed lawyers (9.0 percent); and (5) partners (9.0 percent). The distribution of practicing attorneys across these categories by areas and age is shown in tables 4.7a, 4.7b, and 4.7c. On the basis of these tables, we can make the following observations.

Generally speaking, Japanese practicing attorneys start their careers as employed lawyers.[27] As they grow older, they try to practice independently, but some—especially in Tokyo where rents are higher—find it necessary to share an office in order to accumulate more capital before opening their own practices. After they have achieved independence, if their business prospers and the volume of their work both warrants and demands it, they hire younger lawyers to perform part of the work load. Thus, although Japanese attorneys may associate with others in various ways, their ultimate goal is to be on their own, "the master of a castle, however small it may be."

Partners, most of whom are in their thirties and forties, represent only a small minority among Japanese lawyers. They do not follow the traditional career pattern just described. In fact, partnerships are an innovation. According to our data, there presently are three types of partnership (apart from husband and wife or father and son). The first type comprises law firms specializing in international business transactions and adopting the work style and office organization of the larger American firms. These partners generally have had some legal education in the United States. Indeed, some of these firms were founded by American lawyers. Some have many patent attorneys among their partners. The employer and employee lawyers often are referred to by the English terms "partner" and "associate." Most firms send their young associates to Western countries (not always the United States) for legal studies and training. These firms are located almost exclusively in Tokyo and represent the largest and most modern law offices in Japan. In 1980 they contained eight to fifteen practicing attorneys, and some also had patent attorneys.

The second type of partnership consists of the law firms affiliated with left-wing political parties. They mainly represent labor unions in industrial disputes and defend union members and political leftists in criminal proceedings. In recent years, these lawyers have played an important role in cases concerning environmental pollution. Such cases often require cooperation among a number of committed lawyers sharing a common ideology. Specialization in union cases explains how these law firms can exist, even in the areas where the absolute number of practicing attorneys is very small.

The third type is made up of partnerships oriented to domestic business clients. Such partnerships are increasing in Osaka and Nagoya, and some make a conscious effort both to rationalize their practices through constant mutual consultation within the firm and to develop forms of legal services better adapted to the everyday needs of all Japanese business corporations, and not just the very large ones. These law firms generally are smaller than the first type and sometimes are formed on the basis of a former relationship between a master and an Isoro-attorney.

Most partnerships are fairly small (see table 4.8). One of our respondents belonged to a firm with 20 or more lawyers (partners and associates included), but this is a rare exception. The great majority of partnerships consist of two to five lawyers. This also is true of the offices of office-sharers, although here the average size is slightly larger (see table 4.9).

Table 4.10 shows the distribution of lawyers by area in terms of the number of lawyers in their offices, regardless of whether these lawyers are employed, office-sharers, masters, or partners. Half of Japanese lawyers are solo practitioners, 20 percent belong to a two-lawyer office, and another 20 percent belong to an office with three to six lawyers. In terms of management, however, office-sharers and masters both practice on their own account. In this sense, it can be said that 73 percent of all attorneys and 89 percent of all principal attorneys practice independently.

Law offices in Japan are small in another respect, too. The average number of clerks per lawyer is little more than one (see table 4.11). The occupation of law office clerk is not well institutionalized, either. There is no organized training or certificate system, as is the case in England and West Germany (Rechtsanwalt und Notar Gehilfe). Correspondingly, the work done by the clerks tends to be limited to secretarial and bookkeeping functions. Only a few regularly execute simple, patterned legal tasks. Practically no clerk is entrusted with work requiring independent legal judgment. Most are young women, who leave when they marry, or young men preparing for the Legal Examination, although a substantial minority of clerks are experienced men and women, who are indispensable to their employers. The average numbers of clerks per law office, by gender, education, experience, and area, are shown in table 4.12.

## WORK AND CLIENTS

In order to ascertain the volume and content of the work of attorneys, we asked each respondent to list all open cases[28] and to classify them in terms of various criteria.

Table 4.13 shows that criminal matters account for 5 to 10 percent of the attorney's caseload, a proportion that increases as we go from area A toward area D, reflecting the lawyer shortage in peripheral areas (see also tables 4.14 and 4.15). The average number of cases open at the time of the survey (between thirty-two and forty-eight) is rather small; indeed, the national average of pending civil cases is only thirty-seven (see table 4.16). The volume is dramatically higher among the lawyers in their forties and fifties and also higher in peripheral areas, for the reason given above. Civil cases are heavily concentrated among the small number of masters and partners (see table 4.13). Only a few lawyers handle over 100 cases, most of whom are located in peripheral areas, and only 7.8 percent of all lawyers handle more than 80 cases (see table 4.15).[29]

There are four kinds of civil matters: (1) noncontentious (or preventive) cases; (2) disputes handled without the intervention of a court or other public agency (at least at the time of our inquiry); (3) cases brought before a public agency, such as an administrative tribunal; and (4) cases brought before a regular court for either mediation or adjudication. Formal litigation constitutes by far the greatest proportion of the civil work of Japanese practicing attorneys (see table 4.16). Noncontentious matters and out-of-court settlements represent only 15 to 30 percent of all civil cases (about 25 percent of the total work load of attorneys). Dispute settlement before administrative tribunals still is almost negligible. Only Tokyo differs significantly from this pattern because law firm partners specializing in international trade handle a larger proportion of noncontentious matters (see table 4.17).

When current civil cases are classified by subject matter (see table 4.18), the largest categories are debt collection (20 to 23 percent) and payment of debt (7 to 9 percent)—the gap between the two must be due to default cases. Closely related to these are executions of judgments (5 to 8 percent) and bankruptcy (2 to 3 percent). Together these categories account for about 35 to 40 percent. Next in importance are disputes involving rented houses or land (7 to 11 percent) and other cases involving real estate (9 to 15 percent); inheritance (4 to 5 percent) also primarily concerns houses and land. If we combine the three real estate categories, we get another 20 to 30 percent. A third major grouping consists of automobile accidents (4 to 7 percent), medical malpractice (1 percent), and other damages (6 to 7 percent), aggregating another 10 to 15 percent. Fourth place is taken by domestic matters (4 to 5 percent).[30] Those problems that arise in the everyday lives of most people—employment, environmental matters, consumer complaints, and grievances against the government—are not an important source of business for Japanese lawyers. Nor are those bodies of law that affect the daily affairs of larger business enterprises, such as company and economic law, patent and copyright law, and international trade law. Thus, Japanese lawyers depend heavily on debt collection and real estate matters, in which resort to court often is unavoidable.

Consistent with this subject matter emphasis, the main clientele of Japanese lawyers is individuals (who own property) and small and medium-sized enterprises, not large business firms (see table 4.19). Large business firms virtually are monopolized by master lawyers and partners in the major industrial centers (see table 4.20). Except for partners in Tokyo firms and masters everywhere, most Japanese lawyers rely heavily on new "one-shot" clients rather than on the return of habitual customers (see table 4.21).

Some lawyers have retainers (mostly oral) with an organization (very rarely an individual) whereby the lawyer offers daily consultation in return for a fixed annual fee. If the client also asks the lawyer to handle litigation, it will pay the lawyer a separate fee, although usually at a reduced rate. The retaining organization is not obligated to send its cases exclusively to its legal advisor, and some larger companies have several legal advisors (see tables 4.22 and 4.23). To create such relationships is one of the central goals of Japanese lawyers. Retainers ensure a regular income, which, although often rather small, at least covers the rent. They are important sources of work, for the retaining organizations not only give their advisor profitable cases but also refer other clients—and to be the legal advisor of a well-known firm enhances the prestige of a lawyer. Master lawyers have a distinct advantage in getting retainers (see table 4.22).

Very few clients come to the lawyer through public or private counseling bureaus, and only a small number come without any intermediary (see table 4.24). A potential client has to know the lawyer personally or else be able to mobilize a social network that can lead to a lawyer. This established pattern, which is accepted by both lawyers and the general public, undoubtedly limits the access of ordinary people to legal services.[31]

## INCOME

It is difficult to determine the income of practicing attorneys accurately. We asked our respondents to reveal their gross and net income and certain expenses for 1979, as they reported these to the tax authorities (see table 4.25). The average net income of Tokyo Lawyers is ¥7,600,000 (or about $38,000) after deducting expenses of about 60 percent. In Area D, average net income is ¥6,140,000 (or about $30,700), and expenses are 53 percent of gross. These income levels are roughly comparable with those of British solicitors, but there is much greater variability in Japan than in England (see tables 4.26 and 4.27).

The average net income of lawyers peaks earlier in the more rural areas (see table 4.28). This table also can be used to compare the income of lawyers with the salaries of other occupational groups. Data on the income of company directors, independent entrepreneurs, and practicing physicians are not available. However, we do have reliable data on the salaries of employees of nongovernmental organizations (see table 4.29). This gives the impression that practicing attorneys earn much higher incomes than other white-collar employees but a little less than employed physicians.

The salaries of judges increase fairly regularly for each of the first ten years of their careers (as assistant judges) according to a schedule that, in 1980, rose from ¥147,500 to ¥319,600 per month. (Recall that in recent years the average judge has qualified at about age thirty.) In order to obtain a rough estimate of their yearly income, we may assume that they receive an annual bonus of five times their basic monthly salary, for a total of ¥2,510,000 to ¥5,430,000 per annum. Their salaries no longer are determined mechanically after they become full-fledged judges (see table 4.30). If we consider only ordinary full-fledged judges, whose compulsory retirement age is sixty-five (excluding the Chief Judges of District or High Courts and Supreme Court justices), their total yearly income ranges from approximately ¥6,530,000 to ¥14,530,000. It is difficult to draw a definite conclusion from these data, because these averages are not specified by age. Generally speaking, practicing attorneys in their forties and fifties appear to make a little more money than judges, but they do less well in their sixties and seventies, especially when we take into account the pensions judges receive after retirement.

The variation of lawyers' incomes is much greater within the same age group than that of salaries in other occupations, for those employed in organizations receive a similar salary at the same age. The enormous variation in the income of Japanese lawyers according to their status or form of practice is one of the central connotations of the term "free profession" (see table 4.31). The sole principals (masters) who employ one or more other lawyers are by far the richest, although there are very few. Partners in Tokyo, many of whom specialize in international trade, also are among the top profit-makers.

## CONCLUSION

Our survey of the present condition of Japanese practicing attorneys reveals that they still play a limited role within the legal order. Their professional activities are largely confined to representation before courts. This partly reflects the traditional predominance of judges in the administration of justice. Noncontentious matters, where practicing attorneys would be the only authoritative representatives of the legal order, generally are not entrusted to them. Outside of court, lawyers also are surrounded by lay competitors. These distinct occupational groups of "quasi-lawyers," each with a legally recognized sphere of competence closely related to law, allegedly often serve as lawyer substitutes for individual citizens. Large business firms, in contrast, have their own "lawpersons," who handle the legal matters arising in the course of their daily business transactions (such as making a contract or resolving a dispute); they use their officially qualified "legal advisers" only when involved in litigation.

Practicing attorneys are not highly professionalized. Their heavy reliance on litigation is reflected in the fact that the bulk of their business involves debt collection or real estate—situations where litigation often is a last resort because the parties either are strangers or have terminated their relationships. These areas of legal practice do not require a very sophisticated level of expertise. The main clients of most lawyers—small and medium-sized business enterprises and propertied individuals—do not constitute a very stable clientele. There is little specialization in lawyers' work, except for the small minority who deal with patent law, international trade, or labor union matters. The great majority of Japanese practicing attorneys are generalists working, or aspiring to work, on their own, with minimal clerical help. The general style of their work and life closely resembles that of their main clients, small business proprietors.

In many respects the activities of Japanese practicing attorneys, and thus the legal system as well, touch only the surface of the social order. They still have not penetrated deeply into the everyday life of either ordinary citizens or the business world, nor have they managed to institutionalize the specifically legal ways of ordering human affairs.

# TABLES

4.1. Survey Sample

| Areas | Population | Sample | Returned questionnaire | Return rate (%) | Weighted sample |
|-------|-----------|--------|------------------------|-----------------|-----------------|
| A | 5,361 | 1,340 | 507 | 37.8 | 789 |
| B | 2,044 | 679 | 326 | 48.0 | 301 |
| C | 918 | 459 | 234 | 51.0 | 135 |
| D | 3,143 | 1,558 | 622 | 39.9 | 463 |
| Total | 11,466 | 4,036 | 1,689 | 41.8 | 1,688 |

4.2. Admissions to and Graduations from ILTR and Graduates' Choice of Position[a]

| Class (starting year) | Number of entrants | Number of graduates | Choice of position at graduation | | | | |
|---|---|---|---|---|---|---|---|
| | | | Assistant judge | Summary court judge | Prosecutor | Practicing attorney | Others |
| 1947 | 140 | 134 (2) | 72 (1) | | 44 1) | 18 | |
| 1948 | 245 | 240 (2) | 106 (1) | | 54 (1) | 78 | 2 |
| 1949 | 290 | 284 (3) | 84 (2) | | 77 | 113 (1) | 10 |
| 1950 | 245 (4) | 246 (4) | 57 (1) | | 79 (1) | 97 (1) | 13 (1) |
| 1951 | 223 (4) | 215 (4) | 51 (2) | | 67 | 84 | 13 (2) |
| 1952 | 234 (1) | 226 (1) | 45 | | 48 | 131 (1) | 2 |
| 1953 | 243 (7) | 236 (7) | 67 (5) | | 59 | 109 (2) | 1 |
| 1954 | 214 (3) | 216 (3) | 73 | | 50 | 89 (2) | 4 (1) |
| 1955 | 257 (9) | 267 (9) | 77 (2) | | 45 | 143 (7) | 2 |
| 1956 | 256 (9) | 256 (10) | 65 (3) | | 45 | 144 (7) | 2 |
| 1957 | 284 (16) | 282 (14) | 69 (3) | | 51 (1) | 157 (10) | 5 |
| 1958 | 291 (5) | 291 (7) | 81 (1) | | 44 (1) | 166 (5) | |
| 1959 | 354 (13) | 349 (11) | 83 (3) | 1 | 48 (1) | 216 (7) | 1 |
| 1960 | 314 (10) | 319 (10) | 75 (4) | | 42 | 202 (6) | |
| 1961 | 333 (15) | 334 (14) | 88 (3) | | 40 (2) | 202 (8) | 4 (1) |
| 1962 | 374 (17) | 365 (18) | 56 (3) | 1 | 45 (1) | 261 (14) | 2 |
| 1963 | 440 (23) | 441 (23) | 68 (6) | 4 | 52 (1) | 316 (16) | 1 |
| 1964 | 485 (27) | 478 (25) | 63 (2) | 3 | 47 (1) | 359 (21) | 6 (1) |
| 1965 | 484 (25) | 484 (26) | 61 (2) | 12 (2) | 49 | 356 (21) | 6 (1) |
| 1966 | 513 (28) | 511 (28) | 77 (5) | 8 (1) | 49 (1) | 369 (20) | 8 (1) |
| 1967 | 520 (18) | 516 (18) | 78 (2) | 6 | 53 | 374 (16) | 5 |
| 1968 | 513 (22) | 512 (21) | 61 (1) | 3 | 38 | 405 (20) | 5 |
| 1969 | 503 (37) | 506 (37) | 63 (1) | 2 (1) | 47 (3) | 388 (30) | 6 (2) |
| 1970 | 503 (36) | 495 (34) | 58 (2) | | 59 (5) | 370 (27) | 8 |
| 1971 | 492 (34) | 493 (33) | 65 (3) | 1 | 50 (4) | 371 (23) | 6 (3) |
| 1972 | 510 (30) | 506 (29) | 85 (5) | | 47 (2) | 367 (20) | 7 (2) |
| 1973 | 543 (26) | 543 (27) | 84 (2) | | 38 (2) | 416 (22) | 5 (1) |
| 1974 | 538 (24) | 537 (24) | 78 (3) | 1 | 74 (3) | 376 (16) | 8 (2) |
| 1975 | 491 (22) | 487 (21) | 70 (3) | 2 | 50 | 363 (18) | 2 |
| 1976 | 461 (31) | 463 (32) | 76 (6) | 2 | 58 (4) | 325 (22) | 2 |
| 1977 | 465 (40) | 465 (40) | 61 (4) | 3 (1) | 49 (4) | 350 (31) | 2 |
| 1978 | 454 (33) | | | | | | |
| 1979 | 485 (32) | | | | | | |

[a] The figure in parentheses indicates the number of women included.

*Source:* 700 *Jurisuto* 122–123 (1979).

4.3. Number of Judges, Prosecutors, and Practicing Attorneys, Absolute and in Relation to Population, 1896–1976

| Year | Judges | | Summary court judges | | Prosecutors | | Practicing attorneys | | |
|------|--------|--|----------------------|--|-------------|--|----------------------|--|--|
| | Number | Population per judge | Number | Population per judge | Number | Population per prosecutor | Number | Population per attorney | Population |
| 1896 | 1,221 | 34,390 | | | 383 | 109,634 | 1,568 | 26,779 | 41,990,000 |
| 1916 | 903 | 59,236 | | | 389 | 137,506 | 2,665 | 20,071 | 53,490,000 |
| 1936 | 1,391 | 50,029 | | | 648 | 107,392 | 5,976 | 11,645 | 69,590,000 |
| 1956 | 1,597 | 55,254 | 730 | 120,877 | 1,717 | 51,392 | 6,040 | 14,609 | 88,240,000 |
| 1976 | 1,912 | 58,740 | 791 | 141,985 | 2,089 | 53,763 | 10,792 | 10,407 | 112,310,000 |

4.4. Pass Rates on ILTR Examination, 1949–1979[a]

| Year | Taking | Passing | Percent passing |
|------|--------|---------|-----------------|
| 1949 | 2,570 | 265 (3) | 10.3 |
| 1954 | 5,240 | 250 (10) | 4.8 |
| 1959 | 7,858 | 319 (8) | 4.1 |
| 1964 | 12,698 | 508 (25) | 4.0 |
| 1969 | 18,453 | 501 (37) | 2.7 |
| 1974 | 26,708 | 491 (23) | 1.8 |
| 1979 | 28,622 | 503 (40) | 1.8 |

[a] The figures in parentheses indicate the number of women included.

4.5. Pass Rates on ILTR Examination by University Attended, 1981

| University | Taking | Passing | Percent passing |
|------------|--------|---------|-----------------|
| National | | | |
| Tokyo | 1,920 | 101 | 5.3 |
| Kyoto | 868 | 44 | 5.1 |
| Osaka | 356 | 13 | 3.7 |
| Tohoku | 484 | 13 | 2.7 |
| Nagoya | 276 | 9 | 3.3 |
| Hokkaido | 284 | 4 | 1.4 |
| Kyushu | 432 | 6 | 1.4 |
| Private | | | |
| Chuo | 6,102 | 58 | 1.0 |
| Waseda | 2,887 | 56 | 2.0 |
| Keio | 1,128 | 19 | 1.7 |
| Meiji | 1,730 | 12 | 0.7 |

#### 4.6. Mode of Remuneration of Employed Lawyers

| Areas | Salary only | Salary and commission | Commission only | Other | Total |
|-------|-------------|-----------------------|-----------------|-------|-------|
| A | 69 | 42 | 20 | 19 | 149 |
|   | (45.8) | (28.1) | (13.5) | (12.5) | (54.4) |
| B | 44 | 15 | 2 | 6 | 67 |
|   | (66.7) | (22.2) | (2.8) | (8.3) | (24.2) |
| C | 12 | 4 | 1 | 1 | 18 |
|   | (64.5) | (22.6) | (6.5) | (6.5) | (6.5) |
| D | 30 | 7 | 2 | 2 | 41 |
|   | (72.7) | (16.4) | (5.5) | (5.5) | (14.9) |
| Total | 154 | 68 | 25 | 28 | 275 |
|   | (56.1) | (24.6) | (9.3) | (10.0) | (100.0) |

[a] Figures in parentheses are percentages within each area.

#### 4.7a. Status of Lawyers, by Area[a]

| Areas | Employed lawyer | Overhead-sharer | Solo | Master | Partner | Total |
|-------|-----------------|-----------------|------|--------|---------|-------|
| A | 153 | 174 | 300 | 79 | 36 | 743 |
|   | (20.5) | (23.5) | (40.5) | (10.7) | (4.8) | |
| B | 69 | 20 | 122 | 23 | 49 | 284 |
|   | (24.4) | (7.2) | (43.0) | (8.1) | (17.3) | |
| C | 18 | 14 | 81 | 7 | 6 | 127 |
|   | (14.6) | (11.0) | (64.4) | (5.5) | (4.6) | |
| D | 42 | 20 | 294 | 33 | 48 | 437 |
|   | (9.5) | (4.6) | (67.3) | (7.7) | (10.9) | |
| Total | 287 | 229 | 798 | 143 | 138 | 1,590 |
|   | (17.7) | (14.4) | (50.2) | (9.0) | (8.7) | |

[a] Figures in parentheses are percentages within area.

4.7b. Status of Lawyers, by Age[a]

| Age | Employed lawyer | Overhead-sharer | Solo | Master | Partner | Total |
|---|---|---|---|---|---|---|
| 20–29 | 55 | 6 | 4 | 2 | 5 | 73 |
| | (75.7) | (8.8) | (5.9) | (2.1) | (7.5) | |
| 30–39 | 173 | 70 | 171 | 9 | 66 | 489 |
| | (35.3) | (14.4) | (35.0) | (1.7) | (13.5) | |
| 40–49 | 29 | 73 | 242 | 56 | 41 | 442 |
| | (6.6) | (16.6) | (54.7) | (12.7) | (9.3) | |
| 50–59 | 12 | 54 | 135 | 47 | 15 | 262 |
| | (4.4) | (20.8) | (51.5) | (17.8) | (5.6) | |
| 60–69 | 2 | 11 | 96 | 15 | 5 | 129 |
| | (1.2) | (8.8) | (74.3) | (11.9) | (3.8) | |
| ≥70 | 11 | 11 | 140 | 15 | 6 | 182 |
| | (6.0) | (6.0) | (76.9) | (8.0) | (3.1) | |
| Total | 281 | 227 | 788 | 143 | 138 | 1,577 |
| | (17.8) | (14.4) | (50.0) | (9.1) | (8.7) | |

[a] Figures in parentheses are percentages within cohort.

4.7c. Status of Tokyo Lawyers, by Age

| Age | Employed lawyer | Overhead-sharer | Solo | Master | Partner | Total |
|---|---|---|---|---|---|---|
| 20–29 | 31 | 3 | 0 | 2 | 2 | 37 |
| | (83.3) | (8.3) | (0.0) | (4.2) | (4.2) | |
| 30–39 | 86 | 50 | 50 | 3 | 14 | 202 |
| | (42.3) | (24.6) | (24.6) | (1.5) | (6.9) | |
| 40–49 | 20 | 56 | 107 | 28 | 9 | 221 |
| | (9.2) | (25.4) | (48.6) | (12.7) | (4.2) | |
| 50–59 | 5 | 47 | 48 | 26 | 6 | 132 |
| | (3.5) | (35.3) | (36.5) | (20.0) | (4.7) | |
| 60–69 | 2 | 9 | 44 | 9 | 3 | 67 |
| | (2.3) | (14.0) | (65.1) | (14.0) | (4.7) | |
| ≥70 | 9 | 8 | 45 | 11 | 2 | 75 |
| | (12.5) | (10.4) | (60.4) | (14.6) | (2.1) | |
| Total | 153 | 173 | 294 | 79 | 36 | 735 |
| | (20.8) | (23.5) | (40.0) | (10.8) | (4.9) | |

[a] Figures in parentheses are percentages within cohort.

4.8. Number of Partners in Partnerships, by Area[a]

| Areas | Number of partners | | | | | Total |
| | 2 | 3–5 | 6–9 | 10–19 | ≥ 20 | |
|---|---|---|---|---|---|---|
| A | 19 | 15 | 0 | 0 | 2 | 36 |
| | (52.2) | (43.5) | | | (4.3) | |
| B | 20 | 18 | 9 | 2 | 0 | 49 |
| | (41.5) | (35.8) | (18.9) | (3.8) | | |
| C | 4 | 2 | 0 | 1 | 0 | 7 |
| | (60.0) | (30.0) | | (10.0) | | |
| D | 22 | 18 | 5 | 1 | 0 | 46 |
| | (48.4) | (38.7) | (9.7) | (1.6) | | |
| Total | 65 | 53 | 14 | 4 | 2 | 138 |
| | (47.6) | (38.8) | (10.1) | (2.3) | (1.2) | |

[a] Figures in parentheses are percentages within areas.

4.9. Number of Principals in Shared Offices, by Area[a]

| Areas | Number of principals | | | | | Total |
| | 2 | 3–5 | 6–9 | 10–19 | ≥ 20 | |
|---|---|---|---|---|---|---|
| A | 84 | 58 | 25 | 6 | 2 | 174 |
| | (48.2) | (33.0) | (14.3) | (3.6) | (0.9) | |
| B | 14 | 5 | 0 | 1 | 0 | 19 |
| | (71.4) | (23.8) | | (4.8) | | |
| C | 9 | 5 | 1 | 0 | 0 | 14 |
| | (62.5) | (33.3) | (4.2) | | | |
| D | 11 | 7 | 1 | 0 | 0 | 19 |
| | (57.7) | (38.5) | (3.8) | | | |
| Total | 118 | 74 | 26 | 7 | 2 | 227 |
| | (51.9) | (32.7) | (11.5) | (3.0) | (0.8) | |

[a] Figures in parentheses are percentages within areas.

4.10. Number of Lawyers in Law Office, by Area[a]

| Number in office | Number of lawyers in offices of this size | | | | |
|---|---|---|---|---|---|
| | A | B | C | D | Total |
| 1 | 304 (40.5) | 122 (42.2) | 82 (64.3) | 298 (68.0) | 806 (50.2) |
| 2 | 171 (22.8) | 66 (22.7) | 29 (22.6) | 77 (17.5) | 342 (21.3) |
| 3 | 89 (11.8) | 45 (15.7) | 10 (7.7) | 32 (7.3) | 176 (10.9) |
| 4 | 54 (7.3) | 18 (6.1) | 3 (2.3) | 16 (3.7) | 91 (5.7) |
| 5 | 31 (4.1) | 6 (2.2) | 3 (1.8) | 6 (1.4) | 46 (2.9) |
| 6 | 16 (2.1) | 9 (3.2) | 1 (0.5) | 4 (1.0) | 30 (1.9) |
| 7 | 26 (3.5) | 15 (5.1) | 0 | 1 (0.3) | 43 (2.7) |
| 8 | 19 (2.5) | 4 (1.3) | 0 | 1 (0.2) | 23 (1.4) |
| 9 | 14 (1.9) | 0 | 0 | 1 (0.3) | 16 (1.0) |
| 10 | 6 (0.8) | 1 (0.3) | 0 | 1 (0.2) | 8 (0.5) |
| 11 | 5 (0.6) | 0 | 0 | 0 | 5 (0.3) |
| 12 | 2 (0.2) | 3 (1.0) | 1 (0.5) | 0 | 5 (0.3) |
| 13 | 2 (0.2) | 0 | 0 | 0 | 2 (0.1) |
| 14 | 2 (0.2) | 0 | 0 | 0 | 2 (0.1) |
| 15 | 2 (0.2) | 0 | 0 | 0 | 2 (0.1) |
| 16 | 0 | 0 | 0 | 0 | 0 |
| 17 | 0 | 0 | 0 | 0 | 0 |
| 18 | 2 (0.2) | 0 | 0 | 0 | 2 (0.1) |
| 19 | 0 | 0 | 0 | 0 | 0 |
| 20 | 3 (0.4) | 0 | 0 | 1 (0.2) | 4 (0.2) |
| 21 | 0 | 0 | 0 | 0 | 0 |
| 22 | 2 (0.2) | 0 | 0 | 0 | 2 (0.1) |
| 23 | 3 (0.4) | 0 | 0 | 4 | 3 (0.2) |
| 24 | 0 | 1 (0.3) | 0 | 0 | 1 (0.1) |
| Total | 750 (100.0) | 289 (100.0) | 128 (100.0) | 439 (100.0) | 1,606 (100.0) |

[a] Figures in parentheses are percentages within area.

4.11. Number of Clerks per Lawyer, by Status and Area

| Status | A | B | C | D | Total |
|---|---|---|---|---|---|
| Office-sharer | 0.91 | 0.82 | 0.69 | 0.77 | 0.88 |
| Solo | 1.59 | 1.43 | 1.42 | 1.18 | 1.40 |
| Master | 1.09 | 1.17 | 1.15 | 1.01 | 1.09 |
| Partner | 1.50 | 1.00 | 1.10 | 1.12 | 1.18 |
| Total | 1.31 | 1.25 | 1.29 | 1.14 | 1.25 |

4.12. Number of Clerks per Law Office, by Characteristics of Clerks and Area[a]

| | A | B | C | D | Total |
|---|---|---|---|---|---|
| Male | 0.88 | 0.84 | 0.38 | 0.42 | 0.69 |
| | (32.5) | (34.9) | (21.8) | (26.3) | |
| Female | 1.75 | 1.58 | 1.36 | 1.18 | 1.52 |
| | (65.5) | (65.1) | (78.2) | (73.7) | |
| University graduates | 1.23 | 1.04 | 0.60 | 0.56 | 0.88 |
| | (45.4) | (43.2) | (34.5) | (35.0) | |
| Others | 1.40 | 1.37 | 1.14 | 1.04 | 1.33 |
| | (54.6) | (56.8) | (65.5) | (65.0) | |
| ≥ 7 years in office | 0.58 | 0.45 | 0.41 | 0.35 | 0.46 |
| | (21.4) | (18.7) | (23.6) | (21.9) | |
| 3–6 years in office | 0.93 | 0.91 | 0.63 | 0.62 | 0.81 |
| | (34.3) | (37.8) | (36.2) | (38.8) | |
| < 3 years in office | 1.12 | 1.05 | 0.70 | 0.63 | 0.94 |
| | (44.3) | (43.6) | (41.4) | (39.4) | |
| All clerks | 2.63 | 2.41 | 1.74 | 1.60 | 2.21 |

[a] Figures in parentheses are percentages within category and area.

4.13. Average Number of Open Criminal and Civil Cases, by Age and Area

| | Number of cases | | | | | | | | | |
|---|---|---|---|---|---|---|---|---|---|---|
| | A | | B | | C | | D | | Total | |
| Years | Criminal | Civil | Criminal | Civil | Criminal | Civil | Criminal | Civil | Criminal | Civil |
| 20–29 | 1.2 | 14.8 | 2.2 | 19.0 | 3.7 | 20.3 | 4.2 | 31.2 | 2.3 | 19.6 |
| 30–39 | 1.6 | 23.8 | 2.5 | 31.5 | 2.9 | 36.0 | 4.9 | 40.5 | 2.8 | 31.2 |
| 40–49 | 1.8 | 42.6 | 2.0 | 46.7 | 3.8 | 69.9 | 6.7 | 56.7 | 3.2 | 48.7 |
| 50–59 | 1.9 | 37.6 | 4.0 | 39.4 | 8.0 | 52.0 | 4.1 | 56.0 | 3.3 | 44.1 |
| 60–69 | 1.0 | 26.3 | 1.7 | 33.4 | 2.8 | 52.1 | 6.5 | 37.4 | 2.6 | 32.2 |
| ≥70 | 1.4 | 16.7 | 1.3 | 34.6 | 2.8 | 15.1 | 3.5 | 20.3 | 2.3 | 20.1 |
| Total | 1.6 | 31.0 | 2.3 | 36.8 | 3.9 | 44.7 | 5.1 | 43.3 | 2.9 | 36.6 |

4.14. Average Number of Open Criminal and Civil Cases, by Status and Area

| | | | | | Number of cases | | | | | | |
|---|---|---|---|---|---|---|---|---|---|---|---|
| | A | | B | | C | | D | | Total | |
| Status | Criminal | Civil | Criminal | Civil | Criminal | Civil | Criminal | Civil | Criminal | Civil |
| Employed | 0.9 | 13.5 | 1.9 | 16.9 | 3.3 | 21.1 | 3.7 | 17.4 | 1.7 | 15.4 |
| Office-sharer | 2.3 | 33.4 | 1.8 | 32.6 | 2.6 | 29.1 | 4.4 | 43.7 | 2.4 | 34.0 |
| Solo | 1.6 | 29.4 | 2.6 | 35.5 | 4.3 | 48.1 | 5.0 | 41.9 | 3.3 | 36.9 |
| Master | 1.3 | 59.5 | 3.9 | 74.3 | 3.0 | 79.1 | 5.8 | 82.5 | 2.9 | 68.2 |
| Partner | 1.8 | 41.4 | 1.9 | 50.0 | 3.7 | 59.3 | 6.0 | 47.4 | 3.4 | 47.2 |
| Total | 1.6 | 30.7 | 2.4 | 36.5 | 3.9 | 44.3 | 5.0 | 43.2 | 2.9 | 36.4 |

4.15. Number of PAs with Different Civil Caseloads, by Area[a]

| Areas | Civil caseload | | | | | | | | | Total |
|---|---|---|---|---|---|---|---|---|---|---|
| | 0–5 | 6–20 | 21–35 | 36–50 | 51–65 | 66–80 | 81–100 | 101–120 | ≥121 | |
| A | 98 | 220 | 198 | 126 | 48 | 23 | 12 | 3 | 12 | 741 |
| | (13.2) | (29.6) | (26.7) | (17.0) | (6.5) | (3.2) | (1.7) | (0.4) | (1.7) | (100.0) |
| B | 31 | 64 | 66 | 63 | 28 | 18 | 8 | 3 | 6 | 286 |
| | (11.0) | (22.3) | (22.9) | (21.9) | (9.7) | (6.5) | (2.9) | (1.0) | (1.9) | (100.0) |
| C | 12 | 24 | 29 | 21 | 13 | 9 | 9 | 2 | 6 | 126 |
| | (9.6) | (19.3) | (22.9) | (16.5) | (10.1) | (7.3) | (7.3) | (1.8) | (5.0) | (100.0) |
| D | 42 | 90 | 91 | 76 | 49 | 33 | 33 | 12 | 16 | 442 |
| | (9.6) | (20.4) | (20.5) | (17.2) | (11.1) | (7.4) | (7.6) | (2.7) | (3.5) | (100.0) |
| Total | 184 | 399 | 383 | 286 | 138 | 84 | 63 | 20 | 40 | 1,595 |
| | (11.5) | (24.9) | (24.0) | (17.9) | (8.6) | (5.3) | (3.9) | (1.4) | (2.5) | (100.0) |

[a]Figures in parentheses are percentages within area.

4.16. Breakdown of PA Civil Work, by Type of Matter and Area[a]

| | Average number of civil cases per PA | | | | |
|---|---|---|---|---|---|
| | A | B | C | D | Total |
| Noncontentious matters | 3.26 | 2.47 | 2.29 | 1.95 | 2.68 |
| | (10.4) | (6.6) | (5.1) | (4.5) | (7.3) |
| Out-of-court settlement | 4.48 | 4.21 | 3.53 | 4.20 | 4.28 |
| | (14.3) | (11.3) | (7.9) | (9.7) | (11.5) |
| Tribunal | 1.32 | 1.18 | 1.48 | 1.09 | 1.24 |
| | (4.2) | (3.2) | (3.3) | (2.5) | (3.4) |
| Court | 22.30 | 29.32 | 37.56 | 36.11 | 28.60 |
| | (71.1) | (78.9) | (83.7) | (83.3) | (77.7) |
| Total | 31.36 | 37.18 | 44.86 | 43.35 | 36.80 |
| | (100) | (100) | (100) | (100) | (100) |

[a] Figures in parentheses are percentages within area.

4.17. Percentage of PA Civil Work Devoted to Litigation, by Status and Area

| | A | B | C | D | Total |
|---|---|---|---|---|---|
| Employed | 62.1 | 82.5 | 88.9 | 84.3 | 73.7 |
| Office-sharer | 77.8 | 83.0 | 86.4 | 80.1 | 79.1 |
| Solo | 69.2 | 80.7 | 83.2 | 83.7 | 78.3 |
| Master | 81.0 | 82.1 | 81.9 | 84.8 | 82.2 |
| Partner | 52.5 | 71.9 | 84.7 | 83.9 | 72.0 |
| Total | 72.3 | 79.3 | 83.3 | 83.6 | |

4.18. Subject Matter of PA Civil Work, by Area[a]

| | Average number of civil matters per PA | | | | |
|---|---|---|---|---|---|
| | A | B | C | D | Total |
| Execution of judgment | 2.52 | 2.50 | 2.77 | 2.12 | 2.47 |
| | (8.5) | (6.1) | (6.3) | (4.9) | (7.0) |
| Bankruptcy | 0.65 | 1.01 | 0.82 | 0.79 | 0.77 |
| | (2.1) | (2.8) | (1.9) | (1.8) | (2.0) |
| International transaction | 1.07 | 0.33 | 0.14 | 0.25 | 0.64 |
| | (3.5) | (0.9) | (0.3) | (0.6) | (1.8) |

4.18. (*continued*)

| | Average number of civil matters per PA | | | | |
|---|---|---|---|---|---|
| | A | B | C | D | Total |
| Family | 1.54 | 1.58 | 1.77 | 2.61 | 1.86 |
| | (5.0) | (4.4) | (4.0) | (6.1) | (5.2) |
| Inheritance | 1.59 | 1.50 | 1.98 | 1.98 | 1.70 |
| | (5.2) | (4.1) | (4.0) | (4.6) | (4.7) |
| Leased land or house | 3.40 | 3.56 | 3.13 | 4.13 | 3.61 |
| | (11.1) | (9.8) | (7.1) | (9.6) | (10.0) |
| Debt (creditor) | 6.33 | 6.95 | 10.09 | 7.98 | 7.18 |
| | (20.6) | (19.2) | (23.0) | (18.5) | (19.9) |
| Debt (debtor) | 2.02 | 2.77 | 3.68 | 3.75 | 2.76 |
| | (6.6) | (7.7) | (8.4) | (8.7) | (7.6) |
| Automobile accident | 1.11 | 2.51 | 2.99 | 3.07 | 2.04 |
| | (3.6) | (6.9) | (6.8) | (7.1) | (5.7) |
| Medical accident | 0.34 | 0.44 | 0.74 | 0.52 | 0.44 |
| | (1.1) | (1.2) | (1.7) | (1.2) | (1.2) |
| Labor, employment | 0.67 | 1.02 | 1.41 | 0.84 | 0.84 |
| | (2.1) | (2.8) | (3.2) | (1.9) | (2.3) |
| Environmental pollution | 0.16 | 0.38 | 0.38 | 0.33 | 0.26 |
| | (0.5) | (1.1) | (0.9) | (0.8) | (0.7) |
| Consumer | 0.19 | 0.15 | 0.26 | 0.19 | 0.19 |
| | (0.6) | (0.4) | (0.6) | (0.4) | (0.5) |
| Complaint against government | 0.41 | 0.47 | 0.60 | 0.59 | 0.48 |
| | (1.3) | (1.3) | (1.4) | (1.4) | (1.3) |
| Company or economic law | 0.86 | 0.86 | 0.78 | 0.67 | 0.80 |
| | (2.8) | (2.4) | (1.8) | (1.6) | (2.2) |
| Patent or copyright | 0.55 | 0.51 | 0.19 | 0.14 | 0.40 |
| | (1.8) | (1.4) | (0.4) | (0.3) | (1.1) |
| Other real estate | 2.76 | 4.67 | 5.24 | 6.42 | 4.30 |
| | (9.0) | (12.6) | (11.9) | (14.9) | (11.9) |
| Other damages | 1.84 | 2.52 | 3.45 | 3.19 | 2.46 |
| | (6.0) | (7.0) | (7.8) | (7.4) | (6.8) |
| Others | 2.57 | 2.45 | 3.74 | 3.56 | 2.91 |
| | (8.4) | (6.8) | (8.5) | (8.3) | (8.1) |
| Total | 30.68 | 36.18 | 43.96 | 43.13 | 36.11 |
| | (99.8) | (98.9) | (100.0) | (100.0) | |

[a] Figures in parentheses are average percentage of total civil caseload within area.

4.19. Type of Client Served by PA in Civil Matters, by Area[a]

| | Average number of civil matters per PA | | | | |
|---|---|---|---|---|---|
| | A | B | C | D | Total |
| Individual | 13.57 | 18.93 | 23.00 | 27.31 | 19.08 |
| | (44.4) | (51.1) | (53.3) | (62.8) | (52.6) |
| Small- or medium-sized business | 9.40 | 10.55 | 12.10 | 10.53 | 10.12 |
| | (30.7) | (28.5) | (28.1) | (24.2) | (27.9) |
| Large business | 5.50 | 5.31 | 4.45 | 2.68 | 4.61 |
| | (18.0) | (14.3) | (10.3) | (6.2) | (12.71) |
| Government agency | 0.42 | 0.52 | 1.57 | 0.85 | 0.66 |
| | (1.4) | (1.4) | (3.1) | (2.0) | (1.8) |
| Other organization | 1.68 | 1.70 | 2.00 | 2.14 | 1.83 |
| | (5.5) | (4.6) | (4.6) | (4.9) | (5.0) |
| Total | 30.57 | 37.01 | 43.12 | 43.51 | 36.30 |
| | (100) | (100) | (100) | (100) | (100) |

[a] Figures in parentheses are average percent of total clients within area.

4.20. Average Number of Matters Handled for Large Companies per Lawyer, by Status and Area

| | A | B | C | D | Total |
|---|---|---|---|---|---|
| Employed | 3.03 | 1.39 | 4.48 | 1.00 | 2.21 |
| Office-sharer | 2.89 | 3.50 | 1.13 | 0.81 | 3.24 |
| Solo | 3.57 | 5.63 | 1.91 | 2.27 | 3.35 |
| Master | 21.93 | 17.25 | 12.38 | 11.89 | 17.55 |
| Partner | 11.43 | 7.40 | 0.11 | 1.64 | 6.40 |
| Total | 5.53 | 5.35 | 4.48 | 2.63 | 4.82 |

4.21. Percentage of Lawyers Three-Fourths of Whose Civil Caseloads Are from New Clients, by Status and Area

|  | A | B | C | D | Total |
|---|---|---|---|---|---|
| Employed | 47.4 | 55.7 | 61.3 | 77.8 | 54.8 |
| Office-sharer | 21.4 | 27.2 | 50.0 | 40.7 | 25.2 |
| Solo | 17.4 | 13.0 | 36.8 | 39.2 | 26.5 |
| Master | 11.7 | 6.7 | 0 | 8.8 | 11.5 |
| Partner | 4.8 | 21.3 | 44.4 | 47.5 | 26.3 |
| Total | 23.5 | 25.6 | 41.4 | 42.0 | |

4.22. Average Number of Clients Who Retain the Lawyer as Legal Advisor, by Status and Area

|  | A | B | C | D | Total |
|---|---|---|---|---|---|
| Employed | 4.46 | 2.78 | 2.46 | 2.95 | 3.80 |
| Office-sharer | 9.05 | 9.24 | 8.64 | 9.17 | 9.05 |
| Solo | 9.37 | 10.98 | 11.92 | 9.56 | 9.95 |
| Master | 16.75 | 28.16 | 26.73 | 20.17 | 19.95 |
| Partner | 13.91 | 19.18 | 10.25 | 9.23 | 14.24 |
| Total | 9.68 | 12.84 | 11.66 | 10.19 | 10.54 |

4.23. Average Number of Clients who Retain the Lawyer as Legal Advisor, by Type of Client and Area[a]

|  | A | B | C | D | Total |
|---|---|---|---|---|---|
| Individual | 0.85 | 1.15 | 0.87 | 0.84 | 0.91 |
|  | (8.6) | (8.9) | (7.3) | (8.1) | (9.0) |
| Small or medium-sized business | 6.41 | 7.90 | 7.13 | 6.02 | 6.63 |
|  | (65.1) | (61.2) | (59.9) | (58.1) | (62.0) |
| Large company | 1.76 | 2.59 | 2.36 | 1.53 | 1.89 |
|  | (17.9) | (20.1) | (19.8) | (14.8) | (17.7) |
| Government agency | 0.11 | 0.22 | 0.41 | 0.43 | 0.24 |
|  | (1.1) | (1.7) | (3.4) | (4.2) | (2.2) |
| Other | 0.72 | 1.04 | 1.14 | 1.54 | 1.03 |
|  | (7.3) | (8.1) | (9.6) | (14.9) | (9.6) |
| Total | 9.85 | 12.90 | 11.91 | 10.36 | 10.70 |
|  | (100) | (100) | (100) | (100) | |

[a] Figures in parentheses are average percentage of total retainers within area.

4.24. Route by Which the Client Came to the Lawyer in Civil Matters, by Area[a]

| Route | A | B | C | D | Total |
|---|---|---|---|---|---|
| Kin or through kin | 1.39 | 1.69 | 1.28 | 1.77 | 1.54 |
| | (5.0) | (5.0) | (3.0) | (4.2) | (4.6) |
| Client in another case or through another case | 6.26 | 6.30 | 8.96 | 8.78 | 7.17 |
| | (22.6) | (18.5) | (20.9) | (21.0) | (21.2) |
| Retainer | 8.65 | 12.20 | 14.77 | 10.51 | 10.28 |
| | (31.3) | (35.9) | (34.5) | (25.2) | (30.4) |
| Other lawyer | 1.91 | 2.33 | 4.05 | 2.57 | 2.33 |
| | (6.9) | (6.9) | (9.5) | (6.2) | (6.9) |
| Other law-related person | 0.47 | 0.75 | 1.02 | 1.29 | 0.79 |
| | (1.7) | (2.2) | (2.4) | (3.1) | (2.3) |
| Private counseling bureau | 0.37 | 0.76 | 0.65 | 0.77 | 0.59 |
| | (1.3) | (2.2) | (1.5) | (1.8) | (1.9) |
| Public counseling bureau | 0.43 | 0.82 | 0.99 | 1.17 | 0.74 |
| | (1.6) | (2.4) | (2.3) | (2.8) | (2.2) |
| Other personal acquaintance | 6.92 | 7.97 | 7.88 | 10.11 | 8.05 |
| | (25.0) | (23.4) | (18.4) | (24.2) | (23.5) |
| Other | 1.01 | 0.91 | 1.55 | 2.09 | 1.33 |
| | (3.7) | (2.7) | (3.6) | (5.0) | (3.9) |
| No intermediary | 0.26 | 0.26 | 1.43 | 2.70 | 1.02 |
| | (0.9) | (0.8) | (3.3) | (6.5) | (3.0) |
| Total | 27.67 | 33.99 | 42.58 | 41.76 | 33.82 |

[a] Figures in parentheses are percentage of source of all clients within area.

4.25. 1979 Gross and Net Annual Income of Japanese Practicing Attorneys (in ¥1,000)

| | A | B | C | D | Total |
|---|---|---|---|---|---|
| Gross income | 18,890 | 15,440 | 14,240 | 12,980 | 16,350 |
| Net income | 7,600 | 6,830 | 7,110 | 6,140 | 7,030 |
| in U.S.$[a] | 38,000 | 34,150 | 35,055 | 30,700 | 35,150 |
| Rate of expenses (%) | 59.8 | 55.8 | 50.1 | 52.7 | 57.6 |

[a] Assumes exchange rate of ¥200 = $1.00 (U.S.).

4.26. Net Annual Income of Japanese Practicing Attorneys (in ¥1,000), by Area[a]

| | A | B | C | D |
|---|---|---|---|---|
| Highest decile | 14,000 (2.37) | 11,540 (2.16) | 14,790 (2.62) | 11,600 (2.30) |
| Third decile | 8,000 (1.36) | 7,500 (1.40) | 8,440 (1.49) | 7,200 (1.43) |
| Median | 5,900 (1.00) | 5,340 (1.00) | 5,650 (1.00) | 5,050 (1.00) |
| Seventh decile | 4,290 (0.71) | 3,930 (0.74) | 3,440 (0.61) | 3,160 (0.63) |
| Lowest decile | 2,350 (0.40) | 2,150 (0.40) | 1,730 (0.31) | 1,440 (0.29) |
| Average | 7,600 (1.29) | 6,830 (1.80) | 7,110 (1.26) | 6,140 (1.22) |

[a] Figures in parentheses are ratios to median within area.

4.27. Net Annual Profit (in U.K. £) of
British Solicitors in 1976[a]

| Highest decile | 22,701 (1.94) |
|---|---|
| Third decile | 15,224 (1.30) |
| Median | 11,686 (1.00) |
| Seventh decile | 8,862 (0.76) |
| Lowest decile | 5,604 (0.48) |
| Average | 13,581 (1.16) |

[a] Figures in parentheses are ratios to median.
Source: Royal Commission (1979, 2:477).

4.28. Average Net Annual Income (in ¥1,000), by Age and Area

| Years | A | B | C | D | Total |
|---|---|---|---|---|---|
| 20–29 | 3,470 | 3,030 | 3,020 | 2,740 | 3,200 |
| 30–39 | 5,480 | 5,010 | 5,730 | 4,800 | 5,210 |
| 40–49 | 8,380 | 8,530 | 9,400 | 7,910 | 8,360 |
| 50–59 | 11,340 | 8,030 | 9,460 | 8,780 | 10,050 |
| 60–69 | 8,420 | 11,580 | 9,160 | 5,860 | 8,320 |
| ≥70 | 5,300 | 5,910 | 3,750 | 3,830 | 4,690 |

4.29. Yearly Salary of University Graduates Employed in Various White-Collar Jobs by Nongovernmental Organizations with Fifty or More Employees (1980) (in ¥1,000)

| | |
|---|---|
| Clerk (average age 29.4 years) | 3,236 |
| Unit head (average age 36.17 years) | 4,860 |
| Section head (average age 42.9 years) | 6,249 |
| Department head (average age 48.9 years) | 7,825 |
| Medical doctor other than hospital or department head (average age 37.3 years) | 9,342 |

4.30. Monthly Salaries of Full-Fledged Judges
(1980) (in ¥1,000)

| | |
|---|---|
| Chief Justice of Supreme Court | 1,550 |
| Justice of Supreme Court | 1,130 |
| Chief Judge of Tokyo High Court | 1,030 |
| Chief Judge of other high court | 950 |
| Other full-fledged judge | |
| Class 1 | 855 |
| Class 2 | 758 |
| Class 3 | 708 |
| Class 4 | 604 |
| Class 5 | 521 |
| Class 6 | 471 |
| Class 7 | 423 |
| Class 8 | 384 |

4.31. Average Net Annual Income (in ¥1,000) of Practicing Attorneys, by Status and Area

| | A | B | C | D | Total |
|---|---|---|---|---|---|
| Employed | 4,990 | 4,800 | 4,540 | 3,740 | 4,740 |
| Office-sharer | 7,280 | 5,610 | 6,630 | 5,510 | 6,950 |
| Solo | 7,160 | 6,340 | 7,270 | 5,900 | 6,580 |
| Master | 12,520 | 14,570 | 14,620 | 12,260 | 12,830 |
| Partner | 13,880 | 8,490 | 4,840 | 6,160 | 9,050 |

# NOTES

1. In 1980 the Japan Federation of Practicing Attorneys' Associations (see note 5, below) undertook a survey of its members. This was the first systematic effort in Japan to ascertain empirically and statistically the actual state of legal practice. A thirteen-page questionnaire containing sixty-five questions covering a wide range of subjects was drawn up on the basis of preliminary interviews and sent to a stratified random sample of 4,036 practicing attorneys throughout Japan; 1,689 questionnaires were returned with valid answers to most of the questions asked (see table 4.1).

The total population of practicing attorneys was divided into four sub-populations corresponding to the following four areas: A, Tokyo; B, Osaka and Aichi; C, other prefectures with a high court (Hokkaido, Miyagi, Hiroshima, Fukuoka, and Kagawa); D, all the other prefectures where no high court is located. The prefectures in area C are local centers of legal activities because of their high courts; those in area D generally are rural, although they include some highly industrialized prefectures adjacent to Tokyo and Osaka, such as Kanagawa and Hyogo.

Comparison of the respondents with the original sample with regard to the age, the year of registration as practicing attorney, the university attended, the method of qualification, and the prior occupation showed a statistically significant overrepresentation of younger lawyers, those registered more recently, those who passed the present legal examination, and those without any prior occupation, and an underrepresentation of those over seventy years of age and those who attended the University of Tokyo. However, the overall distribution is not greatly distorted. For detail, see *Nichibenren* (1981: 43ff.)

2. For a general account of the history of the Japanese legal system and of the Japanese legal profession in particular, see Rabinowitz (1956), Takayanagi (1963), and Hattori (1963). A good introductory book on the Japanese legal system as a whole is Tanaka (1976), which also contains excerpts from the last two sources cited.

3. For the details of the history of the modern legal system of Japan, see note 2, above.

4. In this chapter the English term "practicing attorney" (sometimes abbreviated "PA") is used to designate the title "bengoshi."

5. Practicing attorneys are required by law to set up a local association for each district court jurisdiction. Accordingly, there is one PA association in each prefecture, except that Tokyo has three, for historical reasons. The Japan Federation of Practicing Attorneys' Associations (JFPAA), also a legally prescribed institution, is constituted by all the PAs and all the local PA associations. All those associations are incorporated, and each PA must belong to one local association *and* the JFPAA. The purpose of both levels of association is "to perform the business in relation to the guidance, liaison and supervision of members in order to

maintain their dignity and to improve and develop the lawyers' business" (PA Act, art. 31).

Under the law, a person who has completed the legal apprentice course at the ILTR (see section entitled "Recruitment.") is qualified to become a PA. Those who were PAs under the former laws are regarded as having fulfilled this requirement. In addition, the law provides for some exceptional ways of qualifying as a PA (PA Act, art. 5), but only a small minority (less than 1 percent) of the present PAs have qualified in these ways. In order to become a PA, a person should be registered in the list maintained by the JFPAA. The applicant should request the registration through the local PA association, which has the power to refuse to forward this request to the JFPAA on certain grounds specified by the law (PA Act, art. 12). The complaint against the refusal eventually may be appealed to the high court (PA Act, art. 16).

Each PA Association has disciplinary powers over its members, which are exercised through a disciplinary committee whose members are selected from among PAs, judges, prosecutors, and persons of learning and experience (PA Act, arts. 52, 69).

6. For a general account of the examination system as well as of the content of the examination and of the training at the ILTR, see Tanaka (1976: 566–582).

7. The number who enter and leave the ILTR, as well as which branch of the profession they enter, are shown in table 4.2. The Legal Examination is not an entrance examination to the ILTR, and some of those who pass it choose not to enter the ILTR, at least immediately. Since those who have passed the Legal Examination can enter the ILTR whenever they choose, the entrants in a given year may include those who passed it some years previously. Those who enter the ILTR immediately after passing the Legal Examination actually do so the following year.

8. The regular judges may be appointed from among those with ten years' experience as an assistant judge, summary court judge, public prosecutor, practicing attorney, and others (Courts Act, art. 42). In actuality, however, most judges are promoted from the ranks of assistant judges. Only a handful of practicing attorneys are appointed to judgeships (Tanaka, 1976: 552).

9. In 1980, former judges and former prosecutors accounted for about 8 percent and 5.5 percent, respectively, of all private attorneys; both percentages were higher in areas C and D than in areas A and B. Some of these lawyers resigned their offices before retirement age, however. The reasons why judges abandon their careers have not been studied systematically, but the following factors are relevant. Judges usually are transferred from one place to another every few years, which causes increasing hardship when children begin to attend school. Some had chosen to serve as judges in order to get experience before becoming practicing attorneys later. After a period of service, some may feel that their career prospects within the judicial bureaucracy are not very bright. As to the relative income of judges and attorneys, see section entitled "Income."

With regard to the career structure of judges and prosecutors, the following account is relevant:

> In Japan, most of the judges have chosen their position as their career job. This means that a typical judge is appointed to an assistant judgeship immediately after having received training for two years at the Legal Training and Research Institute, is promoted to the status of (full-fledged) judge after ten years, and intends (or is expected) to remain as a judge until the compulsory retirement age of sixty-five or seventy. Though it is guaranteed by Article 80 of the Constitution that judges "shall receive, at regular stated intervals, adequate compensation which shall not be decreased during their terms of office" and although the Courts Act provides that they cannot be dismissed or ordered to move to another post against their will, they in fact move from one position to another (usually every two to four years) as civil servants do. This practice is partly related to the graduated wage scale, which is not different in nature from the civil service wage scale, and partly related to tradition.
>
> Public procurators also usually take the procuratorship as their career job. They, like other civil servants, not only in fact move from one position to another but are required by law to do so when requested. (Tanaka, 1976: 549–550; footnotes omitted)

10. In 1979, mediation cases constituted about 36 percent of all civil disputes brought before court, including family matters (General Secretariat, Supreme Court, 1979). For a discussion of the actual working of this system, see Henderson (1965) and Rokumoto (1981).

11. In ordinary civil litigation in courts of first instance, terminating in 1980, about 85 percent of the litigants in the summary court and about 40 percent of those in the district court were not represented by PAs (General Secretariat, Supreme Court, 1980).

12. In mediation cases terminating in 1975 in summary courts (where most mediation takes place), 25.6 percent of plaintiffs and 16.9 percent of defendants were represented by a lawyer and 14.6 percent of plaintiffs and 12.9 percent of defendants by a nonlawyer.

13. An assistant judge has limited power, cannot sit alone (see Tanaka, 1976: 462), and must serve ten years before being appointed to a regular judgeship.

14. According to Tanaka (1976: 556), summary court judges are appointed either (1) from among those who have served for not less than three years as an assistant judge, public procurator or practicing attorney or (2) from among those "who have the knowledge and experience necessary for carrying out the duties of a summary court judge, such as those who have engaged in judicial business for many years" and have been recommended by the Summary Court Judges

Selection Committee. As a matter of practice, about half of the nearly 800 summary court judges had previously served as court clerks for many years.

15. Changes in the size of the legal profession in Japan are shown in table 4.3.

16. In England there were 28,939 solicitors and 4,263 barristers in private practice in 1978 for a population of about 55 million (Royal Commission, 1979, 2:46), and in West Germany there were 36,081 private attorneys or attorney-notaries and 942 nonattorney notaries in 1980 for a population of about 60 million (*Anwaltsblatt*, 1980: 145).

17. The PA Act (1972) grants practicing attorneys a monopoly in the delivery of legal services for pay.

18. Judical scriveners were recognized officially in 1919 and are distinct from notaries public. The latter also exist in Japan. They numbered about 444 in 1981 and were mostly retired judges or prosecutors. Their function is to authenticate legal actions and documents.

19. According to an official statistical report of the Japanese Association of Judicial Scriveners, they handled 17,577,686 cases in 1980, earning fees of about ¥107,043 million; drafting court documents accounted for 178,652 cases and earned the judicial scriveners about ¥1,800 million (124 *Geppo Shihoshoshi* [*Judicial Scriveners' Monthly*] 7 [March 1982]).

20. Judicial scriveners publicly admit that some of them specialize in litigation (ibid.). The relationship between private attorneys and judicial scriveners is naturally antagonistic, the former constantly and vehemently accusing the latter of violating the monopoly of legal services accorded to private attorneys by law (Practicing Attorneys Act, art. 72). In view of the scarcity and maldistribution of private attorneys and the high price of their services, however, the complementary functions of judicial scriveners are generally recognized as inevitable. Courts also tend to construe the attorney's monopoly clause rather narrowly. Some advocate recognizing judicial scriveners as a second private branch of the legal profession. Instances of a business association between an attorney and a judicial scrivener are rare but not unlawful. In our survey, about 6 percent of attorneys indicated that there was a quasilawyer (not always a judicial scrivener) in their office, and another 12 percent had an ongoing relationship with a quasilawyer, which produced referrals in both directions.

The judicial scriveners, for their part, always have been eager to enhance their status, and their effort bore fruit in the 1978 amendment of the Judicial Scriveners' Act, which formalized and unified the qualifying examination administered by the Minister of Justice, so that it now includes some basic legal subjects, such as civil, commercial, and criminal law, as well as procedures for registration, deposit, and litigation (Judicial Scriveners' Act, art. 5). In 1982, 15,103 candidates sat the examination and 382 passed (2.5 percent), of whom 76 percent had a college education (133 *Geppo Shihoshoshi* [*Judicial Scriveners' Monthly*] 16–17 [1982]).

21. In 1979 there were 1,373 judicial scriveners in Tokyo and 1,073 in Osaka. The ratio of practicing attorneys to judicial scriveners in these cities was 3.80 and 1.75, respectively. The national ratio was 0.77, ranging from 0.10 in Kagoshima Prefecture to 0.99 in Aichi Prefecture (Kaneko & Takeshita, 1978: 378).

22. Of the 486 successful candidates in 1980, 70 (14 percent) were university students, 8 were graduate students, 60 (12 percent) had a regular occupation (public servants, employees of private firms, clerks in a lawyer's office, etc.), and 348 (72 percent) had no occupation (Nihon Houritsuka Kyoukai, 1982: 140). A tenth were women.

23. For the curriculum of legal education at the University of Tokyo, a representative institution, see Tanaka (1976: 579–581).

24. In the Faculty of Law of the University of Tokyo, for example, only 90 to 100 students out of a graduating class of about 600 eventually enter the ILTR. For the variation in the success rate in the Legal Examination among universities, see table 4.5.

25. Growing foreign trade, government regulations, and consumer litigation have made Japanese corporations aware of the importance of having a staff specialized in legal matters, and many larger corporations today have such staffs. It seems safe to say that the legal section of the larger corporations have an average of about five employees with university legal education, and some large commercial companies have several dozen. A small proportion of these have passed the Legal Examination without going on to the ILTR. (Registered lawyers need to obtain permission from the Practicing Attorneys' Association before being employed regularly by a business firm, and there still are only a handful of such attorneys in Japan.) Some are sent abroad by the company for legal studies. Although they do not receive special treatment as professionals but are transferred to other sections as they ascend the career ladder within the company (a few may remain in the section for over ten years), these corporation "lawpersons" tend to form a distinct occupational group, conscious of their legal expertise and work ethos. An association called "Friends of Managerial Law" was formed in 1971 and now contains the legal section members of 365 companies.

26. About half of all employed lawyers earn between 2 and 3.5 million yen per year, and another quarter earn between 3.5 and 4 million yen. Today, those seeking employment demand a salary corresponding to that of their fellow graduates at the ILTR who enter the judiciary as assistant judges.

27. The lawyers in area D are an exception: even the youngest lawyers frequently are not employed. This is because in such peripheral areas the number of lawyers is so small that any association among them, including employment, reduces the number of law offices in the locality, which obviously is to be avoided. The scarcity of lawyers also means that newcomers will find clients much more easily than their colleagues do in central cities.

28. This index itself may reflect the characteristic pattern of Japanese legal practice, which is heavily dominated by litigation. Litigated cases can be counted easily and remain open longer in the lawyer's file than noncontentious matters. All litigation, therefore, may be slightly overrepresented in a survey based on this method, and criminal cases, many of which are terminated within a few months, may be underrepresented.

29. In a 1973 German study, by contrast, practicing attorneys reported that they handled 334 civil or criminal matters per year, of which 130 were litigated (Volks, 1974: 252, 265). Australian solicitors and barristers also report receiving larger numbers of briefs (Tomasic & Bullard, 1978: 310). The smaller number of cases generating the income of Japanese lawyers naturally raises the question of whether their work costs significantly more money.

This difference in the volume of lawyers' business reflects the difference in court caseloads. In 1979, there were only 386,563 civil cases in courts of first instance, whereas West German courts heard 2,001,664 similar cases in 1974 (*Anwaltsblatt*, 1976: 81).

30. Divorce by consent is an established Japanese legal institution, accounting for more than 89 percent of all divorces each year.

31. Criminal legal aid functions relatively well, but civil legal aid is only very weakly developed.

## REFERENCES

Dore, Ronald P. 1967. "Mobility, Equality, and Individuation in Modern Japan," in Ronald P. Dore, ed., *Aspects of Social Change in Modern Japan*, pp. 113–150. Princeton, N.J.: Princeton University Press.

Hattori, Takaaki. 1963. "The Legal Profession in Japan: Its Historical Development and Present State," in Arthur von Mehren, ed., *Law in Japan*, pp. 111–152. Cambridge, Mass.: Harvard University Press.

Henderson, Dan F. 1965. *Conciliation and Japanese Law: Tokugawa and Modern.* Tokyo: University of Tokyo Press.

Kaneko, Hajime, and Morio Takeshita. 1978. *Saibanho [The Laws Concerning the Administration of Justice]*. Tokyo: Yuhikaku.

*Nichibenren*. 1981. "Kihon-houkoku Jiyuu to Seigi [Preliminary Report on the Survey of the Economic Basis of the Japanese Legal Practice]," 32(10) *Nichibenren* 43.

Nihon Houritsuka Kyoukai, ed. 1982. *Shiho Shiken*. Tokyo: Gyosei.

Rabinowitz, Richard W. 1956. "The Historical Development of the Japanese Bar," 70 *Harvard Law Review* 61–81.

Rokumoto, Kahei. 1981. "Tschotei (Schlichtung)—eine Japanische Alternative zum Recht: Verfahren, Praxis und Funktionen" in Erhard Blankenberg, Ekkehard Klausa, and Hubert Rottleuthner, eds., *Alternative Rechtsformen und Alternativen zum Recht*, pp. 390–407. Opladen: Westdeutscher Verlag.

Royal Commission on Legal Services. 1979. *Final Report* (2 vols.) (Cmnd. 7648-I.) London: HMSO.

Takayanagi, Kenzo. 1963. "A Century of Innovation: The Development of Japanese Law, 1868–1961," in Arthur von Mehren, ed., *Law in Japan*, pp. 5–40. Cambridge, Mass.: Harvard University Press.

Tanaka, Hideo, ed. 1976. *The Japanese Legal System: Introductory Cases and Materials*. Tokyo: University of Tokyo Press.

Tomasic, Roman, and Cedric Bullard. 1978. *Lawyers and Their Work in New South Wales*. Sydney: Law Foundation of New South Wales.

Volks, Holger. 1974. "Anwaltliche Berufsrollen und anwaltliche Berufsarbeit in der Industriegesellschaft." Inaugural dissertation, University of Cologne.

# 5

## The Rise of Lawyers in the Dutch Welfare State

### KEES SCHUYT

## INTRODUCTION

Because legal science is so preoccupied with the content of legal rules, it pays little atttention to the people who make and administer the law: the jurists. How many jurists are there in the Netherlands? How many cases do they handle, and how many do they resolve? Are there long-term variations in the number of jurists? If so, how can they be explained, and how are they related to other measures of social change?

Answering these questions turns out to be more difficult than one might expect. Introductory texts ignore them altogether. Yet, these quantitative indices may reveal the relative importance of law within different societies. Takeyoshi Kawashima (1964) has interpreted the fact that Japan has few lawyers in proportion to its population to indicate that the Japanese infrequently need the services of a lawyer (however, see Rokumoto, chap. 4, this volume). In order to avoid the controversy frequently generated by "legal" solutions, the Japanese prefer informal means of resolving conflict, often using the family. In Indonesia, however, another Asian country but one influenced by Dutch legal culture, there are many lawyers in relation to the population. There also are surprising differences between western European countries that otherwise appear similar. The ratio of judges and lawyers to population is relatively high in Germany but relatively low in England and Wales and the Netherlands. How can this be explained?

A salutary warning is appropriate in order to avoid overgeneralization on the basis of such quantitative data. The concept of a "lawyer" and how it is subdivided may differ among societies and legal systems. In the Netherlands it is useful to distinguish seven categories:

1. Lawyers (*advocaten*) are members of the Dutch Bar Association and have the exclusive right to represent clients before district and higher

courts. Apprentice lawyers are included in this category. In 1986 there were 5,124 lawyers, of whom 1,185 were apprentices (23.1 percent).

2. Notaries are mainly concerned with real estate transactions. The government appoints a fixed number, who are assisted by a much larger number of candidate notaries. In 1986 there were 860 notaries and about 2,000 candidates.

3. The Ministry of Justice appoints judges selected by a professional committee from law graduates (who then must complete a six-year apprenticeship) and experienced lawyers. In 1986 there were 696 judges and approximately another 200 apprentices, who will qualify at the end of their apprenticeship.

4. Prosecutors (who also are members of the judiciary) qualify and are appointed in the same manner as judges and are responsible to the Ministry of Justice. There were 235 in 1986 (excluding apprentices).

5. Business lawyers (*bedrijfsjurist*) are law graduates who do not belong to the Bar Association and therefore cannot represent clients in court. Most have completed three years as an apprentice lawyer. Large numbers are employed by domestic and international enterprises, of whom only a small fraction (about 1,000) belong to the Association of Business Lawyers.

6. Everyone holding a law degree is a jurist. Many law graduates not classifiable under any of the first five categories (above) work in local or central government agencies or perform nonlegal tasks in the private sector. In the last general census in 1971, there were 14,616 people holding law degrees; today the number is estimated to be 30,000.

7. Bailiffs and legal advisers work in small offices and can represent clients in the lower district courts. They have their own organizations with about 200 members.

A few examples will suffice to demonstrate the difficulties of cross-national comparison. In England and Wales and the United States there is nothing like the continental office of notary. Real estate transactions are handled by solicitors or lawyers, terms that are translated by the Dutch advocaten. In comparing Dutch and English lawyers, therefore, one must also consider notaries and candidate notaries and even real estate brokers. However, Dutch notaries are appointed by the government and are comparable to the "free profession" of lawyer in only a few respects.

In comparing the proportion of university graduates who hold a law degree, one must recognize that an American "university" is totally different from a Dutch "university." The proportion of the population with a university eduation is much lower in the Netherlands because many subjects (e.g., journalism, social work, pedagogy, and the performing and visual arts) are taught in vocational schools rather than universities. Students compete for admission to American law schools on the basis of their performance during a four-year college degree and on an admission test. *All* Dutch students who have graduated from a gymnasium or atheneum can enter a law faculty when they become eighteen. Dutch students finish law school at the age when American students enter it. Thus, it is easy to become a law student in the Netherlands but difficult to enter certain specialized professional categories, such as the bar or the judiciary.

All these differences can make comparison dangerous and sometimes impossible. Quintin Johnstone, who made a thorough comparison of American and English lawyers, concluded with resignation that the more he learned about English lawyers the less he could compare them with the characteristics of those he knew in the United States (Johnstone & Hopson, 1967).

A quantitative approach within one country faces fewer difficulties for an author familiar with its concepts and legal system. Do changes within a single legal profession reveal changes in the role of law in that society? Are there changes within and between different law jobs? Before looking at the Dutch data, I want to address the issue as to whether the position of jurists in Dutch society has become more or less important in recent years.

## ARE JURISTS MOVING FROM CENTER TO MARGIN?

The Norwegian sociologist of law, Vilhelm Aubert (1970), has advanced the thesis that the role of law and lawyers in solving societal problems diminished during the last century. This is a provocative thesis, which calls for further empirical testing, especially when one sees the urgent unmet need for legal services, the overburdening of the court dockets, and the explosion of legislation. The growing number of lawyers and the parallel growth in the demand for their services suggests just the opposite development.

Aubert studied changes in the Norwegian legal profession during the 150 years between 1815 and 1965 and found what he characterized as its rise and fall. In 1815 theologians and military officers outnumbered lawyers. Yet, by the middle of the nineteenth century, the law faculty produced more graduates than all the other faculties combined. The number of law graduates increased by a factor of 17 during this period, while the population increased only fourfold. The civil service staffed with jurists has expanded enormously. The number of pages of legislation enacted annually was five times as great in 1965 as it had been a hundred years earlier (ibid., 290, 293, 300). However, Aubert points to other developments indicating that law has lost its significance. First, the number of Norwegian judges only doubled during this 150-year period (ibid., 290). This contrasts sharply with the growth of other expert service providers, such as physicians, engineers, economists, and architects. Second, there was little increase in the work of the courts: from 4,000 to 9,720 criminal sentences between 1870 and 1965, and from between 3,000 to 4,000 civil cases to 8,000 during this period—both gains merely reflecting population growth (ibid., 294–295).

Aubert offers an interesting explanation for the increased number of lawyers in the twentieth century. He relates this growth to the industrial revolution. Lawyers (and more generally jurists) contributed to the construction of a state apparatus and the predictability of social life. These were the main preconditions for economic growth. Jurists played this role because they were inexpensive to train and legal training met the needs of an industrializing country (which also may explain the growth of legal professions in the third world today). Recently, however, the prominent position of law and lawyers has been undermined from two directions. First, legal generalists have lost ground to scientific specialists. With the increase of scientific insight into regularities governing nature and the socioeconomic life, the relative importance of law as a means for producing predictability has been decreasing rapidly. Second, legal ways of solving conflict (especially adjudication) have given way to procedures in which negotiation and compromise predominate.

Aubert has formulated his thesis in such a way that it can be tested in most Western societies, especially in smaller countries. Let us see whether the Dutch case corroborates it.

## THE HISTORICAL DEMOGRAPHY OF THE DUTCH LEGAL PROFESSIONS

What can we learn from changes in the number of Dutch jurists and the professional sectors within which they work? Tables 5.1 and 5.2 show that the pattern of growth parallels the one found in Norway: the number of jurists grew sevenfold between 1860 and 1970, while the population increased only fourfold. Growth has been concentrated in government, industry, and higher education, while the "typically legal" sector (judges and lawyers) only doubled.

The periodization of growth differs from that described by Aubert. He argued that industrialization produces a sharp increase, followed by a gradual decrease. In the Netherlands, the number of jurists grew roughly in tandem with the population between 1860 and 1930 (the period of rapid industrialization) but then grew much faster between 1930 and 1973 (see table 5.2). Leaving the "rise" of jurists, let us look for signs of their "fall." Aubert uses the size of the judiciary as an index of the significance of the courts. Norway shows no striking changes. The number of judges in the Netherlands increased only from 414 in 1860 to 453 in 1960 (see table 5.3). In some respects, quantitative changes deviate from Aubert's thesis. First, the number of judges increased after World War II, suggesting a growth rather than a decline in the demand for legal solutions to social conflict. Second, the number of judges changed abruptly, dropping 25 percent between 1870 and 1880 (because of changes in the law) and increasing rapidly after 1950 (because apprentice judges began to be paid in 1952). This seems inconsistent with the gradual social processes Aubert viewed as causal: industrialization and growing reliance on scientific expertise.

The number of judges is not a reliable index of the extent to which social problems are presented to the courts. Contemporary judges work in a very different organizational environment from that of judges a century ago. They follow different work patterns and use different technologies. This brings us to a third quantitative indicator that Aubert viewed as confirming his theory: the static number of cases litigated. Here the Dutch data do tend to support Aubert's theory: the litigation rate (cases per 10,000 population) grew rapidly between 1850 and 1925 and has remained static since then (see table 5.4). What matters, therefore, is not so much the number of judges but rather the total number of court personnel and how they are organized. These factors enabled judges to perform much more work, especially between 1875 and 1925, although the number of judges increased only slowly. After 1925 the litigation rate remained relatively stable.

The historical demography of the Dutch bar resembles that of judges (see table 5.5). The ratio of lawyers to population declined in the latter half of the nineteenth century and then remained constant until 1970. The number of notaries is virtually fixed by law; only the number of candidate notaries (those who are qualified but awaiting an appointment) indicates the potential for growth in this branch of the legal profession. The number of lawyers in the Netherlands nearly doubled between 1970 and 1980, from 2,063 to 3,989, an increase that is historically exceptional. I will return to this phenomenon and suggest some explanations below.

Although the Netherlands resembles Norway in being a small industrialized western European country, the history of its legal profession seems very different. There is no evidence to support Aubert's thesis that jurists have been marginalized, especially during the postwar period. Rather, the number of jurists, and especially the number of lawyers, seems related to the degree of state intervention in society. The only decline in the role of jurists since World War II is their representation in Parliament (see table 5.6). During the nineteenth century, which Aubert would characterize as the modern nation-building period, jurists dominated the legislature. Now, 100 years later, their representation has fallen by half, to less than 20 percent of the total. Other experts, especially economists, have taken their place. If Aubert was wrong about the totality of roles of jurists in society, he was right about their role in Parliament.

## SOCIAL CHARACTERISTICS OF THE DUTCH LEGAL PROFESSION

One becomes a jurist in the Netherlands by obtaining a law degree at one of the nine Dutch universities, a process that takes four or five years. Those who wish to become lawyers must obtain a position as an apprentice with a law firm and join the Dutch Bar Association. This confers full rights to represent clients. The three-year apprenticeship is intended to prepare lawyers to work in all substantive fields. After it is completed, the lawyer can establish a law firm or join an existing one. Many become salaried junior partners, but others leave law practice for jobs in banking and industry.

At the end of 1986, 5,124 Dutch jurists were registered as lawyers. This registration requires a formal induction in court and an oath to adhere to the rules of professional conduct. The numbers had increased by nearly 150 percent from the 2,063 lawyers registered sixteen year earlier. Because the size of the legal profession had been quite stable for the half century between 1920 and 1970, this was a remarkable development. This can be partly explained by the increase in the demand for legal services, which the state had not subsidized or even attended to earlier. Part also is attributable to the sharp increase in divorce following the 1971 family law reform. The legalization of social relationships in general has been increasing with the passage of social welfare legislation (1967), a disability law (1976), housing legislation (1974), a new commercial code (1975), a new family law (1978), and a new civil code in the 1980s.

### AGE

Most of the new legal services are provided by young lawyers: nearly 25 percent of all lawyers are serving their apprenticeships. The number of apprentice lawyers increased sevenfold during the decade of the 1970s, from 7 percent of all Dutch lawyers to 28 percent, although the proportion has declined in the 1980s (see table 5.7). Because 95 percent of all apprentice lawyers surveyed in 1970 and 1973 were under thirty-three years of age, a radical shift has taken place in the age distribution of the

Dutch bar. The proportion under thirty-four increased from 17 percent in 1962 to 52 percent in 1982. It is illuminating to compare the age distribution of lawyers with that of all jurists (see table 5.8). Two-thirds of all lawyers have less than ten years of experience. Only 11 percent are found in the middle years (forty to fifty) and 15 percent in the older cohort (fifty to sixty-five). In their middle years, many Dutch lawyers enter the judiciary. In this the Netherlands occupies a position intermediate between that of Germany (where almost all judges begin their judicial careers immediately after graduation and apprenticeship) and England (where all judges are appointed from among the more experienced lawyers).

GENDER

The 1970s also saw a remarkable increase in the number of women lawyers. In 1969, 21 percent of law students were women; in 1980, 41 percent (see table 5.9). When they graduate, a disproportionate number become lawyers (see table 5.10). Private practice historically has been more open to women than other law jobs. The first woman was registered as a lawyer in 1903, but no woman became a judge until 1947. Barriers remain after entry, however: women accounted for 24 percent of apprentice lawyers in 1979 but only 16 percent of fully qualified lawyers; and there were no women judges in the higher courts. Many women judges sit part time, and only recently were they granted rights to advancement equal to those of full-time judges. Women have to make more applications than men to find positions in private practice, are more likely to undertake marginal work (such as family law), and are less likely to become partners in law firms (Schuyt, 1973). Given the age and gender distribution, a young male defendant now has one chance in six of being represented by a young female lawyer (see table 5.11). The public image of the lawyer does not yet accord with this development.

SOCIAL CLASS AND OCCUPATIONAL BACKGROUND

Although Ladinsky (1963) documented the influence of background variables on American legal careers more than 20 years ago, there is little Dutch research on the subject. Surveys of apprentice lawyers in 1973 (Schuyt, 1974) and of the Dutch bar in 1979 (Klijn, 1981) revealed that since 1969 men from less privileged backgrounds have gained considerable access to private practice but not to the judiciary. Women lawyers still come from more privileged backgrounds (see table 5.12). Klijn (1981) found that half of Dutch lawyers were the children of fathers who worked in administrative or governmental jobs, compared to only 15 percent whose fathers were in commerce and 11 percent whose fathers were in industry. A higher proportion of lawyers than law students (22 percent vs. 18 percent) are the children of fathers in governmental jobs, which suggests that private practice is more selective than law faculties. Yet law students also were from privileged backgrounds: 36 percent were upper-class, 28 percent middle-class, 17 percent from the entrepreneurial class, 13 percent upper-lower-class, and only 7 percent lower-class (Roos, 1981).

EDUCATION

Nearly half of all lawyers have graduated from two universities: Leiden (22.5 percent) and Utrecht (20.4 percent). The other university law faculties account for considerably smaller proportions: the Catholic University of Nijmegen (15 percent), the University of Amsterdam (13.4 percent), and the University of Groningen (11.6 percent). These institutions differ in the careers their graduates pursue: Leiden graduates are underrepresented among lawyers (but overrepresented among judges), while graduates of Nijmegen are overrepresented among lawyers. This appears to reflect the more privileged social background of Leiden students compared to those at Nijmegen and Tilburg (see table 5.13). Entry into the legal profession by those from less privileged backgrounds, therefore, can be attributed partly to the emancipation of Catholics and the role of the Catholic University of Nijmegen.

# PROFESSIONAL ASSOCIATIONS AND INTERNAL DIFFERENTIATION

PROFESSIONAL ASSOCIATIONS

The Dutch Bar Association was created by legislation (Advocaten Wet) in 1952, passed at the initiative of the Ministry of Justice. Membership is a concomitant of registration in the bar. Before 1952 every district had its own voluntary association; these now send representatives to the General Council, the governing body of the national association. One reason for the creation of a national body was to centralize disciplinary authority by creating a single body to hear appeals from district boards. Although the Dutch Bar Association is established by public law, it is self-governing, promulgating rules without interference by the government or laypersons. The Board of the Association increasingly has assumed the role of

representing all lawyers in negotiations with the Ministry of Justice concerning the scope of legal practice and especially the organization and
finance of the state-supported legal aid system. Although "honorary
rules" date back to 1661, recent discussions led to their replacement by
"rules of conduct" in 1980. This reform was compelled both by new commercial practices (such as advertising) and the influx of young lawyers,
many of whom belonged to lawyer collectives. In 1979 ninety-four complaints were filed with district boards, fifty-nine of which were dismissed;
discipline was imposed in twenty-nine cases.

## LAW FIRMS

Before 1960, 40 percent of all lawyers were solo practitioners, and 44 percent worked in firms with two to four partners. Since 1970, some firms
have grown to contain more than 50 lawyers (see table 5.14). By 1979,
one out of four lawyers worked in a "large" firm with at least ten lawyers,
most of which were located in Amsterdam, Rotterdam, or The Hague (the
Randstad). Medium-sized firms (five to nine lawyers) contain one lawyer
out of five, small firms (two to four lawyers) still contain about a third,
while the proportion in solo practice has dropped by half (and many of
these are assisted by one or two apprentices).

## GEOGRAPHIC DISTRIBUTION

It is not surprising that the density of lawyers is greatest in the Randstad.
The population per lawyer increases from Amsterdam (1,500) to The
Hague (1,600), Utrecht and Den Bosch (1,700), Heerlen (1,800), Rotterdam and Alkmaar (1,900), and Maastricht and Haarlem (2,100). Most
lawyers are located in cities with district courts. Nearly 70 percent of
jurists live and work in cities of more than 100,000 population, and 60
percent live in the provinces of North and South Holland, the center of
the Netherlands and the heart of its commerce and industry. Some cities
with lower district courts have no lawyers, but legal representation is not
mandatory in them.

## LAWYERS' WORK

Lawyers handle an average of about 250 cases a year. Because some cases
last more than a year, the number of cases completed—an average of
134—is a better index of workload. The 1979 survey found that this

measure varied with experience: 94 for apprentices, 130 for junior (salaried) partners, and 159 for senior (profit-staring) partners (Klijn, 1981). (The increase is attributable partly to assistance by subordinates, partly to specialization.)

A substantial portion of lawyers' work is supported by legal aid payments. The number of legally aided cases doubled between 1958, when the program was instituted, and 1970, and doubled again by 1980. More than half of these cases involve divorce. Consequently, an important part of the demand for lawyers' services is attributable to the declining authority of the Dutch church, which permits the increasing divorce rate. Unlike civil legal aid, criminal legal aid accounts for only a small part of lawyers' practices (notwithstanding the public image of lawyers as defense counsel). Most lawyers handle less than fifteen to twenty criminal cases per year, and there are few specialists in this field.

Klijn (1981) asked lawyers practicing in 1979 to indicate the legal areas to which they gave the most attention and the number of cases they handled in each field. He found that such specialization grouped lawyers into three categories: commercial practice, family practice, and social welfare practice (see table 5.15). Each category of lawyers had distinct social characteristics: commercial law was practiced by men in large firms, family law by women and small-firm lawyers, and social welfare by young lawyers.

INCOME AND TYPE OF PRACTICE

In 1979, Dutch lawyers earned an average net income of DFl 43,825: apprentices earned DFl 33,850, junior partners DFl 45,713, and senior partners DFl 77,100 (see table 5.16). Income varies strongly with law firm size, although the relationship is not perfectly linear (see table 5.17). The average income of lawyers is low compared to other professions, even if apprentices and employed lawyers are excluded. In 1975 notaries and medical specialists earned two and a half times as much as lawyers, pharmacists twice as much, general practitioners and dentists one and a half times as much, and even veterinarians slightly more (see table 5.18).

## LEGAL EDUCATION AND THE NUMBER OF LAW STUDENTS

During the last 150 years the proportion of undergraduates studying law gradually declined to a nadir in 1960, since when it has nearly doubled (see table 5.19). The absolute number of law students increased from

3,014 in 1960 to 18,588 in 1980, more than sixfold in twenty years. This accounts for the dramatic growth of the legal profession in the 1970s.

Law students remained as a large proportion of undergraduates until 1870. Although industrialization reached the Netherlands late, about 1870, this does not explain the decline in the proportion of undergraduates studying law, because their places were taken not by the natural sciences and engineering but rather by medicine, which enrolled 55 percent of all students between 1870 and 1890. Periods of economic growth between 1870 and 1950 appear to be associated with a *decrease* in the proportion of undergraduates studying law.

Between 1964 and 1967 law faculties (but not other disciplines) dropped Latin and Greek as entrance requirements, allowing the number of entrants to rise and changing their educational and social backgrounds. Today the eight law faculties award about 2,000 degrees a year. Although the proportion of women increased from 20 percent to 41 percent of the entering class between 1970 and 1980, their rate of attrition is higher than that of men law students. Most students (83 percent) read Dutch law; 9 percent prepare to be notaries, 4 percent study fiscal law, and the rest combine these subjects.

The 1983 reorganization of the undergraduate curriculum, which reduced it from five or six years to four, stimulated discussion about the quality of legal education. The Dutch Bar Association sought the requirement of a postgraduate course and an entrance examination for all future lawyers. This would represent a dramatic departure from the Dutch tradition that a law degree qualifies for all branches of the profession, and it probably will not be adopted. However, two other developments may have similar consequences. In 1988 or 1989, the Dutch Bar Association, in cooperation with several law faculties (especially those of Leiden, Amsterdam, Utrecht, and Groningen), will initiate a one-year postgraduate course, the "second-phase curriculum," whose graduates will have a better chance to obtain an apprenticeship. In addition, several law professors and large corporations jointly have established a *private* postgraduate law school, whose one-year curriculum in international business law prepares its graduates for both apprenticeships in large firms and positions as in-house counsel. The fees for this year (DFl 25,000) are ten times as high as those for a year at university. Although some student loans are promised, this novel development will intensify the class bias in the composition of the legal professions.

The political preferences of law students in 1975 did not differ greatly from those of the general population: 46 percent would have voted for progressive parties (Labor and Liberal), 27 percent for conservatives, and 14 percent for religious parties. Students with progressive preferences were less inclined to seek positions in the judiciary, and many of them participated in the growth of legal aid in the 1970s.

## THE 1970s: LAW EXPLOSION OR LAWYERS EXPLOSION?

The first law shop was established by progressive law students in Tilburg in 1969, following the model of the North Kensington Law Centre in London. The object was to use law students or apprentice lawyers to provide advice to poor people in the neighborhood. The number of law shops rapidly multiplied to thirteen in 1972 and eighty in 1975. Although the movement peaked in the late 1970s, its lasting influence has been the reform of the official legal aid system (Schuyt et al., 1976; 1977).

The Dutch Bar Association initially was opposed but soon took the initiative to study legal aid for the poor. The official legal aid system established in 1957 had created no offices to serve the poor, and private lawyers found the level of fee reimbursement too low. As a result, many poor clients did not receive the assistance they needed. The legal aid movement achieved three reforms: (1) an increase in the level of legal aid fees, (2) the emergence of about fifty lawyer collectives, and (3) the establishment of Legal Aid Bureaus in every district, staffed by salaried jurists (civil servants rather than private practitioners), who provide initial advice and legal services (van der Beek et al., 1983). Thus, the reforms changed the attitude of the organized bar, created an oppositional group within the profession, and led to the growth of a paralegal profession (with its own association). Young lawyers (many of whom had worked in law shops) continue to support these reforms. Older lawyers participated in committees for the renewal of the legal aid system and the old consultation bureaus.

Perhaps the greatest change has been the lawyer collectives. The first was established in 1974 by a group of law students who had worked in the Amsterdam law shop. When they qualified they opened a collective law practice in Amsterdam, seeking to serve clients in poor neighborhoods. They deliberately rejected some of the rules of professional conduct, advertising their practice widely and participating in many social and political action groups. These collectives remain the principal supporters of the legal aid movement in the Netherlands, especially now that the law shops are declining or even closing.

Between 1974 and 1978 the state established Legal Aid Bureaus in every district to provide initial advice and free representation to those below a certain income level. By 1980, they employed about 300 people, nearly two-thirds of whom were law graduates (see table 5.20). These bureaus tend to concentrate their energies on the needs of disadvantaged groups, such as ethnic minorities, the unemployed, tenants, and migrant workers. They also administer the legal aid services provided by private practitioners.

The three main constituents of the legal aid movement—law shops, lawyer collectives, and Legal Aid Bureaus—all developed within a single decade. These have expanded access to legal aid to citizens at all income levels. Public consciousness of legal rights also has increased enormously. The combined effect of these two variables has caused a spectacular increase in the amount of legal aid rendered. For the large number of recent law graduates, this meant the (inadvertent) creation of low paid work, which they could define for themselves. For the bar as a whole, this meant far higher levels of consumption (see table 5.21).

Total state expenditures on legal aid had reached DFl 225 million in 1982. Even though this was a very small percentage of the national budget, an alarmed Ministry of Justice sought ways to curtail the upward drift by excluding certain categories of cases and lowering the income ceilings on eligibility, which elicited strong protests from the Dutch Bar Association. Most of the increase in legal aid costs is attributable to the rising divorce rate. There were 5,000 divorces in 1960, 10,000 in 1970, 20,000 in 1975, 25,000 in 1980, and 30,000 in 1982. Between 75 percent and 80 percent of all divorces are legally aided. In 1982, legal aid payments in divorce cases were made on behalf of 58,000 parties, totaling DFl 58 million, or 41 percent of all civil legal aid expenditures. Because a lawyer earns about DFl 1,000 for each divorce, collectives and small firms can obtain a substantial part of their incomes from this source. Therefore, the Ministry of Justice has proposed to lower the fee for divorce and to make it possible for couples to dispense with legal representation. The Dutch bar strongly opposed these proposals, which have been withdrawn for revision.

## CONCLUSION: FIGURES IN NEED OF A THEORY

Although the number of lawyers and the quantity of legal services has been growing dramatically in the Netherlands in recent decades, the Dutch still are not a very litigious people. There are only 5,000 lawyers for a population of 14,641,000, or about 3,000 people per lawyer; there are about 20,000 people per judge. These ratios are much higher than those in most other European countries, although the population per police officer (400) is about the same as that elsewhere in Europe. Any interpretation of the recent increase in lawyers must take into account this starting point.

Table 5.22 compares the proportion of law graduates involved in advocacy, adjudication, business counseling and advice, and the civil service in four European countries and the United States. The Netherlands has relatively small proportions of jurists in the first two categories and the highest proportion in the civil service. The famous Dutch welfare state has been legalized, but bureaucratically rather than through adversary contests. Traditional Dutch cultural patterns of law-making also can be seen.

All these figures demand more adequate sociological theories. I suggest four possible lines of argument. First, twenty-five years of economic growth have increased university enrollment, especially in law faculties after 1965. The postwar baby boom contributed to the increased production of lawyers. Because the ideology of professional autonomy allows lawyers to decide whether to render legal aid, many young lawyers have been able to find work within the "market for welfare and well being." Second, increased state intervention increased the legalization of social relations and thus the opportunities for legal work. Third, the dissolution of long-standing social bonds (work into unemployment, marriage into divorce, etc.) multiplied the rapidity of status change. Law is mobilized when people change their status (whether legally or socially). Fourth, economic activity has shifted from the production of goods to the production of services. Compared to medical services, legal services still constitute a very small part of this market. Although the first of these factors may have run its course, the other three are likely to produce further growth in both the supply of and the demand for lawyers.

# TABLES

5.1. Distribution of Jurists among Categories, 1860–1971

| Year | Judges and lawyers | Government | Universities | Private employment | Total |
|------|------|------|------|------|------|
| 1860 | 1,655 | 482 | 16 | — | 2,153 |
| 1900 | 1,672 | 382 | 82 | — | 2,103 |
| 1930 | 2,168 | 649 | 178 | 1,247 | 4,242 |
| 1947 | 2,823 | 1,805 | 251 | 2,279 | 7,166 |
| 1960 | 3,210 | 2,140 | 430 | 3,774 | 9,555 |
| 1971 | 4,326 | 4,063 | 1,491 | 4,736 | 14,616 |

*Sources:* 1860, 1900—*Dutch State Almanac;* 1930, 1947, 1960, 1971—*Population Survey.*

5.2. Relative Growth of Population and Number of Jurists, 1860–1973 (1930 = 100)

| Year | Population | All jurists | Judges and lawyers | Government | Universities | Private employment |
|------|------|------|------|------|------|------|
| 1860 | 42 | 51 | 76 | 74 | 9 | |
| 1930 | 100 | 100 | 100 | 100 | 100 | 100 |
| 1973 | 165 | 345 | 200 | 626 | 838 | 380 |

*Sources:* 1860—*Dutch State Almanac;* 1930—census; 1973—Hövels and Krijnen (1974).

5.3. Relative Growth of Population and
Judges, 1860–1986 (1860 = 100)

| Year | Judges | | Population index |
| | Absolute | Index | |
|---|---|---|---|
| 1860 | 414 | 100 | 100 |
| 1870 | 436 | 105 | 108 |
| 1880 | 315 | 76 | 123 |
| 1890 | 326 | 79 | 136 |
| 1900 | 331 | 80 | 154 |
| 1910 | 365 | 88 | 177 |
| 1920 | 372 | 90 | 206 |
| 1930 | 372 | 90 | 237 |
| 1940 | 327 | 79 | 267 |
| 1950 | 368 | 89 | 303 |
| 1960 | 453 | 109 | 345 |
| 1970 | 503 | 121 | 392 |
| 1979 | 625 | 151 | 423 |
| 1986 | 696 | 168 | 425 |

*Source:* Schuyt (1981: 128).

5.4. Judicial Caseload, 1860–1975 (1860 = 100)

| Year | Criminal case index | Civil case index | Cases per judge | Cases per 10,000 people |
|---|---|---|---|---|
| 1860 | 100 | 100 | 125 | 34 |
| 1875 | 118 | 138 | 144 | 37 |
| 1900 | 346 | 271 | 532 | 54 |
| 1925 | 585 | 754 | 922 | 107 |
| 1950 | 869 | 887 | 1,227 | 90 |
| 1975 | 886 | 1,335 | 935 | 100 |

*Source:* Schuyt (1981: 130).

5.5. Number of Lawyers, Notaries, and Candidate Notaries, 1850–1986

| Year | Number of lawyers | | Notaries | Candidate notaries |
|------|----------|----------------------|----------|-----------|
| | Absolute | Per 100,000 population | | |
| 1850 | 829 | 27 | 676 | 201 |
| 1860 | 758 | 23 | 710 | 127 |
| 1890 | 679 | 14 | — | — |
| 1900 | 725 | 14 | 839 | — |
| 1910 | 796 | 13 | 833 | — |
| 1920 | 875 | 13 | 832 | 477 |
| 1930 | 1,337 | 17 | 859 | 633 |
| 1947 | 1,612 | 18 | 818 | 620 |
| 1960 | 1,851 | 16 | 839 | 679 |
| 1970 | 2,063 | 16 | 842 | 828 |
| 1980 | 3,600 | 26 | 860 | 1,200 |
| 1982 | 3,989 | 29 | 860 | — |
| 1984 | 4,825 | 33 | 860 | — |
| 1986 | 5,124 | 35 | 860 | 2,000 |

*Source:* Schuyt (1981: 131) (updated).

5.6. Jurists in Parliament, 1860–1983 (Percent of Total)

| Year | First chamber | | | Second chamber | | |
|------|---------|-----------------|--------|---------|-----------------|--------|
| | Jurists | Other academics | Others | Jurists | Other academics | Others |
| 1860 | 46 | 3 | 51 | 65 | 6 | 29 |
| 1900 | 64 | 0 | 36 | 42 | 8 | 50 |
| 1960 | 35 | 20 | 45 | 25 | 16 | 59 |
| 1970 | 19 | 40 | 41 | 23 | 31 | 46 |
| 1978 | 15 | 35 | 50 | 19 | 37 | 44 |
| 1983 | 20 | 45 | 35 | 19 | 35 | 46 |

*Source:* Schuyt (1981: 134–135); *Parliament Handbook* (1983).

5.7. Growth in Number of
Apprentices, 1970–1986

| Year | Number | Percent of bar |
|------|--------|----------------|
| 1970 | 142 | 6.9 |
| 1971 | 161 | 7.9 |
| 1972 | 123 | 5.5 |
| 1973 | 416 | 17.7 |
| 1974 | 607 | 24.8 |
| 1975 | 484 | 18.8 |
| 1976 | — | — |
| 1977 | 796 | 26.9 |
| 1978 | 919 | 28.2 |
| 1979 | 995 | 28.4 |
| 1984 | 1,208 | 25.0 |
| 1986 | 1,185 | 23.1 |

*Source:* Klijn (1981: 18): annual reports
of the Dutch Bar Association.

5.8. Age Distribution of Jurists
(1977) and Lawyers (1979)

| | Percent in category | |
|------|--------|---------|
| Age | Jurists | Lawyers |
| 20–24 | 1.9 | 0.7 |
| 25–29 | 23.6 | 19.7 |
| 30–34 | 23.6 | 31.6 |
| 35–39 | 16.0 | 14.4 |
| 40–44 | 4.7 | 6.3 |
| 45–49 | 6.6 | 5.0 |
| 50–54 | 9.4 | 5.7 |
| 55–59 | 6.6 | 4.9 |
| 60–64 | 3.8 | 5.8 |
| > 60 | 3.8 | 6.3 |

*Source:* Klijn (1981).

5.9. Women Law Students,
1969–1980

| Year | Absolute | Percent of law students |
|------|----------|-------------------------|
| 1969 | 482 | 21 |
| 1970 | 495 | 20 |
| 1971 | 587 | 24 |
| 1974 | 647 | 29 |
| 1975 | 792 | 33 |
| 1976 | 788 | 32 |
| 1977 | 954 | 32 |
| 1978 | 1,155 | 38 |
| 1979 | 1,237 | 37 |
| 1980 | 1,416 | 41 |

*Source:* Roos (1981).

5.10. Women in Different Law Jobs (Percent of all Jurists), 1970–1986

| Year | Lawyers[a] | Apprentice lawyers | Judges | Apprentice judges | Notaries | Law teachers |
|------|-----------|-------------------|--------|-------------------|----------|--------------|
| 1970 | 10.5 | 18.9 | 3.4 | — | 1.2 | — |
| 1973 | 12.7 | 22.1 | 6.5 | 22.7 | 1.4 | — |
| 1979 | 15.3 | 24.0 | 7.2 | 32.1 | 2.2 | 16.5 |
| 1984 | 20.0 | 29.0 | — | — | — | — |
| 1986 | 21.3 | 32.0 | — | — | — | — |

[a]Includes apprentices.
*Sources:* Schuyt (1970; 1974; 1981); annual reports of the Dutch Bar Association.

5.11. Gender Distribution of Lawyers
by Experience (Percent), 1979

| Years of experience | Men | Women |
|---------------------|-----|-------|
| < 4 | 75 | 25 |
| 4–10 | 79 | 21 |
| > 10 | 88 | 12 |

*Source:* Klijn (1981).

5.12. Social Class of Lawyers' Fathers (Percent), 1979[a]

| Experience, years | Low | Middle | High |
|---|---|---|---|
| Men | 11.5 | 4.4 | 84.1 |
| < 4 | 16.2 | 5.4 | 78.4 |
| 4–10 | 15.6 | 7.2 | 77.2 |
| > 10 | 4.9 | 1.3 | 93.8 |
| Women | 4.0 | 3.2 | 92.8 |
| < 4 | 5.6 | 3.7 | 90.7 |
| > 10 | 0 | 0 | 100.0 |

[a]Low = working class; high = professions, entrepreneurs, higher civil servants.
Source: Klijn (1981).

5.13. Social Class of Law Students, by University (Percent),
1970–71

| University | High | Middle | Low |
|---|---|---|---|
| Leiden | 48 | 42 | 10 |
| Utrecht | 42 | 47 | 11 |
| Groningen | 43 | 45 | 12 |
| Amsterdam Municipal | 39 | 46 | 15 |
| Rotterdam | 35 | 50 | 15 |
| Amsterdam Free | 33 | 55 | 12 |
| Catholic Univ. Nijmegen | 26 | 57 | 19 |
| Tilburg | 20 | 60 | 20 |

Source: Roos (1981).

5.14. Law Firm Size, 1960–1979

| Number of lawyers in firm | Percent of all firms | | | Percent of all lawyers | | |
|---|---|---|---|---|---|---|
| | 1960 | 1976 | 1979 | 1960 | 1976 | 1979 |
| 1 | 67 | 56 | 50 | 40 | 22 | 18 |
| 2–4 | 29 | 32 | 36 | 44 | 33 | 35 |
| 4–9 | 4 | 9 | 10 | 14 | 21 | 21 |
| 10–15 | 0.2 | 2 | 2 | 2 | 8 | 7 |
| 16–61 | 0 | 1 | 2 | 0 | 16 | 19 |
| N | 1,267 | 1,176 | 1,053 | 1,851 | 2,694 | 3,497 |

Source: Schuyt (1981: 146).

5.15. Subject Matter Practice of Lawyers, 1979

| Subject matter | | | Number of lawyers | |
|---|---|---|---|---|
| Family | Social | Commercial | Absolute | Percent |
| High | High | High | 159 | 15 |
| High | High | Low | 147 | 13.8 |
| High | Low | High | 126 | 11.9 |
| Low | High | High | 98 | 9.2 |
| High | Low | Low | 92 | 8.7 |
| Low | High | Low | 101 | 9.5 |
| Low | Low | High | 164 | 15.4 |
| Low | Low | Low | 175 | 16.5 |
| | | Total | 1,062 | 100 |

*Source:* Klijn (1981).

5.16. Annual Income of Lawyers, 1978 (DFl)

| | Number of lawyers | |
|---|---|---|
| Income categories | Absolute | Percent |
| < 25,000 | 106 | 11.6 |
| 25,000–50,000 | 368 | 40.3 |
| 50,000–75,000 | 157 | 17.2 |
| 75,000–100,000 | 102 | 11.2 |
| 100,000–125,000 | 62 | 6.8 |
| 125,000–150,000 | 42 | 4.6 |
| 150,000–200,000 | 47 | 5.1 |
| > 200,000 | 29 | 3.2 |
| Total | 913 | 100 |
| No answer | 166 | — |
| No full year's income | 147 | — |

*Source:* Klijn (1981).

5.17. Annual Net Income of Lawyers (DFl), by Size of Firm, 1978 (Percent)[a]

| Income categories | Number of lawyers in firm | | |
|---|---|---|---|
| | < 5 | 5–10 | > 10 |
| < 25,000 | 65.4 | 23.1 | 11.5 |
| 25,000–50,000 | 33.7 | 40.1 | 26.2 |
| 50,000–100,000 | 14.4 | 41.6 | 44.0 |
| > 100,000 | 16.3 | 17.7 | 56.0 |

[a]$N = 872$.
Source: Klijn (1981).

5.18. Average 1975 Income of Lawyers Compared to That of Other Professions (DFl)

| Profession | Income |
|---|---|
| Lawyers (excluding apprentices and employees) | 82,006 |
| Veterinarians | 89,761 |
| Dentists | 121,639 |
| General practitioners (physicians) | 122,261 |
| Pharmacists | 162,788 |
| Medical specialists | 203,600 |
| Notaries | 210,209 |

Source: Schuyt (1981: 148).

5.19. Growth of Undergraduates and Distribution between Law and Social Sciences, 1840–1980

| | Total undergraduates | | Social Sciences | | Law | |
|---|---|---|---|---|---|---|
| Year | Per 100,000 population | Absolute | Percent | Absolute | Percent | Absolute |
| 1840 | 49 | | 32 | 451 | 32 | 451 |
| 1850 | 35 | | 46 | | 46 | |
| 1860 | 41 | | 43 | | 43 | |
| 1870 | 37 | | 40 | | 40 | |
| 1880 | 34 | | 28 | | 28 | |
| 1890 | 57 | | 18 | | 18 | |
| 1900 | 48 | 2,816 | 19 | 519 | 19 | 519 |
| 1910 | 83 | | 18 | | 18 | |
| 1920 | 124 | 8,552 | 21 | | 14 | |
| 1930 | 152 | | 22 | | 11 | |
| 1937 | 151 | | 24 | | 11 | |
| 1950 | 267 | 29,736 | 29 | 8,661 | 10 | 2,936 |
| 1955 | 297 | | 31 | | 9 | |
| 1960 | 367 | 40,727 | 32 | 10,200 | 7 | 3,014 |
| 1965 | 536 | | 36 | | 10 | |
| 1970 | 868 | 103,382 | 44 | 45,254 | 12 | 12,763 |
| 1975 | 883 | | 43 | | 12 | |
| 1979 | 1,054 | 147,590 | 43 | 63,455 | 13 | 19,744 |
| 1980 | 988 | 139,335 | | | 13 | 18,588 |

*Source:* Roos (1981).

5.20. Growth of Legal Aid Bureaus, 1975–1982

| | Staff | | |
|---|---|---|---|
| Year | Jurists | Others | Total |
| 1975 | 7 | 2 | 9 |
| 1976 | 23 | 12.5 | 35.5 |
| 1977 | 55 | 28.5 | 83.5 |
| 1978 | 83 | 48.5 | 131.5 |
| 1979 | 116 | 64 | 180 |
| 1980 | 150 | 82.3 | 232.3 |
| 1981 | 180 | 106.8 | 286.8 |
| 1982 | 187.5 | 111.8 | 299.3 |

*Source:* van der Beek et al. (1983).

5.21. State Expenditures for Legal Aid, 1970–1980 (Millions DFl)

|  | 1970 | 1975 | 1976 | 1977 | 1978 | 1979 | 1980 |
|---|---|---|---|---|---|---|---|
| Legal aid fees |  |  |  |  |  |  |  |
| Criminal cases |  | 10.0 | 12.1 | 21.5 | 26.1 | 25.5 | 32.8 |
| Civil cases | 13.0 | 44.5 | 55.0 | 70.0 | 84.0 | 86.3 | 99.3 |
| Legal Aid Bureaus |  | 1.0 | 2.6 | 4.4 | 8.4 | 10.0 | 15.4 |
| Other |  | 2.1 | 3.3 | 3.1 | 3.3 | 5.0 | 4.6 |
| Total | 13.0 | 57.6 | 73.0 | 99.0 | 121.8 | 126.8 | 152.1 |

Source: Social and Cultural Report (1982).

5.22. Distribution of Law Graduates among Professional Categories in five Countries (Percent)

| Country | Lawyers and notaries | Judges | Private enterprise | Civil service |
|---|---|---|---|---|
| Norway | 24 | 16 | 26 | 34 |
| Belgium | 36 | 7 | 42 | 15 |
| West Germany | 35 | 17 | 18 | 30 |
| The Netherlands | 26 | 4 | 32 | 38 |
| United States | 68 | 4 | 14 | 14 |

Source: chapters 2, 3, and 6, this volume; Abel (1988).

# REFERENCES

Abel, Richard L. 1988. "United States: The Contradictions of Professionalism," in Richard L. Abel and Philip S. C. Lewis, eds., *Lawyers in Society*, vol. 1: *The Common Law World*. Berkeley, Los Angeles, London: University of California Press.

Aubert, Vilhelm. 1970. "Law as a Way of Resolving Conflict: The Case of a Small Industrial Country," in Laura Nader, ed., *Law in Culture and Society*. Chicago: Aldine.

Beek, E. C. van der, G. B. M. Engbersen, and C. J. M. Schuyt. 1983. *The Development of Legal Aid Bureaus and Citizens' Advice Bureaus [De hulpverlening van Instituten Sociaal Raadslieden en Bureaux voor Rechtshulp in ontwikkeling]*. The Hague: Staatsuitgeverij.

Hövels, B. W. M., and G. Krijnen. 1974. *Dutch Jurists and Their Law Jobs: A Research Report [Functies van juristen]*. Nijmegen: Institute for Applied Sociology.

Johnstone, Quintin, and Dan Hopson, Jr. 1967. *Lawyers and Their Work*. Indianapolis: Bobbs-Merrill.

Kawashima, Takeyoshi. 1964. "Dispute Resolution in Contemporary Japan," in Arthur T. von Mehren, ed., *Law in Japan*. Cambridge, Mass.: Harvard University Press.

Klijn, Albert. 1981. *De balie geschetst: verslag van een door het W.O.D.C. gehouden schriftelijke enquete onder de Nederlandse advokatuur* [*A Profile of the Dutch Bar*]. The Hague: Staatsuitgeverij.

Ladinsky, Jack. 1963. "The Impact of Social Backgrounds of Lawyers on Law Practice and the Law," 16 *Journal of Legal Education* 127–144.

*Population Survey*. The Hague: Census Bureau and Statistics.

Roos, Nick. 1981. *Juristerij in Nederland* [*All About Jurists and Lawyers in the Netherlands*]. Deventer: Kluwer.

Schuyt, Kees. 1970. "Stagiaires," 50 *Advocatenblad* (October) (Appendix).

———. 1974. "De stagiaire van 1973. Verslag van een enquete," 54 *Advocatenblad* 473–490.

———. 1981. *Recht en Samenleving* [*Law and Society*]. Assen: Gorcum.

Schuyt, Kees, Kees Groenendijk, and Ben Sloot. 1976. *De Weg Naar Het Recht* [*The Road to Law*]. Deventer: Kluwer.

———. 1977. "Access to the Legal System and Legal Services Research," 1977 *European Yearbook on Law and Sociology* 98–120. The Hague: Martinus Nijhoff.

*Social and Cultural Report*. Rijswijk: Social and Cultural Planning Bureau.

# 6

# Legal Experts in Belgium

## LUC HUYSE

This is not a chapter on lawyers in the narrow sense—that is, legal experts who represent clients in the courts. Reducing the scope of inquiry to what some see as the essence of lawyering—the representational function—would be the wrong strategy for describing the legal profession in Belgium. Such an approach would limit analysis to advocates, excluding almost 70 percent of the jurist population. It also would encourage a static perspective, since representation in court is not the most important function Belgian legal experts perform.

Therefore, I have begun by describing the jurist population as a whole and then have focused on the occupational groups that most closely fit the model of the legal profession, namely, advocates and notaries.

## JURISTS IN BELGIUM: AN OVERVIEW

### A HIGHLY DIVIDED "PROFESSION"

In Belgium, the terms for "lawyer" are *jurist/juriste* (all terms are given in their Dutch or Flemish/French versions), but they refer more to a statistical category of degree-holders (*dr./lic. juris*)[1] than to an occupational or professional group. Indeed, the differences between jurists are much greater than the traits they share.

Belgian folk conceptions make a rather sharp distinction between the highly visible legal practice of advocates, judges, notaries, and court clerks and the more "hidden" services of legal experts in the public sector (civil servants) and private employment (house counsel, jurists in nonprofit organizations, etc.).

Advocates, notaries, judges, and jurists in private employment and public administration also are profoundly differentiated in other ways.

First, the various categories are differently "bound" to the exercise of their legal expertise. Many who enter private firms or the public sector (except as judges) cease to be jurists in a narrow sense: they become managers or executives and only infrequently do legal work. By contrast, ethical codes prohibit advocates from combining their practice at the bar with "nonprofessional" activities, such as selling insurance or real estate. Second, lateral mobility is rare, except for occasional movements from the bar to the judiciary or private sector employment. Third, an overarching association of jurists never has existed, and, consequently, there has been no general professional project for "collective mobility," size control, self-regulation, or the formulation of universal ethical codes (Larson, 1977). The various categories of jurists have developed separate associations, of which the corporations of advocates and notaries are the oldest and most powerful. However, differentiation and decentralization also are the rule within each category. Advocates and notaries are organized in highly autonomous local associations, which have relinquished few powers to the national federation. Judges associate with each other on the basis of their positions within the judicial hierarchy. Finally, the battle for control over "production by producers" (Abel, 1988) is not primarily a struggle between jurists and nonjurists. Conflicts over market position often are challenges between neighboring occupations *within* the world of jurists: advocates against notaries against jurists in nonprofit organizations, and so on.

## WHAT JURISTS DO

Membership in the bar (*balie/barreau*), which alone enjoys rights of audience in the courts, is reserved to jurists who are fully self-employed and who conform to the ideal of a legal profession (approximately 30 percent of all economically active jurists in 1984). The bar itself is divided into full advocates (70 percent) and apprentices (stagiaires—30 percent). In their external relations both groups operate as advocates (advocaten/avocats) and have the right to represent clients in court, but within the professional community (orde van advocaten/ordre des avocats) apprentices have the status of minors. The 7,500 advocates now in private practice are distributed among twenty-six local bars, although very unevenly. One in every three Belgian advocates belongs to the Brussels bar; nearly 60 percent practice in Brussels, Ghent, Antwerp, and Liège. Until 1967, advocates had to compete with a small number of *pleitbezorgers/avoués*—a soft version of the British solicitor.

Notaries (*notarissen/notaires*) are public office holders appointed by the Department of Justice. However, as an occupational group they claim the autonomy and status of a liberal profession. Sociologically they resemble advocates much more than civil service jurists. The function of the 1,200 notaries (5 percent of all practicing jurists) is to write, hold in trust, and deliver copies of contracts for the exchange and mortgage of land, wills, gifts, and marriage contracts. They also conduct public auctions of real estate and execute legacies. Finally, they advise about legal and financial affairs.

The careers of judges (*rechters/juges*) and prosecuting attorneys (*openbaar ministerie/ministères publics*) are closely intertwined. Both groups (which total 7 percent of jurists) are called by the same name: *magistratuur/ magistrature*.

The vast majority of jurists in government (15 percent of all practicing jurists) perform functions in the general administration (mostly national). A second group within this category are law teachers (in Belgium all types and levels of school, including "private" schools, are fully subsidized by the government). Both groups are civil servants.

By far the largest subgroup of jurists (approximately 40 percent) work in commerce, finance, industry, and private nonprofit organizations, but they are differentiated by function and degree of self-employment. The first variable divides this group into jurists practicing as lawyers in the narrow sense—house counsel (bedrijfsjuristen/juristes d'entreprise) and legal advisers in the private nonprofit sector—and jurists whose work is predominantly nonlegal (the larger subcategory). The other variable distinguishes a very large group of salaried employees from a tiny segment of legally trained employers or merchants. Privately employed lawyers are not subject to a professional code of ethics; they are responsible only to their employers.

Finally, there is a miscellaneous category of experts who lack formal credentials but perform legal functions: tax consultants, accountants, court and notary clerks, criminologists, and others. Some are included in the prevailing conception of legal personnel; others are not.

## SOCIOGRAPHY OF LEGAL PERSONNEL IN BELGIUM

### Quantitative Developments: Discontinuous Growth

In 1986 there were approximately 30,000 qualified jurists in Belgium, of whom more than 80 percent were economically active. Seen in relation to the total population, that is one jurist for 330 persons. In 1840 there were less than 1,800 legally trained people or one jurist for 2,300 persons. The jurist population thus has expanded considerably: sixteenfold in gross numbers, sevenfold in relation to the general population (see table 6.1).

The rate of change varied greatly during these 150 years. Three growth cycles can be discerned in the history of law school output (and in the accompanying increase or decrease of the jurist population) (see table 6.2). From 1875 to 1890 the annual output of law degrees rose considerably. This was followed by a very long period of decrease (1895–1932) and then stabilization at the level of 1890 (1932–1948). The second growth cycle was much shorter. There was a very high production of law graduates during the early 1950s. Again, this expansion was followed by a fall in output (1956–1963). The last growth cycle still is developing. At first the annual output of law school graduates increased spectacularly: from 496 in 1969 to 1,144 in 1975. Since then, production has stabilized but at such a high level that we may expect the jurist population to increase by half in the next fifteen years (see table 6.3).

The extraordinary growth of the jurist population conceals another development, however: there has been a real erosion of jurists as a proportion of university enrollment. Jurists were more than 20 percent of all persons with academic degrees in 1937, but they were 16 percent in 1961, and only 10 percent of all those graduating from a university in 1984 (see table 6.4).

Of course, figures do not speak for themselves: they must be confronted with other data if we want to understand patterns of quantitative development. The explanatory variables can be dichotomized into pull and push factors. Most research has been devoted to studying the elements that create conditions favorable to legal experts, generate business for jurists, and, thus, *pull* people into law schools and, subsequently, into legal occupations. These include the development of a market economy and the bureaucratization of political rule (Rueschemeyer, 1973: 5; Pashigian, 1977), legal activity (Grossman & Sarat, 1975), population increases (Abel, 1988), and the growth of state regulation (Pashigian, 1977). Various indices have been suggested: real gross national product, the number of active corporations and other measures of industrial and commercial activity, bankruptcies, automobile accidents, the divorce rate, the number and budgets of regulatory agencies, the number of laws and regulations, and the litigation rate. *Push* factors, by contrast, accelerate the influx of prospective students or jurists without the direct intervention of market demand. Measures that relax the entrance requirements for law schools and positive discrimination in the admission of students from minority groups are good examples.

More work needs to be done to understand both the production of lawyers and the demand for their services (Abel, 1988). This is not primarily a problem of gathering data. Many theoretical questions still have to be answered about the causal relation between variables. For example, does a rise in the volume of court cases pull more people into the legal profession, or does an increase in the number of lawyers lead to rising litigation rates? Why has an increase in the legal activity of notaries—238,041 notarized documents in 1899, 559,308 in 1968 (CRISP, 1974: 17)—been attended with a continuous decline in the number of notaries, with no concomitant loss of the original monopoly?

## Two Push Factors

There can be no doubt about the influence of two push factors in the spectacular increase in the number of jurists after 1970. In 1964 a major reform of the entrance requirements for higher education dramatically opened the doors of universities: many high-school programs that previously did not allow access to colleges and universities were promoted to college-preparatory status. This reform, which enabled many more eighteen-year-olds to attend university, had a particularly strong influence on the recruitment pattern of law schools. Classical (Latin and Greek) studies in high school were dropped as an admission requirement. The impact on law school output was felt six to seven years later: an average of 374 law degrees were awarded annually in the 1960s, 671 in 1970, 781 in 1971, and 909 in 1972 (see table 6.2).

A second push factor is related to the emancipation of disadvantaged groups. The dramatic rise in the yearly output of law degrees, from 404 in 1968 to 1,220 in 1982, must be attributed largely to the breakthrough of female students, who received only 16 percent of law degrees in 1968 but 37 percent in 1983 (see table 6.2). Between 1968 and 1983, the number of law degrees earned by men increased 109 percent, but the number earned by women rose 540 percent. In the period following World War II, the Flemish population also attained greater equality (Huyse, 1982). Table 6.5 clearly shows that the recent rise in law school output also expresses the greater participation of Flemish youth in university education in general and legal studies in particular. The Flemish represented 47.5 percent of law graduates in 1968 but 58.1 percent in 1983. (They were about 65 percent of the general population both years.) The combined effect of the two push factors is visible in the fact that the ratio of French-speaking male law graduates to Flemish female law graduates declined from 7.7 : 1 in 1968 to 1.3 : 1 in 1983.

## Older and Newer Types of Legal Experts

We learned in the preceding pages that the total body of legal expertise has vastly increased in Belgium. However, the incidence and rate of quantitative change vary substantially in the various occupations in which jurists are active. True, all branches have grown absolutely, but in proportion to general population, we find different types of development (see tables 6.6 and 6.7). One category of jurist—notaries—exhibited negative growth: there were 4,422 people per notary in 1841 and 8,000 in 1984. Until the 1960s the judiciary followed a somewhat similar pattern, from 7,350 people per judge in 1841 to 8,412 in 1960. This downward trend recently was reversed, when a major reform of the organization of judicial work dramatically increased the size of the judiciary. Three other branches undeniably display real growth. In the last 140 years the number of advocates grew eightfold in absolute terms and threefold relative to population. Jurists in government service realized a similar growth in less than fifty years (1937—1984). The fastest-growing occupation, however, is jurists in private employment, who numbered about 800 just before World War II but are about 10,000 today. Their breakthrough came in the 1950s. Almost 60 percent of the growth of the jurist population between 1947 and 1961 occurred in this branch, which expanded from about 1,500 to about 3,600, while the bar gained an additional 300 members.

The uneven development of the various occupations considerably modified their proportions of the jurist population. Looking at the distribution of jurists among practice settings (see table 6.7), we can see that the traditional categories (advocates, judges, and notaries) constituted more than three-fourths of the profession before 1940 but less than 45 percent in 1984. Jurists in private employment tripled their share in less than fifty years; they now are by far the largest category (about 40 percent of all jurists), followed by advocates (30 percent) and civil service jurists (about 15 percent).

One important consequence of this historical development is a major change in the size and type of the organizations within which most jurists practice. Before 1940, 80 percent of all jurists (advocates, notaries, and judges) worked alone most of the time. Today, 55 percent of all legally trained people unquestionably work in relatively large organizations, such as industrial, commercial, and financial firms and governmental agencies.

On the surface, the Belgian situation contrasts sharply with many common law countries, where most jurists are private practitioners—not salaried employees. It is questionable whether this signifies a substantial difference in the total amount of legal work accomplished and in the translation of legal functions into legal roles. Nevertheless, the margin for professional autonomy necessarily will be much smaller in Belgium than in some common law countries, given the preponderance of private and public salaried employment among jurists.

## Increasing Participation of Disadvantaged Groups

The first woman jurist in Belgium, Marie Popelin, graduated in 1888. Having been denied entry to the bar, she fought a long court battle, which aroused great public controversy. She lost her fight and became a popular leader in the early feminist movement.

Women were admitted to the bar in 1922. However, demolition of the formal barrier did not immediately bring many more women to the law schools. They remained between 1 and 4 percent of the jurist population until the early 1950s. The low proportion of women among all undergraduates before 1950 is only part of the explanation, for other university branches attracted many more women (see table 6.8). When the number of women undergraduates abruptly started to grow in the 1960s, the law schools again were slow to catch up.

The breakthrough came in the 1970s. Between 1970 and 1984 the absolute number of women jurists rose almost fourfold, and their proportion of the profession doubled to about 22 percent (see table 6.9). Extrapolating from the figures in tables 6.2 and 6.3, we may expect that women will constitute more than a third of all jurists in the early 1990s. However, the earlier attitude of women toward legal studies persists: law schools still attract a smaller proportion of women than do the other university schools and departments (except civil and agricultural engineering) (see table 6.8).

What discouraged many educated women from becoming jurists? Formal discrimination ended with the admission of women to the bar in 1922, the judiciary in 1947, and the office of notary in 1950. One explanation may be that women choose studies that lead to jobs women traditionally have held (psychology, pedagogy) or to careers, such as teaching, where discriminatory practices are thought to be limited. If so, the allocation of careers within law may be based on women's expectations about discrimination. A closer examination of the proportion of women jurists in the various practice settings suggests other selection criteria (see table 6.9). There are few women jurists among notaries or in industrial and commercial firms, banks, insurance companies, and estate handling firms. Compared to the proportion of women among law graduates, women jurists also are underrepresented in the judiciary and civil service but slightly overrepresented in nonprofit organizations, legal education, and the bar. Thus, we may hypothesize that women jurists "feel good" in occupations where a career can be discontinuous, part-time work is available and socially accepted, and status devaluation is most probable (law teaching, the bar, and jobs in non-profit organizations). They will be less comfortable in occupations that are high status (the judiciary, notary offices) and where a career must be continuous and work performed full time (in the industrial, commercial, and profit-oriented service sectors and the civil service). The distribution of women, then, probably is not the product of deliberate choices about particular forms of legal work but a gender-bound allocation of career opportunities.

What effects will these demographic changes have on the way legal functions are performed? It would be unwise to expect to see substantial effects from the entry of women within the next twenty years or so. Recently, the proportion of women with law school degrees who remain unemployed (voluntarily or involuntarily) has been higher than that of men law graduates (see table 6.10; also Bonte [n.d.: 26]); more also work part time and have discontinuous careers. These occupational characteristics seriously diminish the influence of women jurists on the profession as a whole. In addition, women jurists still lack full access to influential positions within each occupation: in 1983, women were 15.5 percent of all judges (257/1,659) but only 8 percent in the courts of appeal and 3 percent in the highest court. That year women were about 25 percent of all advocates but only 7 out of the 325 members of the local disciplinary councils and 1 out of the 26 heads of local bars.

In yet another way the composition of the jurist population begins to reflect general emancipatory processes in Belgian society. Until the 1960s the Dutch-speaking Flemings, although a demographic majority, were underrepresented in the major political, economic, and cultural spheres of the country. The French-speaking Walloons and inhabitants of Brussels also dominated many professional groups, not least because of their higher participation in university education. Flemings obtained only 42.5 percent of the law degrees awarded between 1956 and 1965, although they were about 65 percent of the general population. By 1984, however, Flemings obtained 62 percent of law degrees. As a result, Flemish jurists slowly are taking over elite positions within the bar, the Royal Federation of Notaries, and the Belgian Association of House Counsel. This may effect changes in the organization of legal work. Flemish jurists look more to Dutch and Anglo-American models for their professional mores than do their French-speaking colleagues. The result well could be a shift from a Latin to a northern European legal culture. Signs of such a shift can be found in the differences in substance and form between the regional laws (*decreten/décrets*) of the Vlaamse Raad and the Conseil Wallon (the "parliaments" of the northern and southern regions), the divergent jurisprudence of the Flemish and francophone chambers of the Raad van State/ Conseil d'Etat (highest administrative court in Belgium), and the writings of Flemish legal scholars.

## Class Origins Still Are Important

Class always has affected entry into the jurist population and allocation of law graduates to the various legal roles. The first threshold is access to legal studies. In 1965, 65 percent of all students at the University of Leuven Law School (which produces almost a third of all Belgian jurists) came from upper-class families (see table 6.11). The effects of positive discrimination (scholarships for working-class students and more flexible entrance requirements) are clearly visible in later years, which show a substantial decrease in the proportion of students from upper-class families and an even more pronounced rise in the participation of students with lower middle-class origins. This general trend was particularly strong between 1965 and 1973 but since then has slowed down or reversed, and the position of the lowest income group hardly changed. Law school today continues to draw from more privileged backgrounds than other university departments.

The class profile of jurists naturally reflects this situation. Advocates and notaries are even more privileged. Notaries display a particularly high degree of occupational heredity. Claeys (1974) surveyed a representative sample of Leuven law graduates in 1935, 1940, 1950, 1955, and 1960 and found that 67 percent of notaries and 41 percent of advocates had fathers with university degrees, 56 percent of notaries and 28 percent of advocates had grandfathers with university degrees, 43 percent of notaries and 14 percent of advocates had fathers in the same profession, and 18 percent of notaries and 3 percent of advocates had grandfathers in the same profession.

## LEGAL EDUCATION AND SOCIALIZATION: THE MAJOR ROLE OF LAW SCHOOLS

Studies of legal education shed light on such crucial processes as the creation of legal expertise, recruitment into the various legal roles and occupations, preservation of a fairly homogeneous self-image among the branches of the jurist population, and maintenance of the prevailing definition of the professional situation. Ever since 1835, a university degree has been a formal requirement for advocates and judges. From the early years of the Belgian state, a law school degree also permitted entry to the civil service. Only notaries did not need a full academic training until much later.

Socialization of prospective jurists was and is a multiphase process. It starts in the family. We know that 40 percent of all law students at the

University of Leuven in 1981 had upper- and upper-middle-class origins; many were related to a legally trained person. We may assume that in these cases the assimilation of images about lawyers will have started well before the student crosses the doorstep of the university. The law school is the second—and for most future jurists probably the major—socializing influence. The facts that law schools have a monopoly over formal legal training and that there are no subsequent state or bar examinations give those schools considerable weight. Certain characteristics of Belgian law schools increase their impact: legal studies take five years (two undergraduate, three graduate); many faculty members are only part-time teachers and bring to the classroom their professional experience as advocates, notaries, judges, bankers, and similar functionaries; students have no opportunities to take summer jobs in law firms or to work in a government or nonprofit law office and consequently are totally dependent on the image of lawyers and the legal system presented in the classroom.

Other features reduce the socializing influence of the law schools, however: first-year undergraduates start their legal studies immediately after they leave high school and, therefore, often have no strong commitment to the subject; Belgian students return home every weekend; experiences that might encourage anticipatory socialization (such as membership in prestigious law reviews, early job hunting or preparation for a bar examination) are not available.

The first job is the third important socializing agent. In two of the legal roles (advocate and notary) this occurs during a relatively long period of apprenticeship, as we will see later in this chapter.

## RECRUITMENT INTO LEGAL ROLES AND OCCUPATIONS

The allocation to legal roles is mediated by several steplike processes and intervening variables. Although we already have discussed who comes to law school, it is harder to know why they come. A study at the University of Leuven Law School suggests that many first-year students enroll because other subjects require quantitative skills they lack (De Neve, 1983).

In order to describe recruitment into legal roles during and after law school training, we may find it helpful to use Elliott's distinction between individual processes of choice and commitment and the selection mechanisms employed by the profession itself (Elliott, 1972: 75). "[T]he range of alternatives available to an individual is progressively limited until eventually choice takes place within a relatively narrow range" (ibid., 72). This process of reducing alternatives is affected by factors operating inside and outside the professional groups.

In all countries law school performance correlates with the type of law practice a graduate enters after leaving the university. In Belgium it has a much more direct effect: half of all first-year law students never earn a degree. There is no reason to assume that ascriptive characteristics significantly affect performance. Although students have a choice of courses only in their fifth (last) year, ascriptive elements, such as family background, may play a prominent role here.

The range of first jobs open to law school graduates is limited by a variety of factors. When the economy is stagnant and the output of newly graduated jurists is very high, as has been the case since 1970, obtaining *any* job is a victory. Getting *the* job one prefers often is postponed to better times. Law school performance is important, particularly for those who want to join private companies. Ascriptive elements are very influential for those who become advocates or notaries, however, as we will see later. The recruitment of judges and government jurists is based partly on examinations, partly on political patronage (Huyse, 1974). All cabinet ministers can influence who is recruited and promoted as a civil servant in the various administrative agencies that fall within their jurisdiction. They must, however, respect the principle of proportionality, which allocates civil service appointments among the partners of a coalition government. All this facilitates the emergence of political patronage in the recruitment of judges and civil service jurists.

## WEAK SUPPLY CONTROL

It is difficult to speak of a professional project of supply control among the jurist population as a whole. Many of the usual goals of such a project (the elimination of nonacademic modes of entry, the imposition of high standards of training, the introduction of formal compulsory university examinations) already were in place in the early days of the Belgian state. University reforms (which may have affected supply) were not the product of a professional strategy but partly the initiative of medical and law school faculties and partly the resolution of a struggle between the two principal adversaries in Belgium: those who perceived the secular state as the main agency in the production of legal and medical experts and the Catholic party, which defended the autonomy of the denominational University of Louvain. The role of jurists was limited by the absence of an overarching association, and jurists also were divided along the same lines as other political actors. Consequently, restrictions on the production of legal experts never originated *within* the jurist population but rather expressed the characteristics of the political and educational system as a whole. Entrance requirements were rigid, fees were very high, sociocultural forces discouraged women from attending the university, and there was no secondary or higher education in Dutch (Flemish) before 1935. It is not surprising that the number of law students increased dramatically when these hurdles disappeared one after another, starting in 1960.

## LAWYERING AS A LIBERAL PROFESSION: ADVOCATES AND NOTARIES

Most advocates and notaries work within the environment of a liberal profession. They are fully self-employed, they seek to control supply, and their associations have self-regulatory power granted by the state. A third occupational category, house counsel, recently has sought to obtain professional status. An association created at the end of the 1960s now contains half of the approximately 1,000 *juristes d'entreprise/bedrijfsjuristen*. Its short history is characterized by a continuous search for public and private measures that might accelerate the process of professionalization, such as official protection of the title of house counsel (a step toward monopoly and control over entry), self-regulation, and agreements with the bar that would allow house counsel to enter into partnerships with advocates.

### THE SIZE AND SUPPLY CONTROL PROBLEM

Advocates continuously have patrolled the borders of their profession. Their strategy was threefold: establishing and defending their exclusive rights of audience, systematically excluding foreign advocates, and controlling the "production of producers" who formally qualify for the bar. Advocates obtained exclusive rights of audience early in the nineteenth century, although some of the functions of client representation remained the province of pleitbezorgers/avoués. The first real threat to the monopoly surfaced during a general reform of procedural law in the 1960s. The (local) associations of advocates countered this attack by mobilizing their members and fellow advocates in Parliament. A compromise was reached: non-advocates could represent clients before the labor courts, but the role of the pleitbezorger/avoué was eliminated. However, the importance of exclusive rights of audience is being reduced as litigation becomes a smaller fraction of the market for legal services.

The exclusion of foreign advocates from the bar has become an important and difficult task since the birth of the European Economic Community (EEC) and its advocacy of "free" trade for service occupations. Legal technicalities still prevent noncitizens from entering the Belgian bar (unless they hold a Belgian degree), but foreign law firms have bypassed the obstacles by hiring Belgian advocates.

The third goal, controlling the production of qualified producers, has proved to be the most difficult to realize, particularly the efforts to regulate size. Since 1950, advocates twice have confronted a serious growth problem: contraction between 1955 and 1970 and an extraordinary expansion since 1975. Advocates tried to correct underpopulation through a sort of promotion campaign and overpopulation through various techniques of discouragement and an informal numerus clausus for apprentices, but these endeavors were quite unsuccessful. One reason was the absence of a strong national association of advocates, which was created only in 1968. Another is the absence of a bar examination. Advocates also were constrained by their own public rhetoric of "openness" and "free access" for all who qualify. Finally, law schools have little power to reduce or expand their enrollments at the behest of the profession even if they wish to do so, since many of the forces that determine the size of the student body are exogenous (Pashigian, 1977).

The problems that advocates encounter in regulating their numbers do not prevent them from influencing *who* can become an advocate, thereby fostering the homogeneity of the bar. The major screening device here is apprenticeship, which gives the bar a strong voice concerning occupational entry. The disciplinary council of the local bar examines each applicant for inscription on the roll of apprentices for incompatibilities and to ascertain whether the candidate's conduct is flawless. It is impossible to appeal from a negative decision of the council. The apprenticeship itself is a particularistic training environment. The master–pupil relationship, on which it is based, tends to invest the full members of the bar with great moral authority and, thus, with substantial control over entry to the profession. It also is a setting in which universalistic or meritocratic qualifications for recruitment and occupational selection easily can be replaced by such criteria as "social skills," "character," and "social reliability." As an apprentice, the young jurist has the status of a minor within the professional community and a precarious financial position. Background characteristics, such as parental assistance in obtaining access to clients and direct financial support, may ensure that only the "proper" candidates for full membership survive. Yet, apprenticeship no longer can be an effective selection device if the number of apprentices exceeds that of patrons (who must be full advocates with a minimum of seven years seniority), and that is precisely what happened after 1975. Too many prospective advocates now slip through the apprenticeship period without being properly supervised, and their entry soon may bring greater heterogeneity to the bar. Thus, it is possible that the mere size of the law school population, rather than changes in its social composition, is the real threat to the homogeneity of the bar.

The legal occupation that most closely fits the model of the "professional project" (Larson, 1977) is the notary. Notaries originally were not jurists and enjoyed little prestige. They gained status and autonomy during the Napoleonic period, when the notary was redefined as a public office (and a source of taxes and political patronage) with a large degree of professional freedom. During part of the nineteenth century an official nomination by a public authority was needed, but candidates then were selected on the basis of a "moral examination" by the professional elite. No formal training was required. Today a notary must obtain a law degree, serve an apprenticeship, and be appointed by the Department of Justice. Here both the quantitative and qualitative dimensions of supply control have been very effective (as table 6.6 and the earlier description of occupational heredity clearly show). The successful formula seems to be a combination of appointment by a public authority (with which the profession forms an intimate alliance), limitation (by that authority) of the number of notary offices (which is strictly tied to population growth), the maintenance of apprenticeship as a screening device, the requirement of extremely high payments by those taking over an existing practice, and, finally, the early creation of an overarching association. The notary's present share of the market for legal services is only partly based on the original monopoly (writing, preserving, and delivering copies of notarized documents); notaries increasingly hold themselves out as general advisers in legal affairs.

## APPRENTICESHIP AS A SOCIALIZATION AND RECRUITMENT PROCESS

After obtaining a law degree, those wishing to become advocates or notaries serve an apprenticeship (three years at the bar, one for notaries). During this period candidates undergo formal and informal training in two subroles: legal expert (e.g., how to represent a client in court) and entrepreneur (how to run an office). The patronage relationship with an older professional also maximizes the likelihood of socialization to a third subrole: member of the professional community.

To enroll as an apprentice at the bar seems to be a mere formality: the acolyte must swear allegiance to the constitution and laws and apply for inscription. However, we saw above that the disciplinary council of the local bar screens all applicants and that appeal is impossible. The members of the disciplinary council have unlimited discretion in defining the criteria for entry. Another hurdle is the search for a patron. Huyse and Cammaer (1982) found that in 1979, 25 percent of all applicants had to contact three or more advocates before they were accepted as apprentices. Ascriptive elements (such as kinship with lawyers) clearly affect such placements, which have an impact on the subsequent career of the apprentice.

In the United States, first jobs have a very strong influence on lawyer careers (Abel, 1988). That certainly is true for those Belgian lawyers who begin their careers as apprentices, which is based on sponsored, not contest, mobility. In Turner's (1961) definition, sponsored mobility is a process in which "the elite or their agents, who are best qualified to judge, call those individuals to elite status who have the appropriate qualities. Individuals do not win or seize elite status, but mobility is rather a process of sponsored induction into the elite following selection." Huyse and Cammaer (1982) found that the sponsored apprentices got the best and most powerful patrons, received a better training, were allocated more cases, and earlier obtained a decent share of the income they earned for their patron, while the non-sponsored apprentices were harassed with techniques of what Clark (1960) calls "cooling-out."

## PROFESSIONAL ASSOCIATIONS

The organizational structure of the bar and the notariat has three striking characteristics: extreme localism, considerable self-regulatory powers, and problematic interest intermediation between the two branches and governmental agencies and between advocates or notaries and external occupations (see fig. 6.1). Advocates (and to a lesser degree notaries) are organized in highly autonomous local associations, which share little power with the national federation. The self-regulatory powers of the local corporations of advocates and notaries were not acquired through lengthy strenuous efforts by the profession, as was the case for American lawyers. Rather, these corporate associations were created by the state and endowed with their various competences as early as 1803 (notaries) and 1810 (advocates). It is almost impossible to overestimate the range of powers that local corporations exercise; within their judicial district they formulate ethical codes, discipline violators, mediate conflicts between *confrères*, and organize part of the training of apprentices. The national organizations have only secondary powers: they may try to streamline ethical codes, they deliver services the local corporations cannot afford, and they represent them at the national and international levels. The national corporation of advocates has been forced by its constituent elements to work with a Malthusian interpretation of its competences.

The decentralization of the associations of advocates and notaries was unproblematic as long as state intervention in professional activities was limited and sporadic. The absence of a strong national association became a serious handicap as soon as these professions regularly had to articulate their interests before the government, in competition with other occupations, and the internationalization of legal work made supranational contacts essential. The notaries were the first to fill the gap: their national federation, created in 1891 (in the middle of the "organizational revolution") (Schmitter, 1979), was revived in 1946. The advocates were in a more difficult situation. Their official national association (Nationale Orde van Advocaten/Ordre Nationale des Avocats) emerged only in 1968 and immediately was confined to ephemeral activities. True, there is another much older national association—the *Verbond van Belgische advocaten/ Union des avocats belges* (1886)—but its membership is small, it has no public law status, and it never was able to overcome the autonomy of the local corporations.

## THE IMPACT OF RECENT DEVELOPMENTS IN LEGAL SERVICES DELIVERY

The demand for legal services has been modified recently in at least two important ways. Inexpensive legal aid for the less affluent has been requested with increasing frequency, and large bureaucratic organizations have multiplied their demands for expert advice concerning their legal contacts with individuals (as in the case of banking institutions, mail firms, and social security agencies), with other bureaucratic organizations (mainly government agencies, because of the rapid expansion of labor law, social security law, and economic regulations), and with corporate bodies on the international scene (because of the internationalization of governmental and commercial life). Both changes have led to transformations in the quantity and structure of supply.

Recent developments in legal aid have been analyzed by Breda (1983). Belgium has no state-supported system of public legal aid. Each local bar has a statutory obligation to provide representation to indigents (the pro deo system), a task usually performed by apprentices. The autonomy of local bar associations also extends to setting the income levels for free legal aid. In 1984 for the first time, the national government provided $800,000 to pay the pro deo work of apprentices ($10.08 per capita, compared to $3.20 in the United States). Law shops came into existence in the early 1970s, mostly in cities with a law school. They are staffed by volunteer law students and jurists but never succeeded in attracting the collaboration or even the sympathy of the bar associations. Their main function has been to articulate the issue of legal needs in the media and before policy makers. However, the greatest expansion occurred outside the state apparatus, the bar, and the law faculties. Private nonprofit organizations, such as trade unions and consumer movements, multiplied their activities in the field of legal aid. Labor unions, in particular, provide highly accessible, routinized, cost-effective legal services, which handle at least 100,000 cases a year (mostly rendering advice but also representing clients in labor court). Legal aid also is offered by local and national politicians (political patronage is widespread in Belgium) and by Public Assistance Agencies serviced and subsidized by local authorities. Breda (1983) concludes that Belgian legal aid combines characteristics that are very traditional (the pro deo system), Anglo-Saxon (the law shops), and Italian (clientelism and patronage).

The new demands, coming from large organizations, have been met by the organizations themselves, which have hired more jurists. Only a few law firms have emerged in the big cities, and American law firms have opened branch offices in Brussels.

Have there been meaningful changes in the conception of the lawyer's role? The most striking fact is the almost total absence of innovation on the part of advocates (still 30 percent of the profession). They could have used the law shops as ice-breakers (i.e., demand creators), as the British and Dutch private practitioners did, but they chose to fight them instead. They could have tried to reach agreements with other legal occupations to share the expanding markets. Again, advocates decided to antagonize these other occupations, sponsoring legislation that would have extended the advocates' monopoly to all legal advice. This conservation is difficult to understand. A more sympathetic attitude toward the legal aid movement, in particular, would have provided additional business for lawyers and enhanced the legal profession's reputation for altruism and the legitimacy of the legal system (Abel, 1988). Moreover, there was a very clear model: ten years earlier the Belgian medical profession succeeded in converting a major policy reform that made health care almost free into a mechanism for demand creation, without losing its professional autonomy.

The factors underlying the advocates' negativism are manifold. The Balkanization of the professional community into twenty-six local republics is responsible for the lack of a coherent strategy. However, there also is the fact that the bar elites, men in their forties and fifties, started their careers in the very comfortable market situation of the 1960s, when the bar was shrinking rapidly and demand was increasing. Consequently, they are well established in the market, monopolizing the most interesting clients (such as banking and insurance companies) and unmotivated to innovate. But profit margins are narrowing. Private firms and government agencies are hiring more jurists, who send advocates only the work that employed jurists cannot handle, namely, pleading a case in court. Even the elite members of the bar will learn the lesson soon: innovate or disappear, at least as a liberal profession. Notaries already have switched to demand creation, launching information campaigns, giving free advice to indigent people, and even "inventing" demands (such as the need for a cohabitation contract).

# CONCLUSION

With one qualified jurist for every 330 inhabitants, Belgium seems to rest on a web of legal expertise. However, several factors make it extremely difficult to determine the precise social significance of all the legal expertise and its recent spectacular growth. It certainly would be unwise to regard that growth exclusively as a response to the demand for jurists in society. The output of law schools also is the product of what Larson (1989) calls "the autonomous logic of the market for educational services." In the 1960s and 1970s the political debate about equality of educational opportunity led to a policy of increasing access to the university (including the law schools) for disadvantaged groups such as women, Flemish speakers, and lower-middle-class youngsters. This substantially augmented the production of jurists. Furthermore, law schools are not merely vocational; they also are seen as the source of a liberal education, a ticket to the culture of the higher strata. The ratio of population to jurists also must take account of the fact that many legally-trained persons now are women, who are more likely than male jurists to work part-time and have discontinuous careers. Finally, we should note that the extraordinary growth of the jurist population conceals the rapid decline in the proportion of undergraduates studying law.

The mere fact that jurists share a common education and practical training and speak the same technical language facilitates their collective mobilization for purposes of social engineering. Yet, what divides jurists in Belgium is much greater than what unites them. In the past the heterogeneity of occupational forms and of the legal work performed was reflected in and reinforced by the folk conception of what jurists do and, equally, by the self-definition of the professionals. Strict incompatibility rules guarded the boundaries between the various legal occupations. Lateral mobility was rare. Moreover, localism and functional specialization of associations reduced the capacity of jurists for unified, collective action. Recent changes in the demography of the group have added new sources of heterogeneity. The influx of women, of Flemish speakers, and of persons with lower-middle-class origins has substantially reduced the dominance of men, French speakers, and those from upper-class backgrounds.

Before 1940, 80 percent of all jurists practiced solo. Today, more than half of all economically active jurists are either employees in relatively large organizations or, among advocates, members of associations and partnerships. Thus, more jurists than ever before now experience the division of labor and the problems of working together with paralegal and nonlegal experts.

# TABLES

6.1. Total Number of Persons with Law or Notary Degree,[a] 1937–1985[b]

| Year | Total | Average yearly percent increase | Total economically active | Percent economically active | Population per jurist | Population per economically active jurist |
|------|-------|--------------------------------|---------------------------|-----------------------------|----------------------|-------------------------------------------|
| 1937 | 8,460 | — | 7,360 | 87 | 988 | 1,136 |
| 1947 | 9,358 | 1.1 | 8,143 | 87 | 909 | 1,045 |
| 1961 | 13,701 | 3.3 | 11,554 | 84.3 | 670 | 795 |
| 1970 | 15,803 | 1.7 | 13,463 | 85.2 | 611 | 717 |
| 1985[c] | (30,000) | (6.0) | (24,900) | (83) | (330) | (400) |

[a]Before 1969 a notary degree was received after two to four years of college and university training. Since 1969 a law degree is required before the year of notary training.

[b]Before 1937 the national census did not count degrees.

[c]Figures in parentheses are estimates.

Sources: 1937–1970—Department of Economic Affairs, National Census Reports; 1985—estimate.

6.2. Law Degrees, 1840–1984[a]

| Year | Total Number | Total Annual percent change | Men Number | Men Annual percent change | Women Number | Women Annual percent change | Percent of total |
|------|------|------|------|------|------|------|------|
| 1840 | 44  |     |     |     |     |     |     |
| 1850 | 90  |     |     |     |     |     |     |
| 1860 | 96  |     |     |     |     |     |     |
| 1865 | 98  |     |     |     |     |     |     |
| 1870 | 81  |     |     |     |     |     |     |
| 1875 | 136 |     |     |     |     |     |     |
| 1880 | 186 |     |     |     |     |     |     |
| 1885 | 185 |     | 184 |     | 1   |     | 0.5 |
| 1890 | 200 |     |     |     |     |     |     |
| 1895 | 150 |     |     |     |     |     |     |
| 1900 | 130 |     |     |     |     |     |     |
| 1905 | 129 |     |     |     |     |     |     |
| 1910 | 142 |     |     |     |     |     |     |
| 1920 | 184 |     |     |     |     |     |     |
| 1925 | 198 |     |     |     |     |     |     |
| 1926 | 196 | −1  |     |     |     |     |     |
| 1927 | 197 | 0.5 |     |     |     |     |     |
| 1928 | 205 | 4   |     |     |     |     |     |
| 1929 | 229 | 18  | 214 |     | 15  |     |     |
| 1930 | 240 | 5   | 225 |     | 15  |     | 6   |
| 1931 | 229 | −5  | 220 |     | 9   |     |     |
| 1932 | 222 | −3  | 211 |     | 11  |     |     |
| 1933 | 271 | 22  | 260 |     | 11  |     |     |
| 1934 | 272 | —   | 259 |     | 13  |     |     |
| 1935 | 350 | 29  | 325 |     | 25  |     |     |
| 1936 | 322 | −8  | 295 |     | 27  |     |     |
| 1937 | 317 | −2  | 301 |     | 16  |     |     |
| 1938 | 248 | −22 | 235 |     | 13  |     |     |
| 1939 | 246 | −1  | 228 |     | 18  |     |     |
| 1940 | 267 | 9   | 256 |     | 11  |     | 4   |
| 1941 | 241 | −10 | 226 |     | 15  |     |     |
| 1942 | 270 |     |     |     |     |     |     |
| 1943 | 279 |     |     |     |     |     |     |
| 1944 | 276 |     |     |     |     |     |     |
| 1945 | 284 |     | 264 |     | 20  |     | 7   |
| 1946 | 335 | 18  | 313 |     | 22  |     |     |
| 1947 | 340 | 1   | 314 |     | 16  |     |     |
| 1948 | 273 | −20 | 268 |     | 5   |     |     |
| 1949 | 417 | 53  | 379 |     | 38  |     |     |

6.2. (*continued*)

| | Total | | Men | | Women | | |
|---|---|---|---|---|---|---|---|
| Year | Number | Annual percent change | Number | Annual percent change | Number | Annual percent change | Percent of total |
| 1950 | 550 | 32 | | | | | |
| 1951 | 535 | −3 | 474 | | 61 | | |
| 1952 | 495 | −7 | 427 | −10 | 68 | 11 | |
| 1953 | 514 | 4 | 444 | 4 | 70 | 3 | |
| 1954 | 494 | −4 | 418 | −6 | 76 | 9 | |
| 1955 | 511 | 3 | 449 | 7 | 62 | −18 | 12 |
| 1956 | 495 | −3 | 436 | −3 | 59 | −5 | |
| 1957 | 474 | −4 | 410 | −6 | 64 | 8 | |
| 1958 | 435 | −8 | 380 | −7 | 55 | −14 | |
| 1959 | 418 | −4 | 364 | −4 | 54 | 2 | |
| 1960 | 415 | −1 | 364 | — | 51 | −5 | 12 |
| 1961 | 368 | −11 | 313 | −14 | 55 | 7 | |
| 1962 | 374 | 2 | 302 | −4 | 72 | 31 | |
| 1963 | 301 | −20 | 250 | −17 | 51 | −29 | |
| 1964 | 327 | 9 | 279 | 12 | 48 | −6 | |
| 1965 | 343 | 5 | 293 | 5 | 50 | 4 | 15 |
| 1966 | 358 | 4 | 301 | 3 | 57 | 14 | 16 |
| 1967 | 360 | — | 302 | — | 48 | −16 | 13 |
| 1968 | 404 | 12 | 340 | 13 | 64 | 33 | 16 |
| 1969 | 496 | 23 | 393 | 16 | 103 | 61 | 21 |
| 1970 | 671 | 35 | 509 | 30 | 162 | 57 | 24 |
| 1971 | 781 | 16 | 604 | 19 | 177 | 9 | 23 |
| 1972 | 909 | 16 | 706 | 17 | 203 | 15 | 22 |
| 1973 | 853 | −6 | 617 | −13 | 236 | 16 | 28 |
| 1974 | 977 | 15 | 714 | 16 | 263 | 11 | 27 |
| 1975 | 1,144 | 17 | 761 | 7 | 383 | 46 | 33 |
| 1976 | 1,188 | 4 | 768 | 1 | 420 | 10 | 35 |
| 1977 | 1,117 | −6 | 730 | −5 | 387 | −8 | 35 |
| 1978 | 1,060 | −5 | 711 | −3 | 349 | −10 | 33 |
| 1979 | 1,087 | 3 | 701 | −1 | 386 | 11 | 36 |
| 1980 | 1,118 | 3 | 709 | 1 | 409 | 6 | 37 |
| 1981 | 1,170 | 5 | 756 | 7 | 414 | 1 | 35 |
| 1982 | 1,220 | 4 | 783 | 3 | 437 | 6 | 36 |
| 1983 | 1,121 | −8 | 711 | −9 | 410 | −6 | 37 |
| 1984 | 1,205 | 7 | | | | | |

[a]1840–1935, 1942–1944—Belgians and foreigners; 1936–1941, 1945–1984—Belgians only.
*Sources:* 1840–1935—Department of Economic Affairs, *Annuaire Statistique de la Belgique*; 1936–1984—Universitaire Stichting/Fondation Universitaire, Dienst voor Universitaire Statistiek.

6.3. Law School Enrollment, 1936–1984[a]

| Year | Total Number | Total Annual percent change | Men Number | Men Annual percent change | Women Number | Women Annual percent change | Percent of total |
|---|---|---|---|---|---|---|---|
| 1935–1936 | 1,024 | | 947 | | 77 | | 8 |
| 1936–1937 | | | | | | | |
| 1937–1938 | 876 | | 823 | | 53 | | |
| 1938–1939 | | | | | | | |
| 1939–1940 | 739 | | 704 | | 35 | | |
| 1940–1941 | 832 | | 790 | | 42 | | 5 |
| 1941–1942 | 923 | | 884 | | 39 | | |
| | | | | | | | |
| 1945–1946 | 1,008 | | 958 | | 50 | | 5 |
| 1946–1947 | 1,148 | 14 | 1,070 | 12 | 78 | 56 | |
| 1947–1948 | 1,417 | 23 | 1,302 | 22 | 115 | 47 | |
| 1948–1949 | 1,740 | 23 | 1,546 | 19 | 194 | 69 | |
| 1949–1950 | 1,877 | 8 | 1,648 | 7 | 229 | 18 | |
| | | | | | | | |
| 1951–1952 | 1,832 | | 1,573 | | 259 | | |
| 1952–1953 | 1,788 | −2 | 1,544 | −2 | 244 | −6 | |
| 1953–1954 | 1,791 | 0.2 | 1,555 | 1 | 236 | −3 | |
| 1954–1955 | 1,750 | −2 | 1,533 | −1 | 217 | −8 | |
| 1955–1956 | 1,685 | −4 | 1,474 | −4 | 211 | −3 | 16 |
| 1956–1957 | 1,593 | −6 | 1,393 | −5 | 200 | −5 | |
| 1957–1958 | 1,507 | −5 | 1,313 | −6 | 194 | −3 | |
| 1958–1959 | 1,395 | −7 | 1,209 | −8 | 186 | −4 | |
| 1959–1960 | 1,294 | −7 | 1,107 | −8 | 187 | 0.5 | |
| 1960–1961 | 1,325 | 2 | 1,038 | −6 | 187 | — | 14 |
| 1961–1962 | 1,182 | −11 | 995 | −4 | 187 | — | |
| 1962–1963 | 1,132 | −4 | 957 | −4 | 175 | −6 | |
| 1963–1964 | 1,180 | 4 | 997 | 4 | 183 | 5 | |
| 1964–1965 | 1,221 | 4 | 1,025 | 3 | 196 | 7 | |

6.3. (*continued*)

| Year | Total | | Men | | Women | | |
|------|--------|--------|--------|--------|--------|--------|--------|
| | Number | Annual percent change | Number | Annual percent change | Number | Annual percent change | Percent of total |
| 1965–1966 | 1,341 | 10 | 1,127 | 10 | 214 | 9 | 16 |
| 1966–1967 | 1,491 | 11 | 1,231 | 9 | 260 | 21 | 17 |
| 1967–1968 | 1,847 | 24 | 1,462 | 19 | 385 | 48 | 21 |
| 1968–1969 | 2,321 | 26 | 1,811 | 24 | 510 | 32 | 22 |
| 1969–1970 | 2,866 | 24 | 2,239 | 24 | 627 | 23 | 22 |
| 1970–1971 | 3,036 | 6 | 2,329 | 4 | 707 | 13 | 23 |
| 1971–1972 | 3,327 | 10 | 2,487 | 7 | 840 | 19 | 25 |
| 1972–1973 | 3,572 | 7 | 2,534 | 2 | 1,038 | 24 | 29 |
| 1973–1974 | 3,907 | 9 | 2,692 | 6 | 1,215 | 17 | 31 |
| 1974–1975 | 3,980 | 2 | 2,649 | −2 | 1,331 | 10 | 33 |
| 1975–1976 | 3,914 | −2 | 2,585 | −2 | 1,329 | — | 34 |
| 1976–1977 | 3,807 | −3 | 2,512 | −3 | 1,295 | −3 | 34 |
| 1977–1978 | 4,069 | 7 | 2,744 | 9 | 1,325 | 2 | 33 |
| 1978–1979 | 3,993 | −2 | 2,580 | −6 | 1,413 | 8 | 35 |
| 1979–1980 | 4,106 | 3 | 2,648 | 3 | 1,458 | 3 | 36 |
| 1980–1981 | 4,119 | 0.3 | 2,671 | 1 | 1,448 | −1 | 35 |
| 1981–1982 | 4,216 | 2 | 2,679 | — | 1,537 | 6 | 36 |
| 1982–1983 | 4,184 | −1 | 2,607 | −3 | 1,577 | 3 | 38 |
| 1983–1984 | 4,394 | 5 | 2,692 | 3 | 1,702 | 8 | 39 |

[a]Students in last three years of law school only (approximate equivalent of American law school training); Belgian students only.

*Source:* Universitaire Stichting/Fondation Universitaire, Dienst voor Universitaire Statistiek.

6.4. Jurists in the University-Trained Population, 1937–1984

|  | 1937 | 1947 | 1961 | 1970 | 1984 |
|---|---|---|---|---|---|
| A. Total number of persons with university degree | 40,672 | 55,701 | 91,979 | 152,693 | 11,308[a] |
| B. Persons with law or notary degree | 8,460 | 9,358 | 13,701 | 15,803 | 1,205[b] |
| B/A as a percentage | 20.8 | 17.4 | 15.9 | 11.5 | 10.7 |

[a]Total number of persons graduating in 1984.
[b]Total number of persons graduating in law in 1984.
Sources: 1937–1970—National Census Reports; 1984—Dienst voor Universitaire Statistiek.

6.5. Law Degrees, by Language Group and Gender, 1956–1984[a]

| Year | French | | | Flemish | | | Flemish (%) | |
|---|---|---|---|---|---|---|---|---|
| | Men | Women | Total | Men | Women | Total | Men | Women |
| 1956 | 240 | 37 | 277 | 196 | 22 | 218 | 40 | 37 |
| 1965 | 171 | 34 | 205 | 122 | 16 | 138 | 36 | 32 |
| 1970 | 251 | 90 | 341 | 258 | 72 | 330 | 51 | 44 |
| 1975 | 292 | 185 | 477 | 469 | 198 | 667 | 62 | 52 |
| 1980 | 301 | 205 | 506 | 408 | 204 | 612 | 58 | 50 |
| 1983 | 284 | 188 | 472 | 429 | 222 | 651 | 60 | 54 |
| 1984 | | | 452 | | | 753 | | |

[a]Belgian graduates only.
Source: Dienst voor Universitaire Statistiek.

6.6. Number of Advocates, Judges, and Notaries, 1841–1984

| Year | Advocates | Decennial percent change | Population per advocate | Judges | Decennial percent change | Population per judge | Notaries[a] | Decennial percent change | Total |
|---|---|---|---|---|---|---|---|---|---|
| 1841 | 920 |  | 4,498 | 563 |  | 7,350 | 980 |  | 2,463 |
| 1850 | 813 | −12 | 5,444 | 537 | −5 | 8,242 | 990 | 1 | 2,340 |
| 1860 | 983 | 21 | 4,814 | 561 | 4 | 8,435 | 995 | 0.5 | 2,539 |
| 1870 | 1,149 | 17 | 4,428 | 569 | 1 | 8,942 | 1,011 | 2 | 2,729 |
| 1880 | 1,356 | 18 | 4,070 | 625 | 10 | 8,832 | 1,025 | 1 | 3,006 |
| 1890 | 1,892 | 40 | 3,208 | 666 | 7 | 9,112 | 1,052 | 3 | 3,610 |
| 1900 | 2,184 | 15 | 3,064 | 708 | 6 | 9,455 | 1,087 | 3 | 3,979 |
| 1910 | 2,399 | 10 | 3,095 | 767 | 11 | 9,679 | 1,112 | 2 | 4,278 |
| 1920 | 2,132 | −11 | 3,473 | 861 | 12 | 8,600 | 1,132 | 2 | 4,125 |
| 1930 | 3,023 | 42 | 2,677 | 820 | −5 | 9,868 | 1,172 | 4 | 5,015 |
| 1940 | 3,694 | 22 | 2,245 | 813 | −1 | 10,202 | 1,134 | −3 | 5,641 |
| 1950 | 3,297 | −11 | 2,625 | 1,116 | 37 | 7,754 | 1,128 | −1 | 5,541 |
| 1960 | 3,579 | 9 | 2,564 | 1,091 | −2 | 8,412 | 1,164 | 3 | 5,834 |
| 1970 | 3,827 | 7 | 2,521 | 1,586 | 45 | 6,085 | 1,202 | 3 | 6,615 |
| 1984 | 7,504 | 96[b] | 1,313 | 1,669 | 5[b] | 5,903 | 1,226 | 2[b] | 10,399 |

[a]Before 1969 notaries did not need a full law degree but received a shorter legal training.

[b]Percent change over fourteen years.

Sources: 1840–1970—Van Houtte and Langerwerf (1977: 33–37). 1984—Nationale Orde van Advocaten, Ministry of Justice, Koninklijke Federatie van Belgische Notarissen.

6.7. Distribution of Jurists in Practice Settings, 1937–1984

| | 1937 | | 1947 | | 1961 | | 1970 | | 1984 | |
|---|---|---|---|---|---|---|---|---|---|---|
| | Number | Percent | Number | Percent | Number | Percent | Number | Percent | Number | Percent |
| A. Advocates | 3,627 | 49.3 | 3,309 | 40.6 | 3,641 | 31.5 | 3,827 | 28.4 | 7,504 | 31.3 |
| B. Jurists in private employment | 1,755 | 23.9 | 1,540 | 18.9 | 3,648 | 31.6 | 4,458 | 33.1 | 13,600 | 56.7 |
| C. Jurists in government employment (judges excluded/educators included) | | | 1,052 | 12.9 | 2,008 | 17.4 | 2,390 | 17.8 | | |
| D. Judges | 813[a] | 11.0 | 1,116[b] | 13.7 | 1,091[c] | 9.4 | 1,586 | 11.8 | 1,669 | 6.9 |
| E. Notaries | 1,165 | 15.8 | 1,128 | 13.8 | 1,166 | 10.1 | 1,202 | 8.9 | 1,226 | 5.1 |
| Total | 7,360 | 100.0 | 8,145 | 100.0 | 11,554 | 100.0 | 13,463 | 100.0 | 24,000 | 100.0 |
| Total of "classical" legal professions (A + D + E) | 5,605 | 76.1 | 5,553 | 68.1 | 5,898 | 51.0 | 6,615 | 49.1 | 10,399 | 43.3 |

[a]Figure is for 1940.
[b]Figure is for 1950.
[c]Figure is for 1960.

*Sources:* Advocates and notaries: 1937–1970—*Annuaire Statistique;* 1984—Nationale Orde van Advocaten. Judges: 1937–1970—Van Houtte and Langerwerf (1977: 33); 1984—Ministry of Justice. Jurists employed by government: 1947, 1961, 1970—National Census Reports. Jurists in private firms and government: 1937, 1984—figures are total minus categories A + D + E. Jurists in private firms: 1947, 1961, 1970: figures are total minus categories A + C + D + E. Total: 1937–1970—National Census Reports; 1984—estimate.

6.8. Women in University-Trained Population, 1937–1983

| Degree | Percent women | | | | |
|---|---|---|---|---|---|
| | 1937 | 1947 | 1961 | 1970 | 1983[a] |
| Law | 1.7 | 3.5 | 7.9 | 11.3 | 36.6 |
| Philosophy and arts | 16.8 | 27.8 | 39.3 | 40.4 | 61.7 |
| Sciences | 14.6 | 19.1 | 29.5 | 25.8 | 45.8 |
| Medicine and other health, sciences ... | 4.3 | 9.6 | 15.2 | 23.1 | 42.1 |
| Civil and agricultural engineering | 0.2 | 0.4 | 0.6 | 1.5 | 12.5 |
| Social sciences, economics | 4.2 | 6.5 | 10.8 | 15.1 | 31.2 |
| Psychology, pedagogy | 24.8 | 31.9 | 45.6 | 47.9 | 58.2 |

[a]Percentage of women graduating in 1983

*Sources:* 1937–1970—National Census Reports; 1983—Dienst voor Universitaire Statistiek.

6.9. Women Jurists in the Various Practice Settings, 1961–1983

| Categories | 1961 Number | 1961 Percent | 1970 Number | 1970 Percent | 1983 Number | 1983 Percent |
|---|---|---|---|---|---|---|
| A. Advocates | 286 | 8.0 | 500 | 13.4 | 1,751 | 24.0 |
| B. Lawyers in private employment | | | | | N.A. | N.A. |
|   Primary sector | 0 | — | 2 | 3.4 | | |
|   Secondary sector | 29 | 3.1 | 48 | 5.0 | | |
|   Tertiary sector | | | | | | |
|   Commercial, banking, insurance, estate handling, and transport firms | 83 | 4.6 | 129 | 5.6 | | |
|   Nonprofit organizations | 14 | 5.8 | 34 | 13.0 | | |
|   International organizations | 9 | 7.9 | 18 | 11.0 | | |
| C. Employment by government | | | | | N.A. | N.A. |
|   General administration | N.A. | N.A. | 114 | 6.8 | | |
|   Education | 87 | 19.9 | 157 | 23.4 | | |
| D. Judges | 19 | 1.6 | 73 | 4.6 | 246 | 14.7 |
| E. Notaries | 4 | 0.3 | 12 | 1.0 | 44 | 3.6 |
| Total | 637 | 5.9 | 1,273 | 9.4 | N.A. | N.A. |

*Sources:* Advocates: 1961—CRISP (1971); 1970—Estimate; 1983—Nationale Orde van Advocaten. Lawyers in private and government employment: National Census Reports. Judges: communication from Ministry of Justice. Notaries: communication from Koninklijke Federatie van Belgische Notarissen.

6.10. University Graduates with Job, 1961 and 1970 (Percent)

| | 1961 | | 1970 | |
|---|---|---|---|---|
| Degree | Men | Women | Men | Women |
| Law | 91.1 | 63.8 | 91.9 | 71.4 |
| Philosophy and arts | 90.8 | 76.6 | 91.9 | 77.1 |
| Sciences | 94.3 | 79.1 | 93.9 | 80.9 |
| Medicine and other health sciences | 95.3 | 78.6 | 95.8 | 81.4 |
| Civil and agricultural engineering | 85.0 | 70.0 | 87.0 | 65.0 |
| Social sciences, economics | 91.9 | 63.2 | 92.0 | 67.9 |
| Psychology, pedagogy | 89.9 | 72.4 | 91.6 | 74.5 |

*Source:* National Census Reports.

6.11. Social Stratification of Law Students[a] and All Undergraduates at University of Leuven, 1965–1981 (Percent)

| | Law students | | | |
|---|---|---|---|---|
| Occupation of father | 1965 | 1973 | 1981 | All undergraduates, 1981 |
| *Upper* (occupations requiring college or university degree, employers of 500 or more, top managers in public and private sector ...) | 45.3 | 28.9 | 32.9 | 21.8 |
| *Upper-middle* (junior-high-school teachers, employers of 500 or fewer, chief and senior employees ...) | 19.3 | 25.8 | 18.1 | 17.2 |
| *Lower-middle* (middle-rank clerks, primary-school teachers, artisans, farmers, skilled manual workers ...) | 20.4 | 27.9 | 31.3 | 38.5 |
| *Lower* (lower-rank clerks, small shopkeepers, shop assistants, servants and waiters, unskilled manual workers ...) | 15.0 | 17.3 | 17.4 | 22.5 |

[a](Belgian) students in last three years of legal studies and last two years in criminology.
*Source:* Personal communication from I. De Lanoo, Center for the Study of Higher Education, Leuven.

# FIGURE

| | *Orde van advocaten/Ordre des avocats* | *Kamer van notarissen/Chambre des notaires* |
|---|---|---|
| I. Name of principal professional association | | |
| 1. Territorial base | Judicial district | Judicial district |
| 2. Date of creation | 1810 | 1804 |
| 3. Origin | Created by the state | Created by the state |
| 4. Number | 26 | 26 |
| 5. Corporate status? | Yes | Yes |
| 6. Membership compulsory? | Yes | Yes |
| 7. Authority | Self-regulatory power, licensed by the state (formulation of ethical codes, disciplining of all violators, regulation of conflicts between advocates, organization of apprenticeship, local interest intermediation, etc.) | Self-regulatory power, licensed by the state (formulation of ethical codes, disciplining of small violations, regulation of conflicts between notaries, organization of apprenticeship, etc.) |
| 8. Structure | Chairman/general assembly/disciplinary council/chamber of young advocates | Chairman/general assembly/disciplinary chamber |
| II. National association | | |
| 1. Name | *Nationale orde van advocaten/Ordre national des avocats* | *Koninklijke federatie van Belgische notarissen/Fédération royale des notaires de Belgique* |
| 2. Date of creation | 1968 | 1891–1946 |
| 3. Origin | Created by the state | Created by the profession |
| 4. Corporate status? | Yes | No |

| | | |
|---|---|---|
| 5. Membership | The only members are the local corporate associations | Notaries of local associations automatically become members of national federation |
| 6. Authority | Unification of ethical codes/articulation and aggregation of common interests (de jure representational monopoly before the government) | Articulation and aggregation of common interests (de facto representational monopoly)/professional postuniversity training |
| 7. Structure | Dean/general assembly of local chairmen | General assembly of local chairmen |
| III. Other national associations | | |
| 1. Name | *Verbond van Belgische advocaten/Union des avocats belges* | |
| 2. Date of creation | 1886 | |
| 3. Origin | Created by the profession | |
| 4. Membership compulsory? | No | |
| 5. Activities | Articulation of material and moral interests | |
| IV. International associations | 1. *Internationale unie van advocaten/Union internationale des avocats* (Brussels, 1927) | *Union internationale du notariat latin* (1952) |
| | 2. *Consultatieve commissie van de balies van de Europese Gemeenschap/Commission consultative des barreaux de la Communauté Européenne* (Brussels, 1960) | |

Fig. 6.1. Professional associations.

## NOTES

I am grateful to Robert Dingwall and Filip Reyntjens for their comments on an earlier version of this chapter.

1. The degree lic. juris (dr. juris before 1971) is obtained after five years of university training in one of the seven Belgian law faculties. Students enter university at the age of eighteen or nineteen.

## REFERENCES

Abel, Richard L. 1988. "United States: The Contradictions of Professionalism," in Richard L. Abel and Philip S. C. Lewis, eds., *Lawyers in Society*, vol. 1: *The Common Law World*, chap. 5. Berkeley, Los Angeles, London: University of California Press.

Bonte, André. n.d. *Universitaire studies in een economisch recessieklimaat [University Training in a Time of Economic Recession]*. Ghent: Rijksuniversiteit.

Breda, Jef. 1983. "Legal Aid in Belgium," 4 *Nieuwsbrief voor nederlandstalige rechtssociologen* 360–361.

Claeys, Urbain. 1974. *Universitair onderwijs als mobiliteitskanaal [University Education as a Channel for Upward Mobility]*. Louvain: Universitaire Pers.

Clark, Burton R. 1960. "The 'Cooling-Out' Function in Higher Education," 65 *American Journal of Sociology* 569–576.

Centre de Recherche et d'Information Socio-Politique (CRISP). 1971. *Le monde des avocats*. Brussels: CRISP.

———. 1974. *Le monde des notaires*. Brussels: CRISP.

De Neve, Hubert. 1983. *Profiel van de opleiding in de rechtsgeleerdheid en in de criminologie [Law School and Criminology Students]*. Louvain: Dienst Universitair Onderwijs.

Elliott, Phillip. 1972. *The Sociology of the Professions*. London: Macmillan.

Grossman, Joel J., and Austin Sarat. 1975. "Litigation in the Federal Courts: A Comparative Perspective," 9 *Law & Society Review* 321–346.

Huyse, Luc. 1974. "Patronage en makelarij in het Belgisch benoemingsbeleid [Patronage in the Civil Service]," 10 *Civis Mundi* 222–229.

———. 1982. "Political Conflict in Bicultural Belgium," in Arend Lijphart, ed., *Conflict and Coexistence in Belgium*, pp. 107-126. Berkeley, Los Angeles, London: University of California Press.

Huyse, Luc, and Hugo Cammaer. 1982. "Recrutering en selectie in de Belgische advocatuur [Recruitment and Selection of the Belgian Bar]," in André Hoekema and Jean Van Houtte, eds., *De rechtssociologische werkkamer*, pp. 41–63. Deventer: Van Loghum.

Larson, Magali Sarfatti. 1977. *The Rise of Professionalism: A Sociological Analysis*. Berkeley, Los Angeles, London: University of California Press.

————. 1989. "The Changing Functions of Lawyers in the Liberal State: Reflections for a Comparative Analysis," in Richard L. Abel and Philip S. C. Lewis, eds., *Lawyers in Society*, vol. 3: *Comparative Theories*. Berkeley, Los Angeles, London: University of California Press.

Pashigian, B. Peter. 1977. "The Market for Lawyers: The Determinants of the Demand for and Supply of Lawyers," 20 *Journal of Law and Economics* 53–85.

Rueschemeyer, Dietrich. 1973. *Lawyers and Their Society*. Cambridge, Mass.: Harvard University Press.

Schmitter, Phillipe. 1979. "Modes of Interest Intermediation and Models of Societal Change in Western Europe," in Phillipe Schmitter and Gerhard Lehmbruch, eds., *Trends Towards Corporatist Intermediation*, pp. 63–94. London: Sage.

Turner, Ralph. 1961. "Modes of Social Ascent Through Education: Sponsored and Contest Mobility," in Albert M. Halsey, ed., *Education, Economy and Society*, pp. 121–139. New York: Free Press.

Van Houtte, Jean, and Etienne Langerwerf. 1977. *Sociografische gegevens voor een studie van het gerechtelijk systeem [Sociographic Data for the Study of the Legal System]*. Antwerp: Kluwer.

# 7

# The French Bar: The Difficulties of Unifying a Divided Profession

## ANNE BOIGEOL

Until recently, French social scientists rarely were inclined to turn their attention to lawyers. An examination of works published on the legal profession reveals that most have been written by members of the profession themselves and constitute firsthand accounts, reflections on the state of the profession, and historical frescoes. Only since the 1970s have a few scholarly studies by sociologists and historians begun to appear. This chapter presents the current state of knowledge on the legal profession in France.

A discussion of legal professions, or lawyers, in comparative perspective cannot proceed without first raising certain definitional questions. A "lawyer," in the American sense of the term, has no real equivalent in France or in most other European countries, since an American lawyer's sphere of activity exceeds that of the French avocat and includes functions performed by other members of the French legal profession, such as the notary. The problem raised in translating the term "lawyer" is a lesson in the cultural and social specificity of concepts: the literal translation of "lawyer" in French is "lawman" (homme de loi) or even jurist, but those terms refer more to a formal qualification than a profession. Hence, the total body of jurists includes law professors as well as different categories of legal practitioner: avocats (hereafter referred to as "lawyers"), magistrates, notaries, avoués (hereafter referred to as "solicitors"), house counsel, and so on. While jurists as a whole constitute a coherent group with a specific internal structure and an implicit hierarchy, the term nevertheless embraces a set of very different professions. Rather than treating the entire group at once, as has been done in the study of the Belgian legal profession (Huyse, this volume, chap. 6)—whose internal divisions closely resemble those in France—the following overview will survey this diversity before going on to examine more fully the profession of lawyers in France.

# THE LAWYER: A JURIST AMONG OTHERS

The diversity observed among different legal professions pertains not only to different functions but also to different professional statuses. In this respect, one might distinguish among different legal professionals according to whether they receive a salary from an employer under the terms of a work contract. The first category of salaried professionals are those paid by the state—the magistrates (*magistrats*)—including both the judges (juges) who render decisions and the prosecutors (*procureurs*) who defend society and ask the judges to apply the law. Since 1965 the clerks of the court (greffiers), who assist the judge in administering the court, have been members of this salaried group. Salaried legal professionals in the private sector include those employed in offices of house counsel of corporations and insurance companies (juristes d'entreprise) and the notary clerks (*clercs de notaires*). Nonsalaried legal professionals practice as liberal professionals, the significance of which will be discussed below. Among them are the lawyers (avocats), the legal counselors who give advice, draft legal documents, and represent clients before administrative agencies and the commercial court (conseils juridiques), and a certain number of professionals who are also ministerial officers, which means that they enjoy a monopoly, in exchange for which they may not refuse their assistance to those who seek it. This last group includes the solicitors of the appeals court (avoués), who advise litigants before this court and draft the written documents, and the lawyers (avocats) of the Conseil d'Etat and the Cour de Cassation (French equivalents of the Supreme Court), whose role is to argue and to conduct the case before the high courts. Certain ministerial officers also are public officials in that they exercise state power. This is true of the notaries (notaires), whose special task is to authenticate documents that individuals either desire to submit to them or are required to do so, the bailiffs (huissiers de justice), who are responsible for notifying individuals of proceedings in which they are involved and for executing judicial decisions, and the clerks (greffiers) of the commercial courts.

Ministerial officers have a position inherited directly from the Old Regime. Prior to the French Revolution of 1789, the king sold offices responsible for public functions, including juridical and judicial duties (but excluding the position of avocat). These positions had become venal: they could be sold or bequeathed, like property. Notaries, bailiffs, clerks of the court, and magistrates bought their "position" or "office." The revolution abolished venal offices, and magistrates were compensated for the loss. At first they were elected; after 1800, they were appointed by the government, which paid them. However, this hardly changed the situation of the other legal professions. In fact, bailiffs, clerks of the court, and notaries had the exclusive power to perform certain legal procedures and therefore had a guaranteed clientele, which itself gave value to the position. After the revolution, the titles of notary, bailiff, and clerk of the court were taken off the market, but the office-holder obtained the right to pass his title to his successor. Only the state could confer the title, but it generally conferred it on the person recommended by the former office-holder. The right to pass on one's title, therefore, acquired a value that replaced the price of the office. This system remains in effect today for notaries, bailiffs, and clerks of the commercial courts, solicitors of the appeals courts, and lawyers of the Conseil d'Etat and the Cour de Cassation.

This mode of operation makes these professions particularly inaccessible. The number of positions is restricted by a quota (numerus clausus). Only the state can decide to create or eliminate offices. As a rule, an office is abolished when there no longer is a candidate for the position. Thus, the decrease in the number of offices held by notaries and bailiffs (see table 7.1) corresponds to the elimination of offices located in rural areas or small towns. In contrast, the relatively small number of offices at the top of the legal pyramid (solicitors of the appeals courts, lawyers of the Conseil d'Etat and of the Cour de Cassation) or in particular sectors (clerks of the commercial courts) remains relatively stable. The most remarkable case is that of the lawyers of the Conseil d'Etat and the Cour de Cassation, whose number has remained at sixty since 1817! However, despite the restriction on the number of *posts*, a rise in the number of *professionals* is observed in all the legal professions. Whereas the office-holder once had to be a physical person, ministerial officers now may join together into a professional civil society, according to a law passed in 1966.[1] Thus, it is the corporation which holds the office or title. This new form of responding to the demands of a more collective professional practice has permitted some expansion of recruitment. Nevertheless, access remains very difficult. Aside from the obvious financial requisites, the acquisition of a post is contingent on the completion of an assistantship, success in an examination, and, in most cases, a university degree. Having reviewed the diversity of legal professions, I will turn my attention to the avocats or lawyers (in the French sense of the term), noting, where appropriate, the ties that bind them to other members of the legal profession.


## THE LAWYER: SEVERAL DEFINITIONS

Defining a lawyer in France is not as easy as it may seem at first glance; rather, there are several definitions, depending on which aspect of the profession is emphasized. Lawyers may be defined by their positions in the social hierarchy, by the formal stipulations that protect their titles, by their institutional positions, or by the nature of their activities.

## A SOCIAL POSITION

The profession of lawyer refers not only to a technical competence but also to a position in the social hierarchy. Law is a highly esteemed profession, which enjoys considerable social capital. This prestige was, and is, associated with its status as a liberal profession. "The profession of lawyer is a liberal and independent profession" according to the law of 31 December 1971, which reformed certain legal and judicial professions. Defining a liberal profession is a delicate and strategic operation.[2] An eminent jurist maintains that "the liberal professions are characterized more by a spirit than by a statute" (Savatier, 1966: 458). According to the *Grand Larousse Dictionary of the French Language*, "a liberal profession is a profession based on intellectual work effected in the absence of a relationship of subordination between the person who performs the work and the person for whom the work is performed, the remuneration for which, as a rule, is not commercial or speculative in nature." Thus, a liberal profession is defined more by what it is not—the absence of a relationship of dependence, a system of remuneration that differs from a salary or a commercial system of profit—than by what it is.

The difficulty of defining a liberal profession may be due to the implicit meaning of this concept as a social classification of individuals. In the hierarchical structure of occupational categories, the liberal professions occupy a position of dominance by virtue of their economic and symbolic capital (Bourdieu, 1980: 140–141). Traditionally, there were only a few liberal professions: lawyers, notaries, and physicians. Today, numerous professions have appropriated the legal and fiscal status of a liberal profession, resulting in a certain inflation, and hence devaluation, of the term. However, while professions like medicine also can be performed by salaried employees, and the title of notary is defined just as much by its bearer's capacity to act as a ministerial officer, the lawyer remains the archetype of a liberal profession. Yet the profession of lawyer is defined not only by social position and legal status but also by title.

## A PROTECTED TITLE

A certain number of conditions must be fulfilled in order for one to become a lawyer. First of all, one must hold the university degrees required by law: a minimum of a masters in law awarded by the university after four years of study and a certificate of legal aptitude awarded by a specialized professional training center after a year of practical training. Next, it is necessary to take an oath before the court, which constitutes a charter of good conduct with respect to the profession, judicial institutions, and society.[3] Finally, one must belong to a bar, that is, a professional organization connected to the judiciary.

## AN INSTITUTIONAL POSITION

Lawyers also may be defined by their institutional position as auxiliaries of justice (*auxiliaires de justice*), which means that they participate in "the administration of justice, in which they are the partners as well as the guarantors" (Law of 31 December 1971). This also means that although lawyers do not provide a public service, as notaries do, they are connected to public law. From the perspective of organizational sociology the term "auxiliaries" confers an ambiguous institutional position. The auxiliary, according to the dictionary, is one who assists but is not always indispensable. This ambiguity can create problems, especially with respect to the relation between lawyers and magistrates (CSA, 1982).

## LAWYERS: AN ACTIVITY IN THE PROCESS OF BEING REDEFINED

A final way of defining lawyers is by the nature of their activity. The lawyer is that member of the legal profession who represents and defends litigants before the courts and who advises, consults, and drafts legal documents. These are the functions performed by the lawyer today, but they differ considerably from those performed at the beginning of the century and even twenty years ago. A brief historical digression will show that changes in the scope of the lawyer's functions are at the heart of recent transformations of the profession.

### THE LAWYER'S FUNCTIONS AS AN EXPRESSION OF DIVERGENT PROFESSIONAL INTERESTS

Until 1971, when a litigant wished to initiate a legal proceeding (e.g., divorce), it was necessary to engage the services of two professionals: the solicitor (avoué), who would advise the client, and the lawyer, who would argue the case in court. The solicitor was responsible both for managing the different stages of the case and for informing the magistrates in writing of the client's claims; the solicitor acted in the name of the client. Lawyers, in contrast, spoke only in their own names, and what they said did not implicate their clients. Until the end of the nineteenth century, these two professions had exclusive rights of access to the judicial forum.

At the beginning of the twentieth century, the lawyers, who had a monopoly of rights of audience before the courts, allowed other occupations to intrude, which later were to become competitors in the areas of business and labor law. "The lawyers of the upper bourgeoisie considered that they could not appear before the inferior jurisdictions, such as the commercial court and the *conseil des prud'hommes* [a body that hears labor disputes] or justices of the peace [whose jurisdiction is petty disputes and misdemeanors]" ("Caldus," 1969: 150). Occupations emerged whose members filled the vacancy left by the bourgeois lawyers. The *agréé* of the commercial courts is an example. At first, the agréé was merely a private party who had obtained permission from the commercial court to appear before it on behalf of the litigant. The agréé combined the role of the solicitor with that of the lawyer, whose involvement was not, and still is not, required in this jurisdiction. The agréés obviously did not enjoy a monopoly, but their acceptance by the court recommended them to the prospective litigant. This profession, which arose de facto, obtained legal status in 1941 and ultimately was integrated into the new profession of lawyer in 1971. In other instances, nonprofessionals acted in the absence of the auxiliaries of justice—an example is trade union delegates before the conseil des prud'hommes. Finally, the bar's hostility toward lawyers who engaged in counseling rather than advocacy and the fact that lawyers long had preferred to remain aloof from economic life created conditions favorable to the development of a new professional category, the legal advisors (conseils juridiques) (Trouillat, 1979). This profession, which was barely regulated, catered to a market that turned out to be very important: advising the economic and financial world.

## THE HISTORY OF A REFORM: LAWYERS AND OTHERS

After World War II, this situation began to worry some lawyers, who found that the narrow judicial market did not offer sufficient scope for their energies and who decried the competition of an unregulated profession like the legal advisors. In 1952 five members of Parliament, who also were lawyers, drafted a bill to establish a monopoly of legal counseling for the benefit of the lawyer and several of the organized legal professions (law professors, notaries, and solicitors) but excluding legal advisors. This protectionist impulse reveals the concern on the part of a profession that seeks to reinforce its specificity—only lawyers have the legitimacy and competence to give legal advice in the face of rising competition. A decade later, when it had proved impossible to prevent legal advisors from giving consultations, the Association nationale des avocats (ANA) proposed to incorporate them, with certain conditions, into the "Great Profession" modeled after that of the American lawyer. The ANA aimed to regroup the entire body of legal and judicial professions: solicitors, lawyers, agréés of the commercial courts, and legal advisors. Notaries were excluded because they had been delegated "state authority which they enjoy in the authentication of legal documents, such delegation of state power being incompatible with the principle of absolute independence which the larger profession had to protect in its dealings with the state" (ANA, 1967: 601).

In place of the "excessive complexity" arising from the redistribution of tasks to several professions, the "anarchy of structures," the resulting "feeling of insecurity" on the part of the litigant, and the "artisanal" nature of work practices, a single "judicial and juridical" profession of a "liberal" nature was proposed, which would enjoy a broad monopoly. The creation of such a monopoly was to hold together a combination of professions, among which relations had not always been harmonious. In particular, relations between lawyers and both solicitors and legal advisors often were characterized by contempt (ANA, 1967; Trouillat, 1979). The establishment of a monopoly, created "in the service of justice" and of the litigant, would ensure control of the judicial and juridical market and avoid the unchecked growth of legal professionals. Defense and representation, legal consultation, and the drafting of legal documents all were to be subject to this monopoly (although the last would be shared with notaries).

This attempt to establish a great profession failed in part during the parliamentary debates. The outcome was the fruit of many compromises: the new profession of lawyer excluded the legal advisors but did not gain a monopoly on consultation, which was to remain completely open. It is not possible to analyze here the reasons for the failure of this plan. Some have emphasized technical problems: the difficulty of delimiting legal consultation; the incompatibility of the commercial form, often assumed by legal advisors, with the "liberal and independent" practice of a liberal profession; and the difficulty of establishing a monopoly when "the professors, the university lecturers (maîtres de conférence agrégés) and the former magistrates of the judicial or administrative orders also had the right to give counsel" (Raguin, 1972: 168). These analyses also stress questions of professional competence: it was essential not to confuse the auxiliaries of justice with "auxiliaries of commerce and industry," so as to preserve the autonomy of the judiciary. Finally, the hostility of a large part of the organized bar toward the plan to incorporate legal advisors into the new profession certainly had something to do with the failure of the project.

In defining the new profession of lawyer, the reform of 1971 eliminated certain other professions—both the agréés of the commercial courts and the solicitors of the lower courts (première instance)—although the solicitors of the appeals courts were preserved. Since then, lawyers have had "a monopoly on representation before the courts in those areas formerly reserved to solicitors before the reform, the monopoly in principle on pleading, [and they] give legal consultations together with other professionals, notably the legal advisors and the notaries.... Finally, the lawyer draws up legal documents except for those within the monopoly of the notaries" (Hamelin & Damien, 1981: 31). Insofar as representation before the courts is concerned, the lawyer is subject to the rule of territoriality, as solicitors used to be: that is, lawyers may only represent clients before the court to which they are attached through membership in the bar. In contrast, the lawyer is not subject to any territorial limit whatsoever in pleading. Those lawyers who, at the time of the reform, did not wish to engage in these new activities had the option of continuing to pursue their former fields of specialization. The "great profession," which was to control and oversee the totality of legal activities, was far from being realized.

Together with the traditional professions already mentioned (solicitors of the appeals courts, notaries, and bailiffs), the lawyers coexist with the legal advisors, whose title alone is regulated by the Law of 31 December 1971. In order to be included in the list of legal advisors, a candidate must meet certain standards of morality and hold university degrees, almost the same as the requirements for lawyers. Less burdened by the weight of tradition, this profession recognizes three fields of specialization: fiscal, social, and corporate law.

Unlike the legal advisor, the French lawyer does not officially have a legal specialty. In fact, however, specialization does exist and even structures the profession. Karpik (1985) shows how factors such as income, qualification, and prestige impose a hierarchical structure on different areas of law and hence on the professionals who practice within them. This diversity does not mean fragmentation, however, either because different specialists practice together, "which forges the bonds of a generalized interdependence" (Karpik, 1985), or because there are implicit professional interests associated with the symbolic unity of the profession.

## SOCIOGRAPHY OF LAWYERS

Having defined lawyers in terms of their legal and professional positions and their fields of competence, I will now describe the size of various groups, their different modes of practice, and their geographic distribution. Then I will turn to the role of lawyers in politics and their public image.

## HOW MANY ARE THERE?

With more than 15,000 members, lawyers constitute the largest group of legal professionals, not counting unorganized professionals such as house counsel for corporations and insurance companies (for whom no figures are available). The following numbers were recorded for 1983:

15,757 lawyers
    80 lawyers at the Conseil d'Etat and the Cour de Cassation
4,264 legal advisors
7,001 notaries
  288 solicitors at the Court of Appeals
2,796 bailiffs
5,640 magistrates

Had the great profession envisioned in 1971 been realized, it would have included approximately 20,000 members.

The number of lawyers has grown considerably in the recent past, nearly doubling in ten years, from 8,307 in 1973 to 15,757 in 1983. This profession, like others, has been affected by the demographic upsurge of the postwar years and invaded, "as a result of the democratization of higher education, by a mass of young graduates" (Mialon, 1978: 289). The rapid increase had two causes: entrance to the profession was relatively easy, and the profession was responding to the demands of greater judicial activity (Ietswaart, 1985). In spite of this increase, the population per lawyer remains relatively high (3,600) when compared to the ratios of neighboring countries having similar legal systems: 1,400 in Belgium, 1,300 in Italy, and 1,000 in Spain.

## TOWARD A MORE COLLECTIVE PROFESSIONAL PRACTICE

Lawyers may practice in a traditional individualist fashion or more collectively, sharing part or all of the means of production. This is where the notion of a liberal profession acts as a constraint. Lawyers have had to reconcile economic realities with the freedom required for professional practice. The difficult dialectic of these two imperatives has generated a broad spectrum of legal solutions that can be divided into two categories: logistical groups and associative groups. In the first, lawyers share common expenditures, which may be more or less substantial, but not fees. This participation may be limited to office-sharing arrangements (*cabinet groupé*) or extended to the collective management of offices and administration, known as a partnership of means. Associative groups, or partnerships, imply real professional cooperation. When this cooperation is limited, the group is an *association* in the strict sense of the term. Professional cooperation is loose enough to preserve the individuality of each participant (all participants retain their own fees) but strong enough to prevent members from representing opposing parties. When such cooperation is close, the group is considered a *civil professional society* or a *corporation*. The client no longer deals with a single lawyer but with a corporate body represented by one of its members. The lawyers share their fees according to their previous agreement. This last form of organization may contain the germ of the degeneration of liberal practice. This form of practice, which satisfies the demands of economic rationality and functional specialization, also has been favored by activist lawyers, for whom common ownership and profit-sharing have positive social and professional significance. On the whole, legal professionals remain attached to a mode of operation that preserves at least a minimum of liberal practice. In 1981, 84 percent of lawyers still practiced individually. Nonetheless, collective practice is on the increase. According to Pédamon (1982), in Paris in 1981, there were:

135 office-sharing arrangements containing 338 lawyers
 71 partnerships of means containing 262 lawyers
182 associations containing 534 lawyers
117 civil professional societies containing 367 lawyers

Thus, 30 percent of Parisian lawyers practice in some form of collectivity.

A final form of practice also should be mentioned: the associate (collaborateur d'un confrère). A lawyer who either is or is not serving an apprenticeship may contract "to devote all or part of his activity to another lawyer who agrees to provide the associate with a fair remuneration" (Article 74 of the Decree of 9 June 1972). This is a necessary stage in the training of a lawyer serving an apprenticeship, but it may well survive the end of the formal apprenticeship period. Theoretically, the "contract of collaboration" excludes a subordinate relationship, since associates technically have relative freedom in their work. In reality, however, it has become increasingly common for lawyers to be subjected to the authority of the colleague for whom they work. As an indirect consequence, some lawyers have demanded a salaried position, since the benefits of liberal practice are negligible (Mialon, 1978).


UNEVEN GEOGRAPHIC DISTRIBUTION

The distribution of lawyers throughout France is very uneven, since the city of Paris alone contains more than a third (about 36 percent, or 5,542 practitioners in 1983). Economic and political centralization, which are unusually pronounced in France, account for the relative overdevelopment of the Paris Bar. This bar attracts lawyers by its proximity to the loci of power and by its membership, which includes most of the luminaries of the legal profession. The resulting growth poses a problem for the Paris Bar and for its relations with neighboring bars, which are pointedly illustrated by the way in which the Paris Bar preserved its privileged rights of audience. I noted above that lawyers must be members of a bar and may not represent litigants outside the jurisdiction of the court to which their bar is connected. When new courts were established in the suburbs of Paris, new bars also were created, which became responsible for representing litigants before these courts. Since these new bars were not entirely ready to function at the moment of their creation, a transitional measure was adopted, which allowed Parisian lawyers to represent clients before suburban courts for a period of five years (and members of suburban bars to appear in Paris). When this time limit expired in 1979, the Paris Bar succeeded in obtaining a five-year extension; and in December 1984 its privileges were extended indefinitely.

The provincial bars are on a scale different from that of the Paris Bar, since the largest is little more than a tenth the size of that of the capital (1983 figures):

| | |
|---|---|
| Marseilles | 600 |
| Lyon | 440 |
| Nice | 367 |
| Bordeaux | 355 |
| Toulouse | 307 |
| Strasbourg | 290 |
| Lille | 238 |

The smallest bars have fewer than ten lawyers. The size of the bar is related to the relative importance of the court; the larger a court's civil caseload, the more lawyers there are, and the former variable is a function of the size of the tertiary sector of the economy (service industries, administration, etc.) (Desmyterre, 1981).

## LAWYERS AND POLITICAL LIFE

As stressed above, lawyers are not only people of justice (*gens de justice*) but also individuals with a particular social standing. The participation of lawyers in politics constitutes an important aspect of the insertion of this professional group in social life. However, analysis of this participation is complicated because it can take many forms, whose meanings are far from simple. A single example must suffice: the changing role of lawyers in the National Assembly (see table 7.2). Lawyers occupied so many seats in the National Assembly at the beginning of the Third Republic that it was referred to as a "Republic of Jurists." At the end of the nineteenth century, more than one in every four deputies was a practicing lawyer when elected (Gaudemet, 1970). At the time, the bar seemed to be a privileged stepping stone to seats in Parliament or government positions. By the end of the Third Republic, however, this proportion had dropped to one deputy in six, leading the jurist Gaudemet to observe that a "Republic without Masters" had replaced the "Republic of Jurists" (in France, lawyers and ministerial officers are referred to as "master" by reason of their university degree). The numerical importance of lawyers in the National Assembly diminished further during the Fourth and Fifth Republics and now is very small in comparison to the weight they had in the first third of the twentieth century. It is not possible to provide a global interpretation of this change, which would require an analysis of political institutions as well as of the social and political strategies of lawyers. The best I can do is offer a few partial hypotheses. The social position lawyers enjoyed under the Third Republic as notables and the monopoly they held allowed them the freedom to participate in political life, and they were especially well suited to this role by reason of both their competence (Gaudemet, 1970) and their tradition of opposition to authoritarianism (Karpik, 1985). Lawyers today no longer enjoy a comparable freedom of movement, for they are subject to a large number of constraints, especially economic ones. The withdrawal of lawyers from the political arena thus appears to be part of the redefinition of the profession (Karpik, 1985).

The diminished representation of the bar in Parliament also can be interpreted as the result of competition from other groups whose social power has expanded, such as the higher civil servants who have graduated from the Ecole Nationale d'Administration (created in 1946). But the reduced role of lawyers in the National Assembly does not mean that they are absent from political life: the bar, and especially the Paris Bar, remains an important pressure group. Yet, whether this participation is a collective action, such as a strike,[4] or a political declaration by the professional associations and trade unions, it remains defensive in nature.

## LAWYERS AND PUBLIC OPINION

An analysis of the social position of lawyers brings us to an examination of their image in public opinion. The rather flattering image of lawyers, who occupy the top of the social hierarchy, is offset by the clearly negative view of their role and social utility. In a survey by a consumer group of the image of twenty-nine professions (shopkeepers, artisans, and liberal professionals), it was immediately apparent that the legal professions (lawyer, solicitor, notary, and bailiff) were far from popular, ranking between twenty-fifth and twenty-ninth place in descending order (Cinquante millions de consommateurs, 1983). Lawyers continue to be viewed by most people as "defenders of the rich and of crooks." This is not surprising when analyses of the image of criminal and civil justice are considered, which also reveal a rather negative view of the lawyer, who is regarded as a "necessary evil." "This image is explained by a strong ambivalence in the public perception of the lawyer's role, the important role played by the notion of money in the relations between lawyer and client, and also by the scapegoat role that many ascribe to the lawyer with respect to the legal system as a whole" (Actes, 1974: 5). The image of the lawyer is dependent on the overall perception of the judicial institution, which is identified primarily with the penal. That image also varies directly with the social position of the observer: the closer the observer is to the lawyer socially, culturally, and economically, the more positive the opinion of the profession (Baraquin, 1975).

## DEMOGRAPHIC PROFILES: MEN AND WOMEN, YOUNG AND OLD

The first woman was admitted to the bar in 1900, some forty-six years before the magistracy would open its doors to women in the wake of the progressive reforms of the postwar period. However, it would be at least another twenty-five years before significant numbers of women became lawyers. Today women constitute nearly one-third of the profession. Nonetheless, there still are a few bars without a single woman lawyer and more that have only one (a token woman?). Women constitute a higher proportion of the bars in large cities than in small towns, where the traditional division of social roles on the basis of gender still is observed.

The admission of women to the bar can be seen as evidence of sexual equality within the profession. However, the unusually high proportion of women lawyers in the suburbs of Paris suggests that the feminization of the bar may mean something quite different (see table 7.3).

These observations enable us to advance the following hypothesis: the bars of the Paris suburbs are most open to women because the recent date of their establishment allows greater institutional innovation. These bars also are less prestigious than the Paris Bar because they lack tradition and serve a more proletarian population. Thus, if the profession has effectively been opened to women, their entry is uneven, it has its costs, and it leaves them in a subordinate position. The number of women at the head of a bar proves this point: in 1983 there were only five women bâtonniers for 174 bars! While this ratio may be explained in part by the fact that most women lawyers are relatively young, age alone cannot account for such a disparity.

Finally, I must note the existence of a rather crude and elementary sexism, which regularly appears in firsthand accounts by members of the profession. These writers question the capacity of women to practice law, given their so-called "natural tendencies" (Cau, 1978), and hold women more or less directly responsible for the "decline of the bar" (Damien, 1974).

Half of all women lawyers are less than thirty-five years old (see table 7.4), which reveals the effects of both the massive entry of women into the profession in the last ten years and the postwar baby boom. The age structure of men lawyers is more complicated. First of all, there is a relatively large proportion of older men lawyers. Economic reasons explain why some continue to practice so long; for others, it is an enduring passion for the profession! There also is a parallel with the age structure of women lawyers, for half of the men are less than forty years old. There is underrepresentation of those between forty-five and fifty-five years old—the generation born between 1928 and 1938—which seems attributable not to specific demographic events but rather to variations in the recruitment policies of the bar and the law schools.


## AN ORGANIZED PROFESSION

The profession is structured by two types of organization: the first shapes the lawyer's activity and is situated on a local level—the bar (barreau or ordre des avocats); the second represents the interests of subgroups of lawyers and has a national dimension—the professional associations and trade unions.


### THE BARS

Lawyers are grouped into bars attached to a high court (tribunal de grande instance). Every lawyer must belong to a bar. Until the eighteenth century, the role of the bar was limited to the practical organization of lawyers: the bars were an integral part of the courts of justice, which at that time were the Parliaments. It was Parliament that organized the bar and exercised discipline (Damien, 1974). In the course of the eighteenth century the bars became independent of the Parliaments and the masters of their own "roll" (or tableau, an official listing of lawyers). "By accepting or refusing new members, by eliminating those who have become unworthy" they controlled access to the profession and performed a disciplinary role (Damien, 1974). The bars were abolished by the Revolution of 1789 and then restored in 1810 as part of the new judicial organization established by Napoleon.

Each bar is autonomous: no regional or national organization controls it. Two elected entities within each bar are responsible for governing it: the bâtonnier and the Conseil de l'Ordre.[5] The bâtonnier represents the bar before both the judicial and administrative courts and the public authorities and is responsible for its management and effective organization and for certain disciplinary and conciliatory tasks. The Conseil de l'Ordre presides over the admission of lawyers to the bar, manages its financial resources, defends the principles and safeguards the interests of the bar, and also has a disciplinary role (Lemaire, 1975). The size of the Counseil de l'Ordre is proportional to the size of the bar; in Paris, most of its members are wealthy lawyers with an extensive network of social and professional contacts (Karpik, 1986).

The bar's power to control entry to the profession theoretically is limited, since there is no numerus clausus and the bâtonnier must admit all candidates who meet the necessary requirements. Moreover, since the middle of the nineteenth century, the bar has not had ultimate control over membership, since its decisions are subject to review by the appeals court. Nonetheless, the actual authority exercised by each bar is a function of its size: smaller bars often pursue a protectionist policy through their control of the professional market, which makes it difficult for a new lawyer to obtain business, and through their power to award apprenticeships, which can dissuade undesirable candidates. These protectionist policies are more difficult to implement in the larger bars, which depend on the difficulty of the bar examination to restrict entry to the profession. This, in turn, accounts for their interest in recent reforms concerning the training of lawyers (discussed below).

The bars have acquired an increasingly important role in professional training, either by creating new areas of specialized training (advocacy, pleading) or through their financial and intellectual contributions to the professional training centers established in 1971.

One important function of the bâtonnier and the Conseil de l'Ordre is to ensure that lawyers observe the rules of professional ethics, with respect to their clients on the one hand and their colleagues and the magistrates on the other, and do not exceed the bounds of their competence. The bâtonnier receives all complaints from clients, prosecutors, or other lawyers and decides what measures to take. The bâtonnier can either present the matter to the disciplinary committee of the Conseil de l'Ordre or deal with it directly if it involves a dispute over the amount or payment of fees. In both cases it is possible to seek review before the appeals court or the high court.

An analysis of professional misconduct punished by the disciplinary committee of the bar reveals both the image that the bar wants to project and certain dysfunctions in the process. Elsewhere I have argued that professional deontology not only is a structural necessity but also serves as a buffer against the citizen and the state (Boigeol, 1980). In the absence of research on this topic, I will cite the following:

> A review of disciplinary action within the legal profession as described in professional textbooks and treatises reveals that actions that threaten the honor of the lawyer and respectful relations with colleagues and magistrates are punished more often than failures of impartiality and independence in the daily life of the lawyer. It is especially important not to call into question the honor of the profession, and thereby to inspire confidence. The misconduct that elicits the most serious sanctions are offenses against "probity": falsifying one's professional status in order to obtain economic or social advantages, compromising by fraudulent dealings with a client, making false statements before the bench.... On the other hand, fees and the justification of them remain protected by professional secrecy. (Raguin, 1972: 181)

An analysis of sanctions imposed between 1973 and 1981 by the Conseil de l'Ordre of the Paris Bar, briefly reported in the weekly Bulletin of the Bâtonnier, shows that most offenses involve embezzlement, fiscal fraud, and acts against probity and honor. Sanctions against illicit dealings with prisoners and lack of discipline (aggressive and insulting behavior) also are noted. Problems arising from financial relations with the client are described by the euphemism "failure in delicacy" and are not referred to the disciplinary committee unless coupled with an infraction, for unfair fees do not, in themselves, constitute a professional offense within the jurisdiction of the bâtonnier (see table 7.5). Little is known about the disciplinary role of the bâtonnier in matters concerning legal fees, since the entire issue is cloaked in secrecy.

## PROFESSIONAL ASSOCIATIONS AND TRADE UNIONS

The role of professional associations and trade unions is all the more important in the absence of a professional structure that represents lawyers on a national level. However, the principle of a national organization of lawyers is not new. The oldest organization is the Conférence des Bâtonniers, created in 1902. It represents the various bars rather than the lawyers directly and originally was conceived by the provincial bars as a counterweight to the Paris Bar. Associations of lawyers began to be organized after World War I, with the creation in 1921 of the National Association of Lawyers (Association national des avocats [ANA]) by Appleton (a prominent lawyer and treatise writer) and of the first Associations of Young Lawyers (Union des jeunes avocats [UJA]). The emergence of the latter reflects the specific difficulties young lawyers have encountered from this time on. In 1944 the various local associations of young lawyers were united in a national federation (Fédération nationale des unions des jeunes avocats [FNUJA]). Until 1971, the ANA and the FNUJA were the only large associations of lawyers.

The agitation of the bar at the time of the 1971 reform stimulated lawyers to form new associations to defend their particular interests or to oppose the reform in principle (see table 7.6). Thus, one association fought the fusion of the professions of lawyer and solicitor (Union nationale des avocats [UNA]), another represented former solicitors who had become lawyers (Rassemblement national des avocats de France [RNAF]), and a third spoke for those lawyers who opposed the redefinition of the profession and continued to function in their former capacity as pleaders only (Association professionnelle des avocats [APA]). Since that time these associations have redefined their aims: the UNA presents itself as an association that defends "tradition," and the APA seeks the abolition of territorial limits on representation so that lawyers may represent their clients before any court.

The greatest innovation occurred in 1973 with the founding of the first lawyers' trade union, the Trade Union of French Lawyers (Syndicat des avocats de France [SAF]). This union, which shares the left-wing politics of its members, was created in the wake of the "common program" signed by the communist and socialist parties in 1972. The trade union form of organization later became more widespread. In 1977, two former professional organizations (the ANA and the RNAF) combined to form the Trade Union Confederation of Lawyers (Confédération syndicale des avocats [CSA]). The choice of syndicalism at that time was justified by the fact that "nothing is useful, lifelike, constructive in the twentieth century without syndicalism," which alone can "improve the lot of a profession in the process of being pauperized," according to the president of the RNAF (Bedel de Buzareingues, 1977). Finally, the local associations of young lawyers which belonged to the FNUJA increasingly adopted a trade union form.

Without offering an overall explanation for this process of syndicalization, I can advance some partial interpretations. The movement was initiated by lawyers on the political left who were favorable to syndicalism from the outset. But were lawyers politically more radical than they had been? We cannot answer this question fully, but it is probable that changes in the demography of the profession had some effect on the political positions of its members. From another perspective, these same de-mographic changes may have created a market situation favorable to the birth of trade unionism. Because of the relative democratization of the law schools and the arrival of the postwar generations on the labor market, the profession was partially colonized by young people from the middle class. Since the only market open to them was insufficient (or at least in-sufficiently prestigious or remunerative because the most attractive work was the preserve of upper-class lawyers), part of the profession was faced with the prospect of limited economic rewards, much more meager than the expectations with which they had become lawyers. Professional frus-trations and disappointments can promote the process of syndicalization.

Other mechanisms also can explain the growth of trade unionism among lawyers. Lawyers were neither the first, nor the only, legal profes-sion to be affected by a syndicalist movement. As early as 1968, the mag-istracy experienced an identical evolution with the creation of the mag-istrates' trade union (Syndicat de la magistrature [SM]) and later with the transformation of the professional association of magistrates (Union fédérale des magistrats [UFM]) into another magistrates' trade union (Union syndicale des magistrats [USM]). By introducing syndicalism into the legal system, which previously had been hostile to such movements, the magistrates' trade union paved the way for the other legal profes-sions. The lawyers then followed suit, especially since it was in their in-terest not to leave the field entirely to the magistrates.

The syndicalist movement also should be analyzed in terms of the growing intervention of the state in the affairs of the profession. The trade union form of organization was the most appropriate in view of the fact that the state increasingly was becoming the employer of lawyers (l'Etat patron). Because the absence of a body representing the whole pro-fession created problems in the relations between lawyers and the state, an informal structure for collective action was established: L'Action na-tionale du barreau (National Action of the Bar). This body combines the professional associations and trade unions and has become the interlocutor of the government for all reforms concerning the profession.

## ACCESS TO THE PROFESSION: INCREASED CONTROL

At the beginning of the century, candidates who had insufficient income from landed property were discouraged from entering the profession by the explicit requirements of social class, as confirmed by a university de-gree ("Caldus," 1969). The first specific examination for entry to the bar, the certificate of legal aptitude (Certificat d'aptitude à la profession d'avocat [CAPA]), was not established until 1941 (an entrance examination for the magistracy was established in 1906) (Rousselet, 1957). The CAPA is a test of knowledge taken immediately after completion of law studies at the university. It does not change the traditional system of professional training, which takes place "in the field" during an apprenticeship (stage) and through practical courses offered by the bar, such as the "Apprenticeship Seminar" (Conférence du stage), in which prospective lawyers learn to debate specific subjects. During the apprenticeship, an experienced lawyer agrees to train a probationary lawyer, who works for little or nothing. For this system of reciprocity to function, it must satisfy an economic, or at least a symbolic, interest of each party, a situation that actually existed when lawyers were, and could be only, notables, largely free of the demands of productivity. This traditional form of training lasted until the early 1970s. Since then the training system has been institutionalized, and the scholarly credentials necessary to enter the profession have increased. Professional training centers attached to each appeals court were created in 1971. In 1981, more importantly, a year of specialized training before the CAPA was added to university studies. Those who wish to become lawyers now take a highly selective entrance examination at a professional training center (there were 600 admissions out of 3,000 candidates in 1982), receive a year of practical and theoretical instruction, and take an undemanding, final examination (CAPA) after completing their studies (see table 7.7). Having acquired a certificate of legal aptitude, the new lawyer must serve an apprenticeship for a minimum of two years. The apprentice works with a legal professional, attends hearings, and participates in workshops organized by the professional training center, after which the lawyer is qualified to perform all the tasks of the profession. The apprentice's choice of a supervisor is very important for the future of the young lawyer and depends largely on the applicant's network of social and professional relations.

The year of specialized legal training appears primarily oriented toward private practice (Retière, 1984). It includes courses taught mostly by lawyers and apprenticeships taken with lawyers or other legal professionals. Half the cost of this training is provided by the state and the other half by the profession.[6]

This drive to increase scholarly credentials and professional training is not unique to lawyers. The training of magistrates followed the same evolution; as early as 1958 they created a national center for judicial studies, which was transformed into the National School of the Magistracy in 1970. There are several ways to qualify as a notary; the principal ones are through internal promotion or university studies leading to a notarial degree. However, it is apparent that university degrees are becoming increasingly necessary to the entire profession (Avenirs, 1979).

There are several possible interpretations of this evolution, particularly that observed in lawyers. Beyond the explicit desire of the bar to improve the competence of lawyers lurks a Malthusian concern to restrict access to the profession (Retière, 1984). In the beginning of the 1970s, the profession recruited many young graduates as a result of the increase in the university-educated population among the postwar generation and the heightened judicial and juridical activity. In France, of course, a university education is free: anyone with a high-school diploma in the appropriate subject may enroll in law school. The more prestigious universities have an initial selection process, however, admitting only those who had earned their high-school diplomas with honors. The number of law degrees awarded after four years of university studies (the minimum requirement to become a lawyer) tripled in twenty years, from 1,940 in 1960 to 6,200 in 1980, and the law student population actually quadrupled during the same period (see table 7.8). This disparity results primarily from the increase in the number of intermediate degrees granted after two or three years of university studies.[7] Despite the poor quality of available statistics, it is clear that the number of people entering the profession rose sharply between 1967 and 1980 (table 7.9) and more gradually between 1981 and 1985. The persistence of this rise could have been perceived as a threat to the profession as a whole and to its management of the professional market, prompting a defensive reflex to restrict access to the profession by raising educational and training requirements.

The requirement of a year of on-the-job legal training also must be understood in relation to the earlier creation of a school for training magistrates, which rendered access to that profession more difficult and also raised the competence of the magistracy (Pauti, 1979). Because lawyers and magistrates have complementary but competitive relations, lawyers could not fail to respond by changing their own educational system. Since a national school for lawyers would not have been a viable solution, given the decentralized structure of their profession, professional training was situated in regional centers. Thus, the training of lawyers and magistrates tends to be similar in terms of the total number of years of preparation (university and professional) and the requirement of specialized instruction. Nevertheless, there are differences of institutional framework, and lawyers' instruction is more technical (Retière, 1984).

Finally, there is a more general hypothesis that takes into account the increase in schooling in all social groups. In the face of this development, if professions such as lawyers and magistrates want to maintain their positions of relative dominance within the social hierarchy, they have to increase the educational portion of their social capital—that is, the professional and educational requirements for entry (Bourdieu & Passeron, 1970).

These different hypotheses permit us to show that beyond those arguments usually advanced by lawyers (the growing complexity of the law, the laxity of the earlier system), the establishment of a new means of recruitment and a new system of education reflects the presence of important social and professional interests.

## ECONOMIC ASPECTS OF PROFESSIONAL PRACTICE: FEES

The concept of fees that prevailed during all of the nineteenth and part of the twentieth centuries and still informs the professional discourse is that the lawyer's fee is "a spontaneous testimony of the client's gratitude" (Cresson [1896], citing rulings by the Conseil de l'Ordre of Paris). Because the lawyer's work is of "inestimable" value, "no amount of gold could justly compensate it" (Camus, 1772). This theory, advanced by the Paris Bar in the seventeenth century, eventually became known as one of "the oldest practices of the bar" (Labouret, 1906). In 1931 a provincial lawyer criticized this concept of fees as expressing "excessive pharisaism" and complained "that it would be absurd if it were not hypocritical" (Gardenat, 1931: 170). The definition of fees offered by Cremieu eight years later, in his treatise on the profession, reveals an evolution in thinking: "fees are the just remuneration for work done" (Cremieu, 1939: 235).

Today, discussion focuses on the mechanism of "just remuneration." Since 1971, fees have consisted of two parts: the remuneration of the lawyer, which is set by the market, and charges for representation, which are fixed by law. The fee charged theoretically must take into account several parameters: the work performed, the financial and moral importance of the case, the situation of the client, the seniority, competence, and credentials of the lawyer, and the results of the case (Hamelin & Damien, 1981). In reality however, there are large disparities in the fees charged for the same work, which do not necessarily reflect the criteria mentioned above (*Que Choisir*, 1976).

For several years now, some bars have elaborated price scales suggesting the range of fees that should be charged for each kind of case. In fact, a sort of minimum tariff gradually came into effect. In divorce cases, for example, the fees do not always seem related to the amount of work performed. The divorce market is substantial and functions as a kind of guaranteed income for a large percentage of the profession. Thus, monopolistic tariff practices have been established. The Committee on Competition and Prices of the Finance Ministry issued an unfavorable opinion on these practices, criticizing the suggested price scales as a form of price-fixing. Since then, some bars have abandoned the price scales, although others have maintained them.

The establishment of suggested price scales by the bars appears to be an opportune professional practice. On one hand, it clarifies the question of fees for the client, who was, and remains, extremely disoriented by the mystery surrounding the payment for legal services. On the other hand, the institutionalization of monopolistic practices promotes better collective management and prevents "price-cutting" as a result of the heightened competition produced by the influx of the new lawyers in the 1970s.

However, the hostility toward fixed tariffs remains intense, and the freedom to set one's own fees is endlessly invoked. The profession attacks price-fixing on the grounds that prices will be fixed too low and that price-fixing represents an intrusion of the state into the affairs of the profession. Yet given the increasing pressure for economic rationality, the profession appears to accept the need for some clarification of the way in which fees are determined (if not actual price-fixing), provided this process is controlled by the lawyer, the bar, or the professional association. Thus, an hourly rate set by each lawyer according to the parameters used to determine fees seems to be developing. A long-standing practice in law firms working for business clients, it now is being adopted by a growing number of lawyers. Some associations suggest a method for determining a lawyer's hourly rate (FNUJA, 1983).

The question of fees remains unresolved, however, because there are obstacles to the normalization of professional practices: (1) the underwriting of lawyers' fees by insurance companies is complicated by variations in the fees different lawyers charge for the same service; (2) French lawyers currently are debating whether the winning parties may recover part or all of their legal expenses from losing parties and, if so, on what basis; and (3) the opening of national borders to lawyers from other members of the EEC presents the problems of reconciling different systems of remuneration and standardizing legal fees.

## THE INCOME OF LAWYERS

Given the way in which fees are paid to members of the liberal professions, little is known about the income of lawyers. The average income lawyers declared to the tax authorities in 1978 is similar to that of upper-management personnel and general medical practitioners (see fig. 7.1). However, lawyers fail to declare much of their income. According to a study estimating real profits (CERC, 1980), the average income of lawyers is 50 percent higher than the figure declared to the tax authorities (see fig. 7.2). This study also shows that the income declared by lawyers has grown significantly despite the influx of new members into the profession, while the income of other professions, such as architects, has diminished in responsed to the same phenomenon. However, these averages do not reveal the large disparity of incomes, which reflects the heterogeneity of the bar; the incomes of lawyers who work for wealthy clients or corporations are far greater than those of lawyers who serve a working-class population, often in a legal aid setting.[8]

## THE IMPACT OF LEGAL AID

If the defense of poor clients represents a professional obligation, it also contributes to the legitimacy of the judicial institution. On several occasions the state was forced to intervene to guarantee poor people access to the courts. In 1851 a system of legal assistance was instituted through an office staffed by various professionals, so that representation no longer depended entirely on the lawyer's personal opinion. The beneficiary of such aid was exempted from court costs, and the lawyer assigned rendered services free of charge.

This form of legal assistance lasted until 1972. In its last few years, the system had lost much of its effectiveness: the number granted legal assistance dropped from 41,790 in 1950 to 28,639 in 1970. The offices followed a very restrictive policy, helping only those clients with open-and-shut cases and virtually no financial resources (Boigeol, 1976), although surprising variations were found among different offices (Laroche de Roussane, 1976). Moreover, legal assistance became the exclusive responsibility of lawyers serving apprenticeships and those in need of clients. "In these conditions, justice for the poor is no more than cut-rate justice" (Raguin, 1972: 184).

Since this situation threatened the legitimacy of the institution, the state was compelled to act. In 1972 a legal aid program was established with two new features: clear economic criteria defined eligibility for full or partial legal aid, and lawyers received a standard sum per case for representing legally aided clients. Initially intended for civil or administrative cases, legal aid was extended to criminal matters in 1983. The 1972 law provoked an extremely hostile reaction from the profession. Lawyers saw this form of compensation for legal aid as the beginning of state regulation of the price of their services. Today, the principle of legal aid is thoroughly accepted; debate turns only on the amount of compensation and the criteria for client eligibility.

In order to understand the impact of this reform on the profession, it is necessary to review the central role of the ideology of disinterest and the behavior this inspired (Boigeol, 1981). The ideology of disinterest and the institutions and attitudes that gave it social credibility contributed to the production of symbolic capital that conferred important social benefits on members of the profession and helped to justify the economic privileges they enjoyed. Of course, the burden of generating this symbolic capital was unequally distributed: it fell largely upon lawyers serving their apprenticeships and those less well integrated into the network of bourgeois relations. Yet the important point is that the introduction of a third party who pays the bills—the state—seems to have undermind the coherence of the profession's social strategy. On one hand, the disinterest of lawyers was eclipsed by the extension of the welfare state into the legal sphere, as a result of which the state acquired part of the symbolic capital formerly appropriated by legal professionals. On the other hand, the profession's economic gains did not offset the loss of this symbolic capital. The state fixed the payment for legal aid at a low level, which barely defrayed the lawyer's cost, exploiting the absence of a professional fee schedule and what remained of the ideology of disinterest. Thus, it is not surprising that lawyers reproached the state, and continue to do so, for promoting social justice at their expense.

The present situation appears to be unstable. Yet, the analysis presented here should be tempered by three considerations. First, the reform conferred immediate economic benefits on those lawyers who were in the greatest financial difficulties. Even if legal aid fees are small compared to those paid by private clients, they are significant for some professionals, who are threatened by relative pauperization. The compensation for a simple divorce in 1985 was 2,140 francs; a single lawyer representing two parties divorcing by mutual consent is paid twice that amount. It also is important to recognize that the relative pauperization of some lawyers threatened the social position of all. Thus legal aid may have averted a dangerous development, even if the profession had to pay a price. Second, if the development of legal aid has increased access to justice for a large portion of the population, it also has contributed to regularizing a market that is likely to expand in the future. Finally, legal aid prompted lawyers to examine the timely question of how they set their fees.

## CONCLUSION

Forced to adapt to transformations in social and economic life, the legal profession in France has changed considerably over the last two decades. Lawyers had to expand their legal competence, modify their criteria of economic activity, and accept some degree of state intervention. The few studies undertaken by sociologists have analyzed some of these changes, such as the redefinition of the professional ideology of disinterest and the differentiation of professional practice. Now researchers seem to be more concerned with the actual work of lawyers, as this is influenced by their position within the profession and type of law practice (Dezalay, 1987), and with the construction of professional knowledge.[9] Finally, it must be remembered that although lawyers constitute an "independent" profession, they still are located in a network of legal professions, with which they have both complementary and competitive relations. An understanding of the significance of the bar for law and justice will require further research on the division of labor among the various professionals involved in the dispute process.

# TABLES

7.1. Evolution of the Principal Legal Professions

| | 1973 | 1974 | 1975 | 1976 | 1977 | 1978 | 1979 | 1980 | 1981 | 1982 | 1983 |
|---|---|---|---|---|---|---|---|---|---|---|---|
| **Lawyers** | | | | | | | | | | | |
| Number of practitioners | 8,307 | 10,365 | 11,169 | 11,869 | 12,408 | 13,959 | 14,480 | 15,170 | 15,715 | 15,315 | 15,757 |
| **Lawyers at the Conseil d'Etat and at the Cour de Cassation** | | | | | | | | | | | |
| Number of practitioners | 60 | 60 | 60 | 60 | 60 | 62 | 62 | 64 | 67 | 74 | 80 |
| Offices | 60 | 60 | 60 | 60 | 60 | 60 | 60 | 60 | 60 | 60 | 60 |
| **Solicitors at the Court of Appeals** | | | | | | | | | | | |
| Number of practitioners | 245 | 247 | 250 | 257 | 262 | 266 | 270 | 267 | 280 | 291 | 288 |
| Offices | 233 | 233 | 233 | 233 | 233 | 233 | 233 | 228 | 228 | 232 | — |
| **Legal advisers** | | | | | | | | | | | |
| Number of practitioners | — | — | — | — | — | 4,047 | 4,153 | 4,142 | 4,312 | 4,271 | 4,264 |
| **Clerks of the commercial courts** | | | | | | | | | | | |
| Number of practitioners | 213 | 224 | 236 | 228 | 234 | 249 | 264 | 234 | 236 | 240 | 244 |
| Offices | 227 | 227 | 227 | 227 | 227 | 227 | 228 | 228 | 228 | 228 | 227 |

7.1. (*continued*)

| | 1973 | 1974 | 1975 | 1976 | 1977 | 1978 | 1979 | 1980 | 1981 | 1982 | 1983 |
|---|---|---|---|---|---|---|---|---|---|---|---|
| Bailiffs | | | | | | | | | | | |
| Number of practitioners | — | 2,544 | 2,501 | 2,607 | 2,637 | 2,671 | 2,687 | 2,764 | 2,763 | 2,765 | 2,796 |
| Offices | 2,417 | 2,393 | 2,350 | 2,342 | 2,311 | 2,282 | 2,268 | 2,263 | 2,256 | 2,236 | — |
| Clerks of the court | | | | | | | | | | | |
| Number of practitioners | 4,028 | 4,436 | 4,617 | 4,670 | 4,876 | 5,047 | 5,355 | 5,939 | 5,928 | 5,948 | 5,944 |
| Magistrates | | | | | | | | | | | |
| Number of practitioners | 4,685 | 4,919 | 5,029 | 5,113 | 5,215 | 5,286 | 5,301 | 5,542 | 5,584 | 5,634 | 5,798 |
| Notaries | | | | | | | | | | | |
| Number of practitioners | 6,333 | 6,348 | 6,352 | 6,416 | 6,448 | 6,539 | 6,585 | 6,686 | 6,785 | 6,897 | 7,001 |
| Offices | 5,764 | 5,580 | 5,444 | 5,338 | 5,267 | 5,189 | 5,145 | 5,134 | 5,111 | 5,108 | 5,091 |

*Source:* Ministère de la Justice (1983).

7.2. Lawyers in the National Assembly

Third Republic

|  | Deputies | Lawyers | |
|---|---|---|---|
|  |  | No. | % |
| Chamber of 1881 | 560 | 153 | 27 |
| Chamber of 1906 | 580 | 144 | 25 |
| Chamber of 1924 | 584 | 140 | 24 |
| Chamber of 1936 | 618 | 110 | 18 |

*Source:* Gaudemet (1970).

Fourth Republic

|  | Deputies | Lawyers | |
|---|---|---|---|
|  |  | No. | % |
| 1st National Constituent Assembly (October 1945) | 586 | 76 | 13 |
| 2d National Constituent Assembly (June 1946) | 586 | 80 | 14 |
| 1st Legislature (November 1946) | 618 | 86 | 14 |
| 2d Legislature (1951) | 627 | 91 | 15 |
| 3d Legislature (1956) | 596 | 77 | 13 |

*Source:* Manigand (n.d.).

Fifth Republic

|  | Deputies | Lawyers | |
|---|---|---|---|
|  |  | No. | % |
| 1st Legislature (1958) | 546 | 56 | 10 |
| 2d Legislature (1962) | 482 | 37 | 8 |
| 3d Legislature (1967) | 487 | 36 | 7 |
| 4th Legislature (1968) | 485 | 27 | 6 |
| 5th Legislature (1973) | 490 | 37 | 8 |
| 6th Legislature (1978) | 491 | 29 | 6 |
| 7th Legislature (1981) | 491 | 23 | 5 |

*Source:* Bureau des informations parlementaires, Assemblée nationale, Recueil statistique.

7.3. Number of Women Lawyers by Location

| Bar | Women/total | Percentage of women |
|-----|-------------|---------------------|
| Hauts-de-Seine | 88/159 | 55.3 |
| Seine-Saint-Denis | 40/115 | 41.7 |
| Val-de-Marne | 78/156 | 50.0 |
| Versailles | 110/247 | 44.5 |
| Evry | 42/114 | 41.7 |
| Paris | 2,044/5,542 | 36.8 |

7.4. Distribution of French Lawyers by Age and Sex

| Age Groups | Men | | Women | |
|------------|------|------|-------|------|
| | No. | % | No. | % |
| 20–24 | 32 | 0.3 | 44 | 0.9 |
| 25–29 | 1,022 | 9.7 | 1,161 | 23.8 |
| 30–34 | 2,171 | 20.6 | 1,493 | 30.6 |
| 35–39 | 2,181 | 20.7 | 863 | 17.7 |
| 40–44 | 980 | 9.3 | 351 | 7.2 |
| 45–49 | 590 | 5.6 | 200 | 4.1 |
| 50–54 | 601 | 5.7 | 239 | 4.9 |
| 55–59 | 916 | 8.7 | 234 | 4.8 |
| 60–64 | 990 | 9.4 | 175 | 3.6 |
| 65–69 | 421 | 4.0 | 54 | 1.1 |
| 70–74 | 369 | 3.5 | 39 | 0.8 |
| 75–79 | 179 | 1.7 | 20 | 0.4 |
| ≥ 80 | 84 | 0.8 | 5 | 0.1 |
| Total | 10,536 | 100.0 | 4,878 | 100.0 |

Source: Centre nationale des barreaux français, listing by age and bar (30 November 1983).

7.5. Disciplinary Measures Taken by the Conseil de l'Ordre of the Paris Bar

| Type of sanction | 1979 | 1980 | 1981 |
|---|---|---|---|
| Expulsion[a] | 4 | 2 | 2 |
| Suspension[b] | | | |
| 3 years | | | 1 |
| 18 months | 1 | | |
| 12 months | 2 | 1 | |
| 6 months | 1 | 2 | |
| 3 months | 5 | 2 | |
| 2 months | 2 | 1 | 1 |
| 1 month | 2 | | |
| Reprimand[c] | | 1 | 3 |
| Warning[c] | | | 1 |
| Paternal admonition | | | |
| by the bâtonnier[d] | | 1 | 1 |

[a] Expulsions are primarily for embezzlement and acts against probity.

[b] Suspensions are for violations of etiquette, misue of funds, and infractions of fiscal law.

[c] Reprimands and warnings pertain to various acts of negligence, such as carelessness in the drafting of legal documents.

[d] Paternal admonition by the bâtonnier pertains to errors such as carelessness in accepting documents submitted by the client.

*Source: Bulletin du Bâtonnier* (n.d.).

7.6. Professional Associations and Trade Unions

| Name | Year founded | Claimed membership | Objectives |
|---|---|---|---|
| CSA—Trade Union Confederation of Lawyers | 1977 | 4,500 | Apolitical; to defend the profession as a whole |
| FNUJA—National Federation of Young Lawyers' Unions (83 in 1983) | 1944 | 4,500 | To defend the interests of lawyers under 40 |
| SAF—Trade Union of French Lawyers | 1973 | 1,500 | To include defense of the profession in a "left-wing" political platform |
| UNA—National Union of Lawyers | 1968 | 2,000 | "To defend tradition" |
| APA—Professional Association of Lawyers | 1972 | 600 | A principal demand is the elimination of territorial restrictions on representation |

7.7. Number Enrolled in Professional Training Centers and Awarded the CAPA[a]

| Year | Number enrolled[a] | Number awarded the CAPA | % |
|---|---|---|---|
| 1981–1982 | 604 | 585 | 97 |
| 1982–1983 | 654 | 644 | 98 |
| 1983–1984 | 643 | 639 | 99 |
| 1984–1985 | 666 | | |

[a]Those enrolled already have passed the entrance exam required by the professional centers.
Source: Association française des centres de formation professionnelle.

7.8. Changes in the Number of Four-Year University Law Degrees[a]

| Year | Number | Year | Number |
|---|---|---|---|
| 1960 | 1,943 | 1972 | 8,710 |
| 1961 | 1,894 | 1973 | 7,870 |
| 1962 | 1,992 | 1974 | 7,890 |
| 1963 | 1,803 | 1975 | 7,788 |
| 1964 | 1,766 | 1976 | 7,610 |
| 1965 | 2,138 | 1977 | 7,436 |
| 1966 | 2,246 | 1978 | NA |
| 1967 | 2,573 | 1979 | NA |
| 1968 | 3,881 | 1980 | 6,430 |
| 1969 | 5,011 | 1981 | 6,827 |
| 1970 | 6,215 | 1982 | 6,978 |
| 1971 | 7,980 | 1983 | 7,363 |

[a]Until 1977, this degree was known as the "licence." Since 1977, the licence has been granted after three years (as in other disciplines), and the four-year degree has been the maîtrise (masters).
Source: Service informatique, gestion, statistique (SIGES), Ministère de l'éducation nationale.

7.9. Changes in the Number of Certificates of Legal Aptitude (CAPA)[a]

| | | | |
|---|---|---|---|
| 1960 | 162 | 1971 | (790) |
| 1961 | (200) | 1972 | (915) |
| 1962 | (230) | 1973 | (1,010) |
| 1963 | (220) | 1974 | 1,025 |
| 1964 | (220) | 1975 | 890 |
| 1965 | (225) | 1976 | (1,040) |
| 1966 | 322 | 1977 | (1,090) |
| 1967 | (390) | 1978 | NA |
| 1968 | 610 | 1979 | 986 |
| 1969 | 648 | 1980 | 1,283 |
| 1970 | (700) | 1981 | 471 |

[a]Figures in parentheses are based on estimates for universities not providing information.
Source: Service informatique, gestion, statistique (SIGES), Ministère de l'éducation nationale.

# FIGURES

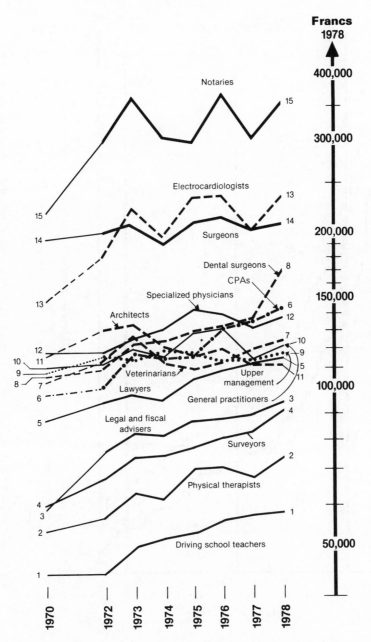

Fig. 7.1. Change in average income, by profession, 1970–1978 (expressed in 1978 francs). (*Source*: Centre d'étude et de recherche sur les coûts [1980].)

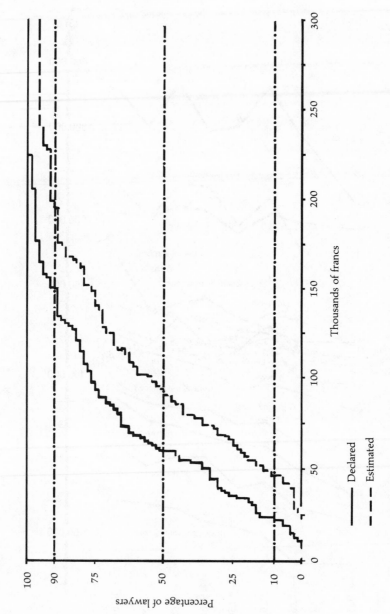

Fig. 7.2. Declared and estimated net income of lawyers, 1974. (*Source:* Centre d'étude et de recherche sur les coûts [1980].)

# NOTES

1. Law of 29 November 1966. The implementation decrees appeared in 1967 for notaries, 1969 for bailiffs and solicitors of the appeals court, and 1978 for lawyers of the Conseil d'Etat and the Cour de Cassation.

2. It is important not to confuse the French concept of a "liberal profession" with the Anglo-Saxon designation "profession." "The English word 'profession' does not include the kind of independence subsumed in the adjective 'liberal,' even though it has an obvious and clear connotation of great autonomy: the salaried doctor of a corporation is no longer said, in French, to be a member of the liberal professions, while in English he continues to be a professional" (Benguigui, 1972: 100).

3. The oath is worded as follows: "I swear, as a lawyer, to defend and counsel with dignity, conscience, independence and humanity, in full respect of the courts, the public authorities and the rules of my order, and neither to say nor to publish anything contrary to the laws, regulations, decency, state security, or the public peace."

4. In 1976 lawyers engaged in a strike in opposition to the new civil procedure code, which had been promulgated very quickly and limited the role of the lawyer.

5. On the assimilation of the order of lawyers to private government, see Karpik (1986).

6. State participation consists of a global budgetary allocation (11 million francs in 1983) and financial support for a certain number of students (213 in 1983) at 70 percent of the salary that they had been earning at any job they had held for at least six months. The participation of the bar consists of a budgetary allocation equivalent to that of the state and 300 scholarships (each worth 12,254 francs per year in 1982/83). The bar's contribution is financed from the interest earned on money deposited by the lawyers in a fund that manages all the monetary transactions that are the responsibility of the bar.

7. Law students obtain an intermediate degree after two or three years of study. While this does not qualify them to become avocats, some leave law school at this point to take other jobs or embark on other kinds of training. Another reason for this disparity is the phenomenon of "fictitious" students, who enroll in the university more for the administrative and social advantages of student status than for educational purposes.

8. On the disparities of income among lawyers, see Karpik (1985).

9. I have begun research on the ways in which the recruitment and training of lawyers and magistrates reflects important social and professional interests.

## REFERENCES

*Actes.* 1974. "L'image de l'avocat et de la défense dans l'opinion publique," 4 *Actes* 5.

Association nationale des avocats (ANA). 1967. *Au service de la Justice.* Paris: Dalloz.

*Avenirs.* 1979. "Le notariat," 307–308 *Avenirs* 85.

Baraquin, Yves. 1975. *Les Français et la Justice civile.* Paris: La Documentation française.

Bedel de Buzareingues, François. 1977. *Gazette au Palais* (12–14 June).

Benguigui, Georges. 1972. "La définition des professions," 13 *Epistemologie sociologique* 99.

Boigeol, Anne. 1976. "La profession d'avocat face à l'aide judiciaire ou le libéralisme en question," 27 *L'année sociologique* 261.

———. 1980. "Les avocats et les justiciables démunis: de la déontologie au marché professionnel." Doctoral dissertation, sociology, Université René Descartes, Paris.

———. 1981. "De l'idéologie du désintéressement chez les avocats," 1 *Sociologie du travail* 78.

Bourdieu, Pierre. 1980. *La distinction.* Paris: Les Editions de Minuit.

Bourdieu, Pierre, and Jean-Claude Passeron. 1970. *La reproduction.* Paris: Les Editions de Minuit.

"Caldus." 1969. *Pour une réforme de la Justice.* Paris: Les Editions ouvrières.

Camus, Armand. 1772. Lettres sur la profession d'avocat. Reprinted in Ainé Dupin, ed., *Profession d'avocat.* Paris: Alex-Gobelet, 1832.

Cau, Jean. 1978. "Le procès des avocates," *Paris Match* (30 July).

Centre d'étude et de recherche sur les coûts (CERC). 1980. *Le revenu des nonsalariés.* Paris: CERC, document no. 50.

———. 1981. *Les revenus des Français: 3è rapport de synthèse.* Paris: CERC, document no. 58.

Cinquante millions de consommateurs. 1983. Paris: Institut national de la consommation, document no. 10.

Confédération syndicale des avocats (CSA). 1982. "Les relations avocatmagistrat." Presented at the CSA conference in Dijon.

Cremieu, Louis. 1939. *Traité de la profession d'avocat.* Paris: Pichon-Durand-Auzias.

Cresson, Ernest. 1896. *Abrégé des usages et règles de la profession d'avocat.* Paris: L. Larose.

Damien, André. 1974. *Les avocats du temps passé.* Versailles: Henri Lefebvre.

Desmyttere, Hubert. 1981. *Construction d'un modèle prévisionnel de l'activité judiciaire.* Paris: Iris/Legos, Université Paris IX (research conducted at the request of the Ministry of Justice).

Dezalay, Yves. 1987. "From Bankruptcy to the Reorganization of failing firms:

the redefinition of the division of labor between the notables and the legal professionals and the experts and the importation of the American model of management consultancy." Presented to the annual meeting of the Law and Society Association, Washington, D.C., June.

Fédération nationale des unions des jeunes avocats (FNUJA). 1983. "La Justice à tout prix." Prepared for the Extraordinary Meeting of the Central Committee on February 3.

Gardenat, Louis. 1931. *Traité de la profession d'avocat.* Paris: Editions Gadde.

Gaudemet, Yves-Henri. 1970. *Les Juristes et la vie politique de la IIIè République.* Paris: Presses Universitaires de France.

Hamelin, Jacques, and André Damien. 1981. *Les règles de la nouvelle profession d'avocat.* Paris: Dalloz.

Ietswaart, Heleen. 1985. "Caseloads and What They Can Tell Us About the Litigation Explosion." Presented to the annual meeting of the Law and Society Association, San Diego, June.

Karpik, Lucien, 1985. "Avocat: une nouvelle profession," 4 *Revue française de sociologie* 203.

———. 1986. "Démocratie et pouvoir au barreau de Paris," 4 *Revue française de science politique* 496–517.

Labouret, Henri, 1906. *Des honoraires des avocats.* Lille: E. Dufrenoy.

Laroche de Roussane, Paul. 1976. "De l'assistance judiciaire à l'aide judiciare... et au-delà," 27 *L'année sociologique* 225.

Lemaire, Jean. 1975. *Les règles de la profession d'avocat et les usages du barreau de Paris.* Paris: Librairie Générale de Droit et Jurisprudence.

Manigand, Patrice. n.d. "Les deputés de la IVè République." Doctoral dissertation, Institut des sciences politiques, Paris.

Mialon, Marie-France. 1978. "Le salariat dans les professions libérales," 7–8 *Droit social* 288.

Ministère de la Justice. 1983. *Annuaire statistique de la Justice.* Paris: Ministère de la Justice.

Pauti, Monique. 1979. *Les magistrats de l'ordre judiciaire.* Nanterre, Université de Paris X: ENAJ.

Pédamon, Michel. 1982. "La profession d'advocat en mutation (in German)," in Hein Kötz, Wolf Paul, Michel Pédamon, and Michael Zander, eds., *Anwaltsberuf im Wandel: Rechtspflegeorgan oder Dienstleitungsgeweibe.* Frankfurt: Alfred Metzner Verlag.

*Que Choisir?* 1976."Oui maître mais combien?" 112 *Que Choisir?* 3.

Raguin, Catherine. 1972. "L'indépendance de l'avocat. Réflexion sur deux réformes: la rénovation de la profession et l'aide judiciaire," 2 *Sociologie du travail* 164.

Retière, Jean-Noel. 1986. "Les avocats," in Pierre Cam and Alain Suppiot, eds., *Les dédales du droit sociale.* Paris: Presse de la fondation nationale des sciences politiques.

Rousselet, Marcel. 1957. *Histoire de la magistrature*. Paris: Plon.

Royer, Jean-Pierre. 1979. *La société judiciaire*. Paris: Presses Universitaires de France.

Savatier, Jean. 1966. "Qu'est-ce qu'une profession libérale?" 4 *Projet* 451.

Trouillat, Robert. 1979. *Les conseils juridiques*. Paris: Presses Universitaires de France.

# 8

# The Lawyers of Geneva: An Analysis of Change in the Legal Profession

BENOIT BASTARD AND LAURA
CARDIA-VONÈCHE

This chapter examines lawyers (avocats) in the Swiss canton of Geneva in light of a reform recently undertaken by the cantonal authorities. That reform, which is particularly important for the Geneva bar, presents an opportune occasion to grasp the transformation of the legal profession and to understand how it operates. In addition, this study illuminates the adjustments—political as well as professional—accompanying the elaboration of rules of professional practice.

The judicial system of Switzerland, like its administrative and political organization, is characterized by diversity: the principal branches of Swiss law are contained in federal codes, but the judicial law remains cantonal, which gives the legal profession a distinctive characteristic in each canton. Thus, entry into the legal profession in certain cantons (such as Solothurn) does not require the practitioner to demonstrate juridical competence by obtaining a university diploma, whereas other cantons demand a license in law—Vaud actually insists on a doctoral thesis. In some cantons (Valais, Ticino, Neuchâtel), the lawyer is also a notary, whereas in others the two functions are strictly separated. The professional association—the Order of Lawyers (l'Ordre des avocats)—is an official organization enrolling every member of the bar in Ticino and Jura but a voluntary association created by private law in Geneva. We will focus on the canton of Geneva in order to describe the legal profession and distinguish the different conceptions of the lawyer's role that emerged in course of the recent legal reform.

The canton of Geneva is largely urban and situated in the extreme west of Switzerland, like an enclave within France. Its incorporation within the Confederation in 1815 followed a period of French occupation, which profoundly affected the law and organization of the judiciary. This historical influence has been counterbalanced by the membership of the canton in the Confederation and the impact of federal law on juridical activity at the local level. The conjunction of two contrasting juridical traditions within an entity of such limited geographic and political dimensions (350,000 inhabitants) underlines the interest of studying the passage of the recent legislative reform. In addition, Geneva, like the two other major Swiss cities Zurich and Basel, has experienced rapid economic development and witnessed the emergence of businesses requiring broader knowledge and foreign contacts, which confers an international dimension on the occupation of the lawyer.

The elaboration of a law intended to regulate the activities of the bar was entrusted to a commission of experts in 1979. The rough draft submitted in 1982 became the basis of consultations with various groups and then was debated by the Geneva Parliament, before being enacted on 15 March 1985. The new law on the legal profession took effect on 1 September of that year.

In order to analyze the functioning of the legal profession and expose the options retained in the rough draft and the discussions concerning successive amendments, we interviewed members of the expert commission and analyzed the parliamentary debates. These data were supplemented by a study of the demographic characteristics of the Geneva Bar in 1984. The lengthy legislative process made it possible for the drafters to discover the common will and produce a legal text that could gain approval not only from the professionals concerned but also within the political arena. At the same time, it revealed the persistence of different and often conflicting perceptions of the role of the lawyer.

## THE LAWYERS OF GENEVA: SEVERAL HISTORICAL BENCHMARKS FOR UNDERSTANDING THE SIGNIFICANCE OF THE REFORM

We will begin by outlining the constitution and evolution of the legal profession in Geneva in order to provide a historical context for understanding what was at stake in the reform. If a legislative reform appeared to be necessary in 1979, it was because certain inconsistencies had appeared, especially with respect to use of the title of lawyer and the exercise of discipline by the bar. These gaps between the legal definition of the lawyer's role and the actual behavior of the profession had been deepening ever since the beginning of the twentieth century. Therefore, we will analyze the development of the profession up to the end of the nineteenth century before showing how recent changes in the behavior of lawyers signify a break with the historical definition of their status and role.

## THE CONSTITUTION OF THE LEGAL PROFESSION

Solicitors (Procureurs) and Lawyers (avocats) in the
Old City of Geneva (1450–1794)

From the first mention of their existence, in 1450, lawyers in Geneva have been jurists attached to judicial institutions. The occasion for the reference was a regulation concerning the defenders who appeared before the ecclesiastical tribunal (l'Officialat) created by the bishop for the exercise of contentious jurisdiction (Cornu, 1945: 594). These practitioners belonged to two distinct professional bodies: the sworn solicitors (procureurs jurés) and the lawyer jurists (avocats juristes).

In Geneva, as in neighboring France, the judicial organization distinguished between the preliminary stages of litigation—which were the domain of the solicitors (procureurs, later called "avoués")—and the actual appearance before the tribunal, which was reserved for the lawyers (avocats). The preliminary stages consist of preparing the procedural steps and assisting the presentation of the lawsuit: solicitors introduce the cases and instruct the lawyers, represent the parties, and embody their positions in formal documents submitted to the court.

The distinction between the two functions has existed since before the Reformation (1536), although that event modified the judicial organization in Geneva. In the seventeenth century, the office of solicitor became a venal tax (i.e., it could be bought and sold); in exchange, solicitors obtained a first monopoly, the exclusive right to plead (*postuler*) before the councils and tribunals (Cornu, 1945: 595). Rules gradually were developed to regulate both entry to the profession of lawyer and the activities of lawyers. After different proposals had been placed before the Geneva Parliament (the Magnificent Council of Two Hundred) in 1644, 1657, and 1674 in order to "regulate yet more thoroughly the career of the bar," the text of a law was passed on 5 June 1674, requiring those who wished to belong to the profession to submit to an examination, matriculate, and take an oath (Perrot, 1980; Ordre des avocats de Genève, 1984a).

The project of regulating entry to the profession was resumed in 1695 and submitted to a commission, which worked for ten years without result (Choisy, 1904: 6). Finally, a "Regulation concerning the Matriculation of Lawyers" was adopted in 1711, supplemented by orders pertaining to the organizational principles of the association of lawyers, giving it a legal status that attached them to the judicial institutions (ibid.). This regulation not only reiterated that those who wished to become lawyers had to pass an examination, be inscribed as matriculates, and take an oath, but it also conferred on lawyers the monopoly of conducting litigation before the councils.

This stage of the institutionalization of the profession occurred during a period that saw the reform of instruction at the Faculty of Law[1] and a rebirth of the activity of guilds. The community of lawyers organized themselves, as shown by the fact that they elected some of their members to the Council of the association, which exercised disciplinary power together with the judicial authorities (Choisy, 1904: 8). In 1774, for example, Parliament and the "Association of Gentlemen Lawyers" (Corps de Messieurs les avocats) punished one of their members (Cornu, 1945: 596).

The position of the bar in Geneva society is well illustrated by the links it maintained with the city authorities. The first matriculation ceremony at the City Hall in May 1712 was attended by fourteen members of the Little Council (the municipal government)—all of whom were lawyers, although they could not practice because of the incompatibility of their political functions. Lawyers distinguished themselves by the suppers they gave, which also attracted notables: in 1727, for example, the first Syndic of the city, who was himself a lawyer (Cornu, 1945: 598).

The regulation concerning the matriculation of lawyers remained in force until the French Revolution. In 1712, fifty-one lawyers were enrolled (fourteen of whom could not practice because they served on the Little Council). Between 1712 and 1798, 195 additional members of the bar matriculated (see table 8.1).

## The Dissolution of the Bar during the Revolution and the Annexation of Geneva by France (1794–1813)

Resolutely hostile to guilds, the revolutionary ideas first embodied in the new Geneva constitution of 1794 began to promote the dissolution of the guild of lawyers, as well as those of solicitors and notaries (Cornu, 1945: 600). In order to continue to exercise their functions, especially the defense of prisoners, lawyers could present themselves before the tribunal only with the title of *"défenseurs officieux"*—individuals without any official status or juridical recognition.

The annexation of Geneva by France in 1798 made the city part of the department of Leman and had the effect of subjecting the judicial professions to French law. The profession of lawyer was reestablished in 1804, and the organization of the bar, dissolved in 1794, was reconstituted by the Decree of 14 December 1810. This decree, passed by the emperor, Napoleon I, created the Order of Lawyers so as to regulate the activity of its members more thoroughly. The Order established Disciplinary Councils charged with "maintaining loyalty to the monarchy and to the constitutional institutions." The power to exclude or to strike a lawyer from the roll was conferred on the minister of justice (Cornu, 1945: 601). Moreover, the new regulation specified that the lawyer's functions were incompatible with those of the solicitor or notary. The status of solicitors (procureurs), who had become "avoués" in accordance with French usage, was regulated by a decree of 1812 confirming their monopoly of pleading.

### The Restoration of Geneva and the Development of Modern Legislation Concerning the Legal Profession (1813–1850)

The restoration of Geneva in 1813 and its subsequent incorporation into the Swiss Confederation in 1815 marked the beginning of the process that has given the legal profession its present configuration. The first law on the judicial organization, passed in 1816, decreed the oath that lawyers still take. The lawyer must swear:

> to be faithful to the Swiss Republic and the Canton of Geneva; never to be disrespectful to the tribunal or the authorities; never to advise or support any cause that does not appear just or equitable, unless it concerns the defense of an accused; not to employ knowingly, in support of the causes entrusted to the lawyer, any untruths and not to seek to mislead the judges by any artifice or by a false exposition of the facts or the law; to abstain from all offenses against the person [such as assaults or abusive language] and to allege no facts against the honor and reputation of the parties if unnecessary to the cause with which the lawyer is charged; not to encourage either the initiation or prolongation of a lawsuit from motives of passion or self interest; not to refuse, for personal reasons, the cause of the weak, the alien, or the oppressed.

This new legislation required those who wished to become lawyers to obtain the diploma of a "doctor in law." It still distinguished, however, between the functions of the lawyer and those of the solicitor. The unification of the profession was the work of the Geneva reformer Pierre-François Bellot. Bellot had been the moving force behind the rebirth of the Order of Lawyers, of which he was the first president from 1822 to 1836. An Edict of 25 May 1821 reestablished the Order as an organization containing all the lawyers listed on the roll. Membership in it became a condition of entry to the profession. The Order was governed by a president and a secretary. Disciplinary power was entrusted to a Disciplinary Council composed exclusively of lawyers (the president of the Order, the secretary, and a third lawyer), which was responsible for ensuring conformity to the laws and regulations concerning the bar. They had the power to censure, suspend, and strike from the roll (the last two penalties requiring confirmation by the judicial authorities).

As the head of this reconstituted and powerful professional organization, Bellot succeeded in fusing the professions of lawyer and solicitor. He himself had practiced both the activities of pleading (postulant) and advocacy between 1800 and 1810, and he felt that the monopoly had benefited the solicitors, giving them control of all litigation and forcing lawyers to seek their patronage (Cornu, 1945:606). He supported his proposal for fusion with the examples of Prussia, Austria, the United States, and other Swiss cantons, in which lawyers alone controlled every procedural step. In the rest of the Confederation, the distinction between lawyer and solicitor effectively had disappeared in the fifteenth century (Siegrist, 1985).

Those opposing Bellot's project argued that the divided profession had existed for a long time in Geneva, that it was necessary in order to prevent lawyers from being entirely preoccupied with procedural formalities, and that the bar would be invaded by people attracted by the prospect of material gain and thereby discredited (Cornu, 1945:606).

Opposition to the project of fusion, voiced most strongly by the solicitors themselves, failed to prevent the passage of a new law concerning lawyers, solicitors, and bailiffs (huissiers) on 20 June 1834. A critical step in the process of modernizing the profession, this law united pleading and advocacy in the hands of lawyers.[2] Solicitors, of whom there had been five, disappeared by 1846 (Cornu, 1945:603; Choisy, 1904:10). The following years were marked by an increase in the number of lawyers enrolled: 111 took the oath between 1814 and 1851, and in 1850 the bar contained about fifty members (see table 8.1).

The movement of institutionalizing the legal profession thus was concretized in the grant of extended professional prerogatives (the fusion of pleading and advocacy, the monopoly of representing parties before the tribunal), and the constitution of a professional association whose power was strengthened by compulsory membership.


The Restoration of the Free Profession of the Man of Law (1850–1863)


In 1850 the movement to reinforce the professional and social position of Geneva lawyers was confronted a second time by the democratic and antipatrician sentiments that deeply characterized the Swiss Confederation. Under the direction of a new head of government, the tribune James Fazy, the Geneva revolution of 1846 dissolved the Order of Lawyers, thereby placing in question the criteria for entry to the profession. During discussion of the reform proposals that had been laid before parliament, Fazy did not hide his hostility toward lawyers:

> The regime of 1834 is a dangerous one for Geneva. We should not believe that the number of lawyers will remain at the present total of 50. In a dozen years we will have a hundred. Then they will form a veritable order within the state.

They are a body that stimulates opposition, and one cannot imagine the harm they do. They seek to dominate the country. (Record of the meetings of the representative council, 1850–1851, title 2, p. 1173)

Without adopting all of Fazy's views, the Geneva Parliament, after long hesitation, passed the Law of 4 June 1851 concerning the free profession of the man of law (homme de loi), which abolished the requirement of any academic credential for entry to the legal profession. This law also abrogated all previous regulations concerning the Order of Lawyers and subjected their activities to supervision by the judicial authorities alone (Cornu, 1945:610). These measures signified the brutal disappearance of lawyers as a profession. It would take several decades for the body of lawyers to reconstitute itself and recover its place in Geneva society.


## The Reestablishment of Geneva Lawyers and Defeat of Proposals to Unify the Profession under a Federal Scheme (1863–1925)

Once efforts to reestablish the legal profession had commenced in 1863, the rest of the nineteenth century was entirely occupied with redefining its activities. This evolution occurred within a general tendency toward developing and unifying federal legislation, a movement affecting constitutional law and the principal bodies of substantive law as well as the organization of the profession. Thus, the federal constitution of 1848 had given the country its present organization, and the success of the constitutional revision of 1874 reconfirmed the enthusiasm for unity.

The movement to codify the juridical structure, visible in the cantons from the beginning of the century, was accelerated in the 1870s by the push for federal unification. The most notable result was the promulgation of the Swiss Civil Code in 1912 and, finally, of the Penal Code in 1942. In several cantons the movement was accompanied by the creation of law schools, which could be found in Bern, Zurich, Vaud, Fribourg, Valais, Neuchâtel, Basel, and Geneva by about 1920 (Siegrist, 1985).

The unification of law did not yet include the rules of procedure or the organization of the judiciary, which remained within the exclusive competence of the cantons. The structure of the legal profession also expressed the tension between national unification and the maintenance of cantonal specificities. The large cantons named above developed legal professions founded on scientific competence controlled by the state. By contrast, the smaller cantons, especially those in central Switzerland, opposed any formalization of the rules of entry to the profession, preferring to leave it entirely uncontrolled. In 1898 the tendency toward unification was expressed by the creation of the Swiss Federation of Lawyers, whose goal was the creation of a federal license for lawyers and the passage of professional legislation valid in all the cantons. All the efforts of the new organization were directed toward promoting a scientific process for qualifying lawyers (requiring both an apprenticeship and an examination) as well as toward enhancing professional autonomy.

Nevertheless, this project, like the unification of the judiciary law, never succeeded. In preparation since 1876, the first proposal was advanced in 1901 but rejected by the federal tribunal in 1905. Other proposals were put forward in 1912–1913, 1924, and finally 1942 without any greater success (Chaulmontent, 1970: 137–140). The unification of the profession, which was incompatible with cantonal sovereignty, was strongly opposed by certain French-speaking cantons, which feared that the establishment of a federal examination would achieve unification by lowering the entry requirements (Siegrist, 1985).

Although the proposed federal unification failed, the campaign had the effect of reinforcing the different cantonal laws and restoring regulation in cantons where entry to the profession had remained entirely free. The number of these latter cantons fell from thirteen out of twenty-five in 1873 to six in 1920 (Solothurn, Graubunden, Appenzell, Shaffhausen, Glaris, and Zug).

The legal profession, codified by nineteen distinct laws, thus remained characterized by great local diversity, in contrast to the medical profession, which was unified under a federal scheme.[3] Lawyers are regulated by article 5 of the temporary provisions of the Constitution of 1874, which granted the cantonal authorities control over both entry and conduct. In a concession to federalism, these cantonal orders prescribed that every Swiss lawyer who had obtained a license after completing legal studies and a year's apprenticeship could, in principle, practice in any canton in the Confederation (Chaulmontet, 1970: 141).

At the beginning of the twentieth century, the Swiss legal profession was firmly organized. In Geneva, rules governed admission as well as the conditions for practicing the profession (Cornu, 1945: 614). The Law of 1863 had reintroduced the mandatory apprenticeship (stage) in the form in which it exists today.[4] In 1878 the functions of lawyers again were specified. They were charged: "in penal matters, to represent the parties and to advocate for them before the tribunals and, in civil matters, to perform all the procedural actions and instructions, represent the parties and advocate for them before the tribunals" (Cornu, 1945: 612). A commission also was established that year to oversee the behavior of lawyers; it was composed of nineteen members: magistrates from the judiciary as well as members named by Parliament, the executive, and the lawyers themselves. In 1891, the membership of this commission was reduced to nine, two of whom were named by the lawyers. In 1900 the requirements of the apprenticeship were specified (Cornu, 1945: 613). The last important element, the examination for the lawyer's license at the end of the apprenticeship, was introduced in 1925.

The Order of Lawyers was reconstituted in 1895 as an unofficial private voluntary association (Ordre des avocats de Genève, 1977: 8). Thereafter, the Order constantly sought to regain its former status. The action of lawyers who favored officialization was illustrated by the reconstruction and publication, in 1904, of the ancient register of lawyers, attesting to the long lineage of the professional organization (Choisy, 1904).

The matriculation examination allows us to evelute the very sharp increase in the number of lawyers between 1863 and 1904. The number taking the oath exceeded the level attained before 1850 (an annual average of about five, compared to three previously), and it increased further after 1890 (see table 8.1). In Geneva, as in Zurich, Basel, and Saint-Gall, women were admitted to the bar around the turn of the century. Their number remained very low, however: there were seven women among the 1,170 members of the Swiss Federation of Lawyers in 1928, two of whom practiced in Geneva (Keller-Huguenin, 1929).

## The Geneva Lawyer at the Beginning of the Twentieth Century

The Geneva lawyer at the beginning of this century was primarily a judicial lawyer, an officer of the court. The requirements for entry to the profession (a law degree, two years of apprenticeship, and successful completion of the examination at the end of the apprenticeship) as well as the conventions of practice were governed by the law of judicial organization. The lawyer had a monopoly over the representation of parties before the civil and criminal courts. Lawyers were generalists; like artisans, each performed the totality of functions incumbent on the bar: pleading, advocacy, and counseling. Lawyers are organized into a professional association, which contained the majority of practitioners even though it remained unofficial. A commission attached to the judicial authorities exercised supervision over the profession, with the participation of the lawyers themselves. Finally, lawyers played an important role in Geneva politics: ever since the liberal movement of 1830 they had taken a dominant part in the governance of the canton.

## THE EVOLUTION OF THE LEGAL PROFESSION

### The Diversification of Lawyers' Activities

Urbanization, the economic development of the city of Geneva, and the expansion of international relations, which occurred after World War I, profoundly changed the nature of legal work. As a result of the evolution of insurance and banking, as well as the industrial sector, lawyers diversified their activities. Their participation in the administration of commercial and industrial enterprises, which had been drawn to Geneva and the other large Swiss cities ever since the nineteenth century, increased in the 1930s. Keller-Huegenin (1929) stated, "The Basel bar has just achieved a great victory. High finance has resigned itself to putting at the head of two great Basel banks a lawyer and a jurist who until then had directed a fiduciary society. Zurich timidly begins to follow the same path." The same author also notes that this evolution amplified the importance of noncontentious matters for lawyers and was accompanied by a rise in income.

The development of the extrajudicial aspects of the work of Geneva lawyers also is described by Cornu (1945:616).

> This profession, it frankly must be acknowledged, no longer is dedicated solely to "representing parties before the tribunals." The power of lawyers to plead before courts—a power they inherited from the former solicitors—no longer is their entire reason for being. Today, the lawyer is called on to give advice and directives not just to litigants but also to a great many other people. The public address themselves to him to draft a contract, for example, or to conduct negotiations of a civil or commercial nature. When performing these new functions, lawyers no longer can claim the title of public officials, a title in which they are clothed when they represent parties before the tribunals. They assume, instead, the title of business agents [mandataires ad negotia] of private persons, a title that could be assumed by any other person.

The diversification of the activities of lawyers, then, has been accompanied by some neglect of judicial activities and the life of the courts, among those who have preferred the world of business. This evolution has not always been approved and accepted by the public and the other professionals conerned. The following extract from an anonymous pamphlet published in 1907 well expresses the hostility engendered by lawyers:

> Outside of the court, where they do not talk enough (at least in the minds of their clients), lawyers talk too much, and of matters that do not concern them. They are too deeply involved in politics, in the Great Council, in the city councils, in various commissions, especially in administrative councils, and in business. Unconsciously, the public is angered by encountering them at every turn of the road and nurses an ill-defined jealously toward them.

Some of the lawyers themselves deplored this diversification of their activities and wished to return to the traditional definition of the lawyer as the auxiliary of justice. This theme runs throughout the work of the great Geneva jurist, Martin-Achard, who describes, with nostalgia, the role of the defender:

The lawyer is called to defend. His fundamental role is defense. Defense of a man, of his physical life, of his honor, of his goods, of his rights, defense of interests. The lawyer defends, counsels, and assists.... The lawyer "explains" the judge to the client and the client to the judge. He is the intermediary who frees the magistrate from all the superfluous verbiage of his client. The lawyer knows the language of his client, that is to say the language of life, but he also speaks the language of science, that of the judge. (Martin-Achard, 1950: 12, 17)

This nostalgia and this preoccupation persist today and are found at the heart of discussions about the proper direction for reforming the profession. In 1977, for example, a lawyer asked rhetorically, in a speech during the ceremonies opening the new judicial term, whether lawyers should not grieve that the bar had abandoned its historic role.

Have we not been wounded, perhaps mortally, by the central criticism that we have become divorced from the Defense? Our services here [in court] are more and more mediocre in quality, often frankly lamentable.... We have distanced ourselves from the court, where our presence often is only formal, whereas many among us, and not the least prominent, are becoming involved in business matters, associating together and practicing more and more arbitration.... We often are only indifferent businessmen. The judgment is rendered and we find ourselves uninterested. (Crettaz, 1977)

## Competition with Other Professions

In distancing themselves from the court, lawyers have entered into competition with an increasing number of other legal professionals. In their extrajudicial activities, they find themselves competing with everyone who gives advice of a juridical character, regardless of whether these are jurists. Even in their strictly judicial activities lawyers who appear within the newly created jurisdictions and commissions must compete with agents who lack formal qualifications. Consequently, they must fight to obtain recognition of the fact that they are better qualified to give legal advice than other jurists, while simultaneously seeking to preserve their exclusive right to represent parties before the tribunals.

In order to regulate the provision of legal advice more precisely and comprehensively, lawyers began in 1937 to seek passage of a law defining the respective competences of the different professions. The professions of notary and business agent had just been regulated following the enactment of the Swiss Civil Code. Notaries were charged by the law of 6 May 1912 with responsibility to "receive all acts and contracts to which the parties must give or wish to give the character of authenticity." They were placed under the authority of the Council of State (the Geneva executive). The profession of business agent had been created by a Law of 2 November 1927, which required a preliminary examination of juridical knowledge and practice and the submission of character references to the Council of State. In addition, other professional groups and occupations were beginning to offer legal advice, as were friendly societies, banks, and insurance companies.

In reaction against this proliferation of consultative activities, the strategy of lawyers has been to try to reserve the monopoly of giving legal advice, if not to themselves, at least to categories of jurists organized into distinct and regulated professional bodies. They persuaded the Council of State to accept and the Geneva Parliament to pass in 1943 a law that purported to regulate all juridical professions—lawyer, legal apprentice, notary, bailiff, and business agent—and to reserve the right to practice law to those formally authorized. When this law was submitted to a referendum, however, it was rejected by the people, despite the fact that it enjoyed the support of the majority political parties.

Lawyers also had to compete with other professions in defending their monopoly of representing parties before the tribunals. The bar asserted that the representation of litigants could not be entrusted to anyone who was not formally qualified; it dismissed challenges to its monopoly based on the "pretext" that others could represent litigants more cheaply or on criticisms of lawyers for complicating the procedure or creating misunderstandings between the party and the magistrate. Martin-Archard (1951: 197a) stated, "We do not think it possible to justify the sentimental view that everyone can act in his own defense. The lawyer has been specially prepared to represent the parties in judicial matters, and it would be absolutely abnormal for others to be charged with this essential mission."

Following the creation of new jurisdictions, various nonjurist agents were admitted to represent the parties. Today, therefore, the lawyer is excluded from some jurisdictions, such as the trade councils (tribunaux de prud'hommes); in others, lawyers must compete with a variety of people whose qualifications are not always specified: the commission of appeals in tax matters (accountants, fiduciaries), the commission of appeals for building permits (architects), the tribunal of leaseholds (managers, land stewards), the appeals commission for old age insurance, and the administrative tribunal. It is unclear whether these developments reflected the lack of interest among most lawyers in matters that are more technical than juridical and for which they are poorly trained, or whether they represented a resurgence of the view that laypersons can defend litigants, in matters with which they are familiar, just as well as lawyers and perhaps even better.

## Abandonment of the Project of Transforming the Order of Lawyers into an Official Body

The desire to unify the bar, thereby restoring it to the status of an official organization, was manifest in 1937, 1941, and 1956 and championed by certain prominent figures in the Geneva judicial milieus. Thus, for example, the head of the judicial hierarchy, Attorney General Cornu, argued (1945: 517): "A new authority should be instituted, one that permitted the professions to police themselves, while guaranteeing the security of the tribunals and the public." [5]

However, this pressure to create a body endowed with the power of self-discipline in the French manner (Martin-Achard, 1951: 150a) constantly was counterbalanced by those who objected to the bar again becoming an official entity. The project of 1937, which was submitted to an extraparliamentary commission, came to naught. In 1941, when the officialization of the Order was included in a proposal to regulate all the judicial professions and accepted by both the judicial milieus and political authorities, it was rejected by a popular referendum. Finally, the project of 1956, which was concerned exclusively with this question, was withdrawn by the Order of Lawyers itself after having been accepted by the Council of State. This last rejection underlined the fact that even lawyers disagreed about the status of the Order. Some believed that officialization would assure the independence of the Order, permitting it to control the activities of all lawyers and restoring it to the prestige it had enjoyed in the time of Bellot. However, others feared that an official Order would tend to impose a dominant conception of the lawyer's occupation and limit the development of alternative ways of practicing law.

The project of making the Order an official body was abandoned, therefore, not only because of divergent opinions and successive rejections of the legislative plan but also because the heterogeneity of lawyers was an inescapable fact. Several new organizations of lawyers were created beginning in the 1970s. The most important, the Association of Progressive Jurists (affiliated with the Swiss Association of Democratic Jurists), included lawyers, magistrates, and jurists employed by the government. This association described itself as defending the professional interests of its members and, more generally, promoting "the social transformations encompassing the body of the juridical profession" (Association des juristes progressistes, 1974).

Without organizing themselves into a competing association, other lawyers remained outside the Order or withdrew from it in order to express their disagreement with the dominant norms of legal practice. These acts of discrete individual opposition recently found public expression in the participation by several lawyers in the spectacle of televised debates, a practice that violates the ethical rules of the Order, which prohibit all publicity by members of the bar (l'Hebdo, 1986).

## The Increase in the Number of Lawyers

It is not only the activity of lawyers and the organization of the profession that have been transformed but also the very structure of the legal profession, insofar as this is affected by the number of lawyers and the way they practice their profession.

The number of lawyers has increased considerably. This can be seen by analyzing the distribution of lawyers enrolled in the bar as a function of the years in which they took the oath (see fig. 8.1). The average number of lawyers admitted annually between 1961 and 1965 was nine. (This cohort had about 20 years of experience in 1984.) More than five times as many—an average of fifty-one per year—began to practice between 1979 and 1983. This increase is more rapid than that observed in Switzerland as a whole. There were 2,426 lawyers practicing in the Swiss Confederation in 1960 and 3,688 in 1980, constituting an increase of 52 percent. In Geneva, the number doubled in the same time, growing from 235 to 472 (Annuaire Statistique de la Suisse).[6] In Geneva, 271 lawyers belonged to the Order in 1970: 171 principals, 58 salaried lawyers, and 42 apprentices (Association des juristes progressistes, 1974). The total had reached 567 in 1984: 308 principals, 139 salaried lawyers, and 120 apprentices (Ordre des avocats de Genève, 1984b).

This unprecedented increase is attributable to the feminization of the legal profession beginning in 1970, as shown by the growing proportion of new entrants who were women (see fig. 8.1) as well as by the shape of the age–gender pyramid of the profession (see fig. 8.2). From this point of view, Geneva in unique, even when compared to the other urban cantons, which contain the largest concentrations of practicing lawyers (Zurich, Basel, Berne, Tessin, and Valais). Women today represent 15 percent of the Geneva Bar (see fig. 8.3).

The increasing youthfulness of the legal profession and its feminization have influenced the forms of practice at the bar. The number of principals has increased much less rapidly than that of either salaried lawyers (who have obtained their certificates and are working for other lawyers or associations of lawyers) or apprentices. Most salaried lawyers (64 percent) are thirty to thirty-nine years old; most apprentices (79 percent) are under thirty (see table 8.2).

Figure 8.4 is a bar graph showing the actual distribution of practicing lawyers across professional positions,[7] as far as we have been able to reconstruct it from the table provided by the attorney general, with the help of knowledgeable informants. These data show that the inclusion of women in the legal profession has not yet affected all professional positions, which leads us to wonder whether the composition of law offices does not still adhere to a model in which the senior partner and his fellow partners remain the center of activity, assisted by a limited number of salaried lawyers.

## Modernization of the Conditions of Law Practice

The last aspect of the transformation of the profession, the modification of the conditions of law practice, is manifest in the diversification of the ways in which law offices are organized and in the modernization of the techniques of work. In addition to the lawyers who practice by themselves, which is the traditional form (more than half of the 256 law offices consist of a lawyer practicing alone), other organizational structures have developed. For many years, association between lawyers was limited to sharing common facilities and dividing expenses. The partnership form appeared between 1955 and 1960; it included the sharing of business—in principle, all the partners are responsible for the files and interchangeable—and the division of the profits among the partners. This mode of organization is more common among the larger offices, but their number and size remain limited. In 1984 only 6 percent of Geneva law offices contained more than three principals, together with several salaried lawyers and apprentices. The largest contained twenty people.

This form of association permits the incorporation of young lawyers. Indeed, although law remains largely artisanal, the work of the lawyer is becoming increasingly complex, entailing higher costs and stimulating the search for new forms of organization. The elaboration of technical solutions (means of communication and information processing), organizational solutions (secretarial pool, common documentation), and professional solutions (professional foresight, emergency treatment, substitution, and specialization) is facilitated by the structure of the partnership. This type of organization, found in other professions also, allows the client to consult different specialists for different needs.

The actual composition of law offices confirms that Geneva practice remains strongly attached to the liberal conception of the legal profession (see table 8.3). Solo practitioners constitute 35 percent of the 135 heads of offices, and offices have expanded by simultaneously increasing the number of partners, salaried lawyers, and apprentices. The large offices, for example, contain seventy-seven partners, thirty-five salaried lawyers, and thirty-nine apprentices.

In contrast to this type of association, which emphasizes the rationalization of function in order to enhance efficiency, there is another form of sharing resources that leads to a more self-reflective practice and tends to transform the lawyer's relationship with the client. The actions of the Association of Progressive Jurists, in Geneva and other cantons, have opened the way for the creation of new organizations—"lawyer collectives" or associations employing specialized lawyers, such as ASLOCA, the association for the defense of tenants. These employ a total of twelve lawyers. They are more politicized than other law offices, collectively choose which causes to defend, adopt a more egalitarian division of labor—secretaries are involved in the development of the office and in discussions about business—and reject hierarchical salaries.

In addition to these forms of law practice, both traditional and modern, alternative structures and experiences are emerging, which tend to affect the lawyer's practice.

## The Gap Between the Historical Definition of the Lawyer and the Actual Practice of Law

Since the beginning of this century, the practice of law in Geneva has changed considerably in all the ways discussed above. The lawyer's activities have diversified with respect to both legal advice and the representation of litigants. Whereas lawyers previously had shared the function of rendering legal advice only with the former solicitors and notaries, now they compete with other legal professionals, both because of the diffusion of juridical competence throughout the commercial and industrial sectors and because other agents are representing litigants in court. Moreover, the composition of law offices also has diversified, and the techniques of work have been modernized. Finally, the authority of the Order of Lawyers has been challenged by competing organizations and unorganized lawyers.

The totality of these changes has had the effect of increasing the already existing gap between the regulations ostensibly governing the legal profession and the actual practice of law today. Indeed, the legislation in force until 1985 persisted in viewing the lawyer exclusively as an officer of the court. Everything continued as though lawyers, like their nineteenth-century predecessors, still were generalists capable of mastering all the various forms of business and the entire corpus of laws, as though the lawyer truly enjoyed a monopoly and dominated the market for legal advice (see, for example, the prohibition of all publicity), as though partnerships among lawyers did not exist, and as though the Order of Lawyers remained, for the judicial authorities, the sole interlocutor and the sole depository of the rules governing the legal profession (Perrot, 1980).

The gap between the rules and conceptions that supposedly guided the legal profession and the concrete practice of law explains why the uncertainties and difficulties of application have led the lawyers and judicial authorities of the canton to seek to modify the legislation concerning the legal profession. These are the stakes; the story and the outcome of this reform will occupy the rest of this chapter.

## GENEVA LAWYERS: KEY POINTS IN ELABORATION OF THE REFORM

The reform carried out between 1979 and 1985 is the product of both a diffuse preoccupation within the judicial milieus and an assertion of will by the political authorities who supervise the judicial organization of the canton and, consequently, the legal profession. The preoccupation of the judicial milieus was expressed in various demands prior to 1979. In 1976 a commission constituted by the Order of Lawyers and the association of magistrates had proposed a reform on one particular point, the taxation of costs. Then, in 1977, the Order of Lawyers made other proposals regarding the totality of arrangements concerning the bar.

These proposals gradually attracted the interest of those with political power. At the beginning of 1979, a deputy submitted a bill concerning responsibility for the roll of lawyers. Then the head of the Department of Justice and the Police created a commission charged with reconsidering all the rules pertaining to the legal profession. It is possible to distinguish two stages in the elaboration of the law: the formulation of the rough draft by the Expert Commission (1979–1982) and the discussion of a definitive text and the passage of the law by the Geneva Parliament (1983–1985).

The Expert Commission charged with drafting the proposal contained nine members: three magistrates, three representatives of the lawyers (chosen by the bâtonnier of the Order), a representative of the Association of Progressive Jurists, a former federal judge called as an expert by the commission, and the representative of the Department of Justice and the Police. This commission operated for eighteen months and held thirty meetings. In 1982 it published its draft, accompanied by an explanatory report (Projet de loi sur la profession d'avocat, no. 5475).

This draft, submitted to Parliament on 20 April 1983, after consultation with the interested professional milieus, was examined by the judicial commission of the Great Council (the Geneva Parliament). The legislative phase of the decisional process was marked by long and sometimes heated debates. The judicial commission held nearly twenty meetings. It was composed of deputies from different parties and also included the head of the Department of Justice and the Police, as well as two members of the

Expert Commission. The parliamentary commission proceeded to hold numerous hearings. The Order of Lawyers was consulted again, as well as the Association of Progressive Jurists, government jurists, professors at the Law Faculty, and representatives of two large law offices. The work of the judicial commission of the Great Council ended with the unanimous adoption (except for two abstentions) of a bill (PL 5475-A) on 12 December 1984. The bill was accompanied by a majority report presented by a deputy of the Liberal party. A minority report also was submitted by a deputy belonging to the extreme right-wing party (Vigilant).

The presentation of reports and the discussion of the bill occupied three sessions of the Geneva assembly, two on 14 February and one on 15 March 1985 (Mémorial du Grand conseil). The final text of the law on the legal profession, dated 14 March 1985, took effect on 1 September of that year. Two appeals since have been lodged with the Swiss Federal Court; on 18 October 1985 the first resulted in the suppression of a paragraph concerning incompatibility (art. 7, para. C); the other, concerning use of the title of lawyer, has not yet been decided.

In order to study the passage of the law we will examine the intentions and strategies of all the actors concerned: the Department of Justice and the Police (the responsible cantonal administration, subordinate to a Councillor of State, who is a member of the Geneva executive), the Expert Commission charged by this Department, the Order of Lawyers, the Association of Progressive Jurists, as well as the Parliament (the Great Council), with its various political divisions. We will show how the determination to obtain the approval of both the interested professional milieus and the political forces, despite their divergent orientations, permitted the creation of a consensus on the principal points under discussion. Finally, we will analyze the reemergence of opposition during the parliamentary debate, before identifying the changes introduced by the new law and evaluating the results obtained by the different participants.

This analysis will deal successively with the following key points of the reform: the redefinition of the role of the lawyer and the question of use of the lawyer's title, the activity of lawyers and especially the problems posed by incompatibility with other roles and by the partnership form, the organization of the profession, and the modification of disciplinary procedures.

## REDEFINITION OF THE LEGAL PROFESSION

Geneva lawyers, as we have emphasized already, were treated as officers of the court by the laws in force until 1985. Their functions, defined by the law of judicial organization (Loi d'organisation judiciaire of 22 November 1941 and regulations of 16 June 1956), consisted essentially of representing parties before criminal and civil jurisdictions and preparing pleadings (art. 127 of the Law of 22 November 1941, reenacting the Law of 22 June 1878).[8]

The title of lawyer could be held by all Swiss citizens who had completed their legal studies (a law degree [license en droit]) obtained in Geneva or in another Swiss university or even an equivalent credential) and had taken the oath before the Council of State. Supplementary conditions—the professional apprenticeship of two years and the examination at the end of the apprenticeship (the lawyer's "brevet")—were required only to represent parties in civil matters (Loi d'organisation judiciaire, 21 November 1944, art. 125).

Various problems resulted from these arrangements. The gap between the legal definition of the lawyer and actual professional practice made it difficult to account for the lawyer's nonjudicial activities and led to self-questioning about the status of those lawyers who, because they were increasingly involved in offering legal advice or conducting arbitrations, also were distancing themselves from judicial activity and no longer were interested in being attached to the court.

Moreover, the imprecision of the arrangements concerning use of the lawyer's title caused all kinds of difficulties. A small number of jurists or apprentices, who had not passed the professional examination, nevertheless called themselves lawyers, which tended to confuse the public. Furthermore, certain lawyers enrolled in the bar no longer actually practiced law but instead engaged in other activities (as journalists or jurists in the public administration, for instance). The law was equally imprecise with respect to the situation of lawyers from other cantons when they practiced in Geneva and lawyers from other countries who sought to associate with local law firms. As late as 1985, for example, the Order of Lawyers had initiated a prosecution "concerning a French national who had no right whatever to use the title of lawyer" (Ordre des avocats de Genève, 1984b).

To remedy the gaps in the legislation, the Expert Commission decided to draft an entirely new law rather than amend the existing text. This solution appeared "judicious and necessary to assure a complete regulation of the profession," especially of the extrajudicial aspects of the lawyer's activity (Projet de loi sur la profession d'avocat du 20 avril 1983, exposé des motifs, p. 21).

The goal was to redefine the mission of the lawyer and the conditions under which a jurist (i.e., a law graduate) could be called a lawyer. The definition of a lawyer evoked conflict within the commission. Some felt that the lawyer's mission should remain narrowly limited to representing litigants before the tribunals. For others, it was necessary to integrate the increasingly diversified activities of the lawyer, which implied that legal oversight should be extended to lawyers' extrajudicial activities.

In opposition to these definitions, which assigned different weights to the judicial and extrajudicial activities of lawyers, the progressive movement proposed to reconsider the lawyer's mission, making it depend less on the hopes of lawyers and more on the needs of litigants. The progressive jurists emphasized that knowledge of the public's wishes was the prerequisite for adapting professional services to public needs:

> We continue to regulate the profession because it is there and not by taking as our point of departure the needs to which it responds. . . . What are the needs of litigants for defense, for legal aid, for the intervention of a specialized professional? This reflection had no place in the deliberations. (A lawyer on the Expert Commission)

The elaboration of the proposal failed to reexamine the totality of judicial functions or take account of demands that still had not reached the tribunals—disputes between landlords and tenants, for example, or consumers' problems. The debate was preoccupied with modifying the existing conditions of law practice.

The question of what limits to place on the activities of lawyers did not receive a clear solution. The recent transformation of practice—the growth of legal advice, the role of lawyers in administering businesses or international affairs—was thoroughly described and discussed, but it had been integrated only partially into the new legislation.

Thus, article 1 of the proposal, defining the lawyer's mission, made legal advice subordinate to the representation of parties before the tribunals. The other functions of Geneva lawyers—such as arbitration or participation in the activities of industrial or commercial companies—are referred to only later, as limitations:

> Article 1. The mission of lawyers is to assist and to represent litigants and claimants before the judicial and administrative authorities. They give advice in juridical matters. (Projet de loi sur la profession d'avocat du 20 avril 1983)

This outcome made it seem that the Expert Commission had not been able to choose between the different conceptions that have shaped lawyers' work more or less explicitly. The participants understood that the activities of lawyers have become increasingly diverse as they have expanded into new professional markets. Whether the participants were magistrates or lawyers, however, they emphasized their preference for legislation that affirmed the continuing attachment of lawyers to judicial institutions, either because the commissioners were concerned to ensure the efficacious functioning of those institutions or because they wished to preserve the historical role of the lawyer as a guaranty of the defense of accused in criminal matters:

We look with nostalgia at the lawyer who rises in a hearing to undertake the defense of someone. This is one of the most magnificent aspects of the profession: to fight against injustice with talent and honesty. This, truly, is the role of the lawyer. (A lawyer belonging to the Expert Commission)

If the mission of the lawyer became the focus of a difficult compromise, the question of who could claim the title of lawyer offered a common ground for all the commissioners. This agreement was founded on a shared objective—the defense of the interests of litigants. Consider, for example, the following extract from our interviews:

The public has an interest in being represented by competent people. It is necessary to be particular about the competence of those granted a monopoly of representing parties before the tribunals. There must be technical competence, proper behavior, and security with respect to the people whom the lawyers represent.... The goal is the protection of the public. It requires preventing just anyone from using the title of lawyer in the public view once this law is passed. (A magistrate belonging to the Expert Commission)

To protect the litigant against the "charlatans" and "sharpers" who "encumbered" the profession—to invoke some of the expressions actually used—it was necessary to restrict entry to the profession (through apprenticeship and the professional examination) and insist that lawyers belonging to the bar (i.e., those named in the Roll) really be "those practicing the profession." Thus, the litigant would be protected against those calling themselves lawyers without joining the bar and against apprentices who claimed the title of lawyer without having acquired sufficient professional experience.

The proposed law reserved the title of lawyer to jurists who had completed their apprenticeship, passed the professional examination, and were inscribed in the Roll of the Attorney General (art. 5, Project de loi sur la profession d'avocat). Enrollment would become a prerequisite for practicing law even though, previously, it had constituted only a logical consequence of membership in the bar (art. 130, Loi d'organisation judiciaire du 22 November 1941).

The Expert Commission had scarcely explored even the definition of the legal profession. It had strongly emphasized the selection (the "purification" according to one magistrate) of those practitioners (jurists, apprentices) who occupy the periphery of the profession. Furthermore, apprentices seemed to be the real victims of restrictions on the use of the lawyer's title. In effect, the Expert Commission introduced a new stage in the process of becoming a lawyer. Apprentices are forbidden not only to use the lawyer's title (art. 5, Projet de loi sur la profession d'avocat du 20 avril 1983) but also to attract and serve their own clientele—which they could have done in criminal matters under the previous law (art. 9 of the regulations of 16 June 1956)—yet apprentices still must represent indigent accused and those without lawyers:

> Apprentices cannot perform procedural acts or take instructions, present themselves or plead in civil or penal matters except in the name of and under the supervision of the lawyer to whom they are apprenticed, unless they are required to do so by virtue of their office. In the latter case, they enjoy, according to the cantonal plan, the same rights as lawyers. (Projet de loi sur la profession d'avocat du 20 avril 1983)

The parliamentary debates did not modify the proposed law with respect to the definition of the lawyer's activities or use of the lawyer's title. The judicial commission of the Great Council thoroughly considered whether one could separate the judicial and extrajudicial aspects of law practice in order to regulate them differently. It rejected that alternative, however: law practice forms a whole, and the judicial phase of a matter often is preceded by an extrajudicial phase.

The judicial commission then ratified the compromise elaborated by the Expert Commission, advancing the same scheme for the representation of parties before tribunals and for the lawyer's extrajudicial activities:

> It is not normal to consider the activity of the lawyer as though it ought to be located exclusively within tribunals.... It is important, however, not to forget that the profession of lawyer was created, above all, to assure the representation of parties in litigation, and that this role should continue to constitute the basis of the regulation in this domain. (Rapport de la commission judiciaire chargée d'étudier le projet de loi sur la profession d'avocat, rapport de la majorité, p. 4)

The first article of the proposal, modified in this way, was passed without discussion by the Geneva Assembly:

> Lawyers attend and represent litigants and administrative applicants before the judicial and administrative authorities. They represent their clients with respect to third parties and give advice on juridical matters. (Article 1, Loi sur la profession d'avocat du 14 mars 1985)

The proposal concerning use of the lawyer's title generated strong opposition among jurists employed in the administration, who would have been prevented from using the title of "lawyer" in Geneva. In response, the proposal was modified by the judicial commission to prohibit use of the title only in professional activities: "No one can use the title of lawyer in professional activities unless inscribed on the Roll of lawyers" (art, 5, Loi sur la profession d'avocat du 14 mars 1985).

This arrangement allowed great flexibility in the actual use of the title, as shown by the commentary of a councillor of state who had initiated the reform proposal: "The bankers and functionaries who used to be lawyers and who write to a duchess in order to send her flowers or to a magistrate to send their best wishes will be able to attach their personal visiting card containing the title of "lawyer"; such usage involves purely private correspondance and personal relations" (Mémorial du Grand conseil, 15 mars 1985, p. 1475).

The same councillor suggested that lawyers who were unhappy with this solution have recourse to the federal tribunal, which they subsequently did (the case still is pending).

## THE REGULATION OF PROFESSIONAL PRACTICE

The Expert Commission found itself confronted with various problems as a result of the evolution of law practice. The diversification of the lawyers' tasks confers on them functions identical with those of other legal professionals, with whom they must compete. Moreover, the assumption by lawyers of such nonjudicial functions as the administration of industrial or commercial companies puts them in situations not foreseen by either the legal texts or the professional customs. The partnership form, which has become an economic imperative, leads the lawyer to collaborate with people, such as members of other professions or foreign lawyers, who may not have the same professional ethic or the same economic interests. These problems will be described successively.

### The Question of the Monopoly of Lawyers

For the lawyers, and especially for the representatives of the Order, recognition of their monopoly of giving legal advice (even with numerous exceptions in favor of the other specialists with whom they have shared this function) would have helped to distinguish the profession of lawyer from the other juridical professions:

> Our goal always is to anticipate the protection of the litigant.... What seems dangerous is that, today, anybody can open an office and give advice without holding any diploma whatever. We propose to improve the regulation of extrajudicial advice. Only the lawyer and the other recognized juridical professions—such as notaries, bailiffs, business agents, and law professors—should be able to give advice outside of court. We make exceptions for professional organizations and trade unions, as well as charitable organizations.... We would be ready to add those who hold law degrees because they have

convinced us that they also are jurists and that it is necessary to allow them this privilege. (A lawyer belonging to the Expert Commission)

After having "broken several lances" in the body of the Commission in order to obtain an extension of their monopoly, the lawyers and the other juridical professions rapidly admitted that their demand was unrealistic, given the opposition of both the political milieus and the public. This opposition, which was revealed by the failure of earlier reform projects (see the preceding discussion of competition with other professions), was characterized by a magistrate in the following manner:

> The lawyers wished to enjoy an extended monopoly. But they knew in advance they would be beaten. In the political arena, both left and right were united in refusing such an extension of the monopoly.... I personally support the monopoly of representing parties before the judicial and administrative authorities. But it is self-delusion to seek to extend it to legal advice. Everyone gives legal advice! (A magistrate belonging to the Expert Commission)

Although they sought a monopoly that they knew in advance probably could not be attained, the lawyer members of the Commission wished at least wished to formalize the organization of the judicial market: "We said: not an absolute monopoly for lawyers, but let us seek regulation of the juridical market, so that those who offer legal services must indicate what title they hold" (a lawyer member of the Expert Commission).

Such a regulation of the activity of other legal professionals does not appear in the proposal. The measure confirms the monopoly lawyers already enjoyed, without extending it to legal advice. These arrangements have left the commissioners dissatisfied and stimulated various reactions among the members of the bar. The issue of monopoly was not revised further during the legislative process despite the arguments of the Order of Lawyers. Before the judicial commission, the Order repeated that it would like "the monopoly of legal advice, so that lawyers could divide it with notaries, bailiffs, trade unions and other professional organizations." The report of the judicial commission emphasized that such a rule, which would entail difficulties of application, was not properly within the domain of the law on the profession (Rapport de la majorité, pp. 2, 5).


## Activities Incompatible with the Practice of Law

The diversification of their activities has led lawyers to engage in several kinds of activity simultaneously, which poses the question regarding which combinations are incompatible with professional ethics. Two opposed tendencies emerged within the Expert Commission.

Both the promoters of the proposal and the magistrates wished to extend the definition of activities incompatible with those of the lawyer in order better to control the profession. They particularly supported the exclusion of lawyers from participation in the administrative functions of commercial or industrial enterprises and from all forms of salaried employment. This again expresses the conception, previously visible in the debate concerning the lawyer's mission, that lawyers ought to be officers of the court and preserve their economic independence.

By contrast, both the Order of Lawyers and the progressive lawyers wished to preserve the existing arrangements, which, by their silence on this point, permitted the simultaneous practice of diverse professional activities. The Order of Lawyers sought to allow members of the bar to sit on the administrative councils; the progressive lawyers wished to safeguard the situation of practicing lawyers as well as the salaried lawyers in the new forms of partnership.

The Expert Commission, in order to satisfy all its members, chose the intermediate solution of extending the definition of incompatibility without excluding any other activity:

> Given the diversity of situations in which the administrative agency of a commercial company can be exercised, it does not appear consistent with the freedom of commerce and industry to prohibit lawyers from exercising such agency, but, in certain cases, acceptance of such an agency can run afoul of the incompatibility restrictions resulting from the exercise of a commercial or industrial profession. (Projet de loi sur la profession d'avocat, 20 avril 1983, exposé des motifs, p. 24)

The proposal by the Expert Commission adopted the previously existing incompatibilities (with the professions of notary and bailiff) and introduced the prohibition against practicing "a commercial and industrial profession" as well as "all salaried administrative functions except those concerning legal education." Nevertheless, this arrangement constituted an important change, as was emphasized by the statement of legislative intent accompanying the proposed law: "These innovations have a particular importance, because they restrain the liberty of the lawyer to practice another professional activity in addition to law" (Projet de loi sur la profession d'avocat, 20 avril 1983, exposé des motifs, p. 24).

These transformation still did not satisfy everyone. Those who wished to preserve access to the increasingly varied professional market feared the new restrictions. Those who emphasized the judicial role of the lawyer had secured the incorporation of certain additional incompatibilities, but they had not succeeded in normalizing all the activity of lawyers. These dissatisfactions were expressed repeatedly at every stage of the legislative process.

During the analysis of the proposed law by the judicial commission of the Great Council, the tendency toward opening the profession prevailed under pressure from the Order of Lawyers. The Order had suggested language that would allow lawyers to engage in other activities, provided these did not "preponderate" over the practice of law, and the clause was adopted without too much controversy.

During the parliamentary debate, this clause was the object of further discussion, in the course of which the manner in which it had been introduced was strongly criticized by a deputy who favored limiting the extrajudicial activity of lawyers:

> On this question of incompatibility, which would have merited a long debate, suddenly, in a meeting of the Geneva parliament, this proposal of the Order of Lawyers was presented and passed without sufficient reflection about its consequences. This clause was passed very quickly during a meeting, in the course of which, all at once, one of our colleagues made the proposal appear in his hand, like a magician. (Mémorial du Grand conseil, 14 février 1985, p. 559)

An amendment was proposed, without success, that would have restored the proposal of the Expert Commission: a stricter limitation of the activities of lawyers in order to guarantee control over these and "the possibility of intervening against abuses with respect to administrative councils" (Mémorial du Grand conseil, 14 février 1985, p. 558).

The text of the law adopted in March 1985 included the modifications concerning salaried employment proposed by the Order:

> Article 7. The practice of law is incompatible with: a) the functions of the magistrate of the judicial power, except for judges of the Cour de Cassation, the President of the Tribunal des conflits, deputy judges, and members of the labor tribunals; b) the functions of notary and bailiff; c) all profitable activity that preponderates over the practice of law, with the exception of legal instruction; d) all activity contrary to the dignity of the bar.

This formulation, which would have enlarged the activities of the lawyer and presaged difficulties of interpretation, did not survive in the final text, however. A challenge to paragraph (c) on the ground of its inconsistency with the constitutional protection of freedom of commerce and industry was filed in the Federal Tribunal and accepted on 18 October 1985. It was brought by a second-year law student who feared that because he lived entirely on his earnings as a music teacher he might be prevented from serving his apprenticeship. This appeal, like the judgment with which it concluded, emphasized that the rules governing incompatibility could adversely affect a particular category of jurists, the apprentices. Indeed, the proposed measures especially affected the young lawyers who earned their subsistence from salaried employment at the time when they entered the profession. Thus, it was the perspective of actors who were neither consulted nor associated with the reform that finally prevailed over the partisans of more rigorous regulations and the corporatist strategies of the Order of Lawyers.

## The Problem of Partnership

A final point concerning the diversification of lawyers' activities, which excited tensions and pressures during the legislative phase, was the question of partnerships among lawyers, with other jurists, and with foreign jurists.

The proposal of the Expert Commission allowed lawyers to enter into partnership with each other in order to practice law but prohibited partnerships with anyone practicing another profession, such as a business agent, a real estate agent, or an insurance agent (art. 11 of the proposal). This text survived the strongest opposition and the longest debates in Parliament.

The Order of Lawyers was concerned that the measure was insufficient to protect the legitimate interests of Geneva lawyers. It demanded that partnerships between Geneva lawyers and foreign lawyers be prohibited:

> The Council of the Order is resolutely opposed to the possibility of partnerships between members of the Geneva bar and foreign lawyers residing in our canton (though their employment by those partnerships is perfectly acceptable). Associations between Geneva and foreign law firms are more likely if guarantees are given... that foreign colleagues cannot practice regularly in our canton. (Ordre des avocats de Genève, 1984a: 5)

By contrast, certain Geneva lawyers who belonged to the largest offices in the city and long had been engaged in collaborations with foreign lawyers practicing in Geneva were opposed to any limitation on the modes of association between Swiss and foreign lawyers.

In the course of the parliamentary debates, various solutions were proposed but finally abandoned in favor of the text elaborated by the judicial commission: "Lawyers inscribed in the Roll can form partnerships or share an office only with those practicing the same professional activity" (art. 11, para. 1, Loi sur la profession d'avocat du 14 mars 1985). The tone of this article, while enlarging the possibility of partnerships with jurists who are not lawyers, remains imprecise, particularly with respect to relations with foreign lawyers.

The outcome of these debates regarding the regulation of professional practice reveals the dissatisfaction of both those who wanted recognition of the exclusive right of lawyers to render legal advice and those who wished to make the practice of law the only activity of lawyers. Lawyers did not obtain an extension of their monopoly. However, the reformers also did not obtain a more precise definition of the activities incompatible with the practice of law. Inertia and conservatism preserved the existing regulations concerning monopoly, incompatibility, and partnerships.

## THE ORGANIZATION OF THE PROFESSION AND THE MODIFICATIONS OF THE DISCIPLINARY PROCESS

As a result of the evolution of the profession, Geneva lawyers were subordinated to two authorities: the Council of the Order of Lawyers and the Disciplinary Commission (Commission de surveillance) of the bar. The Council of the Order, elected by its members, exercises authority over only those members, who constitute about 70 percent of the bar. The Disciplinary Commission, composed of magistrates and lawyers and presided over by the Attorney General, has jurisdiction over all lawyers (art. 135 of the Loi d'organisation judiciaire du 22 novembre 1941).

Although the principles that guide the intervention of both these bodies —namely, the "usages and customs of the bar" (Perrot, 1980)—are identical, as are certain of the matters they handle, the disciplinary practice of each assumes a different form. The measures taken by the Council of the Order—expulsion of a member, for instance—have little direct impact on the lawyer's professional activity as long as they are not confirmed by the Disciplinary Commission, which can expel the lawyer from the bar. Whereas the Order has the will to intervene but not the power, the Disciplinary Commission is empowered to act but does so only in exceptional circumstances. By virtue of its composition, its decisions receive wide publicity and entail consequences that extend beyond the profession and risk harming the image of the entire judicial institution:

> The Disciplinary Commission unites those inside the court. They are solidary. They always tend to minimize the need for intervention. (A lawyer belonging to the Expert Commission)

> The Disciplinary Commission is lax. There must be true catastrophes and a great deal of insistence on the part of the Order for them to prohibit a lawyer from working. (A lawyer belonging to the Expert Commission)

This dysfunction of the disciplinary procedures has led all those concerned to seek to transform the structures of the profession. In order to coordinate the action of the two regulatory institutions and to make disciplinary measures more effective, the Geneva executive sought to make the Order of Lawyers an official body. The Order, by contrast, felt that the harmonization of control could be realized more effectively if both institutions were composed exclusively of members of the bar.

It is interesting to describe the process that led to codification of the status quo with respect to one of the issues that had stimulated the legislative revision. The members of the Expert Commission quickly reached a conclusion about making the Order an official body. They agreed unanimously not to decide this question: "Since the second meeting, the question of the official status of the Order has been settled. We have decided to propose a law that disregards this question" (a magistrate belonging to the Expert Commission).

Everything proceeded as though the sidestepping of this problem constituted a presupposition of the Commission. It had been concerned since beginning its work to avoid formalizing different conceptions and thereby crystalizing conflict, whether this divided the Order of Lawyers and the progressive jurists, the government and the bar, or the Order of Lawyers itself. This decision conforms to the teachings of history and also is confirmed by informal consultations with both lawyers and members of Parliament. It ended with the maintenance of a status quo acceptable to the entire profession.

Because the question of officialization remained undecided, however, all the work of the Expert Commission was characterized by what one lawyer called a "handicap." In particular, how could it resolve the problems posed by the supervision of lawyers without first having defined the status and competence of the Order? The experts proposed to formalize certain rules previously contained in the usages and customs of which the Order is the sole guardian, thereby specifying the criteria for intervention by the Disciplinary Commission. However, these modifications, which subordinated the two procedures to identical substantive principles, are not sufficient to guarantee agreement regarding the application of these rules as long as they are interpreted sometimes by the lawyers themselves and sometimes by an external body. The composition of the Disciplinary Commission was debated within the Expert Commission, but it was not changed; the Attorney General retained the presidency of this institution, as he insisted.

Although the participants had expressed the wish to transform existing practices, the reform proposal still did not modify either the status of the Order of Lawyers or the composition or function of the Disciplinary Commission. It reaffirmed the existing regulations while incorporating within the legal text certain "usages and customs," for example, those concerning professional secrets (art. 13, Projet de loi sur la profession d'avocat, 20 avril 1983).

During the legislative phase of the process, this reaffirmation of the status quo had been questioned with respect to the composition of the Disciplinary Commission. Although the judicial commission maintained the size of the Disciplinary Commission at nine, it reallocated the membership. The Order of Lawyers had revived the issue by arguing that the

Disciplinary Commission "ought to be composed of a majority of lawyers, and its president ought to be the bâtonnier or another lawyer" (Rapport de la majorité, p. 483). Instead, the judicial commission modified the composition of the Disciplinary Commission in the following manner:

Article 18: A commission of the bar is established containing 9 members, of Swiss nationality, as follows: a) 3 members named by the lawyers inscribed in the Roll; b) 3 members named by the Great Council; and c) 3 members named by the Council of State. Two of the members mentioned in clauses (b) and (c) shall be chosen from among the career magistrates of the judicial power and at least two other members shall be chosen from outside the legal profession. (Texte du Projet de loi issu de la commission judiciaire du Grand conseil, Mémorial du Grand conseil, 14 février 1985, p. 500)

The bar thus obtained a guarantee that at least three lawyers would sit on the commission instead of just two. The number of magistrates was reduced from three to two, and the Attorney General no longer was a member of the commission by right. Nevertheless, the lawyers had to accept at least two lay members, who could be neither lawyers nor magistrates. Despite appearances, this measure actually reduced the potential power of lawyers within the commission. Given the prominent role of lawyers in Swiss politics, the process of appointment by the Great Council and the Council of State previously would have assured them six members out of nine (two lawyer members by right and four others designated by the two councils); now they could count on no more than five members (three members by right and two others designated by the cantonal authorities).

The Order of Lawyers reacted by proposing an amendment during the parliamentary debate, which—by eliminating the clauses concerning the presence of both magistrates and laypersons—could have produced a commission composed exclusively of lawyers (three designated by the bar, three by the Council of State, and three by the Great Council). This amendment was rejected, although not without stimulating lively debate. In opposing a commission formed entirely of magistrates and lawyers— "who are part of the same world"—critics asserted the need to ensure the openness of the decisions of the Disciplinary Commission. We can illustrate this with the following extract from the debate:

We think it is indispensable to complete the commission with laypersons who can represent the litigants, which will be a pledge that the body is a disciplinary commission and not a corporatist commission designed to protect special interests against the public. (Mémorial du Grand conseil, 14 février 1985, p. 566)

The composition of the commission thus remained that proposed by the judicial commission of the Great Council (see the discussion of art. 18 above). The Disciplinary Commission of the bar began functioning on 1 March 1986. It consists of five lawyers, two magistrates, and two laypersons, one of whom is a journalist. Yet, despite the presence of two nonjurist members, a skeptic might well ask whether this commission does not remain "a closed circle where only people who think well of each other are represented" (Mémorial du Grand conseil, 14 février 1985, p. 527).

## CONCLUSION

The preceding analysis emphasizes the interdependence of the constitutive elements of the professional system: change in the activities of lawyers, in ethics and the regulation of the problems of internal functions, in relations with other juridical professions, and in more diffuse currents within the local judicial society. Every partial change has repercussions on the total functioning of the profession. The modifications discussed and proposed in the course of the reform, even minor ones, entailed the ongoing redefinition of professional structures. The interdependence of the elements composing the profession thus can result in reproducing the existing situation, as shown by the entire process of elaborating the law concerning lawyers.

The work of the Expert Commission as well as that of the judicial commission and the debates of the Great Council are characterized less by the desire to impose a particular conception of the legal profession, whatever it might be, than by the wish to take account of change and diversity within the contemporary legal profession.

Thus, the proposal to revive the traditional definition of the lawyer as uniquely attached to the judicial institutions—still present in the text proposed by the Expert Commission, if in attenuated form—disappeared from the final version of the law: in effect, the extrajudicial activities of lawyers have been given equal recognition with their judicial activities. Similarly, the conception of the progressive jurists, which would have required a rethinking of the foundations of the profession in order to take account of the needs of litigants, has not been embodied in the reflections accompanying the elaboration of the law.

Instead, the new legislation reflects the actual practices of lawyers. The reform has been the occasion for reflection and confrontation, in the course of which there was constant concern to take account of the diverse conceptions about the occupation of lawyer. During the debates in the commissions and in Parliament, amendments were adopted in response to the preoccupations of different professional concerns: the Order of Lawyers (relaxation of the rules concerning incompatibility), the large law offices (an increase in the possibility of partnerships with foreign lawyers), and jurists in the administration (permission to use the lawyer's title).

Although the new law did not satisfy the expectations of every component of the legal profession, it still presents a snapshot of contemporary Geneva lawyers. Its merit, without doubt, is in reducing the gap between the legislation in force and the actual practice of the legal profession.

# TABLES

8.1. Growth of the Geneva Bar, 1712–1903

| Lawyers enrolled during | Number |
|---|---|
| 1712–1721 | 39 |
| 1722–1731 | 20 |
| 1732–1741 | 19 |
| 1742–1751 | 20 |
| 1752–1761 | 12 |
| 1762–1771 | 23 |
| 1772–1781 | 30 |
| 1782–1791 | 18 |
| 1792–1798 | 14 |
| 1814–1823 | 26 |
| 1824–1833 | 35 |
| 1834–1843 | 16 |
| 1844–1851 | 34 |
| 1863–1872 | 35 |
| 1873–1882 | 52 |
| 1883–1892 | 38 |
| 1893–1902 | 83 |
| 1903 | 11 |

*Source:* Choisy (1904).

8.2. Distribution (in Percent) of Geneva Lawyers by Age and Professional Status, 1984

| | | Professional Status | | |
|---|---|---|---|---|
| Age | Principal[a] | Salaried lawyer | Apprentice | Total |
| < 30 | 4 | 32 | 79 | 27 |
| 30–39 | 37 | 64 | 17 | 37 |
| 40–49 | 25 | 4 | 4 | 16 |
| 50–59 | 15 | — | — | 9 |
| ≥ 60 | 19 | — | — | 11 |
| N | 392 | 125 | 161 | 678 |

[a]The age of the lawyer is not given in three instances.

8.3. Distribution of Geneva Lawyers by Professional Status and Type of Office, 1984[a]

| Composition of offices | Principal | | SL[b] | | Apprentice | |
|---|---|---|---|---|---|---|
| | No. | % | No. | % | No. | % |
| SP[c] | 137 | 35 | — | — | — | — |
| SP with a single SL or apprentice | 25 | 6 | 10 | 9 | 15 | 11 |
| SP with several SLs or apprentices | 18 | 5 | 16 | 14 | 29 | 20 |
| 2 principals | 32 | 8 | — | — | — | — |
| 2 principals with ≥ 1 SLs or apprentices | 52 | 13 | 33 | 30 | 33 | 23 |
| 3 principals with ≥ 1 SLs or apprentices | 54 | 14 | 17 | 15 | 27 | 19 |
| > 3 principals with ≥ 1 SLs or apprentices | 77 | 19 | 35 | 32 | 39 | 27 |
| Total | 395 | 61 | 111 | 17 | 143 | 22 |

[a]Excluded from this table are fourteen lawyers (either salaried members of collectives or lawyers looking for employment) as well as eighteen apprentices (two not attached to a law office and sixteen serving their apprenticeships in the Geneva tribunals).

[b]SL = salaried lawyer.

[c]SP = solo practitioner.

# FIGURES

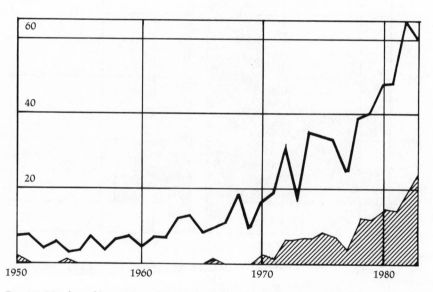

Fig. 8.1. Number of lawyers enrolling in the Geneva bar each year, total and women, 1950–1983.

Benoit Bastard and Laura Cardia-Vonèche

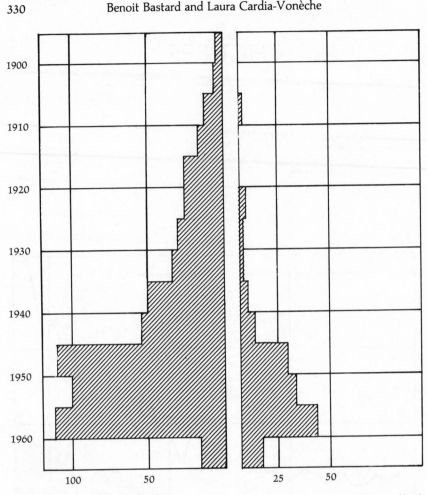

Fig. 8.2. Men and women lawyers and apprentices in the Geneva bar in 1984, by year of birth.

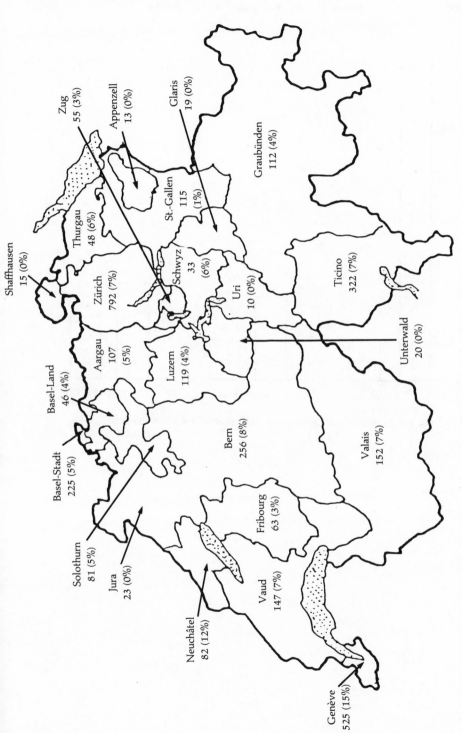

Fig. 8.3. Membership of the Swiss Federation of Lawyers, 1984, by canton (figures in parentheses represent proportions of women). (*Source*: Fédération suisse des avocats [1984].)

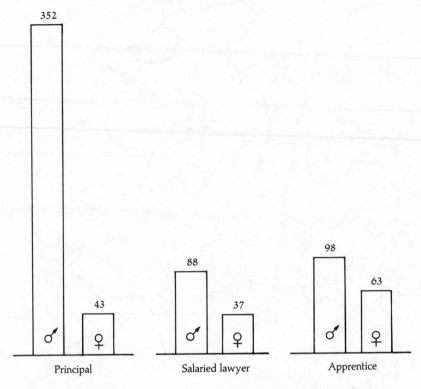

Fig. 8.4. Distribution of Geneva lawyers by professional status and gender, 1984.

# NOTES

Translated from French by Richard L. Abel. We wish to thank the Geneva lawyers and magistrates who took part in this study, as well as Jean-François Perrin, professor at the Faculty of Law of Geneva, and Jeanne Durlemann, for urging us to carry it out.

1. At the beginning of the eighteenth century, legal education within the University of Geneva—the former Academy created by the Reformation—had become more practical, especially by virtue of the publication and study of civil legislation—the Edits (Choisy, 1904).

2. Fusion of the professions of lawyer and solicitor occurred in France only in 1971, following a long and difficult reform (Boigeol [this volume, chap. 7]; Raguin, 1972).

3. Ever since 1878, the Swiss Confederation had subjected the medical professions, both physicians and pharmacists, to national regulation by virtue of a law prescribed by article 33 of the Constitution.

4. The law of 1863 kept a place, next to the lawyers (who held a license in law and had completed a two-year apprenticeship in Geneva or abroad), for another category, the "agréés," who represented a survival of the "free profession" sought by Fazy. The agréés did not have to obtain a diploma but only had to demonstrate their legal knowlege in an examination conducted by a special commission composed of magistrates and professors of the University of Geneva. The profession of agréé lasted until 1878, at which time the title was held by only eight people. However, the possibility it offered to enter the juridical professions without an academic degree, although rarely used, survived in Geneva and appeared, after several metamorphoses, in the law passed in 1985 (art. 29): "Exception to the requirement of a diploma: citizens without a juridical diploma who show that they have acquired the necessary knowledge, practical and theoretical, can be given a dispensation from the condition prescribed in Article 24 (license in law) if they have undertaken an examination about the law."

5. Here, as in all the following texts, the title of "Attorney General" designates the magistrate who, as in France, conducts criminal prosecutions and brings actions on behalf of the public. In Geneva, the Attorney General is the highest magistrate in the judicial hierarchy.

6. The number of lawyers in Geneva differs according to the source used. We are concerned here exclusively with the lawyers enrolled in the Swiss Federation of Lawyers and those who are members of the Order of Lawyers of Geneva.

7. There are 588 lawyers who have fulfilled the required conditions and been inscribed in the Roll of the Attorney General, to which we must add 161 apprentices. Nevertheless, more than 10 percent of the lawyers enrolled no longer practice law, because they are retired, have another activity, or are practicing outside Geneva. These lawyers have been excluded in the sociodemographic data presented (see figs. 8.1, 8.2, and 8.4 and tables 8.2 and 8.3). These data were

constructed by synthesizing various sources of information, and the authors alone are responsible for their accuracy. This explains the differences between our data and those provided by the Order of Lawyers: the Order does not include all the lawyers who practice and belong to a law office. By contrast, the Order may include lawyers who no longer practice but remain inscribed on the Roll.

8. It is necessary to emphasize that legal representation is not obligatory in Geneva, except in matters concerning the assize court. "No one is required to have recourse to the services of a lawyer" (art. 3 of the law on the legal profession, 14 March 1985). However, the right to appear in person before the tribunals rarely is exercised by Geneva litigants.

# REFERENCES

*Annuaire Statistique de la Suisse*. 1984. Bern: Birkhauser.

Association des juristes progressistes. 1974. *Sur la profession d'avocat*. Geneva: Association des juristes progressistes.

Chaulmontet, Philippe. 1970. "Contribution à l'étude de la profession d'avocat (Examen de la jurisprudence relative aux articles 31 et 33 de la Constitution Fédérale et 5 des dispositions transitoires)." Thesis for the License in Law, Faculty of Law, University of Lausanne.

Choisy, Albert. 1904. *La matricule des avocats de Genève*. Geneva: Société générale d'imprimerie.

Cornu, Charles. 1945. "La législation génevoise et l'exercice de la profession d'avocat," 39 *Semaine judiciaire* 593–618.

Crettaz, Jean-Marie. 1977. "Défense du barreau, défenseur de l'homme ménace," in Ordre des avocats de Genève, *Séance solonelle de rentrée (7 October)*. Geneva: Ordre des avocats de Genève.

Fédération Suisse des Avocats. 1984. *Mitglieder Verzeichnis, Tableau au ler janvier 1984*. Bern: Staempfli.

*L'Hebdo*. 1986. "La cité des avocats. Portrait du barreau génevois," *L'Hebdo* 38–42 (16 January).

Keller-Huguenin, Emile. 1929. *Le barreau en Suisse*. Geneva: Kundig.

Martin-Achard, Edmond. 1950. *Le rôle de l'avocat*. Geneva: Georg.

———. 1951. "La discipline des professions libérales," in *Actes de la Société des juristes*. Basel: Helbing and Lichtenhahn.

Ordre des avocats de Genève. 1977. *Séance solonelle de rentrée* (7 October). Genèva: Ordre des avocats de Genève.

———. 1984a. *Les cahiers de l'Ordre*, Vol. 1. Geneva: Ordre des avocats de Genève.

———. 1984b. *Bulletin d'information*, vol. 76. Geneva: Ordre des avocats de Genève.

Perrot, Raymond 1980. *Le serment de l'avocat et les us et coutumes du barreau de Genève*, 2d ed. Geneva: Ordre des avocats de Genève.

Raguin, Catherine. 1972. "L'indépendence de l'avocat. Réflexion sur deux réformes: la rénovation de la profession et l'aide judiciaire," 2 *Sociologie du travail* 164–184.

Siegrist, Hannes. 1985. "Gebremste Professionalisierung—Das Beispiel der Schweizer Rechtsanwaltschaft im Vergleich zu Frankreich und Deutschland im 19. und fruhen 20. Jahrhundert," in Werner Conze and Jürgen Kocka, eds., *Bildungsbürgertum im 19. Jahrhundert*. Stuttgart: Klett-Cotta.

# 9

# The Italian Legal Profession:
# An Institutional Dilemma

VITTORIO OLGIATI AND
VALERIO POCAR

## INTRODUCTION

A sociological analysis of the legal profession in Italy is difficult because
the scarce empirical research has been limited to certain aspects and problems. Although we use that literature whenever possible, we also have had
to rely on and incorporate our personal judgments. We define legal professionals as social actors equipped with a body of esoteric technical legal
knowledge, who operate with some autonomy, discretion, and authority.
This definition has two elements. First, a specific and socially recognized
working *activity* that individuals or social groups either are institutionally
required to perform or may perform within the legal system by reason of
their ascribed or acquired qualifications and expertise. Second, a specific
*role status*, usually attained through rigorous and selective technical, practical,
and ideological *rites de passage* that construct, legitimize, and control the
social distance between legal professionals and laypersons (Johnson,
1972). This definition locates all legal professionals within the widest
possible framework of the processes of professionalization and the mechanisms of institutionalization and social stratification (Parsons, 1954). More
particularly, it highlights the basic element that all these professionals
share: their organic dependence (Gramsci, 1971) on the bureaucratic-
administrative apparatus of the state. This tie is clearly visible in Italy:
formally in the legal matrix and substantively in the cultural base of every
legal profession. It assumes fundamental importance when, as recent socio-
legal literature shows, it defines the overall conditions of the performance
of the legal system and its interactions with society.

The degree of relative autonomy from the state distinguishes two large
categories of legal professionals, which differ in legal competence, structural prerequisites, and the manifest and latent outcomes of their activities.
One category includes the ideal-typical traditional "free" professionals—

lawyers and notaries. The other includes the professional legal operators: judges, juridical officials, agents of public safety, and so on. There are similarities between them. Legal professional operators—mainly state-employed agents or officials—can invoke some of the same sources of privilege and institutional power as lawyers and notaries. Furthermore, ideological, economic, and other indicators locate "free" professionals and some professional operators (high officials, magistrates) close to each other within the class structure. Nevertheless, the first category not only is assumed to possess the "classic" professional attributes (such as a theoretical–practical specialist qualification, a consciously held ideal of service, and status supports) but also has managed to attain and preserve, in both fact and law, relatively autonomous power over access to the professional market. Within the category of "free" professionals, lawyers differ from notaries less because of what they do (both offer legal advice) than because lawyers belong to an exclusive order, which gives them alone the right to meet certain socio-legal needs. Thus lawyers can be differentiated from notaries less by their prerogatives and institutional guarantees than because, legitimately and relatively autonomously, they can define both those socio-legal needs and how to satisfy them.[1]

This chapter examines the Italian lawyers from an evolutionary perspective. We describe the historical development of the legal profession after the Unification of Italy. Then we outline current tendencies and examine the typology of activities and socioprofessional interaction. Finally, we advance some thoughts about the definition of the legal professional ("Conclusion" section).

## THE HISTORICAL CLEAVAGE

Leafing through year after year of records on forensic activity, one frequently finds hints and references about the thousand-year continuity of the legal profession. Modernity and tradition, past and present, seem to merge recursively. But is not this self-representation only a means of collectively hiding the real historical cleavages that characterized the process of professionalization? These questions have greater importance: the essential attributes of modern legal professions are not a direct function of contemporary economic and technological processes but tend, instead, to reflect revolutionary political experience. In other words, the most enduring characteristics of modern legal professionalism—unlike those of the other "free" professions, such as physicians or engineers—are historical products of the *institutional* upheavals that occurred in each nation. Legal professionals always have been either protagonists or victims of any institutional change, whether its cause is a national liberation movement, a civil war, or a class struggle (Burrage, 1989).

To substantiate this we do not need to give detailed accounts of what happened in France, Russia, China, Yugoslavia, India, Venezuela, or Mozambique, to name but a few well-known cases.[2] Nor do we have to review the professional careers of jurists such as Robespierre, Lenin, Gandhi, or Castro, who transformed the material and symbolic conditions of their professions. We need only note that the institutional recomposition of the gap between relations of production and productive forces (the dynamic nexus between law, economy, and society) creates moments when the interstices within which legal professionals operate (Parsons, 1954) open or close in radical and often unpredictable ways.

Italy was no exception. After the insurrectional movement and the Wars of Independence (the *Risorgimento*), the proclamation of the Kingdom of Italy in 1861 deeply affected the entire profession. For the first time in the history of modern Italy one could justifiably talk of *Italian* lawyers in both sociological and legal terms. After Unification, the regional structures, practices, and legal systems, which had diverged over the centuries, lost their meaning and soon disapeared. The legislation inspired by these historical developments greatly affected the interests of lawyers during the following century. For example, the laws presently governing the legal profession (RDL 27 November 1933 n. 1578 and 22 January 1934 n. 36) derive from the model introduced by the Professional Law of 8 June 1874 (n. 1938) and the related rules. That law required practitioners to enroll in the Law List, prohibited them from performing both forensic and notarial functions, and distinguished between "avvocato" and "procuratore." That law also required a university degree in *giurisprudenza*. This ended the practice of conferring the title of lawyer on members of the nobility and the bureaucracy by virtue of their status and also discouraged the profession from continuing to train entrants itself. State support for higher education reduced the importance of heredity for entry and also opened the profession to women (art. 8 of the General University Act of 8 October 1876 passed under the Law on Public Education of 13 November 1859). On 9 August 1883 Signorina Lidia Poet of Pinerolo became the first woman to enroll in the Law List of the *Ordine* (bar) of Turin, stimulating adverse reactions and a long, heated debate throughout Italy (Bianchi, 1886).

The professional attribute of "prestige" also was affected by these changes. The duty to provide "honorary and free" legal aid (*gratuito patrocinio*) was established by the Law of 19 July 1880 (n. 5536) and confirmed by Royal Decree of 30 December 1923 (n. 3282). Parliament imposed this duty on the professional for reasons that were totally unconnected to the profession itself and rather reflected the state's severe financial problems during the post-Unification period. This institution, which provides few services (Siena, 1984) but still is invoked as a symbol of the lawyer's "public" function, displaced the ancient institution of the *Avvocatura dei Poveri*—the legal aid program found in all Italian States before Unification. The earlier system paid the lawyer to provide free legal services to the poor. Some programs were managed by a private charity or foundation (e.g., Avvocazia dei Poveri of Alessandria) and others by the state, or local town councils. The institutional change also affected the "systematic body of knowledge" and the attitudes of the professional group. By contributing to the journals, *Annali di Giurisprudenza* in Turin (which first proposed an annual statistical report on the administration of justice) and *Annali Toscani* (renamed *Annali della Giurisprudenza Italiana* in 1860), Italian lawyers in exile before Unification promoted new international cultural exchanges.

After Unification, most lawyers who took part in the Risorgimento encouraged their colleagues elected to Parliament to favor centralizing legislation and abandoned parties and principles for clients and their interests like their American counterparts following the Civil War (Patterson, 1981). Lawyers who did not take part in the Risorgimento only intensified their aversion to centralization, which, by breaking down regional boundaries, created a national professional market, fostering the migration from south to north that is a distinguishing trait of the modern Italian legal profession.

Nothing said so far can explain why Italian lawyers are so closely controlled and supervised by the state. Some of the reasons are political and directly connected to the location of lawyers within the class system and to the profession's roots in civil society. For example, professional fees, although governed by a tariff system, still are subject to judicial discretion when imposed on the losing party. However, autonomy also was restricted for reasons totally unconnected to lawyers' political ideology or professional attitude. For example, the whole legal system, and particularly the judiciary, was heavily affected by the state's financial deficit. That is why the Royal Decree of 23 December 1865 (n. 2700), while simplifying bureaucratic formalities through the use of *Carta Bollata* (stamped paper on which tax was paid), also retained the *Diritti di Cancelleria* (a tax paid by lawyers to the approximately 4,700 chancelleries of the courts of the Kingdom), thereby ensuring that the administration of justice (mainly in the civil courts) would remain as an important source of income for the state.

The professional transformation just described was managed, at both the social and the institutional levels, without either apparent or real trauma. This seems to confirm the widely held view that national unification was a "passive revolution" (Gramsci, 1971). To explain the speed with which the profession accepted the post-Unification government's "Bonapartist politics," however, one has to remember that the first conscious attempt to modernize the Italian legal profession was the Law of 22 Ventose XII (1804), imposed by armed force during the Napoleonic occupation. In the face of strong cultural and material opposition by conservative lawyers, this law sought to unify the profession and abolish some of its old and often anachronistic privileges by establishing a new model of professional organization based on the legally recognized institution of the Ordine (Bianchi, 1886). The Napoleonic law was in force only briefly, but it was enough—at the time of Restoration—to revive among Italian lawyers the ideal image of the French ordre (according to which lawyers were *maîtres de son tableau*—masters of their own roll) and, more particularly, the ancient and strong Italian tradition of *free* law societies, colleges, associations, chambers, and councils, which, in each preunitary state, often derived from medieval and renaissance municipal institutions, which, in turn, can be traced back to the Roman Imperial constitution of Justinian (Zanardelli, 1879).

Once the Independence of Italy was achieved, the Napoleonic law was taken as a model. According to the prevailing ideology, the Ordine was not the representative of a corporation pursuing private ends but a public entity, indissolubly professional *and* institutional, territorially diffuse, compulsory, formally distinct, and (relatively) autonomous, enjoying the power to regulate itself and to represent the entire professional group. This double image, recognized by the professional law of 1874, was viewed by both lawyers and the government as a compromise. The former were convinced they would be able to continue to influence the social and political system, while the latter believed that it now had the opportunity to control, perhaps even destroy, that traditional influence.

The compromise was only apparent, however. The Ordini established in 1874, which persist today, posed a "question" that was to have repercussions on all future development: what is meant by a *free* profession?

## THE CONTROVERSIAL FEATURES

The monopolistic character of "free" professionalism implies both exclusive rights over professional practice and the duty to provide the services required. This two-edged sword, while restraining other social actors from developing or using specific abilities or technical knowledge, does allow them to demand that those abilities or knowledge are made available (Larson, 1977). In their work lawyers encounter another duality: their performances are legally recognized as both public and private. The first aspect derives from the public's need for forensic functions and the correlative obligations imposed on lawyers in the interests of the administration of justice. The second is apparent in the lawyer's autonomy when dealing with extrajudicial matters (Lega, 1957; Satta, 1959). A careful diachronic analysis of the Italian legal system shows that this ambivalence, although constantly evident, never has been systematically resolved by the legislature. Thus, the problem of defining the role and functions of Italian lawyers— and of any other "free" profession in Italy—remains unresolved because the legal system subsumes and codetermines the professional variables (Lega, 1974). Professional jurists have tried to find a solution, if only because they are more qualified to do so than anyone else. Looking through the jurisprudence of the last century, one soon realizes that the controversial relationship between *compulsory public* office and the *free* practice of lawyers has always been resolved "technically" by shifting attention between the individual professional and the institutional environment, thereby achieving a continuous, if incoherent, normative postponement. This solution is formally and substantively questionable, however, for the Ordine itself remains ambiguous. "Even though the Ordine is within the state, it does not identify itself with the state; on the contrary, insofar as it is autonomous, the Ordine opposes the state..." (Satta, 1959: 655). Like each individual lawyer, it also oscillates between an orientation toward the legal system and toward other social systems. We will explore this problem further, concentrating on the Law of 1874, because of its symbolic role as a model for all other "free" professions in Italy, rather than on the professional laws currently in force (those enacted in 1933 and 1934).

It is possible to trace not one (Larson, 1977) but *two* "professional projects" in the formulation and subsequent enforcement of this normative text. One was supported by the professional group and oriented toward overcoming the manifestly corporate, and thus essentially private, aims that had directed the earlier professional associations. The other, supported by the legislature, pursued the same end but also aimed to bring the group into line with the new political program of the state.

The first "professional project" is documented in the reports of the First Italian Forensic Congress, held in Rome in 1872 to discuss the design of the law, and also in the important speeches made by famous jurists such as Francesco Carrara and Giuseppe Zanardelli immediately after its enactment (Norsa, 1872; Carrara, 1876; Zanardelli, 1879). The second "professional project" is apparent in the parliamentary records and influential comments on the final text (Bianchi, 1886). This text also has a dual character. It allows a single lawyer to combine the "necessary and compulsory" office of legal representation and assistance with the "free, supplementary and facilitative" office of consulting and pleading (Bianchi, 1886). This united the two professional categories, avvocati and procuratori, into one com-

pulsory Ordine and Law List.[3] Yet, it maintained different fee systems and
other functional distinctions and failed to integrate the two roles with
codes then in force concerning the supply of work (*prestazione d'opera*) and
the position in court. The law also established the Ordine as a single entity
that was both institutional and professional. It was a state institution in
that it was founded on the *infeudazione* (enfeoffment) of each lawyer within
the territorial jurisdiction of the Tribunale within which the lawyer's Ordine
was established ("forced residence"). The decentralization of each Ordine
at the lower court level (characterized as its "autonomy") was opposed to
the trend toward centralization of the judiciary. The state also used the
Ordine to impose limits on professional self-regulation and practice. These
features were not required for the functioning of the legal system but
rather reflected the political urge to circumscribe a status role that would
conform to the political program of the ruling class (Carrara, 1876). At the
same time the Ordine also was a professional organ because its origins
seem to lie in the far broader requirements transcending political regimes
and their laws (Zanardelli, 1879). The fact that the state acknowledges the
Ordine may demonstrate the role of the legal system in preserving social
order.

The connection between the public–private ambiguity of the Italian
professional monopoly and the two opposed professional projects pursued
by lawyers and the government reveals the difficulty of defining the role
and functions of Italian lawyers as "free" professionals. There are two
alternatives. One is to consider Italian lawyers as a "free" profession, in
light of the autonomy and independence proclaimed and partially achieved
by the professional group in order to meet increasing social demands for,
and expectations of, access to justice. The other is to view Italian lawyers
as an institutionalized office or an integrative state organism that fulfils a
*ministerio* (a public function) in accordance with the principles of hierarchy
and instrumentality that *constitute* the state, so as to ensure the certainty
and comprehensiveness of the legal system and the dominance of raison
d'Etat.

## INSTITUTIONAL PRESSURE AND PROFESSIONAL
## RESISTANCE

The Ordine characterizes all Italian "free" professions. For lawyers, however, the Ordine displays a dual level of institutional integration between
the professional and the state, which is not found in any other "free"
profession in Italy. Lawyers were deeply involved in the processes of
nation building and represent the legitimate organized power of the state
to society (Weber, 1961). Lawyers are the only "free" profession whose

private face arguably is only auxiliary but whose public face is absolutely essential, for it both creates the preconditions of the legal system and permits interaction between it and society. Indeed, what distinguishes lawyers is the fact that they occupy a "boundary role," a position on the border of the bureaucratic-administrative organization of the state.

The fact that the Ordine is established by positive law creates a second and far more complex level of institutionalization. The absence of a compulsory professional body like the Ordine in other countries demonstrates that the relationship between legal professionals and the state does not require it. So do the facts that Italian lawyers can act as judges simply by virtue of their legal skills. For the same reason, any citizen with a law degree can be named an honorary magistrate (Punzi, 1985). A century after its creation it is clear that the formal and compulsory structure of the Ordine has made the relation between Italian lawyers and the state more instrumental.

The combination of formal direct control and informal indirect control has favored the professional "project" of the state's ruling coalition over that of the lawyers. This can be seen in the government's use of lawyer self-regulation (Olgiati, 1985), particularly under Fascism. It also is visible in the government's strong resistance to lawyer efforts to create both a national professional association and a trade union. Only the Fascist legislators created the latter, but for reasons that were totally external to professionalism.[4] The Italian state still views the Ordine as a useful means of control, but Italian lawyers never have relented in their opposition, continuing to pursue the basic objectives of their own professional project.

In the first phase of their project, lasting more than half a century, lawyers concentrated on overcoming the deficiencies associated by Carrara (1876) with the uncoordinated and fragmented professional Ordini, finally establishing a national body, the Consiglio Nazionale Forense (DL 23 November 1944, n. 382), However, the Consiglio was a disappointment because it was located in Rome at the Ministerio di Grazia e Giustizia—and consequently under the control of the government— and it had only limited powers over the Ordini. The second phase responded to this disappointment by creating extrainstitutional "intermediate" professional bodies, such as the Unione delle Curie Forensi and the Unione delle Camere Penali. These were followed by the spontaneous appearance of private associations throughout Italy. The Federazione dei Sindacati degli Avvocati e Procuratori Italiani, founded in 1964 and organized on a territorial basis, united about seventy of these local voluntary private associations with about 6,000 members in 1979. In 1986 it became a Sindacato Unico Nazionale with local sections. The Associazione Italiana Giovani Avvocati, founded in 1966 on both a territorial and a national basis, is affiliated with the Association Internationale des Jeunes

Avocats, which organizes lawyers under forty-five years old. The recent founding of the Associazione Giuriste Italiane indicates the impact of women's entry into the profession. Finally, there are associations united by politics or ideology and open to all those connected with the law, such as the Associazione Italiana dei Giuristi Cattolici and various Commissioni Giustizia connected to political parties. These later associations seek to reform the profession or substantive legal areas, such as family law, whereas the other private associations resist the state's efforts to use the Ordini instrumentally.

Because their existence is not officially recognized, these associations have been pursuing two strategies. They seek to strengthen the representational power of the professional group by cooperating with other legal workers who also are feeling the effects of social change and the crisis of the state. Furthermore, they are trying to develop alliances with other "free" professions, to which end some Associazioni Sindacali of lawyers have joined the Confederazione Sindacati Liberi Professionisti, and some lawyers have joined the Associazione Liberi Professionisti. However, different levels of ideological and cultural consciousness among lawyers and other professionals, as well as limited economic means, result in participation by only a small elite. Nevertheless, there is a strong cultural commitment, indicated by both the frequency with which congresses are held and the wide circulation of publications, and an equally strong political commitment to influencing the only officially recognized associations, the Ordini and the Consiglio Nazionale Forense, especially by electing members to their governing bodies. Thus, the "battle of ideas" and the "long march within the institution" define the private associations as true "pressure groups" acting outside, and in opposition to, the formal legal system. That is why some Ordini recently established a Federazione degli Ordini Forensi d'Italia, in order to contrast private and syndicalist unionism.

## THE SOCIOPROFESSIONAL FRAMEWORK

Italian lawyers are experiencing a structural and functional change of their profession. This transformation has three components: (1) the displacement of lawyers from their traditional political role and social position as an "eminent class"; (2) their increasing identification of the professional as a technical specialist; and (3) a consequent redefinition of their duties, functions, and operational models.

### EDUCATION AND ACCESS

A lawyer must obtain a university degree in giurisprudenza from one of the twenty-nine law faculties. Between 1938 and 1969 the *curriculum studiorum* in all Italian law faculties required examinations in eighteen compulsory and three optional subjects. Since then students have been able to choose twenty-one subjects out of all those offered, subject to the approval of the faculty council. In response to this liberalization, many Ordini have imposed their curricular requirements.

A century ago there were fewer than 3,000 students enrolled in Italian law faculties; as recently as 1969 there still were only 13,839. That year saw the repeal of requiring a secondary school diploma in *Liceo Classico* or *Liceo Scientifico* for admission to the university. In 1977 there were 128,604 law students out of a total of 935,795 in all Italian universities, making law the third most popular subject after medicine and science (Cassese, 1978). There were more law students in Central and Southern Italy than in Northern Italy. In 1974, for example, there were 16,290 in Naples, 15,275 in Rome, 11,163 in Bari, and 8,870 in Palermo, compared to 4,290 in Turin, 7,546 in the two law faculties in Milan, 3,242 in Genoa, and 1,654 in Trieste.

Law courses traditionally have had three main objectives: research, training law teachers, and general legal education. Legal education still is formal, focused on the interpretation of doctrine, as is the Italian legal tradition itself. Consequently, it is not directed toward vocational preparation (Merryman, 1966; 1967; 1968; Cappelletti, 1974). Most instruction is through lectures; case studies and the seminars and practical exercises that have developed recently remain marginal. Because attendance is not compulsory and an increasing proportion of students are employed, the numbers at lectures are fairly low. A degree in giurisprudenza offers numerous occupational opportunities in government, banks, insurance companies, and so on. Only a small number of graduates actually enter the legal professions, and even fewer become lawyers.

Graduates who wish to be lawyers must enroll in the register of praticanti procuratori and begin a two-year apprenticeship in a lawyer's office. In fact, the apprenticeship rarely is less than three years, and because of the difficulty of the state exams the average period is between four and five years (Pocar et al., 1978; Pocar, 1983). The experience does not give the future lawyer the necessary technical and professional expertise. Rather, it is simply a means of reproducing traditional lawyers. The conditions are poor: little or no income, the exclusion of those who lack sufficient means, and acceptance by a studio on the basis of family relationship or friendship rather than merit. Thus, the apprenticeship reflects a corporative conception of the legal profession and a corporative defense of professional interests (Pocar et al., 1978; Pocar, 1983).

Once the period of training is over, the praticante can take the state examination to become a procuratore. This consists of two written papers (one on civil and administrative law and the other on civil and criminal procedure) and six oral examinations (civil, criminal, administrative, and fiscal law and civil and criminal procedure). Two new substantive areas—industrial and international law—are not examined. The examinations are theoretical, and the pass rate varies from 13 percent to 70 percent across locales. The examination commissions, appointed annually by each court of appeal, are composed of three magistrates (one of whom is made the president), one law professor, and two lawyers. Those who pass can enroll in the professional Law List and, as members of the Ordine, start practicing law as procuratori. A procuratore becomes an avvocato after practicing for six years or passing another examination.

## HOW MANY LAWYERS?

It is impossible to specify the number of active lawyers in Italy because those enrolled in the Law List may not be practicing. There were 39,415 lawyers enrolled in 1968, 46,620 in 1980, 46,610 in 1981, and 46,401 in 1982. Changes in the number of lawyers and the ratio of population to lawyers over the past 100 years are shown in table 9.1. As can be seen the number has remained fairly constant in recent years. The number of lawyers enrolled in the Cassa Nazionale di Previdenza Forense (Forensic National Health Insurance) is a more reliable index because only practicing lawyers may belong.[5] There were 32,468 in 1982. That year, 34,998 declared their incomes to the Cassa. Lawyers are the second largest "free" profession; although they are less than a third the number of physicians, they are more than three times the size of the next largest group (see table 9.2).

In 1982 the geographic distribution of enrolled lawyers was as follows: Northern Italy, 16,446 (35 percent); Central, 10,930 (24 percent); Southern, 13,064 (28 percent); and the Islands, 5,962 (13 percent) (Ricciardi, 1982). The distribution of those who paid income tax to the Cassa was similar: Northern Italy, 13,703 (39 percent); Central, 8,433 (24 percent); Southern, 8,698 (25 percent); and the Islands, 4,154 (12 percent). Table 9.3 shows a more detailed distribution a decade earlier, when the proportions of the three major regions were equal; thus, lawyers multiplied more rapidly in Northern Italy in the 1970s. Lawyers are geographically mobile and concentrated in the cities; Milan, for example, has about 3,500 enrolled in its Law List.

## ECONOMIC CONDITIONS

While there is considerable internal stratification within the profession, by clientele and especially income, its overall economic condition is poor.

Since most professional activity still is concerned with litigation, two opposed developments are relevant. On one hand, the public is reluctant to look to the courts for redress largely because of the delay and cost of a trial (Giovannini, 1969; Ferrari, 1979). (Fluctuations in litigation are presented in table 9.4.) On the other hand, some lawyers take advantage of the delays and cost and the complexity of procedure to prolong litigation (Castellano, 1968; Ferrari, 1979). That is why the public often views them as social parasites. Legal underemployment probably has been worsening recently. In 1961 the average lawyer handled only 4.9 civil cases, a figure that speaks for itself even if we acknowledge that not all enrolled lawyers practice. Although lawyers in Northern Italy handled an average of 8.2 civil cases, the number fell to 3.3 in Central Italy and 3.2 in Southern Italy. That even these figures are inflated by unfounded lawsuits is clear from the fact that judges in Central and Southern Italy reject 34.2 percent and those in the North, 15 percent. The distribution of criminal proceedings somewhat reduces the regional disproportion.

In the last few years the net average income declared by Italian lawyers has been fairly low, often below the average incomes of industrial and white-collar workers and only slightly above the national average. However, not all lawyers enrolled in Law Lists or the Cassa Nazionale di Previdenza declare their income deriving from professional activities. The total of income in 1981 subject to *IRPEF* (income tax) was 392,937,824,769 lire for 31,499 persons or 12,665,094 lire per capita (U.S.$7,500) (excluding declarations of negative or zero income). The total subject to IVA (value-added tax) was 604,080,974,085 lire for 29,226 persons or 20,669,300 lire per capita (U.S.$12,300). The difference can be explained partially by the fact that associated professionals declare IVA together (Ricciardi, 1982). It is interesting to note that individual declarations of income for 1981 showed an increase over the preceding year of 28 percent for *Irpef* and 21 percent for *IVA*, while the value of the lira fell by 19 percent, and the gross national product rose by 16 percent. However, if the number of practicing lawyers is more accurately represented by enrollment in the Cassa, then the average per capital income (*Irpef*) was 13,704,412 lire, the average per capita volume of business (*IVA*) was 22,051,069 lire, and they increased by 27 percent and 18 percent, respectively, over the previous year. Lawyers often are accused of widespread and major tax evasion. However, these accusations probably are exaggerated and too indiscriminate. Only a few lawyers have a lucrative clientele, while many earn barely enough to survive (see table 9.5). One consequence is that an unknown but probably quite high number of lawyers have a second job.

The professional income of lawyers is strongly influenced by a tariff structure. Since only those enrolled in the Law Lists can insist on payment for legal services, lawyers who work "illegally" cannot be paid. The lawyer's right to be paid does not depend on the outcome of the lawsuit. The tariff structure still is based on the fundamental distinction between the activity of avvocati and procuratori.[6] A lawyer who performs both functions is entitled to be paid for each. Tariffs establish both maxima and minima. Lawyers and clients can ask the council of the Ordine to evaluate the appropriateness of the fee whenever controversy arises. The maximum and minimum tariffs are modified only in special cases, but the fee actually paid can vary greatly from that established by the tariff since the lawyer and the client are free to reach a private agreement between themselves. In principle, the fee is based on the level of jurisdiction and the subject and value of the case. At the same time, the judge in charge of a case enjoys wide discretion over professional fees (Ruperto, 1973).

## SOCIAL COMPOSITION

Lawyers are drawn mainly from the upper-middle classes (Prandstraller, 1967). This earlier study recently has been confirmed by examining a more limited sample (Pocar et al., 1978; Pocar, 1983). In Lombardy, 33 percent of praticanti procuratori had fathers with university degrees, and 54 percent had fathers who were professionals, managers, or entrepreneurs; the proportions in Milan were even higher (40 percent and 59 percent, respectively). The proportion of women still is quite low but increasing rapidly: in Lombardy they are about 11 percent of practitioners but more than one-third of praticanti procuratori (Pocar, 1983). Religious, ethnic, and political variables do not seem to have much influence on recruitment, even though they do affect the lawyer's choice of career. A disproportionate number of lawyers and other legal actors come from Southern Italy, migrating northward.

Lawyers both enter and leave the profession at a fairly late age. The former observation is explained by the difficulty of entry. The latter reflects the autonomy of the profession, particularly with respect to income, which increases to age forty, remains constant to sixty, and then declines only gradually (see table 9.6). According to the Cassa Nazionale di Previdenza, the age distribution of lawyers who declared an income for 1981 (excluding praticanti procuratori) was as follows: 5 percent below thirty, 12 percent thirty to thirty-five, 12 percent thirty-six to forty, 30 percent forty-one to fifty, 13 percent fifty-one to fifty-five, 12 percent fifty-six to sixty, 5 percent sixty-one to sixty-four, and 20 percent over sixty-four (Ricciardi, 1982). These data suggest that the number of entrants is falling and the age of entry rising.

## DECLINE OR RECONVERSION?

These data on income, numbers, entry, and work make it clear that the profession has severe difficulties in achieving supply control, creating demand, and inspiring public trust. This crisis of the lawyer's role has become almost a platitude (Indovina, 1968; Giovannini, 1969; Ferrarese, 1975; Pocar, 1983). The profession often makes a defensive corporatist or protectionist response, which only exacerbates its social isolation and resistance to change. The crisis, then, is simultaneously a cause and an effect of the poor social image of lawyers, which is related to the weakening of their status supports. The proliferation of legislation characterized by incoherence and woolly reasoning not only affects the technical competence of lawyers but also has threatened the rule of law and the administration of justice, lowering the prestige of the entire legal system. A survey in the late 1960s revealed that 82 percent of the lawyers interviewed felt that they had lost prestige, and 34 percent of these attributed the loss to the public's mistrust of legal procedures (Prandstraller, 1967). During the 1960s lawyers began to fear "proletarianization," and the dangers of progressive decline were expounded at almost every professional meeting (Giovannini, 1969).

In reality, however, there has been no generalized decline. The profession remains a *constituent* element of both the social and legal systems. We argue, instead, that the profession is experiencing a reconverson from an organic socioprofessional position based on the *principle of social stratification* to a technical service-oriented position based on the *principle of functional differentiation* (Luhmann, 1983). This has occurred along the three variables previously mentioned: the weakening of the political role; the self-identification with technical-scientific professionalism; and the redefinition of duties, functions, and operating models.

### WEAKENING OF THE POLITICAL ROLE

Several observers have contended that the political role of lawyers has been weakened (Farneti, 1971; Carocci, 1964). The legal profession previously enjoyed considerable political and cultural prestige, which enabled it to influence the behavior of the entire legal system. Today the profession no longer is perceived as the social and political representative of the ruling class—its "organic" intellectuals (Gramsci, 1971; Irti, 1985).

One index of this change is the decline in the number of lawyers involved in political activities (see table 9.7). Between the 1913–1919 legislature (the first with almost universal suffrage) and that of 1958–1963, the proportion of lawyer members of Parliament fell from 42 percent to 21 percent. In the first legislature of the Republic (1948) there still were 184 lawyers and 54 other law graduates in the *Camera dei Deputati* (House of Representatives) and 144 lawyers and 29 law graduates in the *Senato* (Senate). In the sixth legislature (1972), although both chambers were larger and contained more representatives of other professions (e.g., physicians, engineers, and architects), there were only 141 lawyers and 76 law graduates in the Camera and 73 lawyers and 38 law graduates in the Senato (Ferrarese, 1975; Casalinuovo, 1974). Despite this decline, however, the role of lawyers in Parliament remains significant. Yet, there has been a change in the basis of their membership in Parliament, from class or status to functional characteristics and expertise. The requirement in the electoral law of 1882 that parliamentary candidates possess a certificate of education provided a functional basis for the professional's role in Parliament until education became more widespread. The emergence of the professional party politician also reduced political activity by lawyers (Farneti, 1971) and deprived them of their central role in mediating between law, economy, and society. Thus, most of their status symbols have disappeared, along with the power that derived directly from the social position they previously enjoyed.

## LAWYERS AS TECHNICIANS?

A principal reason for lawyers' increasing identification with technical-specialist professionalism is the loss of political authority. Evidence of their new self-image can be found in almost any recent professional conference. Civil lawyers consider themselves technicians with whom other technicians consult and interact (Grande Stevens, 1981). Yet, lawyers remain generalists. Among 382 solo practitioners who responded to a survey, 110 indicated no specialty (Prandstraller, 1981); and Indovina (1968) emphasizes lawyers' concern about the low level of specialization and the fact that what little specialization does occur is not economically advantageous. This trend toward technical specialization, then, is mainly an aspiration (presently achieved only by the elite), which reflects the contradiction between the actual role of lawyers and social demands.

## REDEFINITION OF STATUS ROLE

The causes of this last element of the professional reconversion include the quantitative decline in legal proceedings together with the increasing demand for legal transactions and advice, the growth of extralegal means of social control, and the contradictions between individual and collective interests. Because lawyers do not control these forces, legal professionalism suffers from deep uncertainties and growing ambivalence. For some lawyers the profession is gaining renewed functional relevance, while others complain that the functions are residual. For example, the lawyer is portrayed as the judge's invaluable collaborator, who acts on behalf of the judge to collect evidence in lawsuits and to translate the fragmentary and disconnected statements of the parties into technical language (Calamandrei, 1920). However, lawyers often fail to represent either the client or the law, advancing their own interests instead (Ferrari, 1979) or going to extremes in an attempt to assert an alternative use of law (Barcellona, 1973). If we adopt Johnson's (1972) concept of professionalism as a means of control, we see that the current reconversion affects the body of knowledge still shared by all lawyers, the material organization of lawyers' activity, their value systems and criteria of rationality, and the cohesion of the professional community.

The legal profession in other countries also finds itself in a period of transition. "Most of the authors interpret these changes as a new stage in the process of professionalization, as a movement from a strategy of supply control to a strategy of demand creation" (Szelenyi & Martin, 1989). Abel (1981) identifies two ways of creating demand: increasing access to justice through either public subsidy or private market strategies. Szelenyi and Martin suggest two other responses to deprofessionalization: efforts to regain supply control and a broader, neocorporatist, collective mobility project. These hypothetical alternatives have not yet become part of the ongoing debate within the Italian legal profession. Indeed, a study of the problems of training and access reveals no awareness of the future among legal professionals (Pocar, 1983). Today, as in the past, Italian lawyers who seek to justify their place within the framework of class relations and the hierarchy of occupations appeal uncritically to the necessity and usefulness of the service they render society.

## PRODUCTION AS A SERVICE IDEAL

Any attempt to predict the future development of the profession will have to take into account a wider range of considerations, particularly how the profession is legitimated. Until the middle of the last century professional claims for the necessity or social utility of lawyers referred less to the importance of their work than to the preeminent moral value of social integration through stratification. Today the profession seeks legitimacy through its role, function, specialization, and duties—by referring to the division of labor as it distributes the members of society among different types of production. As "free" professionals, lawyers always have sought sources of legitimation outside the legal system, which institutionalized them and which their activities support. The ethical rules of conduct, for example, are based on criteria of rationality that are equally opposed to the irrationality of certain state powers and to the formal or substantive rationality of the bureaucracy (Olgiati, 1985).

However, the strategic resource that both legitimates and changes the legal profession does not appear to be society's demand for legal services. We should look, instead, at the three elements that constitute the nomos (law): the *institutionalized* social processes of production, distribution, and appropriation (Polanyi, 1957; Schmitt, 1972). The profession's legitimating resource is its structural-functional congruence with these institutions. In the past, for example, there was an obvious congruence between the rise of the *noblesse de la robe* and the appropriation and division of land: the ethical maxim "the noble art (*ars boni et aequi*) makes the spirit noble" was related to precapitalist struggles over property rights. The hypothesized professional reconversion and the cultural change it entails are also reciprocally interconnected with the contemporary articulation of production, distribution, and appropriation. What is the impact of this articulation on the profession today?

## THE LOGIC OF ORGANIZATION

The profession views the redefinition of its status-role with ambivalence. Ambiguity may be characteristic of all contemporary legal experience (Capograssi, 1953; Resta, 1984). However, this ambiguity may be accentuated today by the difficulty of defining the relationship between the production, allocation, and appropriation of resources, given the marriage of convenience between *laissez-faire* and the welfare state. The ambiguity of law may reflect the fact the state guarantees the conditions for private appropriation at the same time that it distributes collective resources. Legal professionalism accommodates itself to the current patterns of production, distribution, and appropriation by an organization that makes the ambiguity "latent and bearable." In the absence of consensus or stable values or interests that are (legally) noncontigent, it is the logic of its organization— whatever society's demands—that motivates and justifies the existence and usefulness of the contemporary legal professions.

Since the legal profession initially established a close relationship with the capitalist mode of production, one might expect a trend toward increasing homology between the organization of the professional office and that of the business firm as lawyers become the entrepreneurs of legal services (Olgiati, 1983). In Italy, however, 51 percent of professional offices still are solo practitioners (Prandstraller, 1981). Although the number of offices containing more than one person is growing, the dominant object is to share, and thereby reduce, rising costs (personnel, rent, equipment, and books). Lawyers express their individualistic culture by retaining full autonomy and competing for clients with others in the office. There is a trend toward specialization among lawyers practicing labor law, administrative law, and criminal law (Pocar, 1983), but no significant division of labor within offices, although some commercial lawyers form partnerships that enable them to offer services in complementary sectors (Prandstraller, 1981).

One reason for the lack of specialization is the high level of competition for clients among new entrants. Many clients are acquired through personal acquaintance and social relationships. A beginning lawyer may welcome an appointment by a judge as *difensore d'ufficio* for an accused, which can ripen into an ongoing relationship. Although advertising and the use of intermediaries violate professional ethics, clerks, members of the clergy, prison guards, police, and insurance agents do perform that role. Unions also supply a fairly large clientele. In such cases lawyer and client do not identify with each other. However, professionals do identify with clients, such as commercial enterprises or artisans. Perhaps because of this identification people recently have begun to view lawyers as artisans or small entrepreneurs. The profession also has begun to debate such matters as competition (advertising), productivity (fees and the time and cost of their services), risk (insurance), the formation of partnerships (legal firms), and the professional monopoly (particularly the procedural requirements for expelling from the Law List those who do not practice on a regular basis) (Fontana, 1969). This debate indicates that the more thoughtful sectors of the Italian legal profession, at least, are relinquishing the traditional picture of the profession as engaged in allocating and appropriating goods (a pretense justified by the part played by lawyers in distributing resources ever since the beginning of agriculture) and acknowledging that lawyers *produce* services. This acknowledgment also has an organizational and productive dimension that lies at the origin of an entirely different and opposite phenomenon: the *incorporation* of professionals within public, semipublic, and private organizations (Tomasic, 1984).

## THE ITALIAN ANOMALY

Unlike any other advanced Western capitalist country, Italy has no public agencies for delivering legal services. A large part of lawyer—client relations and intermediation between law, economy, and society—long the nearly exclusive province of professional jurists—has been located within private organizations, such as trade unions and political parties, which have assumed responsibility for the civil, economic, and political protection of social groups (not just individuals), thereby "solving" the problem of legal aid and public legal assistance. The formal legal aid system (gratuito patrocinio) (RD 30 December 1933 n. 3282) is almost totally ineffective (Siena, 1984). An applicant who can prove not only poverty but also a high probability of a favorable outcome will be excused from paying court costs and obtain free assistance from a lawyer in the legal aid commission established in every court. Nevertheless, an indigent party cannot appeal an unfavorable decision without being reaccepted for legal aid, and it is impossible to obtain free advice before the case commences or outside the context of a lawsuit. The economic burden of legal assistance falls entirely on the lawyer appointed, who also is subject to supervision by the court; both features distort the normal professional relationship. Between 1971 and 1979 the proportion of civil cases in which a party was legally aided fell from 0.8 percent to 0.2 percent (Siena [1984]; see also table 9.8). Family matters accounted for 65 percent of the cases granted assistance.

Unions have been particularly important in providing legal services because of their size, wide geographic distribution, and efficiency. Initially limited to the workplace, the *uffici vertenze* have expanded their activities to the defense of broad collective interests (such as housing) by offering advice out of court. Union lawyers have become specialists in specific substantive areas. In the more important courts, these uffici vertenze have influenced interpretation of the law. Because their position is advanced not by an individual lawyer acting in a single case, but by a group of lawyers in many similar cases, the judges must compare notes and render a uniform "answer." (Insurance companies offering legal assistance in disputes regarding road accidents have adopted a similar strategy.) Lawyers who work for unions are chosen on the basis of ideological orientation; this intensifies ideological divisions within the profession and affects the social orientation of the lawyers, who cannot be "neutral" when supplying legal services. The fact that lawyers becomes permanently dependent on the union as the source of all work affects the organizational structure of the office and explains why such lawyers do not tend to establish law firms.

## THE LAWYER–CLIENT RELATIONSHIP

If the legal system is both a means of social control and a structure of symbolic communication, then lawyers are both "collaborators" within it and transmitters of information. Their training allows them to receive from other social subsystems the information that activates the legal system. The more selectivity they exercise in transmitting this information, the greater their authority and prestige (Parsons, 1962). Yet, the professional who performs such a function gradually acquires attributes that structure the mediation between legal and social subsystems. Thus, the function of the lawyer has its roots in the opportunity to influence the behavior of others by translating the information transmitted and in the continuous exposure to the risks and advantages structurally connected to this professional performance (Luhmann, 1983). This is, by definition, a "clientele" relationship. It arises when one individual or social group represents another; it must satisfy the interests and expectations of both. It is not accidental that the modern concept derives from the image of the professional jurist as an "eminent personage" (Farneti, 1971). Whereas the client relationship used to be based on the social position of the parties, today it also rests on the structure of the legal system, specifically the degree to which social interaction within it is formalized. For example, Italian lawyers cannot act on behalf of clients without a mandate, but sometimes they are legally obliged to act as court-appointed defense counsel. In acting as representatives they can mobilize their acquaintanceship and confidential relationships with judges and bureaucrats.

The clientele relationship has undergone a contradictory process of transformation. The professional's traditional dominance over the client has attenuated as a result of the crisis of the credibility and authority of legal institutional procedures and decisions (Ferrari, 1979). At the same time, the professional has been drawn further into the client's own sphere of activity, following the progressive legalization of the entire social system. Finally, the professional does not directly mediate the political exchange between the state and private clients. Indeed, the services that the individual lawyer performs for the large corporate client are more bureaucratic than communicative.

One decisive element in the contemporary relationship between lawyer and client is the movement away from the legal formalism of the nineteenth-century state to the materialization of welfare state law. This actually reinforces asymmetric power relations and breaks down the congruence of the traditional principles that characterize law, economy, and society (Abel, 1982). The transformation of the lawyer–client relationship compels lawyers to adopt new modes of social interaction (counseling, negotiation, computer-generated legal documents) and to redefine legal ethics. Nevertheless, the symbolic values of the profession still are framed in terms of what lawyers were and are rather than what they do. Thus, professional performance is measured by sociocultural background rather than functional task, and this radically affects the terms of the service offered and exacerbates the difficulty of defining a new identity.

## CONCLUSION

In this chapter we have tried to outline some problematic aspects of the legal profession, interpreting what appear to be unconnected events according to a cluster of theories. We described the professional "reconversion" as a manifestation of the evolution from social stratification to functional differentiation, the institutional and organizational changes resulting from the impact of nomos on the profession, and the professional interaction as an expression of a communicative code.

The lack of sufficiently complex theoretical models often has confused current discussions of legal professionalism. For example, there are contradictory definitions of the lawyer's function and role: is the lawyer an intellectual employing technical skills to safeguard the apparently private individual interests or a collaborator in the administration of justice, a kind of decentralized civil servant? The sociologist cannot accept that statement of the question. Regardless of how the lawyer's role is perceived, lawyers *do* collaborate in the administration of justice. The argument here is not the obvious one that since the right of citizens to legal representation and the duty of lawyers to render it are guaranteed by law, the legal professional is indispensable to almost all civil, criminal, or administrative proceedings and thus inevitably participates in judicial decisionmaking. These are occasions when the lawyer's display of technical skill on behalf of a private party can be effective. Indeed, it is precisely during the trial that legal professionals most closely resemble their ideological, cultural, and political image as mere defenders. There the professional's role as technical consultant is not simply compatible with, but actually corresponds to, the basic requirements of a system of justice based on partisanship and the dialectic of judicial proceedings. Representation in court is not the sole activity of lawyers, however, and appears to be of diminishing significance.

Lawyers also perform a collaborative role in other activities. They often serve as surrogate judges and sometimes have exclusive control over the administration of justice, as when they become honorary judges. Lawyers are the majority of giudici conciliatori, whose competence, although limited, is being extended. In performing these roles, lawyers resolve a fairly large number of cases, thereby freeing the magistrate from innumerable minor, if socially relevant, matters. In addition, a vast number of lawyers work as honorary vicepretori, performing the same functions as professional judges. In some important magistrates' courts the vicepretori have an influence on jurisprudence. In the smaller magistrates' courts they often manage to survive such drawbacks as the rotation of magistrates or under-staffing. Other examples of the subsidiary role of the lawyer in the administration of justice can be found in tax courts, arbitration, and some administrative bodies such as the Regional Department of Labor.

One could argue that, although lawyers participate in and often perform the function of judges, the latter role involves only a very small proportion of all legal professionals and should be considered merely a substitution, since in acting as a judge the lawyer ceases to be a "free" professional. The objection seems insubstantial. Lawyers invariably bring their distinctive professional background and experience to the role of judging. In addition, lawyers are likely to be more independent of those external influences that lead magistrates to assume bureaucratic attitudes. Moreover, lawyers contribute to the development of legal solutions that often have a strong influence on both judicial and legislative decision making. Thus, it seems that the role of legal professionals in the administration of justice is extremely significant and steadily growing as the judiciary's difficulties increase. In other words, lawyers do collaborate in the administration of justice; and since they act as alternatives to judges, they operate autonomously and authoritatively, however informally they may perform their duties. Therefore, they cannot be described simply as the technical advisors of parties, but rather are the equals of judges in resolving disputes and social conflict. This characteristic "social orientation" (Parsons, 1954; 1962) is peculiar to the legal profession.

Given the significance of the lawyer's role it is essential to ensure that it is properly performed. This is obvious when the lawyer substitutes for the judge, whose behavior is tightly constrained. The problem becomes especially acute where the lawyer acts as a private collaborator in the administration of justice. The lawyer, to a far greater extent than the judge, acts with substantive rationality. Yet, even the legal professional is subject to controls. Technical performance is influenced by the requirements for registration in the Law List and by the professional codes of ethics. The client, who may terminate the relationship at will and with no stated motive, controls the lawyer even more rigorously, if less fairly. Still, the powerful force of market demand operates only within the expectations created by specific lawyer–client relationships. Notwithstanding these controls, discipline by the Ordine, officially directed toward safeguarding professional dignity, does not seem to be very intrusive. Nor do the prescriptions contained in the Italian Civil Procedure and Criminal Codes fill this need, since they refer only to behavior during trial.[7] The oath the lawyer must take before beginning to practice is of dubious efficacy and based on the most abstract ethical principles. However, more rigid institutional controls, proposed by such renowned jurists as Chiovenda and Carnelutti, would appear to be unacceptable. Since formal institutions can exercise only limited control over the lawyer's participation in the administration of justice, it is clear that informal controls over quality will be useful and important. A better understanding of the actual professional situation and a clarification of the lawyer's role may provide a useful guideline.

# TABLES

9.1. Number of Lawyers Enrolled and Population per Lawyer, 1880–1982

| Year | Number of lawyers enrolled | Population | Population per lawyer |
|------|---------------------------|------------|----------------------|
| 1880 | 12,885 | 28,709,000 | 2,228 |
| 1881 | 13,518 | 29,953,000 | 2,216 |
| 1898 | 20,361 | 32,554,000 | 1,599 |
| 1913 | 21,488 | 36,178,000 | 1,684 |
| 1914 | 21,163 | 36,707,000 | 1,734 |
| 1921 | 25,000 | 38,449,000 | 1,538 |
| 1958 | 33,059 | 49,640,000 | 1,502 |
| 1965 | 39,415 | 52,931,000 | 1,343 |
| 1982 | 46,401 | 56,590,000 | 1,220 |

*Sources:* Mase Dari (1968); ISTAT (1982).

9.2. Estimated Size of "Free" Professions, 1982

| | |
|---|---|
| Physicians | 180,000 |
| Lawyers | 46,000 |
| Business consultants | 15,000 |
| Architects | 13,500 |
| Accountants | 13,000 |
| Pharmacists | 13,000 |
| Veterinarians | 9,000 |
| Notaries | 5,000 |

9.3. Geographic Distribution of Lawyers, 1971 and 1985

| Court of Appeal | No. of Ordini | Enrolled in Law List | | Change 1971–1985 | | Enrolled in Cassa, 1985 | |
|---|---|---|---|---|---|---|---|
| | | 1971 | 1985 | Absolute | % | Absolute | As % of Law List |
| Torino | 17 | 2,056 | 2,420 | 364 | 18 | 2,097 | 87 |
| Genova | 7 | 1,633 | 1,835 | 202 | 12 | 1,585 | 86 |
| Milano | 11 | 4,514 | 5,344 | 830 | 18 | 4,501 | 84 |
| Brescia | 5 | 860 | 1,127 | 267 | 24 | 932 | 83 |
| Trento | 3 | 375 | 415 | 40 | 11 | 365 | 88 |
| Venezia | 8 | 1,884 | 2,251 | 367 | 19 | 1,855 | 82 |
| Trieste | 5 | 604 | 655 | 51 | 8 | 564 | 86 |
| Bologna | 9 | 2,196 | 2,775 | 579 | 26 | 2,200 | 79 |
| Total North | 65 | 14,122 | 16,722 | 2,700 | 19 | 14,099 | 84 |
| Firenze | 10 | 1,981 | 2,631 | 650 | 33 | 2,169 | 82 |
| Perugia | 4 | 390 | 511 | 121 | 31 | 425 | 83 |
| Ancona | 7 | 672 | 896 | 224 | 33 | 727 | 81 |
| Roma | 8 | 6,636 | 6,834 | 198 | 3 | 5,349 | 78 |
| L'Aquila | 8 | 865 | 1,038 | 173 | 20 | 774 | 75 |
| Total Central | 37 | 10,544 | 11,910 | 1,366 | 13 | 9,444 | 79 |
| Napoli e sez. di Campobasso | 9 | 5,942 | 5,682 | −260 | −4 | 3,801 | 67 |
| Salerno | 3 | 939 | 1,124 | 185 | 20 | 784 | 70 |
| Bari | 4 | 2,039 | 2,254 | 215 | 11 | 1,790 | 79 |

9.3. (*continued*)

| Court of Appeal | No. of Ordini | Enrolled in Law List | | Change 1971–1985 | | Enrolled in Cassa, 1985 | |
|---|---|---|---|---|---|---|---|
| | | 1971 | 1985 | Absolute | % | Absolute | As % of Law List |
| Lecce | 3 | 1,346 | 1,821 | 475 | 35 | 1,351 | 74 |
| Potenza | 4 | 408 | 427 | 19 | 2 | 337 | 79 |
| Catanzaro e sez. di Reggio Calabria | 11 | 1,907 | 2,011 | 104 | 5 | 1,301 | 65 |
| Total South | 34 | 12,581 | 13,319 | 738 | 6 | 9,364 | 70 |
| Palermo | 6 | 1,867 | 2,030 | 163 | 9 | 1,525 | 75 |
| Caltanissetta | 3 | 319 | 330 | 11 | 3 | 258 | 78 |
| Messina | 3 | 752 | 917 | 165 | 22 | 558 | 61 |
| Catania | 5 | 2,087 | 2,085 | −2 | 0 | 1,437 | 69 |
| Cagliari | 6 | 709 | 914 | 205 | 29 | 676 | 74 |
| Total Islands | 23 | 5,734 | 6,276 | 542 | 9 | 4,454 | 71 |
| Total Italy | 159 | 42,981 | 48,327 | 5,346 | 12 | 37,361 | 71 |

*Sources:* 1971—ISTAT, Census (1976); 1985—La Previdenza Forense, Notiziario no. 4 (1985).

9.4. Changes in Number of Civil Cases, 1930–1974

| Year | Office of Conciliation (giudice conciliatore) | Praetura | Tribunale | Court of Appeal | Total |
|------|-----------------------------------------------|----------|-----------|-----------------|-------|
| 1930 | 992,801 | 354,916 | 167,768 | 404 | 1,515,889 |
| 1940 | 483,222 | 164,819 | 87,383 | 567 | 736,991 |
| 1950 | 158,469 | 214,766 | 110,362 | 880 | 484,477 |
| 1960 | 112,722 | 205,930 | 174,483 | 2,450 | 495,585 |
| 1965 | 48,015 | 119,059 | 210,666 | 1,351 | 469,081 |
| 1970 | 54,840 | 222,748 | 227,133 | 1,067 | 505,788 |
| 1971 | 52,422 | 247,154 | 220,882 | 730 | 521,188 |
| 1972 | 44,013 | 265,115 | 240,346 | 1,582 | 551,056 |
| 1973 | 37,788 | 249,956 | 231,573 | 894 | 520,211 |
| 1974 | 30,698 | 394,168 | 142,881 | 1,604 | 569,351 |

*Source:* Ferrari (1979).

9.5. Distribution of Lawyers by Income[a]

| Annual income (lire) | Number | Percent |
|----------------------|--------|---------|
| ≤ 3,000,000 | 5,254 | 19.7 |
| 3,000,001–5,000,000 | 3,983 | 14.8 |
| 5,000,001–10,000,000 | 6,763 | 25.4 |
| 10,000,001–20,000,000 | 5,632 | 21.2 |
| 20,000,001–30,000,000 | 2,363 | 8.9 |
| 30,000,001–40,000,000 | 1,066 | 4.0 |
| 40,000,001–50,000,000 | 1,211 | 4.5 |
| > 50,000,000 | 407 | 1.5 |
| Total | 26,629 | 100.0 |

[a]Individual IRPEF declarations by those enrolled in the Cassa di Previdenza, 1981, excluding those who declared no income.
*Source:* Cassa Nazionale di Previdenza e di Assistenza, Relazione di sintesi 1981–1983 (typescript).

9.6. Age Distribution of Lawyers and Average Income of
Age Groups, 1980

| Age | Percent of group | Average income (declared to IRPEF) (lire) |
|---|---|---|
| ≤ 30 | 5.8 | 4,071,000 |
| 31–35 | 11.4 | 6,584,000 |
| 36–40 | 13.0 | 9,699,000 |
| 41–50 | 29.8 | 11,105,000 |
| 51–55 | 12.9 | 11,263,000 |
| 56–60 | 12.1 | 11,170,000 |
| 61–65 | 4.8 | 10,165,000 |
| ≥ 66 | 10.2 | 9,586,000 |

*Source:* Cassa Nazionale di Previdenza e di Assistenza, Relazione
di sintesi 1981–1983 (typescript).

9.7. Percentages of "Free" Professionals in the Italian, French, and German Parliaments at the End of the Nineteenth and the Beginning of the Twentieth Centuries

| Profession | Italy, 1891–1913 legislature | | | | France, 1889–1897 legislature | | | Germany, 1887–1912 legislature | | |
|---|---|---|---|---|---|---|---|---|---|---|
| | XVIII | XX | XXII | XXIV | V | VI | VIII | IX | XI | XIII |
| Lawyer | 74 | 71 | 71 | 72 | 61 | 60 | 32 | 40 | 31 | 34 |
| Physician | 6 | 7 | 9 | 9 | 16 | 23 | 28 | 12 | 8 | 8 |
| Engineer | 8 | 10 | 8 | 7 | 8 | 8 | — | — | — | — |
| Journalist | 7 | 8 | 8 | 8 | 14 | 9 | 32 | 44 | 57 | 57 |
| Other profession | 5 | 4 | 4 | 4 | — | — | 8 | 4 | 4 | 1 |
| Size of legislature | 282 | 293 | 336 | 347 | 284 | 291 | 35 | 61 | 93 | 105 |

*Source:* Farneti (1971).

9.8. Requests for and Grants of "Gratuito Patrocinio," 1970–1979

| | Magistrate's court | | | Court of Appeal | | |
|---|---|---|---|---|---|---|
| Year | Requests | Grants | Abandoned | Requests | Grants | Abandoned |
| 1970 | 2,795 | 1,579 | 134 | 108 | 58 | 6 |
| 1971 | 4,201 | 2,709 | 186 | 149 | 85 | 7 |
| 1972 | 3,473 | 2,192 | 157 | 107 | 50 | 8 |
| 1973 | 2,159 | 1,733 | 128 | 93 | 53 | 8 |
| 1974 | 2,972 | 1,611 | 164 | 119 | 61 | — |
| 1975 | 2,004 | 1,570 | 170 | 42 | 36 | 3 |
| 1976 | 1,823 | 1,539 | 152 | 73 | 49 | 2 |
| 1977 | 1,844 | 1,412 | 126 | 61 | 42 | 3 |
| 1978 | 1,588 | 1,176 | 145 | 60 | 35 | 4 |
| 1979 | 1,477 | 1,181 | 153 | 42 | 34 | 4 |

*Source:* Siena (1984).

# NOTES

This chapter is the result of a joint effort. Vittorio Olgiati wrote the sections entitled "The Historical Cleavage," "The Controversial Features," "Institutional Pressure and Professional Resistance," "Decline or Reconversion?," and "Production as a Service Ideal"; Valerio Pocar wrote the "Introduction" and "Conclusion" sections and the sections entitled "The Socioprofessional Framework" and "The Lawyer–Client Relationship."

1. The functional unit of Italian lawyers is subject only to some formal limitations concerning the locality and level of court in which they may appear. These create internal differentiation among praticanti procuratori, procuratori, avvocati, and avvocati patrocinanti in Cassazione.

2. No sooner had Mozambique won independence than it abolished the free, private legal profession (Law no. 4 of 1975). This was the first step toward building its new legal system. Equally relevant is the French Revolution (Bills of the Constituent Assembly, 1791) and the Russian Revolution (Decree no. 1 of 22 November 1917).

3. At the beginning of the nineteenth century the situation was as follows:

*Kingdom of Sardinia:* A clear distinction between lawyers and procurators. Only the latter could represent parties in judgments; however, both lawyers and procurators could draft and sign legal acts. Lawyers were organized in a *Collegio* without a Chamber of Discipline; procurators had their own Chamber of Discipline.

*Duchy of Parma:* A clear legal distinction between lawyers and procurators. Lawyers were organized in a Collegio, procurators in a professional body called *Corpo.*

*Duchy of Modena:* No functional distinction between lawyers and procurators. The title of lawyer was purely honorary. Lawyers were organized in a Collegio, procurators in Corpo.

*Grand Duchy of Tuscany:* A merely nominal distinction between lawyers and procurators. Procurators could defend and prosecute at every level of court; a lawyer was *not* considered necessary. Legal professionals were organized in a Collegio with a Law List and Disciplinary Council.

*Pontifical State:* A very clear distinction between lawyers and procurators, whose functions were incompatible. Procurators could only represent clients. Lawyers had a Law Society and Disciplinary Council; procurators had a Chamber of Discipline.

*Kingdom of Naples:* Three functional categories: lawyers, procurators, and lawyer-procurators. Lawyers were authorized to establish a law society but never did so. Procurators were organized in a Chamber of Discipline.

*Sicily:* A clear distinction between lawyers and procurators. However, the procurator could both represent and defend and was the true "dominus litis" (master of the lawsuit). Lawyers were retained by procurators and were not responsible to clients. There was a Chamber of Discipline for lawyers only.

4. Fascism created a single compulsory union, which alone could represent lawyers (Law of 3 April 1926, n. 563). Local professional associations and disciplinary councils were abolished (Royal Decree of 22 November 1928, n. 2580). The Secretary of the Union of Fascist Lawyers and Procurators, addressing the First National Union Council in Rome, said: "If one speaks of independence within our profession, one speaks of something that is very limited.... The best way to have independence ... is to refuse to be your client's slave" (Vecchini, 1931).

5. All lawyers should declare their income to the Cassa, even when they are not enrolled, but not all practicing lawyers do so. Only lawyers enrolled in the Cassa make social security contributions.

6. As in all "free" professions, the tariff is set by ministerial decree, on the basis of proposals by the Consiglio Nazionale Forense. The tariff is updated periodically on the basis of certain parameters, including the cost of living.

7. Consider, for example, "parties and their representatives must behave with loyalty and probity during the proceeding. If their representatives fail to do so the judge must inform those authorities with disciplinary power" (Civil Procedure Code, art. 88).

# REFERENCES

Abel, Richard L. 1981. "Toward a Political Economy of Lawyers," 1981 *Wisconsin Law Review* 1117.
———, ed. 1982. *The Politics of Informal Justice* (2 vols.). New York: Academic Press.

Barcellona, Pietro. 1973. *L'uso alternativo del diritto*. Bari: Laterza.

Bianchi, Antonio. 1886. Sull'esercizio delle professioni di avvocato e procuratore. Testo e commento della Legge 8.6.1874 n. 1938 e del Reg. 26.7.1874 n. 2012. *Raccolta delle Leggi speciali e convenzioni internazionali del Regno d'Italia*, vol. 2, ser. 6. Turin: Unione Tipografica Editrice.

Burrage, Michael. 1989. "Revolution as a Starting Point for the Comparative Analysis of the Legal Profession: France, the United States, and England," in Richard L. Abel and Philip S. C. Lewis, eds., *Lawyers in Society*, vol. 3: *Comparative Theories*. Berkeley, Los Angeles, London: University of California Press.

Calamandrei, Piero. 1920. "L'avvocatura e la riforma del processo civile," 35(3/4) *Studi senesi* 165.

Capograssi, Giuseppe, 1953. *L'ambiguità del diritto contemporaneo*. Milan: Giuffrè.

Cappelletti, Mauro. 1974. *L'educazione del giurista e la riforma dell'Università. Studi, polemiche, raffronti*. Milan: Giuffrè.

Carocci, Giovannini. 1964. *Il Parlamento nella storia d'Italia. Antologia storica della classe politica*. Bari: Laterza.

Carrara, Francesco, 1876. "Il passato, il presente e l'avvenire degli Avvocati in Italia," 6 *Opuscoli di diritto criminale* 51.

Casalinuovo, Aldo. 1974. "Cento anni di storia e di gloria dell'Avvocatura," 16(3/4) *Rassegna Forense* 113.

Cassese, Sabino. 1978. *Guida alla facoltà di giurisprudenza*. Bologna: Il Mulino.

Castellano, Cesare, et al. 1968. *L'efficienza della giustizia italiana*. Bari: Laterza.

Farneti, Paolo. 1971. *Sistema politico e società civile. Saggi di teoria e ricerca politica*. Turin: Giappichelli.

Ferrarese, Maria Rosaria. 1975. "Gli avvocati tra passato e presente," 3 *Rassegna italiana di sociologia* 421.

Ferrari, Vincenzo. 1979. "I tempi della giustizia e la professione forense," 6(1/2) *Sociologia del diritto* 137.

Fontana, Errino. 1969. "Dall'avvocatura artigianale all'avvocatura imprenditoriale," in *Atti IX Congresso Nazionale Giuridico Forense* (Venice, 25–30 September 1967). Padua: CEDAM.

Giovannini, Paolo. 1969. "La professione di avvocato in una fase di transizione," 3 *Sociologia. Rivista di studi sociali dell'Istituto Sturzo* 209.

Gramsci, Antonio. 1971. *Quaderni dal carcere*. Rome: Editori Riuniti.

Grande Stevens, Franzo. 1981. "Esperienza professionale: Diritto privato," in *Cinquant'anni di esperienza giuridica in Italia* 1289. Milan: Giuffrè.

Indovina, Francesco. 1968. "La professione di avvocato in un'area di capitalismo avanzato," *Rivista internazionale di scienze economiche e commerciali* 1054.

Instituto Centrale di Statistica (ISTAT). 1982. *Annuario*. Rome: Instituto Poligrafico dello Stato.

Irti, Natalino. 1985. "Profilo dell'avvocatura nella società industriale," in *Atti IX Convegno Nazionale AIGA* (Verona, 31 May–3 June 1984), 1/2 *Rivista AIGA*.

Johnson, Terence. 1972. *Professions and Power*. London: Macmillan.

Lancellotti, Franco, and Graziano Pini. 1980. *Il laureato in giurisprudenza*. Modena: Stem Mucchi.

Larson, Magali Sarfatti. 1977. *The Rise of Professionalism: A Sociological Analysis*. Berkeley, Los Angeles, London: University of California Press.

Lega, Carlo. 1957. "Avvocati e Procuratori (Diritto Moderno)," in *Novissimo Digesto Italiano* 1666. Turin: Unione Tipografico Editrice Torinese.

———. 1974. *Le libere professioni intelletuali nelle leggi e nella giurisprudenza*. Milan: Editore Giuffrè.

———. 1975. *Deontologia forense*. Milan: Giuffrè.

Luhmann, Niklas. 1983. *Struttura della società e semantica*. Bari: Laterza.

Masè Dari, Federico. 1968. "Alcuni aspetti attuali della professione forense," 22 *Rivista trimestrale di diritto e procedura civile* 272.

Merryman, John H. 1966. "Lo stile italiano: la dottrina," 20 *Rivista trimestrale di diritto e procedura civile* 1169.

———. 1967. "Lo stile italiano: le fonti," 21 *Rivista trimestrale di diritto e procedura civile* 709.

———. 1968. "Lo stile italiano: interpretazione," 22 *Rivista trimestrale di diritto e procedura civile* 373.

Norsa, Cesare. 1872. "Esercizio della professioni di avvocato e procuratore e Tariffe giudiziarie," in *Atti del I Congresso Giuridico Italiano*. Rome: Tipografia Crivelli.

Olgiati, Vittorio. 1983. "La pubblicità: anello debole dell'ordinamento professionale," 5 *Studio legale* 3.

———. 1985. "L'etica dell'avvocato come ordinamento," 12(3) *Sociologia del diritto* 35.

Parsons, Talcott. 1954. "A Sociologist Looks at the Legal Profession," in *Essays in Sociological Theory* 370–385. New York: Free Press.

———. 1962. "The Law and Social Control," in William Evan, ed., *Law and Sociology* 62. New York: Free Press.

Patterson, L. Ray. 1981. "On Analyzing the Law of Legal Ethics: An American Perspective," 16 *Israel Law Review* 28.

Pocar, Valerio, ed. 1983. *Il praticante procuratore. Una ricerca sociologica sull'accesso alla professione d'avvocato*. Milan: Unicopli.

Pocar, Valerio, Paola Mora, Vittorio Olgiati, Antonio Prina, and Silvano Siena. 1978. "Il praticante procuratore. Formazione o deformazione professionale?" 5 *Sociologia del diritto* 75.

Polanyi, Karl. 1957. *The Great Transformation*. Boston: Beacon Press.

Prandstraller, Giampaolo. 1967. *Gli avvocati italiani: inchiesta sociologica*. Milan: Edizioni di Comunità.

———. 1981. *Avvocati e metropoli. Inchiesta sulla professione di avvocato dell'area lombarda*. Milan: Angeli.

Punzi, Carmine. 1985. "Il giudice onorario," in Nicola Picardi and Alessandro Giuliani, eds., *L'Ordinamento giudiziario*, vol. 3, p. 74. Rimini: Maggioli.

Resta, Eligio. 1984. *L'ambiguo diritto*. Milan: Angeli.

Ricciardi, Edilberto. 1982. "Relazione dell'avv. Edilberto Ricciardi, Presidente della Cassa Nazionale di Previdenza e Assistenza a favore degli Avvocati e Procuratori all'Assemblea Nazionale degli Ordini Forensi," 2(3) *La Previdenza Forense* (supplement).

Ruperto, Cesare. 1973. *Gli onorari di avvocato e procuratore*. Milan: Giuffrè.

Satta, Salvatore. 1959. "Avvocato e procuratore. L'ordinamento professionale degli avvocati e procuratori," 5 *Enciclopedia del diritto* 653.

Schmitt, Carl. 1972. "Appropriazione, divisione, produzione," in Gianfranco Miglio and Pierangelo Schiera, eds., *Le categorie del politico*. Bologna: Il Mulino.

Siena, Silvano. 1984. "Il gratuito patrocinio: un istituto in via di estinzione," 11(3) *Sociologia del diritto* 59.

Szelenyi, Ivan, and Bill Martin. 1989. "The Legal Profession and the Rise and Fall of the New Class," in Richard L. Abel and Philip S. C. Lewis, eds., *Lawyers in Society*, vol. 3: *Comparative Theories*. Berkeley, Los Angeles, London: University of California Press.

Tomasic, Roman. 1984."Law as a Bureaucratic Profession." Paper presented to the Working Group for Comparative Study of Legal Professions, Bellagio, July.

Vecchini, Aldo. 1931. "L'avvocato nel regime fascista," in *Relazione I Consiglio Sindacato Nazionale Forense* 237. Rome: Eloquenza.

Weber, Max. 1961. *Economia e società*. Milan: Edizioni di Comunità.

Zanardelli, Giuseppe. 1879. *L'avvocatura. Discorsi*. Florence: Barbera Ed.

# 10

# The Legal Profession in Spain: An Understudied but Booming Occupation

## CARLOS VILADÁS JENE

## TERMINOLOGY

Because the literature on the legal profession in Spain is so limited, it is difficult to know how that concept is generally understood. Many careers share the common requirement of a first degree in law, the *licenciatura en derecho*. Judges, prosecutors, and most law professors[1] are civil servants. Notaries and registrars[2] are a mixture of civil servant and private practitioner.[3] Finally, "abogados" (hereafter translated as "lawyers") and "procuradores"—both of whom clearly fall within the strict definition of the legal profession—are private practitioners, with very few exceptions. Only those who want a career in academe continue their formal education, taking additional courses and writing a thesis in order to obtain a "doctorado en derecho" prior to taking the examinations that must be passed to become a law professor.

## PRIVATE PRACTITIONERS

The distinction between abogado and procurador does not correspond to that between the English categories of solicitor and barrister. The Spanish legal system requires each litigant to name a procurador as an official representative who will handle its relations with the court. Such representation tends to be merely formal: all pleadings, petitions, and briefs submitted to the court by the parties will be signed and presented by the procurador but prepared by the abogado. The procurador is lower in status than the abogado, although not necessarily in income.

Because this role increasingly is a mere formality (such as that of the "avoué," who has been eliminated in France, Belgium, and Switzerland), some people urge its suppression. However, one cannot ignore the fact

369

that some procuradores possess such a thorough knowledge of the procedural rules that they are extraordinarily helpful to lawyers. This is why it is the abogado who chooses the procurador, even though it is the client who pays the latter (a fee that is determined partly by regulations and partly by the procurador).

There are very few procuradores in Spain today. In Barcelona, for instance, there are only 100, compared to approximately 5,000 lawyers. Given the limited functions they perform, it is very easy for procuradores to handle a vast number of cases, especially since the advent of photocopying, computers, and word processors.

Since 1506 the Barcelona procuradores have had their own "Colegio" (association), to which anyone with a law degree can belong on payment of a fee of 225,000 pesetas (Pts) (approximately $1,400). No special training is required, and practitioners may move freely between the categories of abogado and procurador, although they cannot practice both functions at the same time.

An abogado has exclusive rights of audience in all courts located within the territorial limits of the Colegios to which the abogado belongs.[4] Until recently, therefore, only members of the Madrid Colegio could appear before the Tribunal Supremo located in the capital. Today, all lawyers appealing cases for which they have had responsibility below can plead before the Supreme Court (Estatuto de la Abogacía, art. 22).

Although lawyers are entitled to practice all branches of law, they tend to specialize. They also encounter competition in certain areas—for instance, with economists and business consultants in advising and representing individuals and companies in tax matters (although lawyers retain their exclusive rights of audience in court). In labor matters, they also compete with social workers, who can appear before labor courts.

## PUBLIC LAWYERS

*Abogados del estado* must be distinguished from *fiscales* (prosecutors),[5] although both represent the state and are civil servants. The duties of the latter are much broader, covering four areas. Fiscales issue opinions as to whether a court has jurisdiction in a particular case, are responsible for the discipline of judicial personnel, instruct the police, and represent the state and the government[6] whenever those entities have an interest in litigation, unless legislation explicitly assigns such representation to an abogado del estado. In civil cases, they intervene in matters involving status, personality, or family law, represent minors and others who lack legal capacity, and appeal judicial decisions based on a misinterpretation or error of law.

Despite these formal responsibilities, fiscales commonly are perceived solely as prosecutors. Furthermore, their duties in criminal cases are so essential and have become so onerous that they have crowded out most other activities. In 1983, the 540 prosecutors and about 1,694 judges and magistrates in Spain handled 1,633,244 cases and participated in 99,660 trials (*Memoria elevada al Gobierno*, 1985: 24–26, 40, 554). Although most people believe that fiscales are merely prosecutors in criminal matters, they have a legal obligation to represent an accused whom they believe to be innocent, both in private prosecutions and following arrests by the police—and sometimes they actually do so.

Abogados del estado often are asked by administrative bodies or government departments to give opinions about the legally appropriate forms through which goals may be pursued. They audit tax returns in order to ensure that the correct amount has been paid on the sale of goods, land, and shares in corporations. They represent the state when it has a financial interest in litigation (both civil and criminal) and represent civil servants who are sued for acts performed in the course of their official duties.

## NUMBERS AND DISTRIBUTION

At the end of 1982, there were about 32,000 practicing lawyers and about 10,000 non-practicing lawyers in Spain. In addition, many more people hold law degrees and have the right to enter practice at any time. There are about 1,000 people per lawyer in the country at large but only 370 per lawyer in Madrid (which contains 10,800 practicing lawyers—about a third of the total—for about 4 million people) and about 400 per lawyer in Barcelona (5,000 practicing lawyers for less than 2 million people).

## EDUCATION, SOCIALIZATION, AND ALLOCATION

### NUMBER OF LAW STUDENTS

There are twenty-eight universities in Spain, twenty-one of which contain law faculties (three of them are private). In 1978/79, nearly half of the 156,189 university students were enrolled in law faculties. The number of law students increased threefold in the seven years between 1971/72 and 1978/79 (see table 10.1). Students must be registered for a minimum of five years, but few manage to graduate in that short a period.

A recent study of the Faculty of Law at Barcelona confirms the failings of the educational system (Moltó García & Oroval Planas, 1983). Only about 10 percent of the students succeed in graduating within five years; another 7 percent take six years, and a further 7 percent require seven years. These failures of the system impose enormous costs not only on students but also on the state, which heavily subsidizes the public universities. Although a student who graduated in five years would have to spend only 2.5 million Pts, the average expenditure actually is estimated at 8.3 million Pts because of the prolongation of study. Half or more of the students fail their examinations, but not because the academic standards are high. Rather, the level of secondary schooling is low, particularly in the private schools; and very few students really are interested in law—most simply want a credential that, until the mid-1970s, was useful in obtaining a job.

## ADMISSIONS

All students who complete their secondary education and pass a general university entrance examination are admitted to the law school closest to their secondary school. A student who wishes to move to another city usually has no difficulty in obtaining entrance to the law school there. Most students attend the nearest university because they live at home. Only those not situated near a law faculty choose among them on the basis of some factor other than geographic convenience. Even professors seek employment in a university primarily on the basis of the city in which they wish to live.

The creation of new universities during the late 1960s and early 1970s somewhat reduced the importance of those in Madrid and Barcelona, which most students attended in the past. Nevertheless, the incredible increase in law student enrollments did not allow those faculties to contract to the manageable sizes they had enjoyed earlier.[7] Of the 74,117 law students in 1978/79, 14,476 were enrolled in the Universidad Complutense of Madrid and 11,559 in the Unversidad Central of Barcelona—a third of all law students.[8]

Private universities are operated by various orders within the Catholic Church: Deusto (the most prestigious) by the Jesuits; Navarra, by Opus Dei. Both are expensive compared to public institutions. Nevertheless, the quality of the education at Deusto attracts students with superior secondary-school records. Although some feel that private universities offer a better education because they are smaller and less "disorganized," the most prestigious professors in all fields teach at public universities. I also believe that private universities resemble secondary schools in being overprotective of their students.

## FINANCING LEGAL EDUCATION

Both public and private institutions receive state funds, although in different amounts. In the former, annual tuition is about 35,000 Pts (about $250), far below the actual cost. The real expense for the student, therefore, is maintenance. Since most students live with their parents, all those whose families can forego their wages for five years can attend university. Only those living far from the major cities are at a significant disadvantage. The very few scholarships are given to those who demonstrate both need and capacity, on the basis of earlier education and present performance.

## THE CHARACTER OF LEGAL EDUCATION

Both the weight of tradition and the large number of students combine to lower the quality of legal education. It is conceptualistic, exegetic, and dogmatic. Although both Madrid and Barcelona attempted to encourage the discussion of alternative solutions to legal cases in the late 1970s, the rapid increase in enrollments forced a return to ex cathedra lectures. Indeed, the ratio of students to teachers worsened dramatically during the seven years between 1971/72 and 1978/79 (see table 10.1). Even these figures exaggerate the teaching resources available, for only young assistants teach full time; tenured professors maintain a heavy practice, arriving at the university just before their classes and leaving immediately afterward.

# THE STRUCTURE OF THE LEGAL PROFESSION

## THE PROFESSIONAL MONOPOLY

The unauthorized practice of a profession is an offense in Spain (Criminal Code, arts. 321, 572). Although there have been prosecutions of those masquerading as physicians, it is only within the last two years that similar prosecutions have been commenced against lawyers, as a result of complaints to bar associations.

## PROFESSIONAL REGULATION

The legal profession is regulated nationally by the Estatuto General de la Abogacía Española, enacted on 24 July 1982. It defines an abogado as a member of a Colegio who is registered with that Colegio as a practicing lawyer and is practicing in a law office (art. 10).[9] In order to join a Colegio, a candidate must be a Spanish national (or obtain an exemption), be at least eighteen years old, hold a degree in law, be free of any criminal conviction inconsistent with the practice of law, pay an admission fee (about $100), join a compensation and insurance fund for lawyers,[10] and pay the local tax for professionals (art. 15). It is illegal for a Colegio to limit the number of members (art. 13). It is clear that the formal entry requirements do not limit the size of the profession. The real obstacle is beginning practice. Law offices admit new entrants on the basis of acquaintanceship, never exclusively on merit. At the same time, it is economically almost impossible to begin practicing on one's own immediately after graduation, especially since advertising is prohibited.

## BAR ASSOCIATIONS

There is a Colegio de Abogados in the capital of each of the fifty-two provinces. In addition, thirty other local bar associations have been preserved for historical reasons, ten in Catalunya and the rest throughout Spain (art. 2). Lawyers must belong to the Colegio in the jurisdiction within which they practice, but there is no limit on the number of Colegios a lawyer may join. The membership elects a *Junta de Gobierno* (board of directors) and a *Decano* (dean), usually for a term of four years, with the vote of a practicing lawyer worth twice that of a nonpracticing lawyer. The Colegios are less political today than they were during the Franco dictatorship, especially at its end. From the late 1960s, the Colegios in Madrid and Barcelona were platforms for opposition to the regime, publicly and continuously criticizing police methods and the trials of political activists.

## DISCIPLINE AND MALPRACTICE

Bar associations have disciplinary powers over members who violate the code of ethics or commit malpractice and may issue a private reprimand, suspend for up to two years, or expel from the association (Estatuto General de la Abogacía, arts. 107–22). In theory, a lawyer who is suspended or expelled cannot practice anywhere in Spain, but enforcement remains ineffective. It is surprising that such serious sanctions can be imposed without any possibility of appeal and uncertain whether such a procedure is consistent with the Constitution of 1978. This has not been tested, perhaps because bar associations have been cautious in exercising their disciplinary powers, at least until very recently. Client complaints are increasing, however, and bar associations are treating offenders more severely. Bar associations take a grave view of several forms of misconduct: practicing law while holding an incompatible office; offending another lawyer, the board of a bar association, or the dignity of the profession; violating the code of ethics; committing a crime; practicing law while intoxicated or using drugs; or assisting the unauthorized practice of law.[11]

The Barcelona Bar Association initiated 227 disciplinary proceedings in 1983, held 52 hearings, and imposed sanctions in 24 cases (including two expulsions). The following year it initiated 254 proceedings, held 63 hearings, and imposed sanctions in 32 cases (including one expulsion) (*Memoria dels esdeveniments*, 1983; 1984). In 1983 the Madrid Bar Association reported that it initiated 325 proceedings, held 50 hearings, and punished 24 lawyers; the following year it initiated 284 proceedings, held 51 hearings, and punished 30 lawyers.

The provisions concerning competition among lawyers are so strict that they are not rigidly enforced. Lawyers must avoid all forms of direct publicity or advertisement and may not even give opinions (without remuneration) to legal periodicals or the mass media (Estatuto General de la Abogacía, art. 31). They also cannot agree with clients to accept payment contingent on the outcome of the matter (art. 56).

Lawyers may be criminally liable for misconduct and civilly liable for malpractice. However, the courts are unsympathetic to charges of malpractice even against physicians, and patients find it very difficult to persuade one physician to testify against another. Because bar associations have mediated claims of malpractice against lawyers, the first case reached court only recently, charging malpractice by judges. This explains why it was only in 1985 that the Barcelona Bar Association negotiated a group insurance policy and urged its members to join.


LAW FIRMS

Very few lawyers practice in partnerships. Although most offices contain several lawyers, they share only the rent, secretarial expenses, and office equipment. Most offices also provide space and offer some training to recent graduates. The Estatuto General de la Abogacía distinguishes such loose associations from law firms (*despachos colectivos*), where lawyers share responsibility for clients, and it limits the number of partners in such firms to 20 (arts. 34–38). It also requires firms to obtain bar association approval of their bylaws and register with the association.

Most law firms offer a wide variety of services to companies, to which they become "permanent counsel" in exchange for a fixed payment, supplemented for negotiating complicated contracts, advising on difficult issues, and conducting litigation. Individual lawyers also seek such agreements, since they offer security without the limits on independence associated with the status of house counsel. Larger companies tend to prefer to employ house counsel, although they continue to retain specialist practitioners when faced with a significant issue. Such specialists charge high fees, especially if they hold a chair in a university law faculty. Most large companies now employ a lawyer at least part time as house counsel. The practice began in banks and insurance companies, and some of the former are considered the best places to obtain legal training, since the heads of those departments used to be prestigious lawyers. Unlike house counsel in France, those in Spain retain their right to appear in court and can even practice privately, if their employer permits.

Lawyers may charge whatever they wish, although the bar associations publish recommended fee schedules (Estatuto General de la Abogacía, art. 56). Bar associations also mediate fee disputes. Madrid lawyers are known to charge the highest fees. Law professors and politicians temporarily out of office also are expensive.

## LEGAL AID

The state pays most of the costs of legal aid. Each bar association organizes the delivery of legal services within the general framework established by law (Estatuto General de la Abogacía, arts. 57–60). All practicing lawyers have the obligation to represent civil litigants who apply to the local bar association for legal aid. Those whom the court finds to be "poor" must be represented free of charge. If the court does not make a finding of poverty, the lawyer is entitled to charge the usual fee. Cases are assigned to lawyers in alphabetical order, but a lawyer who wishes to be excused need pay only the symbolic amount of 1,000 Pts (about $7). In criminal cases, the lawyer who represents a defendant who cannot pay will be reimbursed by the Ministry of Justice according to the complexity of the case. Lawyers must have acquired some experience before they may handle legal aid cases: one year in Barcelona in all civil cases and minor criminal matters, five years in serious criminal cases. In 1982, there were a total of 9,175 legally aided matters in Barcelona, 15,025 in Madrid, and 102,076 in the entire country.

The 1978 Constitution provided legal aid to all those arrested during booking at the police station. It was implemented by legislation of 12 December 1983. Again, lawyers serve in alphabetical order but may be excused on payment of 1,000 to 1,500 Pts. They are paid 10,000 Pts (about $70) each time they serve. In 1982, 4,805 accused were represented in Barcelona, 7,019 in Madrid, and 46,313 in the entire country.

## CONCLUSION

Cultural evidence strongly suggests that Spaniards do not respect lawyers. A Catalan proverb says: "Advocats i procuradors, a l'infern de dos en dos"

("Lawyers and procuradores, to hell by pairs"). In *El Tablado de Arlequin*, a famous twentieth-century novel by Pio Baroja, one character says to another: "In view of your complete incapacity for something useful, be a lawyer." Nevertheless, it may be significant that two of the three presidents elected since the 1978 Constitution have been lawyers, as are the present presidents of both chambers of Parliament, the majority leader, and the leader of the opposition. A 1984 survey revealed that 70 percent of the respondents had a good image of the justice system in general and positive, respectful attitudes toward the legal profession as a whole. Nevertheless, answers to more specific questions were less flattering (Toharía, 1985). Only a third thought that the courts were efficient, just another third felt the opposite, and another third had no opinion. Only 21 percent thought it advisable to solve a conflict by retaining a lawyer and suing; 70 percent thought it better to solve conflicts outside of court, although 25 percent would go to court if litigation were less expensive and more expeditious. One reason for the very poor performance of the judicial system is that resources always have been inadequate—just enough to avoid complete collapse. In 1981, for example, the Ministry of Justice obtained only 0.8 percent of the total budget of the Spanish Government (*Memoria elevada al Gobierno*, 1985: 54ff.).

Despite repeated political discussions of the reform of both the judical system and higher education, no significant new policies have been implemented since the transition from authoritarianism to democracy. This is why the performance of both state institutions has not improved. On the contrary, the massive increase in law faculty enrollments, the subsequent expansion of bar associations, and the increasing number of social conflicts that fall within the jurisdiction of the courts have created a situation that many judges, prosecutors, law professors, and lawyers view as chaotic and close to collapse.

This chapter is not a prescription for improving the legal profession, much less the entire legal system. It would be presumptuous for me to conclude with a superficial diagnosis and cure when the problem is extraordinarily complex and calls for a nuanced response. However, I am not alone in my conviction that there is no chance whatever of reversing the present trends until the government decides that judges, prosecutors, and law professors should be paid civil service salaries sufficient to allow them to relinquish their part-time jobs, which now are absolutely essential to afford them even a minimal standard of living but distract them from their public duties.[12] It is necessary to improve the quality of legal education, which would limit the number of students admitted and the number of graduates who enter a bar association or the school for judges. This also would allow judges to devote all their time to managing court personnel, whom they scarcely control at present, and to attend to the task of sentencing.

# TABLE

10.1. Numbers of Students and Professors in Spanish Law Faculties

|  | Year | | |
|  | 1971/72 | 1975/76 | 1978/79 |
|---|---|---|---|
| Students enrolled |  |  |  |
| State universities | 22,665 | 44,817 | 69,154 |
| Private universities | 2,159 | 2,633 | 4,963 |
| Graduates |  |  |  |
| State universities | 1,625 | 2,458 | 3,923 |
| Private universities | 53 | 246 | 627 |
| Faculty[a] |  |  |  |
| State universities | 1,570 | 1,513 | 1,660 |
| Private universities | 141 | 155 | 214 |
| Student: faculty ratio |  |  |  |
| State universities | 14.4 | 29.6 | 41.6 |
| Private universities | 15.3 | 16.9 | 23.1 |

[a]Includes all faculty, from professors to assistants

Source: Anuario Estadístico de España (1981: 360ff.)

## NOTES

Felip Portabella Cornet, a practicing lawyer who also teaches at the Faculty of Law of the University of Barcelona, has contributed to writing this chapter.

1. Only three private universities offer degrees in law.

2. There are two kinds of registrar: the "registrador de la propriedad" maintains the real estate records, and the "registrador mercantil" maintains the registry of commercial enterprises.

3. A notary or "registrador" must pass a national examination administered by the Ministry of Justice. The number of practitioners is limited. They start their careers in small towns and must compete for promotions to larger towns or transfers to the specific town where they wish to establish practice. However, they are not paid by the state but live on the fees they charge for their professional services.

4. In some lower courts the parties may represent themselves.

5. "Fiscal" is the vernacular term; in court they are called "ministerio fiscal" or "ministerio público."

6. I am using "government" in the American sense rather than in the way the word is used in civil law countries.

17. The Faculty of Law of Barcelona had 1,800 students in 1965 and 3,500 in 1970.

8. In addition, 4,280 students were registered at the Universidad Autónoma of Madrid and 773 at the Universidad Autónoma of Barcelona.

9. A law graduate who does not wish to practice also may join a Colegio and will be registered as a "nonpracticing lawyer."

10. The Barcelona fund was established in 1866; the national fund, in 1950.

11. Bar associations also claim authority to punish nonmembers who practice law, but since the greatest sanction is expulsion, it is not clear how such disciplinary authority could be exercised.

12. The average salary of a high court judge is 200,000 Pts per month; a full-time law professor earns between 150,000 and 190,000 Pts per month.

# REFERENCES

*Anuario Estadístico de España.* 1981. Madrid: Instituto Nacional de Estadística, Ministerio de Economía y Comercio.

*Memoria dels esdeveniments de la vida del Col.legi durant l'any 1983.* 1983. Barcelona: M. I. Col.legi d'Advocats de Barcelona.

———. 1984. Barcelona: M. I. Col.legi d'Advocats de Barcelona.

*Memoria elevada al Gobierno de su Majestad por el Fiscal General del Estado.* 1985. Madrid: Reus.

Moltó García, Tomás, and Esteve Oroval Planas. 1983. *Análisis de la racionalización global de la asignación de recursos públicos a la enseñanza superior.* Barcelona: Gráficas Signo.

Toharía, J. J. 1985. "Actitudes de los españoles hacia la Administración de Justicia," *Poder Judicial* 33–45.

# 11

## The Venezuelan Legal Profession: Lawyers in an Inegalitarian Society

### ROGELIO PÉREZ PERDOMO

## INTRODUCTION: TERMINOLOGY AND HISTORICAL BACKGROUND

I will begin with a brief history of Venezuela. The territory of the present Republic of Venezuela was colonized by Spain during the sixteenth and seventeenth centuries. Its increasing prosperity led the Spanish crown to convert it into an autonomous administrative entity at the end of the eighteenth century. At the beginning of the nineteenth century the long-term effects of the French Revolution and the Napoleonic wars accelerated the independence movement within Latin America, and Venezuela became an important center of the struggle, providing leaders, politicians, intellectuals, and soldiers for the liberation of several other colonies. International difficulties, in part produced by the intense war of independence, as well as the lack of exports that would have integrated it within the capitalist system, combined to make Venezuela of the nineteenth and early twentieth centuries a poor and turbulent country. The population was more than 80 percent rural and sparsely distributed: approximately one million inhabitants at the beginning of the nineteenth century and three million at the beginning of the twentieth. In the last fifty years, the country has been incorporated into the world economy (especially through the export of petroleum, its major product); it has stabilized its political system and established a liberal democracy; it has urbanized and industrialized very rapidly; and its per capita income now is the highest in all of South America. The population has grown dramatically, partly through declining mortality rates achieved by improving sanitary conditions and partly through immigration. The country today has more than fifteen million inhabitants, over 80 percent of whom live in urban areas. Serious problems do exist, however, most notably the very unequal distribution of income and the strong dependence on the centers of world capitalism for the export of the country's main product as well as for the import of foodstuffs and technology.

Manuals of comparative law include Venezuela and the rest of Latin America among the civil law countries. In fact, the country completed codifying its law around 1870 (generally by importing European codes), and legislation clearly dominates the production of legal rules today. Legal writings also are important and, in general, closely linked to the legal thought of the other Latin countries (Spain, Portugal, Italy, France, and other Latin American countries). The formal legal system thus can be considered entirely modern, but clearly there is considerable distance between the legislative models and the actual social practices.

There have been university law graduates in Venezuela since the beginning of the eighteenth century. Law teaching started in 1720, and a law professor occupied one of the first chairs in the Universidad Central de Venezuela (Caracas University). During the colonial period the university granted the degrees of "bachiller," "licenciado," and "doctor" of civil law or canon law (or both). In the 100 years before independence in 1821, 372 persons took law degrees, but the number of law graduates in practice was somewhat greater because several graduates immigrated from other parts of the Spanish empire. The Audiencia—the highest court within the colony—granted the degree of "abogado" (lawyer) after a period of apprenticeship and an examination. For various reasons, less than a third of the law graduates aspired to the degree of "abogado," which was necessary to appear in the Audiencia but not before the alcaldes and the tenientes de justicia (lay judges).

Law graduates played an important role in the independence period. Many joined the independence party, and law graduates were well represented in the independence congresses. They had great influence in designing the institutions in the new Republic because they represented the criollo class (Spanish descendants born in America) and were experts in politics.

After independence the study of canon law declined and law teaching was enriched with such subjects as political economy, international law, and principles of legislation. By the middle of the nineteenth century the only degree that qualified for the practice of law was the doctor of political science. At this time the degree of "abogado" was granted by various courts after a period of apprenticeship. This degree was a mere formality; instead of a real examination, all that was necessary was certification by an established lawyer. Because an abogado no longer was burdened with the responsibilities that had accompanied the degree during the colonial era (such as the obligation to provide free assistance to Indians and the poor and to advise lay judges and other administrators), all graduates in law or political science also obtained the additional qualification. Between 1820 and 1930 only 1,800 degrees were awarded, or sixteen per year. By 1936, there were 740 law graduates (all of whom were both doctors of political science and abogados) in a country with 3,850,000 inhabitants. The legal profession could be considered established: the majority of law graduates had a private practice or eventually became judges, registrars, or notaries.

The year 1936 usually is specified as the beginning of contemporary Venezuela. The death of General Gómez, the dictator, the previous year initiated a period of political liberalization and rapid social change. The number of law graduates increased steadily, and growth became explosive after 1960 (see figs. 11.1 and 11.2).

During the 1950s the legal regime regulating professional qualification changed: the universities themselves granted the title of "abogado," which admitted the graduate to practice. The degree of "doctor" and the recently created titles of "magister" and "especialista" are granted after postgraduate studies and are relevant mainly for law teaching. However, because of heightened competition in the job market for lawyers, graduates are seeking these additional credentials as entree to the official bureaucracy or to enhance their prestige in private practice.

Thus, the word "abogado" (lawyer) designates all those who have earned the qualification as well as the much smaller category of title-holders who offer legal counseling, assistance, and representation to the public. Only about a third of law graduates are in private practice. Another third are judges and public officials within the legal system, and the last third occupy positions for which a law degree is not required. I shall use the word "lawyer" to designate law graduates in private practice, the word "jurist" for all law graduates, and the expression "legal professionals" (or sometimes just professionals) for those law graduates who have a full-time job in the legal system for which a law degree is required (including judges, lawyers, and notaries).

Historically, the relationship between formal legal qualifications, actual occupation, and sources of income has been complex. Even though there were people with the title of lawyer in the eighteenth and nineteenth centuries, legal occupations were not a stable source of income for many. There was far too little legal work to provide a sufficient income for people of high social status. Although the most important judges were qualified lawyers and political appointees, all other judges and all registrars were laypersons (procuradores).[1] Most jurists were letrados (learned people) rather than private practitioners, and their principal occupation was politics, where they discharged very important duties, even though they served caudillos and dictators. In twentieth-century Venezuela, in contrast, a true legal profession has emerged, although the political system continues to provide work for some jurists.

In the following pages I will analyze the current situation and will refer only occasionally to periods prior to 1935. Any statement made without a specific time reference pertains to the present day.

## WHO ARE THE LEGAL PROFESSIONALS?

SELECTION

Law study is located within the university, which constitutes the only route into legal practice. Most students enter the university at eighteen, after completing a minimum of eleven years of mandatory schooling, although many enter later. There are two types of university: public, where tuition is free; and private, supported by student fees and, to a lesser degree, private foundations and the government. The four law schools in public universities enroll 65 percent of the law students—Caracas, Mérida, Maracaibo, and Valencia. There are two private universities in Caracas and a third in San Cristóbal. The total number of law students was 19,000 in 1981/82, or 5.7 percent of the entire university population.

Each school is allowed to set a maximum number of students (fixed by a national planning body for the public universities on the basis of budgetary considerations and physical capacity). Thus, there is selection at two levels: the capacity of the educational system as a whole and competition to enter schools that differ in prestige. In general terms, law schools are more selective than most other schools within the public universities, with the exception of computer science, architecture, engineering, and medicine. Entry to the Universidad de Venezuela (Caracas) is most highly competitive among universities.

The fact that the public universities are free might suggest that socioeconomic background plays no role. However, differences in attitude toward university study and selection and ranking at earlier stages of the educational system already have had had an effect. Few university students (about 5 percent) are of peasant or working-class origin because very few people from this social background are able to afford a long period of study or aspire to a profession in which their lack of personal contacts within the relevant milieu would make success very uncertain.[2]

Background variables other than class probably do not affect entry. The student bodies of both the university as a whole and the law schools are fairly equally divided between the sexes. The Venezuelan population is mestiza (a mixture of European, Indian, and black), any prejudice is covert, and race has no importance in the selection of the students. The vast majority of Venezuelans are Roman Catholic, but religion does not influence university selection or employment.

After admission there is a further screening by the law schools themselves. Although the data are inadequate, we know that student attrition is very high. In law—a subject that is not particularly difficult—less than 20 percent of entrants graduate. Many abandon their studies because they lack genuine interest (remember that tuition is free in most cases).[3] The significance of academic selection is unclear. In my judgment, the most obvious cases of intellectual incapacity are discarded, but creative students are lost as well. The dryness of the material, pedagogical rigidity, and the requirements of memorization probably exclude the most intellectually "alive" students.

## INTELLECTUAL FORMATION

I will analyze briefly the content of the training the schools provide during the five or more years of the law course. This is relatively easy since there is an obligatory list of topics that varies little from one university to another.

The bulk of the assigned courses are designed for private lawyers involved in litigation (private law, procedural law, and legal practice constitute half of the curriculum). The remainder is divided between courses on public law, criminal law, and historical or complementary materials. Students are required to understand and often to memorize principles, concepts, and rules. Most critics feel that legal studies are irrelevant to, and an inadequate preparation for, the activities of professional life. The response (mistaken, in my view) has been to increase the number of courses useful for private practice, instead of modifying the teaching methods to develop the skills of factual investigation, legal reasoning, and problem-solving.

## EDUCATION AFTER THE DEGREE: ON-THE-JOB TRAINING AND POSTGRADUATE WORK

Students most frequently seek to overcome the poverty of their formal legal education through training within the occupation itself. This is entirely informal, since there is no apprenticeship requirement for entry into the profession. Many students begin to work in courts, law firms, or public offices during the final years of their university careers. Others train after the degree by working with lawyers who are relatives, friends, fellow employees, or employers. Many graduates also pursue postgraduate studies, either in law schools (especially the Universidad Central de Venezuela, which has the largest and best organized program) or in other schools with interdisciplinary programs in administration, urban studies, planning, and similar fields. An increasing number seek a postgraduate degree abroad, usually in France, Italy, or the United States, generally in law but also in other disciplines that may be relevant to a bureaucratic career in a specialized area of public or private administration. Postgraduate degrees have gained importance in recent years, probably as a result of greater competition in the job market.[4]

## PROFESSIONAL ORGANIZATIONS

I will now analyze the support systems available to legal professionals: the twenty-one colegios de abogados (bar associations), one in each state capital and one in Caracas, and the national institution that coordinates them, the Federación de Colegios de Abogados. The colegio de abogados was a colonial institution, created in 1788, which has some of the features of a medieval guild. Even though most lawyers belonged to the pro-independence party, the new Republic suppressed the colegios in 1822 as medieval corporations inconsistent with the prevailing ideology of liberalism. Nevertheless, the colegios were revived in 1883, principally as academic institutions to enhance public knowledge of law. Any law graduate can register in a colegio, without further examination, and almost all do so, although only a small group are active and pay their annual fees. Every law graduate who performs any legal professional activity must join a colegio and register with Impreabogado, a form of social security for lawyers. The colegios have multiple functions. Later I will analyze their role in enforcing the legal professional monopoly. They act as interest groups or trade unions to defend the working conditions of their members. Although they possess disciplinary authority and can suspend or expel a member, they almost never impose any sanctions or even reprimands. The colegio functions mostly as a meeting place for lower court judges and young or politically ambitious lawyers who seek to enhance their professional or political prestige or to establish friendships. The most active colegios organize professional refresher courses, publish a magazine and sometimes even books, and maintain a library. They also are social clubs and generally have a bar service and a swimming pool and organize sporting and cultural activities. Some colegios offer free legal assistance to low-income people, but such activity is marginal for both the colegio and the public. The colegio's president frequently is a judge, and political parties are involved in the election of a president. The Federación de Colegios de Abogados is merely an umbrella organization, as its name implies. Within it, judges, litigators, and women have organized their own special-interest groups (the Associación de Jueces, the Associación de

Abogados Litigantes, and the Federación de Mujeres Abogadas); none of these national groupings is very strong.

NUMBER, DISTRIBUTION, AND DIFFERENTIATION OF THE PROFESSION

The number of legal professionals in Venezuela has increased very rapidly: from 543 in 1926 (over 5,500 people per lawyer) to 15,000 in 1980 (1,000 people per lawyer).[5] Growth has been especially rapid since 1950. Approximately 65 percent of legal professionals are based in Caracas, which has 25 percent of the population of the country and is the center of political and economic decision-making (see table 11.1). Recently, however, there has been a redistribution toward the interior of the country, especially to the principal cities of the new areas of regional development.

The division by function is more difficult to determine. There are more than 1,000 courts, the vast majority of which are conducted by a legally qualified judge. Given that some courts have several judges and a number of court secretaries in the major cities are jurists, I estimate that approximately 1,500 professionals are employed in the judicial apparatus. Another 1,000 work in other public offices within the legal system as registrars, notaries, public defenders and prosecutors, and so on. There are approximately 600 law professors in the country, but they are not an important occupational category because less than 25 percent are full-time teachers. The remaining legal professionals are private lawyers, judges, or other officials who devote some time to teaching. We lack data with respect to two very important occupational categories whose size is particularly difficult to estimate: lawyers (i.e., private practitioners) and jurists who work as administrative officials within the government. I would guess that one-third of all law graduates, or about 5,000 people, are in each category. Finally, more than 1,000 law graduates are found in such diverse occupations as housewife, business executive, writer, and military officer. Declared unemployment is insignificant.

Each jurist in Venezuela traditionally occupies several different positions in the course of a lifetime. In analyzing the careers of those who graduated from law school in 1936, I grouped the positions into five categories: private practice; public officials, such as a judge, registrar, or notary; important positions in the political system (those who hold high governmental offices and diplomatic posts, legislators, leaders of political parties); literary activities (scholarship in law, history, literature); and law teaching. I found that 75.8 percent performed activities in three or more categories.[6] This tradition, which reflects the relatively undifferentiated nature of Venezuelan society until the middle of the present century and the absence of progressive careers within each sector, is undergoing modification.

Recent social and political changes have permitted functional specialization. Now a judge expects to remain on the bench throughout a professional career, rising within the judiciary until retirement. The same is true, to a lesser extent, of university professors, public officials, and private practitioners. Job security and the rewards of seniority encourage lawyers to remain within one occupational category (with occasional or part-time activity in another), which is producing a functional segmentation of the profession, such as exists in European countries.

## WHAT DO LEGAL PROFESSIONALS DO?

Legal professionals have a monopoly over the following activities:

1. Representation and assistance of any individual or legal entity before the courts. Furthermore, no party may appear before a judge unless represented by a lawyer.[7]

2. Preparation of registered or notarized legal documents. All documents transferring property, establishing a company, or creating a lien must be prepared and signed by a lawyer.[8]

3. Legal consulting. Only legal professionals may publicly offer legal advice.

4. Important positions in the legal system. The Constitution of Venezuela requires that only law graduates may become members of the Supreme Court of Justice or serve as Contralor General, Fiscal General, and Procurador General.[9] Law is the only profession that enjoys a constitutional monopoly of high public office. The Organic Law of Judicial Power also reserves to legal professionals the position of judge, except in localities where there are no such professionals.[10] Other statutes and regulations require a law degree for the position of registrar, commercial registrar, notary, legal counsel, public defender and prosecutor and so forth.[11]

The colegios de abogados have added their own monopolistic practices to the laws reserving certain duties and positions to law graduates. Among the main ones are restrictions on advertising, the setting of minimum fees enforced by disciplinary action, and rules concerning the collection of fees.[12] Legal professionals do not limit themselves to activities over which they enjoy a monopoly but perform many others as well, most notably mediation and conciliation, business planning, negotiating, and politics.

## SOCIAL AND PROFESSIONAL STRATIFICATION

In the "Introduction" I noted that Venezuelan society is highly inegalitarian. Each stratum retains a distinct type of legal professional and requires characteristic services. The manner of obtaining clients, the lawyer–client relationship, the structures of practice, and the type and quality of services vary with the type of professional. I will examine two extreme categories: the lawyers of the elite and lawyers for low-income people.[13]

## LAWYERS OF THE ELITE

In this section I shall examine the organization and activities of lawyers who serve business and government—large units that require varied and continuous legal services. By including government within the economic elite, I am referring to the central administration, agencies, and public enterprises, which control substantial economic resources and are in frequent contract with entrepreneurs and investors, often adopting many of the forms of activity characteristic of private enterprise.

### In-House Counsel (consultoria jurídica)

Almost all large companies and all public administrative bodies have an office of house counsel directed by one or more professionals. This type of practice may be inconsistent with the image lawyers have of themselves as independent professionals who offer their services to many clients and thus preserve their independence of judgment because they are not economically dependent on any one client. Although the number of lawyers employed is uncertain, it probably is 1,500 or more. The characteristic feature of the house counsel is that the professional really is an employee of a single "client," which actually is an employer. The service is rendered within the offices of the client, which provides all of the operating expenses and pays a salary (not a fee) to the professionals. The professional participates in the most important decisions, usually attends the meetings of the Board of Directors, and also handles routine matters: preparation of documents and contracts, employee relations, and interaction with companies or administrative bodies. When the volume of routine activities is very large, the in-house counsel employs additional professionals ranked within a bureaucratic hierarchy. The object of in-house counsel is to prevent conflicts. When litigation is unavoidable, the client usually will retain outside counsel, often through in-house counsel, although the latter may handle routine matters in court.

The prestige and salary of the employed lawyer will depend on the employer's importance and the employee's ranking among other lawyers within the office. The lower positions usually are occupied by women or by young lawyers seeking training. However, even the higher officials do not enjoy the prestige of elite private practitioners.


## The "Big" Law Firm

There are no law firms in Venezuela as big as those found in the United States. The largest barely has thirty lawyers, and only ten have more than ten lawyers. I call these firms "big" because their model is the large American law firm. Their distinguishing feature is that the practice of law becomes a legal services company: the professional partners pool their work and share the earnings of the company in accordance with previously agreed rules. The company has employees: secretaries, students, messengers, accountants, and sometimes translators. Among the employees are other lawyers, generally recent graduates who expect to become partners of that firm or to establish themselves independently after completing an apprenticeship.

This organizational form appeared in Venezuela during the 1940s and is becoming more common among corporate lawyers. Currently there are many legal offices, containing five to ten lawyers, which have adopted this form with the intention of growing. I estimate the total number of lawyers in firms at about 300.

Some of these firms include litigantes (court lawyers), discussed below. But the basic activity of this type of firm is counseling and business planning. In the event of litigation, they frequently associate with a prestigious court lawyer.


## The Interdisciplinary Service Firm with a Legal Component

This is a very recent development. To my knowledge, there are only two such firms, employing some twenty lawyers between them, although the phenomenon may proliferate. In these firms jurists, economists, engineers, accountants, sociologists, and other professionals collaborate to offer planning and counseling services to a group of related companies. Although these firms could operate independently, they gain expertise and efficiency by working for companies that encounter similar problems. Thus they combine the advantages of the corporate law firm with those of the inhouse counsel. Because they do not appear in court, they refer litigation and other unusual or complex legal matters to a court lawyer or a law firm.

The Prestigious Court Lawyers (Los Litigantes de Prestigio)

Although some lawyers known for their prowess as litigators have joined big law firms, most maintain individual offices or share expenses with other lawyers but not income or clients. Some of these court lawyers practice in the criminal area, which has acquired renewed prestige due to the greater frequency of cases of white-collar crime and of politically motivated prosecutions in a country where the judiciary is very independent of the executive (although not of the political parties, as we shall see later) and where the press enjoys considerable freedom.[14] There is no formal distinction between the litigante de prestigio and the ordinary lawyer. It is a specialization based on professional reputation, and often the distinction is difficult to draw. The category suggests what might happen in England if the barriers between solicitor and barrister were eliminated.

In summary, the most significant forms of economic activity, which are controlled by the ruling class, occupy the energies of the most qualified lawyers. They adopt different organizational structures, depending on the type of services they render. Because their services differ, they complement each other and frequently collaborate.

Finally, I want to highlight the way in which elite lawyers obtain clients. Some of the corporate law firms interested in representing foreign investors appear in the *Martindale-Hubbell Law Directory*. The majority of lawyers appear in the telephone directory, and a small percentage publish advertisements in the yellow pages of the telephone directory or in the major newspapers. Yet one of the oldest, largest, and most prestigious firms, Mendoza-Palacio-Acedo-Bórjas, does not appear even in the telephone directory. This is indicative of how clients are obtained in the majority of instances: through personal contacts within the shrinking Venezuelan elite, to which both the prestigious lawyers and their clients belong, or through contacts with American law firms. The common feature of elite lawyers is the small number of clients they serve, usually big national or multinational corporations. These lawyers generally have an excellent education and come from families of high social status. They earn substantially more than traditional lawyers: the median income of a senior partner in a big law firm is ten times that of any other lawyer.

## LOW-INCOME CLIENTS AND THEIR LAWYERS

Before discussing this topic, I want to explain why I am not describing the lawyers used by clients of moderate means: individuals and small enterprises. These clients use general lawyers, who resemble those legal professionals described in the large literature in Spanish and in other languages. Another account would not reveal anything significant about the structure of Venezuelan society.

I indicated above that wealth and income is very unequally distributed in Venezuela. This has an obvious consequence: an important segment of the population cannot hope to purchase quality legal services from private providers. The usual rate for one hour of quality legal work (not by a lawyer who enjoys particular prestige) is approximately 500 bolivars, which is equal to the average family income for five days. However, the actual situation is even worse because informal mechanisms strongly influence decisionmaking in Venezuela. Much of the work of a lawyer is utilizing one's personal contacts, one's prestige, or the influence of one's client to achieve a favorable or at least a rapid decision. Low-income individuals not only cannot pay a lawyer but also lack the personal contacts necessary to persuade lawyers, judges, and administrators to pay attention to their cases.

## Private Lawyers

Our research showed that in Caracas, and to a smaller extent in other large cities, a number of lawyers serve low-income clients. One group offer their services for ideological and political reasons. Lawyers active in politics, especially within the leftist parties, are involved in labor law, counseling and representing both unions and individual workers. The parishes of some Catholic churches, some universities, and some of the colegios de abogados also render legal services. Lawyers with ties to religious organizations are concerned with matters involving minors, the family, housing, and illegal immigrants. Those working with the Federación de Mujeres Abogadas tend to serve women and cases involving minors and the family.

Although the quality of the services varies from one institution to another, most lawyers serving low-income clients are dedicated to them. The number of lawyers rendering such services is low, and those who do are overworked. Therefore, although the services are little known, they are not publicized further in order to avoid aggravating the case overload.

Another group of private lawyers is motivated by profit, seeking to handle a large number of cases or documents at moderate prices. The offices of these lawyers are characterized by numerous secretarial employees who actually interview the client, make decisions, and prepare documents. The lawyer's role is limited to signing the document prepared by his employees after giving it a cursory reading.

The manner of attracting the client is illegal, or at least a violation of professional ethics. These lawyers advertise in the press, usually offering "free legal counseling" and listing the types of case handled, such as marriage certificates and requests for exemption from military service. The client finds that the "counseling" is free but payment will be demanded for the document prepared. Some lawyers contract with lay intermediaries who haunt places frequented by people with specific legal needs: jails, certain notaries' offices in downtown Caracas, and public offices that issue identity cards or other official documents. The intermediary looks for a confused or disoriented person and offers the services of the lawyer, telling the prospective client that the lawyer can resolve the problem. The intermediary then conducts the potential client to the lawyer's office and receives from the lawyer a percentage of the client's fee.

## Public Lawyers

The Venezuelan government pays approximately 500 full-time legal professionals to render counseling, assistance, and representation to low-income clients. Although the duties of public lawyers are similar to those of private lawyers, the manner in which they relate to their clients differs significantly. Despite my reference to public lawyers, there is no such category within the Venezuelan legal system but only particular roles: public defenders, public prosecutors, procuradores de *menores* (minors), procuradores de *trabajadores* (laborers), procuradores *agrarios*, (farmers), lawyers from the Housing Regulation Office, lawyers with the Children's Institute, and so on.[15]

The most notable characteristic of these services reflects the basis fact that public lawyers are paid by the government, not by the client, and receive a fixed remuneration regardless of the quality of the services rendered. This, together with the very high caseload, tends to make the professional insensitive to the needs of the client. Thus, although particular lawyers are deeply dedicated to fulfilling their duties (especially those within the procuradores de menores), most have little motivation. Because the services are free, however, clients know that they cannot demand too much, even though the law requires the lawyer to be as diligent as possible and holds the lawyer responsible for negligence, if only on paper. Clients must queue up, often standing for extended periods, and the office personnel, including the receptionist and the secretaries, treat the clients with arrogance or condescension.

The services rendered by public lawyers are shaped by the interests of the lawyer, not the needs of the client. Thus, problems related to health, welfare, and education do not generate claims through the public lawyers. Low-income people do not perceive their problems as legal. The welfare system for Venezuelan workers, administered by the Social Welfare Institute, is an example. There are two million paying members and another six million dependents, who together account for more than half the population. However, we did not find any claims against the Institute made by the procuradores de trabajadores and very few made by other lawyers (Acedo Machado, 1986). This lack of claims is not testimony to the excellence of the welfare services, which generally are held in low esteem. Rather, it reflects the low quality of the legal services ostensibly rendered by public lawyers. Van Groningen (1980) evaluated the quality of the services performed by the public defenders and found them to be very poor. Among people accused of homicide, those represented received sentences averaging more than seventeen years, while upper-class defendants represented by private lawyers received an average sentence of 5.1 years.

Recently, a coalition of university researchers and politicians has proposed a radical restructuring of the delivery of legal services to the poor, based on an empirical investigation of the deficiencies of the present system (Pérez Perdomo, 1986). We advocated greater involvement by universities, colegios de abogados, unions, municipalities, and other intermediaries, supported by public funds and subject to government evaluation. The services provided by lawyers within these institutions progressively would replace much of the work presently performed by civil servants. Law students and recent graduates would be required to render free legal assistance as a prerequisite to qualifying as a lawyer, and qualified lawyers would be encouraged to do so. Mediation centers, staffed by specially trained legal professionals, would be given jurisdiction over many of the matters that concern poor people and would have the power to compel the parties to attend without their lawyers, even though the centers could not render judgments.

The proposal has elicited strong and widespread opposition. Public defenders and other public officials who provide legal assistance to the poor were deeply resentful of the highly critical evaluation of their work and anxious about losing their positions. Colegios de abogados and associations of trial lawyers (abogados litigantes) within the colegios also feared that these proposals would deprive them of paying clients. Although there has been little public discussion, discreet lobbying by both of these groups and the absence of countervailing support by equally powerful proponents has led to legislative inaction.

## POLITICS AND THE LEGAL PROFESSION

I will conclude with an analysis of the place of the legal profession within the Venezuelan political system. I am consciously rejecting the commonly accepted distinction between professional and political activity. Legal professional activity, in the strictest sense, *is* political; its apparent neutrality and independence from the political system is a myth constructed by lawyers for their own purposes. Legal professionals are politically more active than other occupations because of their professional roles—and the political activity of lawyers is important for understanding the meaning of their professional roles.

Lawyers are viewed as independent of politics because their income is received from clients who choose lawyers on the basis of experience and professional prestige. As already mentioned, however, those who retain the more capable and prestigious lawyers are precisely the most powerful business executives. The resulting professional activity will favor those interests. However, those social sectors that cannot retain lawyers or can retain only the least prestigious will be at a disadvantage whether engaged in litigation or in actions designed to prevent conflict through mediation.

In the "Introduction" I pointed out that Venezuelan jurists have a long tradition of political participation, dating back to the end of the eighteenth century. This is not peculiar to Venezuela: jurists were prominent in the medieval and Renaissance Church, in the constitution of the national states, and in the bourgeois revolutions of the seventeenth and eighteenth centuries. In Spanish America, jurists have been the civil leaders par excellence. From 1936 to the present, five of the fourteen presidents of Venezuela were jurists and two were law students who abandoned their studies because of political persecution. Between one-third and two-thirds of all cabinet members have been jurists. Between 25 percent and 40 percent of the members of the National Congress are jurists. In the two major political parties, 47.4 percent and 36.7 percent of their Boards of Directors are jurists. In this regard we can speak of the law schools, especially those of the Universidad Central de Venezuela and, more recently, of the Universidad Católica, as centers of training and recruitment for the political elite. I will not speculate about the consequences for Venezuelan politics and government of the fact that so many leaders have had a legal background. I am concerned, rather, with the fact that the lawyers of the economic elite overlap with the political elite and that the two groups share common training and friendships. This is important for the study of the legal profession because the political contacts of legal professionals are an important factor in explaining the significance of law practice, especially in a country where the government wields such vast resources.

High government officials who usually are lawyers or are closely advised by lawyers maintain very close relationships with big-business lawyers. Consequently, lawyers are the main architects of a society that has been able to combine democratic political practices, the rule of law, and enormous social inequality.

# FIGURES

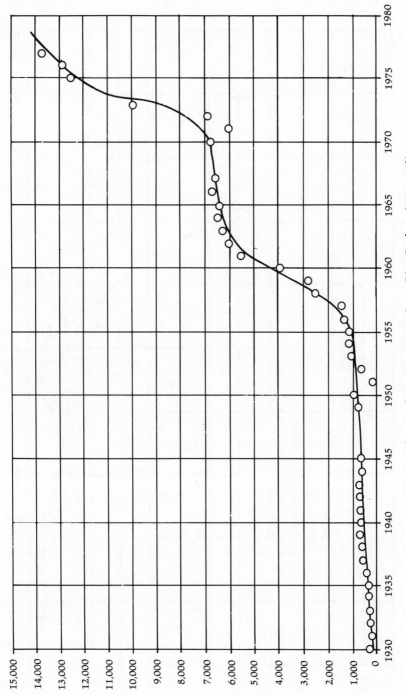

Fig. 11.1. Number of law students, 1930–1980. (*Source:* Pérez Perdomo [1981:182].)

395

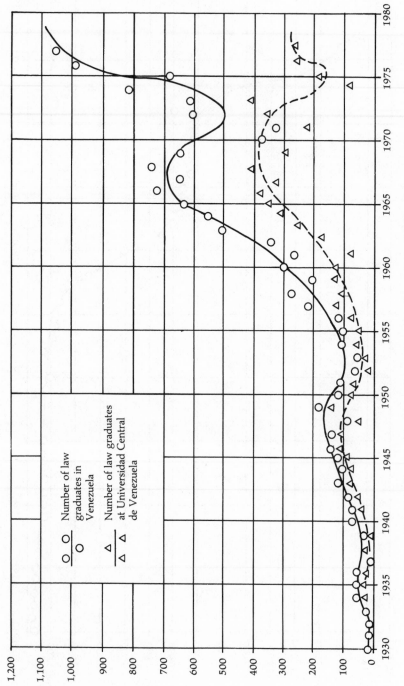

Fig. 11.2. Number of law graduates, 1930–1980. (*Source:* Pérez Perdomo [1981: 188]).

The following labels appear in the figure:

O O Number of law graduates in Venezuela
O

△ △ Number of law graduates at Universidad Central de Venezuela
△

# TABLE

11.1. Historical Trends in the Geographical Distribution of Law Graduates in Venezuela

| Year | Population of the country (1,000s) | Law graduates in the country | Law graduates in Caracas (%) | Population of Caracas as percent of the country | |
|------|------|------|------|------|------|
| 1840 | 1,000 | 120 | 51.7 | 3.6 | |
| 1894 | 2,445 | 246 | 48.4 | 3.0 | |
| 1926 | 3,027 | 543 | N.A. | 5.5 | |
| 1961 | 7,524 | 4.256 | 68.7 | 17.8 | |
| 1971 | 10,722 | 8.102 | 63.0 | 20.4 | |
| 1978 | 12,800 | 14.000 | 67.6 | 23.7 | (est.) |

*Source:* Pérez Perdomo (1981: figures 6, 7, 15, 16).

## NOTES

The present chapter is based on my two books (Pérez Perdomo, 1981; 1986); for this reason, sources are not stated.

1. Registrars are public officials who record title to real property and maintain other public records. Today they are law graduates. In the nineteenth century, the term "procuradores" referred to laymen authorized to practice law. The category no longer exists and should be distinguished from procuradores agrarios, procuradores de menores, and procuradores de trabajadores—legally trained public officials charged with protecting the interests of disadvantaged groups (these are discussed further below).

2. A survey of university students (Instituto de Investigaciones Educativas, 1978) did not reveal a relationship between social background and academic achievement, probably because much of the selection occurs prior to entering university. Nevertheless, my personal experience as a teacher confirms that the best students are not from working-class origins.

3. There is no study of attrition, but the generally accepted view of student careers is as follows. After a year or two of school, most students begin working at one of a wide variety of jobs (wealthier students to gain experience, poorer students to support themselves and their families). Job pressures and university demands determine attrition. Many students who leave at this point return to the university after a few years, often to a different institution with lower academic standards, and graduate in law or another subject. The most desirable jobs from the point of view of law students are those in courts, in law offices, and with notaries. The number of good jobs that advance a student's career is limited, however, and usually only the well-connected students obtain them. At the same time, academic success in the Central University or the Catholic University makes demands on students that are compatible only with part-time work. These are the structural reasons for the high rate of failure and attrition.

4. I estimate that there were 400 postgraduate students and 1,000 jurists with postgraduate training in a population of 15,000 law graduates in 1980.

5. The estimates are very rough. Even if the number of law graduates could be calculated from university statistics and the registry of Impreabogado, that would tell nothing about their functional distribution. There are no figures for the number of private practitioners or for law graduates employed in government. Among the latter I have included law graduates in the central administration, the legislature, the Contraloria General, the Procuraduria General, and regional bureaucracies, even though not all those positions require legal training. For this reason I confine the category of "professional practice" to private practice and those positions in the judicial system and in other forms of employment that demand legal training.

6. Although I have no quantitative data on the sequence of positions, most lawyers begin as lower-court judges and lower- or middle-level administrative officials and either move up within those bureaucratic hierarchies or, following a political disgrace, return to private practice. Teaching and writing pay poorly and generally are part-time positions.

7. The profession's monopoly extends to administrative tribunals, with the exception of labor tribunals, which the petitioner can approach alone or with a lay assistant (usually a friend or trade union official).

8. A private lawyer must prepare the document, and the registrar or notary must read it and, unless it contains some obvious illegality, transcribe it in a public register of documents. Registrars and notaries are public functionaries and cannot practice privately.

9. The Contralor General oversees the legality and appropriateness of public expenditures. The Fiscal General is the head of the ministère public and performs some of the functions of an ombudsman. Both are elected by the National Congress for five-year terms. The Procurador General is legal advisor to the executive and represents the Republic in litigation in civil and administrative cases (hence equivalent to the solicitor general in common law countries). The Con-

tralor General is appointed by the President, subject to the approval of Congress, and is a member of the Cabinet.

10. In 1985 only ninety-two of the judges in the 1,064 tribunals were not law graduates.

11. Registrars keep records of transactions concerning real property, wills, and university titles. Commercial registrars maintain records of incorporation and other commercial transactions. Notaries record private documents and certify the signatures of those signing them. All three are public officials.

12. The minimum fee scale was established by the Federación de Colegios de Abogados in 1971, but not all colegios accepted it. At first, the Colegio of Caracas refused to enforce it. Following a change in the board of governors in 1983, the colegio promulgated a scale and required that a percentage of the charge be paid to it, justifying both as a means of allowing the colegio to provide legal aid. A group of members now has challenged the minimum fee scale as an unlawful monopoly, an improper use of funds, and an invasion of the constitutional rights of lawyers. In fact, the conflict is between low-status lawyers and judges, who control the colegio and use it for their own purposes, and elite lawyers and judges, who have no use for the colegio but resent their inability to control it.

13. There are no quantitative data on the stratification of private practitioners, so these remarks necessarily are more qualitative.

14. There is no overt political repression in Venezuela, and control of the government changes periodically through free elections. However, politicians, especially those challenging the incumbent, use the criminal process to disqualify their opponents. Recently, two former presidents, serveral cabinet ministers, and many high officials have been charged with a variety of economic crimes ("corrupción administrativa"), but few have been convicted.

15. The three types of procurador are public officials charged with representing minors, workers, and peasants in court and with giving them legal advice.

## REFERENCES

Acedo Machado, Clementina. 1986. "Necesidades jurídicas y acceso a la justicia en un nuevo sector: Beneficiarios del Seguro Social," in *Estudios Laborales ... en Homenaje al Profesor Rafael Alfonso Guzmán*, pp. 35–66. Caracas: Universidad Central de Venezuela.

Instituto de Investigaciones Educativas, Universidad Simon Bólivar. 1970. *El rendimiento estudiantil universitario*. Caracas: Equinoccio.

Pérez Perdomo, Rogelio. 1981. *Los Abogados en Venezuela: estudio de una élite intelectual y política 1780–1980*. Caracas: Monte Avila.

———, ed. 1986. *Justicia y pobreza en Venezuela*. Caracas: Monte Avila and Universidad Central de Venezuela.

Van Groningen, Karin. 1980. *Aplicación de la Ley Penal y Desigualdad Social*. Caracas: Ed. Jurídica Venezolana.

# 12
## Lawyers in Brazil

JOAQUIM FALCÃO

## INTRODUCTION

An understanding of Brazilian lawyers requires some knowledge of Brazilian history. Brazil was a Portuguese colony from the time of its discovery by European explorers in 1500 until the Proclamation of Independence in 1822 by the Portuguese Prince Dom Pedro I, then acclaimed as its first emperor. One of the first challenges for the new country was to build a national elite capable of administering internal affairs, representing Brazil abroad, and defending it. Until then, this had been the task of the foreign Portuguese elite in both Lisbon and Rio de Janeiro. During the colonial period, the Brazilian elite had been educated in Coimbra (Portugal) or in England. In 1823, therefore, the first legislature discussed the creation of Brazilian universities (Camara dos Deputados, 1977). In 1827, however, the General Assembly and Emperor Pedro I decided instead to create two law schools: the Olinda Law School in the northeast and the São Paulo Law School in southern Brazil. Both sought not only to prepare lawyers, judges, prosecutors, or attorneys but also to train the political, bureaucratic, and administrative elite of the new country. Since then they have molded deputies, senators, civil servants, ministers, police officers, customs officers, and financiers, building the elite of a sovereign nation (Falcão, 1978b: 85).

Brazilian law schools were modeled on the academic program, the readings, the teaching methods, and the subjects of Coimbra Law School. Although directed by the central government (even the required readings were established by the government) and entirely free, only the heirs of the economic and political elite could attend them. From 1827 until approximately 1920, law schools were the principal path toward a higher degree for students not attracted to the study of medicine or engineering or preparing for the church or the military (Steiner, 1971). They offered a

400

liberal education—the humanistic conception of politics, law, and social relations that an educated person would need to perform almost any role in the government of a traditional society.

Two aspects of Brazil's independence are more directly related to the creation of both law schools. First, independence meant the rejection of absolutism and the adoption of liberalism and constitutionalism—initially monarchical and subsequently republican—as the national ideology. Second, the already feeble bonds of economic dependence on Portugal were cut as ties with England strengthened. If Brazil previously had exported its agricultural products exclusively to Portugal, economic liberalism freed the country to export anywhere in the world.

From these intimate connections between the creation of the law schools, the appearance of law graduates (the *bachareis*) as the dominant professionals within the national elite, and the political independence of the country we derive four fundamental characteristics of legal practice in Brazil: (1) law graduates engage in both legal and nonlegal professional activities; (2) law graduates perform their activities in both the public and the private sectors; (3) although advocacy is a liberal profession, the government and not civil society provided its educational institutions, created its associations, and influenced its job market; and (4) law graduates are committed to the liberal ideology of the constitutional state, with its notions of civil liberty and political sovereignty—but this does not ensure the economic independence of the profession or its opposition to social inequalities.

For the purposes of this study I have constructed three analytic categories:

*Law graduates* (bachareis) are those who hold a law degree from a law school, regardless of whether they practice law or are registered in the Brazilian Bar Association (Ordem dos Advogados do Brasil [OAB]).

*Legal professionals* are law graduates whose occupation primarily involves implementing law or teaching or conducting research on it. This category includes judges, prosecutors, attorneys, justices, jurists, and law professors.

*Lawyers* are law graduates registered in the Brazilian Bar Association whose main occupation is advocacy as defined in the statutes of that association: someone who represents the interests of another in court or outside and who has the exclusive right to draft and sign pleadings.

Although I will focus my attention on lawyers, I also will touch on law graduates and legal professionals, not only because this typology is not an exact reproduction of reality but also because, without a comprehensive knowledge of all those who hold a law degree, it is not possible to understand lawyers, their educational institutions, and legal practice. For, contrary to appearances, state regulation of legal practice and legal education and the tendencies of the job market are determined not only by the actions of lawyers but also by the interests of law graduates and legal professionals.

The modern conception of the legal profession, although controversial, derives from its nuclear occupation: the prevention and settlement of social disputes through the implementation of rules established by state power (executive, judiciary, and legislative). If we accept this definition, two principal characteristics of Brazilian legal practice emerge as significant.

First, the great majority of Brazilian citizens can neither hire a lawyer nor rely on a state-supported legal aid lawyer to protect their rights. They have no voluntary access to the judiciary. Legislation frequently means political and economic submission rather than tools to protect their interests. They cannot buy a house, get a decent job, earn enough to live in good health, obtain an adequate education, or enjoy some leisure. In 1983, for instance, 21.9 percent of those over fifteen were illiterate: 15.2 percent in urban Brazil and 41.5 percent in rural Brazil. In 1984, 10 percent of Brazilians received 46 percent of the national income. This society is divided into two groups: those who can hire lawyers, go to court voluntarily, and defend their interests through legislation; and those whose disputes are not settled in courts or through the implementation of legislation. Nonspecialized "professionals" implementing informal or unofficial "law" in multiple noninstitutionalized "courts" dominate this world. There is a peculiar and at least potentially contradictory "conviviality" between the law of the "asphalt" and the law of the "favelas" (squatter settlements) (Santos, 1977).

The consequences of this dual reality are quite significant for the legal profession. In designing its market strategy—supply control or demand creation—the Brazilian Bar Association must take into account fluctuations in per capita income, for in a developing country even a small reduction seriously affects the demand for lawyers' services.

Second, our legal profession historically has been linked to political independence, liberalism, and constitutionalism. Except for the Vargas dictatorship (1930–1937), all other Brazilian constitutions have proclaimed their commitment to liberal ideology, political democracy, and republican ideals. This does not necessarily mean that all citizens have enjoyed the rule of law. On the contrary, the majority are deprived of those benefits by reason of their poverty, the chronic inefficiency of the judiciary, and the culture of legal formalism. Since 1930, legal formalism has meant an uncritical attitude toward the political regime, the economic system, and the legal order itself.

There are almost no quantitative data concerning the Brazilian legal profession. This is due not only to the size of the country and the absence of national data banks but also to the dominant juridical doctrine, which is both formalistic and idealistic. Instead of seeking to understand social reality inductively, lawyers idealize it deductively. In fact, the profession knows very little about itself. Lawyers write more about what they *should* be than what they *are*. Social reality counts less than ideological aims. Consequently, I have sought to produce a descriptive analysis based on the limited empirical data available and on the common sense of the legal community itself. If this strategy is successful, it may produce knowledge characterized by bright and dark areas, similar to the lights and shadows of an impressionist painting.

## LEGAL EDUCATION

### THE LAW SCHOOL

The bachelor of law degree is obtained by graduation from a law school. Public law schools are supported by the federal, state, and municipal governments. If they are directly and totally controlled by the government, they assume the legal form of autarchy; otherwise, they are public foundations, enjoying greater autonomy concerning staff recruitment and salary policies. Those who belong to the private sector may be either secular or religious, for in Brazil the Catholic Church maintains its own schools.

Both public and private law schools may be part of a university or a federation of schools, or they may be independent (see table 12.1). In 1980, fifty-six law schools were part of the sixty-five universities (of which forty were public, fourteen religious, and six private but secular). Another ten law schools belonged to one of the fifty federations of schools (of which forty-seven were private and three were public). Finally, sixty-four law schools were independent (CFE, 1983). Public law schools generally are free or heavily subsidized, requiring students to pay much less than the monthly fees of $20 to $70 charged by private schools. Although educational institutions are not supposed to be profit-oriented, some of the independent law schools behave like business enterprises. Table 12.1 reveals that private enterprise is responsible for most of this education: two-thirds of all law schools and three-fourths of all law students. Some schools place up to 120 students in a single room (Mello Filho, 1981: 119), indicating the thoroughly commercial character of private law schools.

Although Brazil is a federal republic, composed of twenty-three states and three territories, the regulation and inspection of university education is the responsibility of the federal government. The agency charged with this task is the Federal Council of Education (Conselho Federal de Educação [CFE]), connected to the Ministry of Education (Ministério de Educação e

Cultura [MEC]). This Council issues standardized regulations for the entire country with respect to almost all aspects of legal education, such as enrollments, the courses and subjects to be taught, and the minimum requirements for the faculty. It also conducts (or at least should conduct) periodic inspections. Each diploma issued by a law school must be recognized by the Ministry of Education, independently of its registration by the Brazilian Bar Association. In fact, the Council's activities have been purely formal. It rarely reviews the quality of the teaching offered. Most students who have passed the entrance examination for law school will finish the course and receive the degree if they wish. Examinations within law school are not difficult. A few students will drop out for lack of interest or because they have come to prefer some other career. During the recession years of 1979 to 1984 a few dropped out for economic reasons.

In 1828, there were only two government-owned law schools and fewer than seventy students. In 1971 there were approximately ninety law schools, public and private, with some 53,000 students (Steiner, 1971). By 1980, the economic boom of the 1970s had increased these numbers to 130 schools containing 135,026 students, representing 9.0 percent of all university students. Yet, this is far less than the 23.7 percent of all university students who were studying law in 1961 (Falcão, 1978a: 85).

The factors that stimulated this decrease are multiple and vary historically. They include the appearance of competing professions; the dwindling social and political prestige of lawyers; the poor quality, formalism, and conservatism of legal education; and the saturation of the job market, which directly affects legal fees and salaries.

The number of law students would have decreased more except for four other considerations: the historical and cultural role of law school in preparing not only lawyers but also bachareis (law graduates), through a humanistic and unspecialized education with little emphasis on professional skills; the slow expansion of schools of applied, biological, and agricultural sciences, which have been unable to meet the demand; the big gap between the salaries of those holding a university degree and those with only a technical degree; and the fact that the number of university students is below the international average. In 1970 Brazil had 4.7 percent of its university-age students in universities, while the international average was 5.5 percent (Falcão, 1978a: 100). In 1980 this ratio had dropped to 4.6 percent according to the Ministry of Education.

In fact, the law schools play three competing, and sometimes conflicting, functions: a *residual* function—absorbing the university students who were not accepted for enrollment in the subjects they preferred; a *historical and cultural* function—providing humanistic and unspecialized training for many different professions; and, finally, a *legal-technical* function—preparing professionals to practice.

## CURRICULUM AND DEGREES

Law schools may offer four degree programs: bachelor, specialization, master, and doctorate. The first satisfies the prerequisite for enrolling in the Brazilian Bar Association and practicing law. About 90 percent of the law schools offer only the bachelor's degree in morning, afternoon, or evening courses.

Since 1972, every bachelor's degree course must include at least 2,700 class hours during a period of four to seven years (Resolution 162/72, CFE-MEC). The minimum curriculum established by the Federal Council of Education is divided into two parts. The "basic cycle," lasting two semesters, includes introduction to the study of law, economics, sociology, and other subjects not directly related to law. The "professional cycle" includes constitutional, civil, criminal, commercial, and administrative law, civil procedure, practical legal training, and studies of Brazilian problems, plus two elective subjects. Of the nine subjects in the first curriculum in 1827, six remained in the curriculum of 1980. The law schools may add other subjects to complement the curriculum but rarely do so. Cross-registration in other faculties is rare, but allowed. Thus the minimum curriculum also is the maximum curriculum. It represents at least 90 percent of the curriculum adopted by almost all 130 schools. The curriculum of a law school in the Amazon is very similar to that of a school in southern São Paulo or in Caruaru, in the interior of Pernambuco in the Northeast. There is almost no regional, ideological, or market differentiation. This standardization is attributable not only to centralized regulation but also to the demand for unspecialized professional training (reflecting the residual and historical-cultural functions of the law school) and the profit orientation of those two out of three law schools that are private. The Brazilian Bar Association recently has been pressing the Federal Council of Education to disapprove new law schools and to make instruction more modern and practical. In response to these requests, the Council has frozen the number of places and law schools.

The OAB battle against formalistic, rhetorical, conservative, and largely unspecialized instruction included a proposal to require practical legal training—an apprenticeship within the law school, the judiciary, or a law office. So far the OAB has failed to implement this reform. Most law schools deem the requirement an unacceptable interference by the bar and one that would increase the cost and administrative complexity of the course. Practical legal training, although required, paradoxically is taught in a "formal and rhetorical way."

The prominence of the residual and the historical-cultural functions over the legal-technical function of the law schools stimulated the development of an informal system of legal education for those who intend to be legal professionals if not necessarily private practitioners. Thus, we may say that the professional socialization of a lawyer results from the confluence of the formal diploma and unsystematic training within an informal system, during and after the law course. A major part of the latter occurs through apprenticeship in law offices for the students enrolled in the law courses. In the past the bar offered a scheme through which students could work as "solicitors" (*solicitadores*) in law firms. Nowadays, any apprenticeship depends solely on the efforts and personal connections of the students, and they are paid little or nothing. Only a small percentage of students, about a tenth, receive this training. Most of them work as secretaries, clerks, or librarians in urban law firms or associations. The nature and extent of training varies from one office to another.

Public agencies, bar associations, isolated professors, unions, and other groups also offer minicourses and seminars in legislation for lawyers. They deal with such fields as corporations, new economic legislation, accounting for lawyers, and tax law—specializations the law school did not cover adequately. The specialization programs require at least 360 hours of work, and they are not a permanent activity of the law schools.

The master's and doctorate programs are permanent activities and are strictly regulated by the Federal Council of Education, which adheres to a North American model. In 1981 there were twenty master's courses and twelve doctorate courses, which together enrolled 2,183 students (Falcão, 1983: 156). Most are located in federal government law schools in Rio de Janeiro and São Paulo. Like the bachelor's degree courses, they also do not diverge by region or legal doctrine. The curricula are traditional, dividing their subjects into two: public and private law. In the last ten years, however, there have been some significant experiments with legal theory and instructional methodology.

Government educational policy directs graduate courses to integrate instruction with research, but this rarely occurs. In 1982 only 28 percent of the graduate professors were engaged in research (Falcão, 1983: 159). Legal research still is not institutionalized. On the contrary, traditional legal research, which tends to be dogmatic and doctrinal, is performed individually by jurists (important lawyers, law professors, ex-supreme court justices, and chief magistrates) in their law offices and generally is based on their professional experience and legal opinions. In addition, several federal agencies, such as the National Council of Scientific and Technological Development, the Coordinating Agency for the Preparation of Higher Education Personnel (CAPES) and the Financing Agency of Studies and Projects (FINEP), recently have funded juridical research groups, both within the law schools and outside, stimulating research based on social reality and empirical data.

## THE LAW FACULTY

Professors of law are not required to have any special training beyond a bachelor of law degree. Since the instruction is rhetorical, generalized, humanistic, and largely unspecialized, every graduate is a potential law professor. This results not only in the poor quality of teaching, which is condemned by all, but also in the debasement of law teacher salaries. Those who work in law schools owned by the federal government follow well-established patterns of recruitment and career progress. However, this is not necessarily true for those working in private law schools. The great majority of professors are paid by the class at the rate of $10 to $20 per hour. Even the privileged few who have part-time (twenty fixed hours per week) or full-time (forty fixed hours per week) positions receive a low monthly salary of $30 to $800. The majority of the latter work in federal government law schools. Therefore, we have the following typical profile of a law professor: a person with only a bachelor of law degree, who offers no individual assistance to his students, does not participate in the administration of the school, and performs his principal professional activities outside the school. Nine out of ten law professors in Rio de Janeiro and São Paulo fit this description (Miralles & Falcão, 1974). In 1969 there were 2,964 law professors in Brazil, and the law professor–student ratio was 1:26; in 1972 it was 1:23; for the university system as a whole, it was 1:7 and 1:10, respectively (Falcão, 1974). This gap between law schools and the university system still persists.

At least three factors motivate a law graduate to become a law professor:

1. A vocation for instruction and research. These professors constitute a minority. Because of the low salaries, they are obliged to teach about seven class hours per day, in two or three different law schools, which is possible only in the larger cities.

2. The search for professional prestige, which is important to judges and lawyers. A lawyer gains prestige and clients from having the title of law professor. The more important law schools have no difficulty recruiting their professors from among prominent lawyers, judges, and prosecutors. For example, professors represent 11.7 percent of the lawyers heading legal departments in large corporations, who constitute the professional elite in the area of corporate and commercial law (Sá & Ferreira Filho, 1982:42).

3. Failure to obtain a position in the job market or the need to supplement an inadequate salary. These generally constitute the faculty of smaller private law schools.

Normally a class takes the form of a lecture and is little different from a class in the University of Coimbra in the seventeenth century. It either concerns a theoretical-speculative issue of legal doctrine or attempts to present a logical-formal description of a statute or a section of a Code. Seminars, debates, case studies, and systematic analyses of legal sentences or contracts are extremely rare. Lectures are based on the text of a "manual," a handbook full of contradictory doctrinal quotations, taken mainly from the European jurists and full of fragmented and sometimes outdated legislation, all mixed up with one or two centuries of Portuguese and Brazilian legal history. It offers a "peculiar" synthesis of all the items required by the Federal Council of Education. Those teachers who have a legal occupation outside the school add unsystematic and generally critical observations on the basis of their professional experience. The dominant testing procedure consists of two or more written examinations per semester, in which the student regurgitates the legal contents of the "manual."

In 1982 there were 240 professors for 1,556 students in the master's and doctorate programs, a ratio of 1:6. According to the more rigorous standards of the Federal Council of Education, these professors should have a master's degree or its equivalent and should teach full time. In 1973 only 21 percent of them taught full time, but by 1982 the proportion had increased to 45 percents (Falcão, 1983: 158). This does not mean that they are exclusively law professors, much less that they devote themselves only to graduate programs. On the contrary, they generally teach on all levels and have another job besides teaching. The instructional methodology is fundamentally the same as for the bachelor's degree, with lectures predominating. However, a greater effort is made to go beyond doctrinal-speculative issues with the help of interdisciplinary perspectives and scientific methodology. A few innovative programs conduct sociojuridical or politicojuridical research.

THE STUDENTS

We conducted a survey of 29,910 students at twelve law schools in Rio de Janeiro and São Paulo, asking them why they chose to attend law school. The principal motivation for two-thirds of the students was the fact that the law course would help them to pursue *other* professional activities; for another tenth, it was the social and economic prestige of the legal professional. In other words, most students only want to obtain the degree; they are not deeply interested in technical and specialized legal training (Miralles & Falcão, 1974). Because legal education is regulated by the federal government, these data reflect the situation throughout the nation, which probably has changed very little during the past ten years. If anything, there has been increased tension between those seeking only the degree (the residual and historical-cultural functions of the schools) and the future legal professionals who desire specialized training (the legal-technical function of the law schools).

Two historical events corroborate this interpretation. First, from 1964 to 1968 the economic recession and federal planning decelerated the expansion of enrollments in the human and social sciences, causing great dissatisfaction in the urban middle class. Prior to 1964, there had been an increase in the number of students who could not find a vacancy in the university system after passing the entrance examinations (*vestibular*), due to the government's imposition of quotas. Between 1960 and 1964, there were university places for 63.9 percent of the applicants; between 1964 and 1968 the proportion fell to 52.7 percent (Arruda, 1983: 18). The resulting dissafistaction led to the political protests of 1968, which threatened to topple the regime.

The federal government yielded, permitting expansion, particularly in the private sector. Between 1963 and 1967, the Federal Council of Education approved 128 new university courses in all fields (63 percent of the applications); between 1968 and 1972, it approved 779 (83 percent of the applications) (Canuto, 1983: 132). In 1968, 6,274 students obtained a bachelor of law degree; by 1973 the number had increased to 15,802. In 1984 the student:professor ratio in federal universities was 7.8:1, but it was 16.6:1 in private institutions. Private law schools flourished in Rio and São Paulo, offering low-quality evening courses and generating substantial profits for their owners. Thus, the political-economic crisis was postponed. Students managed to find places in the university but were unable to find employment after graduation. They attributed their plight to their own intellectual and cultural deficiencies (21 percent of Rio students and 26 percent of those in São Paulo) as well as the excessive number of students (31 percent and 37 percent, respectively) (Miralles & Falcão, 1974). In 1961 there were 23,519 students enrolled in law school. In 1980 there were 135,026, most of them urban middle-class beneficiaries of the economic boom.

The second historical event derives from the first. Since every law graduate (*bacharel*) is potentially a lawyer (free to enter and leave the job market), the excess supply has generated a destructive competition among lawyers. For this reason, the Brazilian Bar Association recently has pressed the Federal Council of Education to limit the opening of new schools and to "professionalize" the bachelors course (OAB, 1981).

The social background of law students does not differ greatly from that of university students generally, both in Brazil and abroad. The first graduating class in 1832 included no women students; even in 1950 the

proportion was only 3.3 percent; but in 1984, 24.6 percent of law graduates were women. The increasing proportion of women in law school and
in the job market can be seen in table 12.2. While 2.0 percent of law
professionals were women in 1950, thirty years later this proportion had
risen to 20.9 percent. Entry to university legal studies is by examination,
which traditionally has included Latin, Portuguese, History, French, and
English. Each law school prepared its own entrance examination, although
some collaborate today.

As is the case everywhere, students from wealthier families have a
better chance of entering a university. In the 1985 entrance examinations
in Rio de Janeiro, while only 13.1 percent of the candidates from families
with the lowest incomes passed, 26.5 percent of those from families with
the highest incomes did so (Fundação Cesgranrio, 1985). Recent research
shows that, paradoxically, candidates from the higher socioeconomic strata
are more successful in obtaining places in the public law schools, which
offer a free education of better quality, whereas those from lower strata are
compelled to attend private law schools (Ribeiro & Klein, 1982). Even so,
the university plays an important role in social mobility. Thus, for
example, only 35.3 percent of the parents of the law students in Rio de
Janeiro and São Paulo were university graduates (Miralles & Falcão, 1974),
and only 32 percent of the parents of students at Recife Law School
between 1930 and 1975 had a secondary school education (Falcão, 1981:
67). In less developed states this percentage is even smaller: in Espírito
Santo only 18.4 percent of the parents of judges in the interior had a
secondary school education (Herkenhoff, 1977: 235).

Since the law schools require only class attendance (to take the examinations each semester, the student must have attended two-thirds of the
classes), the majority of students work as well as study—74.8 percent of
those in Rio de Janeiro and São Paulo (Miralles & Falcão, 1974)—especially
in order to pay the tuition. Most work six to eight hours per day in the
service sector of the economy in unspecialized administrative jobs. These
jobs rarely lead to law jobs. Most students live with their parents. In the
past century, by contrast, the few schools were regional and served the
elite of the neighboring states. The law schools in Olinda (Recife), São
Paulo, and Rio de Janeiro were favored.

In 1981 there were 2,076 law students enrolled in master's programs, of
which 62 percent only attended classes and conducted no legal research.
Of the 112 students who obtained a master's degree in 1980/81, 61 were
teachers. This suggests that the course serves two functions. First, for the
great majority of students who are practicing lawyers, the master's
program allows specialization: less than 10 percent write the thesis required for the diploma. Second, more than half of the small minority who

do write theses are seeking diplomas to advance their careers as law professors (Falcão, 1983: 154).

## THE LAW GRADUATES ("OS BACHAREIS")

Every law graduate (bacharel) may practice law and become a legal professional or a lawyer. Every lawyer may cease practicing and enter one of the many nonlegal careers open to the bacharel, although there is evidence that, historically, this has been less frequent (Hendricks, 1977: 166). This lateral mobility reflects the unspecialized job market in an underdeveloped society and the humanistic and rhetorical instruction in the law schools. Law graduates still become industrialists, diplomats, small-business executives, bank employees, civil servants, police officers, tax inspectors, educators, artists, politicians, scientists, and so on.

It is commonly believed that urbanization, industrialization, and technological development reduce the number of jobs open to law graduates. Even so, we should not underestimate the continued relevance of this humanistic unspecialized education. It not only is connected historically to a traditional and professionally undifferentiated society but also sometimes constitutes the seed of a new profession. Thus, it was not an architect, an artist, a business executive, or an engineer who introduced design as a profession in Brazil and later became the principal designer. Rather, it was a law graduate, Aloísio Magalhães. Similarly, Raymundo Faoro and Vitor Nunes Leal, the precursors of modern Brazilian political science, were law graduates. The first Planning Minister and one of the leading Brazilian planners until recently also is a law graduate: Celso Furtado. All of them enjoy international recognition in their fields.

Table 12.2 offers an overview of the three professional categories: law graduates; legal professionals, including judges, public attorneys, prosecutors, public curators (these terms are explained below); and lawyers. Law graduates greatly outnumber legal professionals. This ratio increased in 1980 (2.3 : 1) because of the expansion of legal education during the late 1960s and the 1970s as a result of the political crisis. Between 1950 and 1980 the number of law graduates increased more rapidly than the number of judges, lawyers, and other legal professionals. The number of law graduates fluctuated between 699 in 1932 and 1,880 in 1952. From then on the figures grow steadily: 12,214 students got law degrees in 1977, 21,685 in 1980. This means that law graduates either are unemployed, perform legal work as a subsidiary activity, or have not yet begun to perform legal functions. In 1980 only 44.5 percent of the 221,321 people holding law degrees stated that law was their principal occupation.

Table 12.3 shows that of the 221,321 law graduates, only 168,245 (71.4 percent) were registered in the Brazilian Bar Association in 1980. Of those registered, no more than 93,846 (55.8 percent) were engaged primarily in legal practice. In other words, being registered in the Brazilian Bar Association does not mean that law is the registrant's main occupation. In São Paulo, for instance, 21 percent of recent law graduates were enrolled in the OAB but did not practice law (Lima, 1984). They enrolled to ensure their right to practice in the future and to claim the prestige associated with being a lawyer—and because there is no fee. My research showed that 62.3 percent of Recife Law School graduates between 1950 and 1975 working in the public sector performed nonlegal activities, as did 59.3 percent of those in the private sector; only 20 percent could be considered private practitioners (Falcão, 1981:59).

It is not possible to understand Brazilian politics, economic life, or culture without noticing the historic role of the law graduate. Although they were much more important in the past, they remain prominent today. Gilberto Freyre, for example, calls the Second Empire (1842–1889) the "empire of the 'bachareis'." The emperor placed greater faith in the legal performance of the bachareis and in their administration of justice than in the delivery of "meat and flour for the oppressed people of the provinces" (Freyre, 1961: 575). Their political influence remains considerable. Between 1831 and 1840, 56.6 percent of cabinet ministers and 71.4 percent of senators were law graduates. Between 1871 and 1889, these proportions increased to 85.7 and 71.7 percent, respectively (Carvalho, 1974). In the Congress elected in 1982, 60.6 percent of the 479 deputies held bachelor of law degrees. However, only 14.2 percent described themselves as legal professionals or lawyers, compared to 17.4 percent of the previous legislature (Fleischer, 1983). Among the governors of Pernambuco between 1930 and 1975, 60 percent were law graduates (Falcão, 1981: 60).

Two characteristics of law graduates deeply affect Brazilian history. First their commitment to liberal political ideals has been extremely important at such crucial moments as the bloodless abolition of slavery, the proclamation of the Republic, the overthrow of the Vargas dictatorship in 1945, and the present redemocratization. Legal professionals and lawyers consider themselves to be the heirs of this liberal tradition. Today, the Brazilian Bar Association is equally active in defense of human rights and political liberties and on behalf of the redemocratization of the country. It is interesting that lawyers and legal education seem to be regaining some of their social prestige. The president of the Bar Association, for example, points to the role of lawyers in redemocratization to explain the fact that demand for law school places in the Cesgranrio system (a consortium of universities with a common entrance examination) rose 30 percent in 1986, while the demand for places in other university subjects dropped 16 percent (*Jornal do Brasil*, 1985).

## THE LEGAL PROFESSIONAL

### JUDGES

During the Empire, judges were appointed by the emperor. Only justices of the peace were elected. Appointment was for life. With the coming of the Republic and the Constitution of 1937, the selection and advancement of judges was based on merit and seniority, as determined by their own colleagues. The only exceptions are Supreme Court justices, who are nominated by the Presidency and approved by the Senate, and the chief justices of the state courts, who are designated by the state governor. According to the Constitution of 1946, magistrates enjoy life terms, and their salaries cannot be reduced. The military regime temporarily suspended these guarantees in 1964. Now, even though they have been restored, inflation has undermined the prohibition of salary cuts.

It is essential to understand three central characteristics of the Brazilian judicial system:

1. Before 1934, each state had its own judiciary and procedural law. After the Constitution of 1934, civil procedure became uniform in all states and throughout all substantive areas.

2. The judicial system remains divided into federal and state courts.

3. Courts are further organized into those administering "common justice" (divided into criminal and civil) and those administering "specialized justice" (divided into labor, military, and electoral courts). The latter are federal at all levels. The former are state on the first two levels and federal on the third. Civil cases involving the federal government are handled in a special court called "Federal Justice," which has a branch in each state. Table 12.4 presents an outline of the judges.

Only judges have legal authority to settle disputes by applying legislation. Judges may not engage in any other professional activity except education. Unlike other legal professionals, who accumulate various occupations and sources of income, the income of the judge is derived almost exclusively from the magistracy. In Espírito Santo, for instance, 97.4 percent of the income of the judges of the interior came from their salaries and only 2.6 percent from capital gains (Herkenhoff, 1977: 233).

There are exceptions to this monopoly, however. In criminal courts, members of the jury do not need to have a law degree. Each year they are randomly chosen from the citizens of the state. The military court is composed of both civil and military judges, who do not have to hold a law degree. The Constitution does not require a law degree for a justice of the Federal Supreme Court but only "outstanding juridical knowledge." Nevertheless, of the 122 justices who served during the Republic (1889–1980), only one was not a law graduate—Justice Barata Ribeiro, a medical doctor appointed by Marshall Floriano Peixoto (1893–1894) (Machado, 1981: 8).

The most notable exception to the judges' monopoly is the *labor court*. It has three members: the professional judge and two "class" judges, an employee representative nominated by the unions and an employer representative nominated by the trade association; both must be approved by the President. The "class" judges need not have law degrees. Finally, in certain courts, such as the Federal Court of Appeals and the electoral court, some members are chosen from among lawyers rather than judges. In 1980 Brazil had only one judge for every 23,489 inhabitants. Like most Brazilian university students, judges generally came from the middle class. In twelve of the twenty-three state courts in 1983, 79 percent of the members were recruited from within the states themselves. Interstate mobility is quite rare in Brazil. The members of the federal, military, and electoral courts, however, are recruited by examination and come from almost all the states. Traditionally, this has been an exclusively male profession. Although there is no de jure prohibition, no woman has served as justice of the Federal Supreme Court. In some states, such as Paraná, Rio de Janeiro, and São Paulo, women may become judges. In others, such as Pernambuco, this is impossible because of the discriminatory use the court has made of its discretionary powers. Monthly salaries range from approximately $140 in the poorer states (Pará) to $1,300 in the richer states (Santa Catarina).

We must take account of two facts so as to gain more than a merely formal profile of judges:

1. In a country with some 130,000,000 inhabitants, where only about 29.1 percent of the total working population earn an income above three minimum salaries (ca. $150 per month), access to the courts is the privilege of a minority. This access has decreased in some cities as the population has increased and income has become more and more concentrated, as has happened in Rio de Janeiro. Between 1975 and 1980 the number of summary and ordinary proceedings and executions of judgment declined by a fourth (Piquet Carneiro, 1983: 147). This means that the majority of disputes involving ordinary people are "settled" outside the judiciary. Recent surveys (Falcão, 1982; Oliveira, 1984; Santos, 1977; Moura, 1983; Aguiar, 1984) show that the role of judging is performed by police chiefs, slum leaders, civil society commissions, and legal aid lawyers.

2. The formal division of the judiciary into electoral, criminal, civil, labor, and military courts reveals very little about its internal power structure, which depends fundamentally on the nature of the political regime. Thus, in recent years the military court manipulated the legal concept of "national security" to assert its authority over others. Theoretically, everything could affect military security and therefore could fall within the exclusive jurisdiction of the military court—and the military court itself defined the concept of national security. As the redemocratization progresses, the military court has lost political prestige as well as doctrinal preeminence.

## PUBLIC ATTORNEYS ("MINISTÉRIO PÚBLICO")

Public attorneys are civil servants in the executive branch employed in preparing, managing, and trying cases. One category acts on behalf of the people, seeking to implement the legal order in the "public interest":

1. In criminal cases they do not represent the interests of the Union or a state but rather those of the people. They have the exclusive right and responsibility to promote the investigation of crimes in the name of the people. If they uncover any, the public attorneys, acting as prosecutors, should perform independently of the executive.

2. In civil cases they perform as *custos legis* (guardians of the law), observing the application of the law as well as representing those citizens who cannot appear in court, such as absentees, minors, and prisoners.

Another category of public attorneys act as government lawyers, defending government interests in tax or social securities cases, for example. Both types of public attorney can be found at the federal, state, and municipal levels. Sometimes the same public attorney acts as custos legis in one case and as government lawyer in another.

At the federal level, public attorneys acting as custos legis staff a special department, administratively subordinated to the Minister of Justice, called the Ministério Público. The attorney general of the Republic is chosen by the president of the Republic. It is the only position in the Ministério Público that does not require a law degree. The attorney general is aided by nine deputy attorneys general. There are a total of 202 attorneys (84 percent of whom are men). They work with the Federal Supreme Court (24 attorneys), the Federal Court of Appeals (24 attorneys), the Federal Military and Labor Courts, and each of the twenty-three states and three territories. A special branch of public attorneys recently was created to protect human rights. They are divided into 140 first-class (junior) and 62 second-class (senior) attorneys. Their monthly salaries in November 1983 varied between $500 and $700, and they are recruited from among law graduates through nationwide competitive examinations.

Each state defines the structure, functions, and form of recruitment (mostly through competitive examination). As long as they do not appear in cases involving the union or the state, public attorneys also may have private clients. In 1983 approximately 20 percent of the 3,912 members of the Ministério Público in fourteen of the twenty-three states were women, and about 80 percent were recruited from within the state. Monthly salaries varied between $170 in the poorer states such as Mato Grosso and $1,050 in the wealthier states such as São Paulo. In each state the attorney general heads the Ministério Público, which includes prosecutors, public defenders, and public curators. In some states, prosecutors who work in specialized jurisdictions are called "curators": of minors, public foundations, the family, bankruptcies, and work-related accidents. Finally, in some states, such as Rio de Janeiro, the initial position is that of public defender, a legal aid lawyer for citizens who do not have the means to pay a private attorney. Public defenders give free representation in both civil and criminal cases. In 1982, in eleven of the twenty-three states, there were 753 legal aid public attorneys (54 percent men) for a population of 37 million, a ratio of about 1:50,000. In Pernambuco in 1984, 12 attorneys had to handle 14,725 cases; 1,536 were settled through negotiation, 3,008 were litigated, and the rest remained unresolved (Silva, 1985).

The most controversial question concerning public attorneys in Brazil is whether they are independent of the executive. The interests of the government do not always coincide with those of the citizens. In Brazil, challenges to the constitutionality of a law do not begin in the courts. The claim first is brought before the attorney general of the Republic, who raises it in the Supreme Court only if he agrees with it. Because the attorney general is nominated by the president and is therefore is subject to the executive, he rarely finds an executive action unconstitutional.


POLICE CHIEFS ("DELEGADOS DE POLÍCIA")

States regulate the position of police officer. Recently, more and more states have required that the chief be a law graduate: twelve of the nineteen states surveyed considered the bachelor of law degree indispensable, while one required it only for the police chiefs of the state capital. As a member of the Civil Police, subordinated to the State Police Department (a branch of the executive), the chief of police has the following functions: (1) administrative-preventive—guaranteeing public order and preventing crime, and (2) judicial-repressive—investigating crimes and capturing suspects. In 1983 there were 2,476 police chiefs in the nineteen states surveyed: 53 percent in the state capitals and the rest in the interior; 61 percent were law graduates, about 6 percent were women (excluding the state of Amazonas), and 75 percent were recruited from within their own states (excluding Pernambuco, Rio Grande do Norte, Mato Grosso, and Amazonas). Monthly salaries varied between $31 in the poorer states (Espírito Santo) and $400 in Brasília.

Police chiefs and their deputies (assistants) are the "judges" who actually settle the day-to-day disputes of most Brazilians quickly, inexpensively, and informally. A survey revealed that most of these cases deal with moral offenses (such as slander or insult), public disorder, and physical aggression within the working-class urban population. The number of these informal settlements in 1982 was at least twenty times greater than the cases handled by the Pernambuco Criminal Court (Oliveira, 1984). Given the authoritarian nature of the 1964 government, the poverty and marginality of the urban centers, and the connections between the political power and the economic power of the large landowners in the interior (Nunes Leal, 1948), the police in general, and also the chief, behave illegally. One example is the "Death Squad" in Rio de Janeiro or the "Rota" in São Paulo—police who assassinated criminals as a means of crime prevention (Bicudo, 1976). Another is the submission of the rural population to the "Colonels" of the Backlands (Villaça & Albuquerque, 1965).

# LAWYERS

## THE SERVICES AND TYPES OF LAWYERS

From the creation of the first law schools in 1827 until the establishment of the Brazilian Bar Association (OAB) in 1930, any citizen could practice law. National legislation did not regulate legal practice. Although states could do so, many imposed no requirements whatsoever. Others simply demanded registration of the diploma in the state court, with the same result: everyone could practice law.

With the creation of the Brazilian Bar Association in 1930 and the subsequent unification of civil procedure, the practice of law became the exclusive privilege of those citizens registered in the Brazilian Bar Association. Today, the requirements to obtain this registration are (1) a diploma from a law school recognized by the government; (2) civil responsibility (which excludes minors, the insane, and Indians); (3) successful completion of either practical legal training or the bar examination; (4) qualification as a voter (eighteen years or older and registered) and satisfaction of the required military service; (5) freedom from any criminal convictions; (6)

abstention from any professional activity incompatible with the function of a lawyer, such as being a judge or a secretary of state. Registration in the Brazilian Bar Association entitles the lawyer to practice in any state by satisfying a few formal supplementary requirements.


## Legal Services

We may divide lawyers' activities into two categories: legal services and political-juridical activities. Legal services are directly related to the application of legislation and include those described in article 7 of the Statutes of the Brazilian Bar Associations: representation in a court and before administrative agencies, extrajuridical representation and legal counseling, and the management of a legal department. The right to participate in judicial proceedings and to act in one's own name or that of one's client is the monopoly of the lawyer. In the labor court, however, the parties may defend themselves personally, although they cannot be represented by a layperson. Research indicates that only 33.6 percent of the complaints before the labor court are mediated by a lawyer (Aguiar, 1984). In the criminal court, the defendant also may appear without representation if there is no lawyer in the region. Finally, any person may apply for habeas corpus for oneself or for others. Besides pleading in court, only one other activity is the monopoly of lawyers: registering the contracts of commercial and civil entities with notaries public in order to make them enforceable against third parties. Notarial activities are state regulated and very profitable. The notary public does not need to hold a law degree—only a state license. Normally a son inherits this license from his father. Notaries public protest notes and bills, attest and certify certain classes of documents, and administer oaths. They also maintain the civil and the real estate registers.

Some legal services may be provided by provisional lawyers and apprentices. A provisional lawyer is a citizen who passes a bar examination and obtains a license to practice law only in first-level courts. The license is valid for four years but can be renewed. Previously, provisional lawyers played an important role because there were too few lawyers. Today, however, provisional lawyers virtually have disappeared. In the eight regional divisions of the Brazilian Bar Association that we surveyed in 1983 (out of a total of twenty-three), there were only 21 provisional lawyers compared to 129,578 lawyers.

An apprentice is a law graduate or a fourth or fifth-year student who is undergoing two years of legal training in a law office or legal department approved by the Brazilian Bar Association or by a law school. The apprentices must be supervised by a lawyer whenever engaging in litigation, except in preliminary hearings. In 1983 there were 11,422 apprentices in the eight regional divisions surveyed, 6 percent of the lawyers registered; 83 percent of these apprentices are in Rio de Janeiro and São Paulo.

The lawyers' monopoly of representation in court is beginning to be challenged, either because it is seen as obstructing access to justice, because of the higher cultural level of the citizen (who is more capable of self-representation), or because of the need for more rapid justice. Congress, for example, recently approved the creation of a new court similar to the New York Small Claims Court, in which lawyers are unnecessary. Another proposal submited to Congress would allow heirs to represent themselves in inheritance matters. Both reforms are strongly opposed by the Brazilian Bar Association, which seeks to maintain and expand the lawyers' monopoly, especially at a time of economic recession and a shrinking job market.

The extrajudicial services of lawyers include (1) representation of public or private interests before the "direct" or "indirect" public administration (a distinction explained below); (2) representation of individuals or entities before private institutions and in negotiations; (3) counseling individuals and institutions concerning public and private law, drafting legal opinions and negotiating and implementing rights, and (4) examining candidates for the judiciary. These extrajudicial services are not the monopoly of lawyers. Attempts to make representation before the public administration the monopoly of lawyers failed in 1963 and again in 1980.

Because of the slowness and inefficiency of some sectors of the Brazilian public administration, relationships with citizens are mediated by the "despachante," a specialist who lacks professional training but has enough information and personal connections to defend the interests of the citizen before the government agency. In the last ten years, lobbying has been growing as a professional activity, mainly at the federal level. So far, lawyer lobbyists have concentrated their efforts on government agencies in the financial and economic sectors of the public administration. However, there is increasing interest in Parliament as the redemocratization progresses. Lawyers are actively lobbying the drafters of the new Constitution.

## Political-Juridical Activities

Political-juridical activities differ from legal services because the former are not devoted to the uncritical technical implementation of legislation. On the contrary, they normally take a highly critical stance toward legislation, the economic system, and the political regime. Legal justification for this activity is found in the statutes of the Brazilian Bar Association (OAB), which commit it to defending the legal order and the Federal Constitution, fighting for the proper application of the laws and the rapid administration of justice and helping to improve juridical institutions. Social and cultural support for this activity is found in the historical commitment of lawyers to liberal ideology, even when this ideology has been characterized by the permanent gap between the egalitarian ideals it defends and the hierarchical practice it obscures. Juridical-theoretical support is found in a concept of law that is not limited to legislation, regardless of whether it is denominated *ius naturalista* or linked to human rights. Justice is not simply government justice. Above all, the political-juridical activities of lawyers challenge official legality divorced from political legitimacy.

In contrast to legal services, which are individualized, these political-juridical activities are collective and pursued through professional associations. The lawyers generally receive no payment or only a nominal sum. In 1980, 52 percent of Rio de Janeiro's 36,000 lawyers believed that the struggle to improve the legal system should be the OAB's first priority. In other words, political-juridical activities are more important than legal-technical ones as far as the OAB is concerned. Lawyers may take political positions, issue manifestos, and make public statements in the press or in public debates. In contrast, legislative drafting is performed by individual lawyers and paid at market rates. These political-juridical activities have helped lawyers to perform their legal services less subordinated to governmental influence.

## Lawyers in the Public Administration

Most lawyers hold two or more jobs, one of which may not be related to law. It is very difficult to find a lawyer who works only in a law firm or a public attorney who works only in government. This is due to at least two main factors: low salaries and the low level of regulation of legal activities. Although there is a trend toward specialization, "general advocacy" still is quite common. In São Paulo in 1984, 53.9 percent of the graduates of the two main law schools were practicing law, 41 percent of whom were generalists (Lima, 1984).

Brazilian public administration is divided into direct and indirect administration. The former is linked directly to the government and includes the state cabinets, city governments, state secretariats, and autarchies (units that enjoy unusual autonomy in accounting and personnel matters and in formulating policy). The legal professional responsible for providing legal advice, conducting negotiations, implementing the law, and appearing in court is called a "public attorney" or a "lawyer." The indirect administration —federal, state, or municipal—may assume very varied legal forms, such as foundations, state-owned corporations, and mixed-capital enterprises. The lawyers of these agencies may or may not be called "public attorneys." Their activities are not clearly differentiated. These professionals defend the public administration in court, offer legal advice, assist in negotiations, collaborate in the implementation and enforcement of administrative law, and participate in inspections. What distinguishes lawyers from public attorneys is more the way they are hired, paid, and employed. Attorneys in the direct administration must be hired through open public examinations, and the appointment generally is for life, since cause for dismissal rarely is found. Lawyers in the indirect administration may be hired through personal acquaintance rather than open public examination and are dismissed more easily. Public attorneys and lawyers working for the Public Administration previously enjoyed lifelong appointments but no longer do so. Most hold a second job or practice privately by themselves.

Lawyers in the public administration are hired either as public officials under the Statute for Civil Servants, which grants them special working conditions, salaries, and benefits, or under the Consolidation of Labor Laws (CLT), like most Brazilian laborers. The duties are the same for both; the main difference is the possibility of dismissal. A lawyer hired under the CLT may be dismissed at will. One hired under the Statute for Civil Servants may be dismissed only after proof of serious fault, through a complex administrative inquiry. The result is that the public attorneys of the direct public administration are lifelong employees, de facto.

The public sector definitely is expanding. The government accounted for 38.1 percent of the gross national product in 1964 but 43.7 percent in 1979 (Reichstuz & Coutinho, 1983: 45). There were 14 public corporations in the federal government at the end of the 1950s but 560 in 1981 (Bresser Pereira, 1982: 58). In 1984, 25 percent of the graduates of São Paulo Law School went to work for the public sector.

## Lawyers in the Private Sector

Lawyers in the private sector are differentiated by the degree to which they specialize in legal planning, counseling, negotiation, mediation, and representation in court or outside. Law graduates usually begin general practice, accepting any case and job. Specialization is gradual and influenced by vocation, the type of clients, and success in an important lawsuit. It is greater in large cities. Approximately 50.2 percent of the lawyers active in Rio de Janeiro in 1980 specialized in only one subject. The main areas are labor law (30.1 percent), commercial law (27.3 percent), civil law (16.5 percent), and real estate law (10.3 percent) (Melo Sobrinho, 1980: 27).

A small group of important lawyers and well-known ex-judges stand out from the rest. Having acquired a reputation as full-time specialists in the course of a long career, these law graduates specialize in legal opinions, attempting to clarify an obscure issue in juridical doctrine and legislation on behalf of important clients. These lawyers generally are called "jurists," "jurisconsults," or "pareceristas" (legal opinion writers), honorific titles in Portuguese. Most also are law professors.

The importance of these opinions for the development of legal interpretation cannot be overestimated. In the common law system, the modernization of law occurs through innovative judicial decisions. In the civil law system, judges may play an innovative role but often hesitate to do so (Souto, 1982: 264). In Espírito Santo, 15.8 percent of the judges from the interior said they never delivered opinions that disagreed with the prevailing law, and 76.3 percent did so only rarely (Herkenhoff, 1977: 241). When innovations occur in the higher courts, these legal opinions are important points of reference, always inserted in a European doctrinal framework.

## PROFESSIONAL ASSOCIATIONS

### The Brazilian Bar Association (OAB)

The Institute of the Order of Lawyers in Brazil was created in 1843 as a private law institution with cultural aims. In 1880 the Chamber of Deputies of the Empire rejected a proposal to create the Brazilian Bar Association, arguing that the Association's powers would violate the principle of equal opportunity by granting privileges to a particular professional group. The Chamber was more radically liberal than the liberal lawyers themselves. The Brazilian Bar Association was created only in 1930, well after the fall of the First Republic, by a decree of the revolutionary government of Getulio Vargas. It was granted the power to select, discipline, and defend lawyers in the courts and the Public Administration and to defend the legal order and help to reform it. A former attorney general, Andre de Faria, took the initiative to convince the new minister of justice that the OAB should be created. According to a former president, Seabra Fagundes, the OAB had become necessary to eliminate abuses committed by unscrupulous persons who illegally practiced law in Rio de Janeiro courts, as well as in other states.

Paradoxically, the decree established that the Brazilian Bar Association, the regulatory entity of a liberal profession, is a federal public service created by the government. The paradox disappears when we observe that liberalism penetrated Brazil mainly through government action and that Brazilian capitalism is characterized less by the free play of market forces than by the permanent intervention in that market by the government, always on behalf of liberal ideals.

The Brazilian Bar Association (OAB) has a federal structure governed by the following units: (1) a Federal Council composed of a president and three representatives from each state or territory; (2) a Board of Directors composed of five lawyers elected biannually by federal councillors; (3) regional Boards of Directors and Councils in each state and territory; (4) subregional Boards of Directors in municipalities (sometimes one board for several cities); and (5) General Assemblies of Lawyers—a meeting of all Brazilian lawyers or of those in regions or subregions.

The powers of the OAB, most of which are exercised by its Federal Council, include (1) regulating entrance to and practice within the profession, including the bar examination and apprenticeship; (2) organizing the registration of law firms; (3) deciding which occupations are incompatible with the exercise of the profession; and (4) granting awards for legal studies.

Although the OAB is a federal public service, it always has been independent of the government. Lawyers gradually established a careful and consistent system of self-regulation insulated from any state interference. The fact that it is a public service, however, serves as a pretext for government challenges to this autonomy, especially when the OAB takes political positions against the government. The authoritarian regime of 1964 tried twice (in 1967 and 1974) to place the OAB under the control of the Ministry of Labor. It failed. Previously, the federal government had tried without success to place it under the control of the Auditing Court (an executive agency that oversees the finances of the Public Administration).

*Legal-Technical Activities.*    The legal-technical activities are directly related to the regulation of entry, disciplinary action, and the defense of lawyers. Here, the OAB encounters two problems: the maintenance of ethical behavior among lawyers, clients, and the public authorities; and the control of entrance into the profession and the inspection of the practice of advocacy.

The Code of Ethics of 1934 states the basic duties of the lawyer. It covers relationships with clients, the court and public administration, the occupancy of public offices, and fees. The OAB Regional Councils punish violators of the Code following complaints, usually by lawyers; the Federal Council hears appeals from these decisions. The most frequent violations currently are the following: (1) retaining documents in judicial proceedings longer than the period permitted by law, (2) failing to inform clients of the progress and outcome of the case, (3) improper conduct and solicitation of clients and disrespect for clients and authorities. The penalties range from warning, censure, and fines to suspension of the registration and dismissal from the bar.

The OAB does not take action against laypersons who illegally practice law. Since representation in court is the sole monopoly of the lawyer, it is regulated by the judiciary. The control of the OAB consists of inspecting the lawyers who represent clients in court or before the public administration but who should not do so because they hold an incompatible public office, such as police officers.

In regulating entrance to the profession and disciplining lawyers, the OAB rarely considered the job market but merely applied the statutes of the OAB and the Code of Ethics to the individual cases. The Federal Council reviews individual cases but rarely frames more general policies toward the job market because its liberal inheritance reduces social relations to individual actions. Yet, this attitude recently underwent radical change when problems arose with respect to the excess of supply.

Entry to the OAB is through the bar examination, or, since 1963, also through apprenticeship—practical legal training in offices or legal departments approved by the OAB. Historically, entry control can be divided into three periods. Until the 1960s, entry was more an initiation rite than a selection process. Then the excessively abstract, rhetorical, formalistic, and conservative character of legal education persuaded the OAB to initiate quality control. The statutes of the OAB in 1963 and subsequent legislation introduced the bar examination and then practical legal training. There were attempts to induce the future lawyers to obtain practical training. Legal education had distanced itself too much from the professional reality. Today, responding to the increasingly deficient professional training of the law graduate and the oversupply of lawyers, the OAB has been obliged to control quantity as well as quality. It took two steps. Regional bar associations began to transform the bar examination from a mere initiation rite into a true selection process, varying in severity according to local conditions. In addition, the president of the OAB and the Federal Council formulated a policy toward legal education and began to press the government to control the number of university places and to modernize the education.

An official document of the OAB (1981: 15a) states that the surplus of lawyers with inadequate professional training is causing underemployment and unemployment, lowering salaries and fees, reducing the lawyer to a mere wage-earner, and curtailing payment of the annual membership fees in the OAB. It is lowering the ethical level of lawyer behavior and stimulating disputes over clients, the appearance of "lawyers at the doors of prisons," and connections to the police to enable lawyers to obtain tort cases. It has led to a decrease in the quality of legal services, the filing of petitions with terrible mistakes, and an increase in complaints of poor service and malpractice. It has reduced the social prestige of legal education and advocacy and eroded the lawyer's self-confidence.

The OAB pressed the Federal Education Council of the Ministry of Education to refuse to license new law schools, limit the expansion of those already licensed, introduce changes in the minimum curriculum and in teaching methods, and inspect the law courses more rigorously. In fact, the number of law graduates had increased by 122.9 percent between 1970 and 1980 (table 12.2). To understand what this means for the job market, consider that the GNP rose 5.3 percent in 1980 but fell 4.3 percent in 1981 and another 1.1 percent in 1982.

*Juridical-Political Activities.* Ever since the Republic (1889), lawyers and the military have been the main leaders of the political process. As such, they have been both the heralds of dictatorship and the shepherds of liberation. The dictatorship of Getulio Vargas relied on the lawyer Francisco Campos to draft its main institutional structures, just as the authoritarian regime of 1964 depended on the lawyers Gama e Silva and Alfredo Buzaid. The lawyers also have had a martyr for democracy in the law student Demócrito de Souza Filho in 1943 and a leader for redemocratization in Raymundo Faoro, president of the OAB in the 1970s. This balanced viewpoint is not shared by the lay community nor, obviously, by the lawyers themselves. On the contrary, the prevailing view portrays lawyers solely as defenders of public liberties and of civil and human rights. This reflects the historical role not only of lawyers but also of the bachareis in general. Lawyers and the OAB have taken credit for the historical liberating performance of all law graduates (bachareis). This confers great moral authority on the OAB in the eyes of both the government and civil society. Above all, it compels the OAB to engage in political activities.

The moral authority secured through juridical-political activities redounds to the benefit of lawyers' legal-technical activities. One of the main tasks of the OAB has been to defend and protect lawyers from embarrassment by public authorities—for example, when the police, abusing their power, prevent lawyers from seeing their clients or prohibit them from entering certain public buildings. This moral authority has been very useful since the 1970s. One characteristic of the authoritarian regime of 1964 was the silencing and dismemberment of the institutions of civil society: unions, political parties, student associations, and professional bodies (Saldanha, 1982:17). One of the few institutions that managed to maintain its autonomy and identity was the OAB. Therefore, it (as well as the Catholic Church) were transformed into the institutional leaders of civil society in the redemocratization of the country. It fought for human rights and the liberalization of the regime: the withdrawal of authoritarian legislation, the granting of amnesty, the restoration of habeas corpus, and the annulment of the national security statute. Today the OAB is struggling for a Constituent National Assembly and direct elections for the president of the Republic. It is interesting to note that the fall of the authoritarian regime established in 1964 was finally accomplished through a mass mobilization in the streets in support of direct election of the president. That mobilization occurred above the political parties. On some occasions about a million people took to the streets to protest against the government. The associations involved in this campaign elected the president of the OAB, Mario Sergio Duarte, as their national leader.

These bar activities are performed through (1) pronouncements of the Federal Council and its president; (2) representation before the proper authorities—the attorney general of the Republic and the judiciary; (3) support for democratic legislation; (4) participation in the Committee for the Defense of Human Rights, the Ministry of Justice, and similar entities; and (5) juridical activism through the Human Rights Commissions created after 1980 in the OAB regional associations. Some regional associations, such as those in São Paulo and Rio de Janeiro, recently opened research departments to pursue the democratization of the legal order and gain empirical knowledge about juridical institutions and legal practice, including the lawyers themselves.

## Other Associations

The other institutions to which lawyers belong may be divided in terms of their goals (cultural and social security) and structure (national, state, or municipal). All are voluntary. The main cultural institution is the Brazilian Lawyers' Institute (Istituto dos Advogados Brasileiros [IAB]), previously called the Institute of the Order of Lawyers in Brazil, created in 1843 to regulate and discipline lawyers. It was modeled upon the "Istituto dos Colegiados" in Lisbon. Despite its declared goals, it had no legal power but was, and is, a private entity. In 1916, IABs were found in various Brazilian states. Today there are eleven. With the creation of the OAB, the IAB limited itself to cultural activities, research, enhancing the prestige of the profession, and reforming the legal order. Until recently it had the right to appoint a third of the members of the regional Councils of the OAB. Besides the IAB, there are dozens of other cultural associations, such as the Brazilian Academy for Juridical Culture (modeled on the Académie de France), the Brazilian Institute for Constitutional Law, and the Institute for Social Law.

Next to the OAB, the most important associations are the regional lawyers' unions (Sindicato dos Advogados), whose purpose is to study, defend, and coordinate the economic and professional interests of all lawyers. The union and its state branches are chartered by the Ministry of Labor and remain under its control. Membership is voluntary. Unlike most labor unions, the unions of the liberal professions, including lawyers, do not have great political power. The OAB wields all the powers that unions normally have. Not all the Brazilian states have lawyers' unions. The most important one is in Rio de Janeiro, but even it has little impact. Recent research on young law graduates from São Paulo shows that the importance of the unions might increase in the future. While only 52.6 percent felt that the OAB represented their interests, 67.9 percent favored the existence of lawyers' unions (Lima, 1984). This is due, no doubt, to the progressive proletarianization of lawyers. Various other professional associations may defend the interests of their members even though they may not represent them legally or engage in collective bargaining. These include the Lawyers' Associations (the most important of which is in São Paulo), the Association of State Magistrates, the Association of Police Chiefs, and the Association of Public Attorneys.

Finally, the main social security institution of lawyers is the "Caixa de Previdência dos Advogados," which provides loans, pensions, and medical, dental, and pharmaceutical services to lawyers, supplementing the benefits a lawyer receives from the government social security service. There presently are eleven of these entities in Brazil, and they have been growing as the quality of government medical services decreases and the cost of private medicine renders it progressively less accessible.

## PROFESSIONAL PRACTICE

This section describes the varieties of law practice, fees and salaries, and lawyers' income and analyzes the present job market. I will focus on individual practice and the private sector generally, although I will include the indirect public administration when dealing with legal departments.

### Types of Law Practice

There are three types of professional law practice: individual offices (solo practitioners), law firms, and legal departments. Solo practice is most consistent with the classic liberal tradition, which stresses autonomy, liberty, and individualism. In the past, the lawyers' offices were in their homes. Differentiation and specialization are minimal. For this reason, solo practice still is quite common in the interior of the country, which is less developed economically and socially. Solo practictioners accept any case and client. In the large- and medium-sized urban centers, these offices still are important, although some are specialized by subject. Very little capital is required to start an individual practice; at most, one needs the funds to rent a furnished room. In 1984, only 19.5 percent of recent young law graduates in São Paulo (less than 5 years since graduation) were solo practitioners (Lima, 1984).

When they first begin to practice, lawyers secure clients through personal contacts, relatives, and local networks; only later is professional performance significant. Advertising is forbidden by the Code of Ethics. There are no comprehensive directories.

Law firms can be divided into de facto and de jure. The former, far more numerous, are merely two or three lawyers sharing office space and common expenses, such as rent and secretarial services. They do not have any legal status, and their members are registered as individual practitioners. By contrast, de jure law firms are regulated by the OAB, must register, and enjoy their own legal status. They are defined by the Civil Code as partnerships and must divide work as well as profits. The assets belong to all the partners.

De jure law firms may include only partners or partners and salaried lawyers. The majority are based in Rio de Janeiro and São Paulo. The main services they render are legal planning, counseling, and representation before the public administration for a clientele composed primarily of multinational or large Brazilian corporations. A law partnership with twenty lawyers (partners and employees) is considered large. A few partnerships now have more than fifty lawyers. In Rio de Janeiro, only 8 percent of the law firms had more than five lawyers in 1980. In São Paulo in 1984, only 17 percent of lawyers who had graduated less than five years earlier worked in law firms with more than three partners (Lima, 1984).

Legal departments are divisions of public and private institutions, most of which are located in the large urban centers. They engage in counseling and negotiation with third parties. They also may represent their employer before the public administration or in court, as often happens with unions. These departments do not have independent legal status, nor must they register with the Brazilian Bar Association; those that do not register are not subject to inspection. Lawyers employed in these department usually do not provide services for other clients. Most employed lawyers specialize in tax, commercial law, and labor law.

The legal departments of the largest national and international, public and private corporations in the states of São Paulo, Rio de Janeiro, Santa Catarina, Minas Gerais, Rio Grande do Sul, Bahia, Paraná, and Brasília D. F. were studied in 1979 by the Fundação Casa Rui Barbosa (Sá & Ferreira Filho, 1982). Of the department heads interviewed, 74 percent entered the department through personal acquaintance and invitation, and 79.3

percent believed that a good knowledge of accounting and business administration was necessary in addition to legal knowledge. Almost all (96.1 percent) felt that the judiciary was not satisfying the expectations of large enterprises. These lawyers mobilized the judiciary primarily in labor disputes with individual employees (55.8 percent) or to collect debts and execute judgments (59.7 percent). Two-thirds of the corporations offered training and continuing education. Only 7 percent of these lawyers considered their professional practice to be identical to that of the prototypical liberal lawyer—the solo practitioner. Of these departments, 65.2 percent employ fewer than ten lawyers, and 38.2 percent occasionally hire outside legal services. Only 14 percent of these departments are registered with the Brazilian Bar Association.

Two other surveys, which, unfortunately, are not comparable, help us to visualize the three varieties of legal practice. The first studied approximately 35,000 lawyers registered in the Rio de Janeiro regional division of the Brazilian Bar Association. This survey revealed that the majority of lawyers engage in two or more occupations. For instance, 44 percent held a full- or part-time job in the Public Administration, only some of which were related to law. Approximately 61 percent were solo practitioners, and 5 percent practiced alone and also were connected with law firms or legal departments. Twenty-four percent were employees of law firms, part-time or full-time. The other survey studied those who graduated from the Recife Law School, in Pernambuco, between 1930 and 1975. Of those who practiced law in the private sector as their main occupation, 27 percent worked in legal departments, while 73 percent worked in individual offices or law firms (Falcão, 1981: 58).

This view of law practice would be incomplete if I failed to mention the emerging practice of lawyers who specialize in the defense of the legal interests of the lower-class urban populations and rural laborers. These "clients" cannot pay a lawyer, and the free legal services provided by the government are totally inadequate. These lawyers work through nonprofit nongovernmental institutions funded by religious groups from abroad, annual fees from their members (such as consumers, environmentalists, or activists within the Catholic Church), and government subventions. The best known are the lawyers of the Commission for Justice and Peace of the Catholic Church. They are engaged primarily in negotiating with the Public Administration and in judicial or extrajudicial representation before public or private third parties. The majority of cases deal with police violence and rural and urban land ownership. A major effort now is being made to integrate these groups into a national organization. A preliminary investigation has identified more than 150 groups throughout the country.

These groups rarely have their own legal personality. The lawyers within them usually have an ideological commitment to the clients they defend and receive a minimum fee or a salary below market value. Many of these lawyers originally worked for the defense of human rights in the period of greatest repression. Today, the battle for human rights is understood as a struggle for economic rights as well, such as the right to a dwelling place. In contrast to public interest law firms in more developed countries, however, the challenge is less defending minority rights than asserting the rights of the large majority. Recently, those groups defending the interests of the urban middle class against the National Housing Bank filed about 200,000 suits against the Bank and its agents.


## Payment Systems

*Fees.*   Fees are the payment for services rendered by any liberal professional, including lawyers. They may be established by contract, arbitrated by the judiciary, or fixed by the judge. The vast majority of fees are set by oral contracts in the individual case. The quantum is determined by bargaining and depends on many factors, such as the economic condition of the client, the economic risk involved, the professional reputation of the lawyer, the complexity of the work, the duration, and competition with other professionals. There is neither a minimum rate nor any government control. The OAB has a fee chart, which varies from state to state, but it rarely is heeded, for it is not compulsory and is far above the market level.

There are two other common ways of establishing fees. Some lawyers have permanent clients who pay them a fixed monthly wage or a fixed amount for each hour of service rendered. Large law firms are most likely to have such retainers. The best law firms of Rio de Janeiro and São Paulo charge about $150 for a senior lawyer. Lawyers also have clients who are habitual rather than permanent. Fees are contracted in each case but are lower than they otherwise would be. When fees are not agreed beforehand, and there is disagreement, judicial arbitration always is available.

The last type of fees are court-awarded—the judge always determines what the loser must pay to the winner. These fees, set by the Code of Civil Procedure, vary between 10 and 20 percent of the value of the case, depending on such factors as the amount of professional zeal, the place the service was rendered, the nature and importance of the lawsuit, the amount of work done by the lawyer, and the time spent on the case.

*Salaried Lawyers.*   Today the majority of lawyers are salaried: 56 percent of lawyers in São Paulo who had graduated less than 5 years earlier, for instance (Lima, 1984). This is true of all professionals with university degrees. In 1950 only 32.9 percent were salaried, while in 1973 the proportion had more than doubled (69.9 percent) (Revista OAB—São

Paolo, 1984). Salaried lawyers include all those who work with the Public Administration, those who work in law firms but are not partners, those who work in legal departments, and finally those who provide legal services for the low-income population through private or public entities. This proletarianization produced a contradictory professional reality. On one hand, there are fewer and fewer "liberal" lawyers, and they are less and less independent. On the other hand, the commitment of lawyers to liberal ideology is much greater, especially as the redemocratization of the country advances.

Two aspects of fees currently are being debated. One is whether salaried lawyers or lawyers who have contracted for their fees have the right to receive court-awarded fees in addition, if they have represented the winning side. It is a controversial demand frequently advanced by the embryonic associations of salaried lawyers, and there is no prevailing practice. The second issue is a minimum wage for the salaried lawyers, as well as other benefits. In 1981 salaried lawyers began to organize nationally to demand: a fixed work week of twenty hours (four hours per day), a minimum salary equivalent to six minimum salaries (about $320 per month), the right to court-awarded fees (in addition to their salaries), registration of all legal departments in the OAB and payment of annuities and inspections by the OAB, and the prohibition of discrimination on the basis of sex or differentiation on the basis of seniority (in the Public Administration).

## Income and the Job Market

*Income.* In a third world country such as Brazil, lawyers clearly constitute a professional and economic elite, as do all university graduates. Table 12.5 compares the average income of all economically active citizens in 1980 with the income of all legal professionals. While 70.9 percent of the working population earned three minimum salaries or less, only 7.3 percent of all legal professionals earned this little. Moreover, while 17.5 percent of all legal professionals earned more than twenty minimum salaries, only 0.6 percent of all Brazilian workers earned this much. In São Paulo, only 6.3 percent of lawyers who had graduated less than five years earlier began by earning less than three minimum salaries (Lima, 1984).

These are not isolated data but are confirmed by consideration of the distribution of national income, as well as by the limited research on legal professionals. Given the strong correlation between educational background and income, it is highly significant that only 4.6 percent of Brazilians hold university degrees. This alone puts lawyers among the best-paid professionals in the country. My survey of the graduates of the Recife Law

School indicated that their average income placed them among the top 5 percent of the economically active population of Brazil, earning an average of twenty-five minimum salaries per month (Falcão, 1981: 65). (A minimum salary was approximately $50 per month in December 1983.) Another survey showed that 73.5 percent of the law professors in Rio de Janeiro and São Paulo received a total monthly income (including income from other legal activities) of approximately $1,000 (about twenty minimum salaries). In Rio de Janeiro, 62.1 percent owned their own homes in 1980 (Melo Sobrinho, 1980: 19). Finally, the recent Gallup Poll in São Paulo suggested that salaried lawyers are beginning to earn more than the private practitioners. In addition, the legal department heads interviewed by the Fundação Casa Rui Barbosa earned more than thirty minimum salaries (Sá & Ferreira Filho, 1982).

Table 12.5 seems to suggest that there is economic discrimination against women lawyers (although some of the differences may be attributable to age). While 21.1 percent of the men earned more than twenty minimum salaries, only 5.2 percent of the women did so, and, inversely, while 5.3 percent of the men earned three minimum salaries or less, 15.3 percent of the women were paid this little. There is sex discrimination even among the privileged lawyers of large firms. While 75.0 percent of the women earned more than thirty minimum salaries, 90.4 percent of the men earned this much (Sá & Ferreira Filho, 1982: 32). In the survey of Rio de Janeiro lawyers, 2 percent of the women and 23 percent of the men were in the highest income bracket.

*The Job Market.*   The fundamental characteristic of Brazilian law practice is that most lawyers do not merely practice law but also perform other activities, which may not be related to law. This was so in the past (Hendricks, 1977; Falcão, 1981), and it remains true today (Miralles & Falcão, 1974; Sá & Ferreira Filho, 1982; Lima, 1984). Like law practice, these other professional activities are related to the needs of the Brazilian elite.

Even though they are part of the Brazilian economic elite, legal professionals—especially lawyers—are suffering from a saturated job market. Recently, for instance, the federal government held a public competition for new attorneys in the Ministry of Finance: 133 candidates competed for each position (*O Globo*, 1986).

This saturation is due not only to the temporary crisis but also to structural features of the Brazilian economy and politics. Given that only 29.1 percent of the Brazilian population earned more than three minimum salaries in 1980 (about $150 per month), more than two-thirds of the Brazilian people cannot possibly hire a lawyer. The free legal aid services of the government are totally inadequate. Furthermore, the progressive concentration of income is not a temporary condition but a structural characteristic of the kind of capitalism that has been implanted in Brazil.

The principal clientele of lawyers, therefore, is the urban middle class and their economic institutions. In recent years, however, because of the economic recession engineered by the International Monetary Fund, the Brazilian middle class contracted, despite the growth of the population. The proportion of the population earning less than five minimum salaries rose 6.5 percent between 1979 and 1982. If we consider the population increase (which should have enlarged the middle class), then this group was 16.3 percent smaller in 1982 than it had been in 1979. According to the São Paulo Economists' Association, the middle class lost about 19.9 percent of its real purchasing power between November 1979 and November 1983 (Polesi, 1984: 16). While the potential demand for lawyers is declining, the supply of law graduates simultaneously increases. The number of law graduates increased by 77.9 percent between 1950 and 1960, 640 percent between 1960 and 1970, and 122.9 percent between 1970 and 1980.

Political as well as economic factors affect the job market for legal professionals and especially for lawyers. Central among these is the performance of the judiciary. The judiciary constitutes an important sector for the absorption of law graduates, an employment area to fall back on. However, authoritarian regimes expand the executive and contract the judiciary. Brazil did not escape this trend during the last twenty years. The budget of the federal judiciary in 1981 was only 0.6 percent of the total federal budget (Albuquerque, 1981: 29). In Pernambuco in 1980, the state judiciary represented only 1.8 percent of the total state budget—only 26.5 percent of the budget of the military police alone (Cavalcanti Filho, 1980: 65).

Another influence of the judiciary on the legal profession derives from the fact that lawyers have a monopoly in the arena where citizens may peacefully settle their conflicts. The Federal Supreme Court has recognized public criticisms of judicial delay and inefficiency in executing judgments (Federal Supreme Court, 1975). Recent opinion polls show that people do not trust the judiciary: 46 percent have little or no faith in the judiciary in São Paulo (*Revista Veja*, April 1984); 48.2 percent believe that people should take justice into their own hands, even if this means beating a criminal to death (*Folha de São Paulo*, April 1984); 48.7 percent of Rio de Janeiro and São Paulo voters believe that the judiciary performs badly or very badly (*Revista Isto E*, September 1984). Without an effective judiciary that can cope with the minimum needs of its citizens, conflicts will be settled in other arenas, where lawyers enjoy no monopoly. For this reason, the crisis in the job market for Brazilian lawyers not only reveals the divergence between declining economic demand and rising law school supply but also reflects the performance of highly unequal social structures and the authoritarian suppression of the judiciary.

## CONCLUSION

A comprehensive overview of Brazilian lawyers thus reveals three apparent paradoxes. First, Brazil has a well-defined and carefully regulated national system of legal education and a powerful bar association that controls legal practice, yet at least half of all law graduates do not practice law. This means that law schools perform educational and cultural functions other than simply preparing legal professionals. There is a close relationship within the job market between those law graduates who perform other roles (sometimes a majority of the total) and practicing lawyers. Second, Brazilian lawyers have a monopoly over the representation of citizens in court, but the great majority of Brazilians have no access to court whatsoever, for cultural, economic, and legal reasons. This means that lawyers do not actually enjoy a monopoly over dispute settlement in Brazil; on the contrary, the role they play is quantitatively quite minor, if symbolically important, in the context of the totality of social disputes. There is an exchange between lawyers, codes, and courts on one hand and other unspecialized professionals, social norms, and informal arenas, on the other hand. Third, Brazilian law graduates, including lawyers, are strongly committed to the Western ideals of the rule of law and liberalism, but their actual legal practice adheres to legal formalism and dogmatics. This means that legal professionals have helped to implement most of the authoritarian legislation that still shapes the daily lives of Brazilians. There is an interaction between the liberating effect of lawyers' political commitment to the rule of law and liberalism and their technical implementation of authoritarian legislation. These three tensions will continue to influence the evolution of Brazilian lawyers.

# TABLES

12.1. Legal Education, 1980

| Sector | Total | | | University | | | Federation | | | Independent Institutions | | |
|---|---|---|---|---|---|---|---|---|---|---|---|---|
| | Number of courses | Number of students Enrolled | Graduating | Number of courses | Number of students Enrolled | Graduating | Number of courses | Number of students Enrolled | Graduating | Number of courses | Number of students Enrolled | Graduating |
| Federal | 27 | 21,810 | 3,077 | 27 | 21,810 | 3,077 | | | | | | |
| | (20.7) | (16.2) | (15.0) | (48.2) | (38.0) | (39.0) | | | | | | |
| State | 7 | 6,089 | 934 | 6 | 5,798 | 893 | | | | 1 | 291 | 41 |
| | (5.4) | (4.5) | (4.5) | (10.7) | (10.1) | (11.3) | | | | (1.5) | (0.5) | (0.4) |
| Municipal | 9 | 6,669 | 1,293 | 2 | 2,398 | 386 | | | | 7 | 4,271 | 907 |
| | (7.0) | (5.0) | (6.3) | (3.6) | (4.2) | (5.0) | | | | (11.0) | (7.2) | (8.8) |
| Private | 87 | 100,458 | 15,295 | 21 | 27,397 | 3,520 | 10 | 18,373 | 2,447 | 56 | 54,688 | 9,328 |
| | (66.9) | (74.3) | (74.2) | (37.5) | (47.7) | (44.7) | (100.0) | (100.0) | (100.0) | (87.5) | (92.3) | (90.8) |
| Total | 130 | 135,026 | 20,599 | 56 | 57,403 | 7,876 | 10 | 18,373 | 2,447 | 64 | 59,230 | 10,276 |

aFigures in parentheses are percentages of columns.
Source: Ministério da Educação e Cultura (1980).

12.2. Population, Education, and Legal Professionals, by Gender, 1950–1980[a]

| | 1950 | | 1960 | | 1970 | | 1980 | |
|---|---|---|---|---|---|---|---|---|
| | Men | Women | Men | Women | Men | Women | Men | Women |
| National population | 25,885,001 | 26,059,396 | 35,059,596 | 35,131,824 | 45,754,659 | 46,586,897 | 59,115,533 | 59,909,067 |
| | (100) | (100) | (135) | (134) | (176) | (178) | (226) | (229) |
| Working population (>10 years old) | 14,630,933 | 2,705,067 | 18,673,167 | 4,076,861 | 23,391,777 | 6,165,447 | 31,392,986 | 11,842,726 |
| | (100) | (100) | (127) | (150) | (159) | (227) | (214) | (437) |
| University graduates | 114,233 | 13,837 | 246,755 | 41,199 | 349,668 | 256,020 | 1,002,706 | 806,812 |
| | (100) | (100) | (171) | (297) | (242) | (1,850) | (695) | (5,830) |
| Law graduates | 30,254 | 1,048 | 51,768 | 3,845 | 79,673 | 11,459 | 166,827 | 54,494 |
| | (100) | (100) | (171) | (366) | (263) | (1,093) | (551) | (5,199) |
| Judges | 2,259 | 6 | 2,298 | 43 | 3,435 | 189 | 4,244 | 380 |
| | (100) | (100) | (101) | (716) | (152) | (3,150) | (187) | (6,333) |
| Prosecutors, public attorneys, public curators | 1,332 | 14 | 1,613 | 27 | 4,225 | 468 | 6,477 | 1,653 |
| | (100) | (100) | (112) | (193) | (317) | (3,343) | (486) | (11,807) |
| Private lawyers and legal aid | 15,566 | 346 | 28,819 | 1,247 | 34,311 | 3,408 | 67,143 | 18,573 |
| | (100) | (100) | (189) | (360) | (225) | (984) | (441) | (5,367) |

[a]Figures in parentheses are in relation to 1950 (= 100).

Source: Istituto Brasileiro de Geografia e Estatística (1980).

12.3. Law Graduates and Lawyers Registered at the OAB, 1980/81

| State | Lawyers registered | | Law graduates 1980 |
|---|---|---|---|
| | Total January 1981 | Registered during 1980 | |
| Acre | 301 | 29 | 25 |
| Amazonas | 1,061 | 42 | 67 |
| Pará | 2,557 | 256 | 433 |
| Maranhão | 2,688 | 137 | 126 |
| Piauí | 918 | 25 | 64 |
| Amapá | 74 | 10 | — |
| Roraima | 62 | 51 | — |
| Total | 7,661 | 550 | 715 |
| | | | |
| Ceará | 3,777 | 222 | 422 |
| R. G. Norte | 952 | 63 | 53 |
| Paraíba | 2,500 | 300 | 620 |
| Pernambuco | 6,860 | 600 | 687 |
| Bahai | 5,243 | 286 | 462 |
| Sergipe | 1,083 | 88 | 78 |
| Alagoas | 1,764 | 114 | 344 |
| Total | 22,134 | 1,673 | 2,666 |
| | | | |
| Minas Gerais | 18,043 | 1,366 | 2,540 |
| Espírito Santo | 3,384 | 238 | 418 |
| Rio de Janeiro | 40,091 | 2,639 | 3,429 |
| São Paulo | 54,727 | 4,912 | 7,729 |
| Total | 116,245 | 9,155 | 14,116 |
| | | | |
| Paraná | 8,040 | 784 | 828 |
| Santa Catarina | 3,900 | 259 | 319 |
| R.G. Sul | 14,265 | 1,357 | 1,401 |
| Total | 26,205 | 2,400 | 2,548 |
| | | | |
| D.F. | 3,936 | 674 | 645 |
| Goiás | 4,740 | 545 | 637 |
| Mato Grosso | 1,269 | 133 | 109 |
| Mato Grosso Sul | 1,259 | 245 | 249 |
| Rondônia | 222 | 51 | — |
| Total | 11,426 | 1,648 | 1,640 |
| | | | |
| Total | 183,671 | 15,426 | 21,685 |

*Sources:* Lawyers registered—Baeta (1981); law graduates—Ministério de Educação e Cultura (1980).

12.4. Judiciary, 1983

| Courts | Levels | | | |
|---|---|---|---|---|
| | Third (justices) | Second (magistrates; desembaradores) | First (judges) | Total |
| Federal | | | | |
|   Supreme Court | 11 | | | 11 |
|   Federal Court of Appeals | 27 | | | 27 |
|   Federal Justice | | | 115 | 115 |
| Military | | | | |
|   Military Superior Court | 15 | | | 15 |
|   Military Justice | | | 22 | 22 |
| Labor | | | | |
|   Labor Superior Court | 17 | | | 17 |
|   Labor Justice | | 172 | 380 | 552 |
| State Justice | | 819 | 4,479 | 5,298 |
| Total | 70 | 991 | 4,996 | 6,057 |

Source: Ministério de Justiça, Departamento de Assuntos Judiciários (1984).

12.5. Average Monthly Income: Working Population[a] and Legal Professionals, 1980[b]

| Income in minimum salaries[c] | Working Population | | Magistrates, lawyers, and other legal specialists | |
|---|---|---|---|---|
| | Men | Women | Men | Women |
| ≤ 1 | 8,573,391 | 5,000,563 | 376 | 219 |
| | (27.4) | (42.2) | (0.5) | (1.1) |
| > 1 but ≤ 3 | 12,897,708 | 4,195,462 | 3,795 | 2,935 |
| | (41.1) | (35.4) | (4.8) | (14.2) |
| > 3 but ≤ 5 | 3,547,843 | 824,352 | 9,269 | 4,754 |
| | (11.3) | (7.0) | (12.0) | (23.1) |
| > 5 but ≤ 10 | 2,305,041 | 499,697 | 20,898 | 6,952 |
| | (7.3) | (4.2) | (26.8) | (33.8) |
| > 10 but ≤ 20 | 1,091,094 | 155,560 | 26,654 | 4,378 |
| | (3.5) | (1.3) | (34.3) | (21.2) |
| > 20 | 570,396 | 34,075 | 16,464 | 1,072 |
| | (1.8) | (0.3) | (21.2) | (5.2) |
| No income or declaration | 2,406,913 | 1,133,017 | 408 | 296 |
| | (7.6) | (9.6) | (0.5) | (1.4) |
| Total | 31,392,986 | 11,842,726 | 77,864 | 20,606 |
| | (100.0) | (100.0) | (100.0) | (100.0) |

[a] Ten years and older. Includes 626,829 men and 337,359 women looking for work.
[b] Figures in parentheses are percentages of columns.
[c] One minimum salary is approximately $50.
*Source:* Istituto Brasileiro de Geografía e Estatística (1980).

## NOTES

This chapter was translated from Portuguese by Elizabeth Portella.

## REFERENCES

Albuquerque, Francisco M. X. 1981. "Conjuntura Política Nacional: O Poder Judiciário." Paper presented at the Escola Superior de Guerra, Rio de Janeiro.
Aguiar, Esther. 1984. "Juntas de Conciliação e Julgamento." M.A. thesis, Economics and Sociology Program, Universidade Federal de Pernambuco.

Arruda, Eduardo L, Jr. 1983. "Notas para uma Sociologia das profissões dos bacharéis em Direito no Brasil" (mimeo). ANPOCS. São Paulo: Aguas de São Pedro.

Baeta, Herman Assis. 1981. "Algumas Questões sobre o papel da OAB no ensino público," 14(29) *Revista da Ordem dos Advogados do Brasil* 72.

Bicudo, Hélio. 1976. *Meu Depoimento sobre o Esquadrão da Morte*, 3d ed. São Paulo: Ed. Pontifícia Comissão de Justiça e Paz de São Paulo.

Bresser Pereira, Luis Carlos. 1982. Economia Brasileira—Uma Introdução Crítica. São Paulo: Brasiliense.

Camara dos Deputados. 1977. *Criação dos Cursos Jurídicos no Brasil.* Brasília: Camara dos Deputados.

Canuto, Vera R. A. 1983. "A Organização do Ensino Superior Brasileiro: Condicionamentos Sociais e Políticos (1930–1970)." M.A. thesis, Economics and Sociology Program, Universidade Federal de Pernambuco.

Carvalho, José Murilo. 1974. "Elite and State Building in Imperial Brazil." Ph.D. thesis, Stanford University.

Cavalcanti Filho, José Paulo. 1980. "O Poder Judiciário e sua Correlação com os demais Poderes. Orçamentos Anuais," in Corregedoria Geral da Justiça, ed., *Poder Judiciário em Pernambuco—Diagnóstico de um Poder Imolado*, vol. 2, p. 65. Recife: Corregedoria Geral de Justiça.

Conselho Federal de Educação (CFE). 1983. *Programa de Avaliação da Reforma Universitária—Detalhamento do Programa.* Brasília: CAPES.

Falcão, Joaquim de Arruda. 1974. *Plano Básico de Desenvolvimento Científico e Tecnológico: Direito.* Rio de Janeiro: SEPLAN/MEC.

———. 1978*a.* "Crise da Universidade e Crise do Ensino Jurídico," 9(24) *Revista de Ordem dos Advogados do Brasil* 79–129.

———. 1978*b.* "Os Cursos Jurídicos e a Formação do Estado Nacional," in Aurelio V. Bastos, ed., *Os Cursos Jurídicos e as Elites Brasileiras*, pp. 65–93. Brasília: Camara dos Deputados.

———. 1979. "Lawyers in Brazil: Ideals and Praxis," 7 *International Journal of the Sociology of Law* 355–375.

———. 1981. "L'enseignement de droit au Brésil: Son idéal et sa pratique à la Faculté de Droit de Récife entre 1930 et 1985." Doctoral thesis, Faculté de Psychologie et des Sciences de l'Education, Université de Genève.

———. 1982. "Justiça Social, Justiça Legal," in *Anais da XI Conferência Nacional dos Advogados do Brasil*, pp. 430–449. Rio de Janeiro: Conselho Federal da Ordem dos Advogados do Brasil.

———. 1983. "Avaliação e Perspectivas: Direito," in Coordenação Editorial CNPq, ed., *Avaliação e Perspectivas*, pp. 156–159. Brasília: SEPLAN/CNPq.

Fleischer, David. 1983. *Um Perfil Socio-Económico e Político do Congresso Eleito em 1982.* ANPOCS. São Paulo: Aguas de São Pedro.

Freyre, Gilberto. 1961. *Sobrados e Mocambos.* Rio de Janeiro: José Olímpio.

Fundação Cesgranrio. 1985. *Dados Sócio Culturais dos Candidatos ao Vestibular—*

85. Rio de Janeiro: Fundação Cesgranrio.

Hendricks, Howard Craig. 1977. "Education and the Maintenance of the Social Structure: The Faculdade de Direito do Recife and the Brazilian Northeast, 1870–1930." Ph.D. thesis, State University of New York at Stony Brook.

Herkenhoff, João Batista. 1977. *A Função Judiciária no Interior*. São Paulo: Ed. Revista Universitária.

Istituto Brasileiro de Geografía e Estatística (IBGE). 1980. *Anuario Estatístico do Brasil e Sinopse Preliminar*. Rio de Janeiro: IBGE.

*Jornal do Brasil*. 1985. "Inscrições para Direito em 86 só ficam atrás das de Medicina," *Jornal do Brasil* (8 December) 24.

Lima, Edmundo, Jr. 1984. "Dados Preliminares—Pesquisa OAB/MEC" (unpublished).

Machado, Mario Brockmann. 1981. *Os Ministros do Supremo*. ANPOCS. Rio de Janeiro: Friburgo.

Mello Filho, Álvaro. 1981. "Impasses e Alternativas dos Cursos de Direito no Brasil," 12(29) *Revista da Ordem dos Advogados do Brasil* 115–131.

Melo Sobrinho, Noeli Correia. 1980. *O Advogado e a Crise na Administração da Justiça*. Rio de Janeiro: Ed. Ordem dos Advogados do Brasil.

Ministério da Educação e Cultura (MEC). 1890. *Sinopse Estatística do Ensino Superior*. Brasília: MEC.

Ministério da Justiça, Departamento de Assuntos Judiciário (MJ/DAJ). 1984. *Annual Report*. Brasília: MJ/DAJ.

Miralles, Tereza, and Joaquim A. Falcão. 1974. *Atitudes dos Professores e Alunos das Faculdades de Direito do Rio de Janeiro e São Paulo Capital, face ao Ensino Jurídico e sua Reforma*. Rio de Janeiro: Ed. PUC/RJ.

Moura, Alexandrina S. S. 1983. "Direito de Habitação às classes de baixa renda," 11(1) *Ciência & Trópico* 71–78.

Nunes Leal, Victor. 1948. *Coronelismo, enxada e voto: município e o regime representativo no Brasil*. Rio de Janeiro: Ed. Rio.

*O Globo*. 1986. "O Jornal de Ibrahim Sued," *O Globo* (23 January) 2.

Oliveira, José Luciano G. 1984. "Sua Excelência o Comissário." M.A. thesis, Economics and Sociology Program, Universidade Federal de Pernambuco.

Ordem dos Advogados do Brasil (OAB)—Conselho Federal. 1981. "Reflexões sobre o Ensino Jurídico apresentado pelo Conselho Federal da 'OAB'," 12(29) *Revista da Ordem dos Advogados do Brasil* 155–160.

Piquet Carneiro, João Geraldo. 1983. "Juizado de Pequenas Causas: A Justiça do Pobre," 1 *Revista da AMAGIS* (Associação dos Magistrados Mineiros) 147.

Polesi, Alexandre. 1984. "A Classe Média vai ao Paraiso," *Jornal do Comercio* (Recife) (26 January) 1C.

Reichstuz, Henri Philippe, and Luciano Coutinho. 1983. "Investimento Estatal 1974–1980: Ciclo e Crise," in *Desenvolvimento Capitalista no Brasil*, no. 2. São Paulo: Brasiliense.

Revista OAB—São Paulo. 1984. "Caem os salários da classe média," 2(9) *Revista*

*OAB—São Paulo* 12.

Ribeiro, Sergio, and Ruben Klein. 1982. "A Divisão Interna da Universidade: posição social das carreiras," 5 *Educação e Seleção.*

Sá, Constança Pereira, and Zefer P. Ferreira Filho. 1982. *O Advogado e a Empresa.* Rio de Janeiro: Ed. OAB/RJ.

Saldanha, Nelson. 1982. *A OAB-PE e Sua Trajetória.* Recife: Ed. Ordem dos Advogados do Brasil—Seção de Pernambuco.

Santos, Boaventura de Sousa. 1977. "The Law of the Oppressed: The Construction and Reproduction of Legality in Pasargada," 12 *Law & Society Review* 5–126.

Serviços de Estatística de Secretaria de Educação e Cultura (SEES). 1983. *Sinopse Estatística do Ensino Superior, 1978/1979/1980.* Brasília: Ministério da Educação e Cultura.

Silva, Maria Betania. 1985. "Um perfil da Assistencia Judiciária no Recife" (unpublished).

Souto, Claudio. 1982. "Teoria Sociológica do Direito e Prática Forense," 72 *Enciclopédia Saraiva do Direito* 264. São Paolo: Saraiva S. A. Livreiros Editores.

Steiner, Henry J. 1971. "Legal Education and Socio-Economic Change: Brazilian Perspectives," 19 *American Journal of Comparative Law* 67.

Supremo Tribunal Federal. 1978. *Reforma do Poder Judiciário—Diagnóstico.* Brasília: Supremo Tribunal Federal.

Villaça, Marcos V., and Roberto C. Albuquerque. 1965. *Coronel, Coronéis.* Rio de Janeiro: Ed. Tempo Universitário.

# CONTRIBUTORS

Richard L. Abel is professor of law at the University of California, Los Angeles. He has written widely about the legal profession, torts, and dispute processes and has been editor of the *Law & Society Review* and *African Law Studies*. He edited *The Politics of Informal Justice* (2 volumes) (Academic Press, 1982). He recently published *The Legal Profession in England and Wales* (Basil Blackwell, 1988) and soon will publish *American Lawyers* (Oxford University Press, 1989).

Benoit Bastard received his license in philosophy and diploma in political science. Since 1974 he has been a sociologist at the Centre de sociologie des organisations in Paris, which is a constitutent of the Centre national de la recherche scientifique. He also has visited at the law faculty of the University of Geneva. His principal studies concern the modernization of courts, the judicial processing of divorce, and family dissolution.

Erhard Blankenburg teaches sociology of law at the Free University of Amsterdam. He received his master's degree in sociology from Oregon in 1964, his Ph.D. degree from Basel in 1966, and his *habilitation* from Freiburg in 1974. He is the author or editor of books on legal services, labor courts, civil litigation, police, and prosecutors. He has contributed to and is an editor of the *Jahrbuch für Rechtssoziologie* and the *Zeitschrift für Rechtssoziologie*.

Anne Boigeol received her *doctorat de IIIème cycle* in sociology and has studied demography. Her earlier research concerned family dissolution in France and the regulation of economic relationships following divorce. She began her work on legal professionals by analyzing legal aid and lawyers and now is studying the recruitment and training of lawyers and magistrates. She is a researcher in Paris at the Centre national de la recherche scientifique.

Laura Cardia-Vonèche studied sociology at the University of Geneva. She has conducted research on sociology of the family and sociology of law at the law faculty of the University of Geneva and at the Institute of Social and Preventive Medicine at the medical faculty. Her present reseach concerns young couples and family functioning, divorce and its effect on the family, and eating habits in families.

Joaquim Falcão received his LL.M. degree from Harvard University in 1968 and his docteur en education from the University of Geneva in 1981. He is professor of sociology of law at the Federal University of Pernambuco, associate professor at the Catholic Law School, Rio de Janeiro, and president of the Fundação Nacional Pro-Memória, established by the Brazilian Ministry of Culture. His principal publications are: *Advogados: Ensino Jurídico e Mercado de Trabalho* (Ed. Massangana, 1984), "Lawyers in Brazil: Ideals and Praxis" (7 *International Journal of the Sociology of Law* 355 [1979]), and "Democratización y Servicios Legales en América Latina." (in *Los Abogados y La Democracia en América Latina*, ILSA, 1986).

Luc Huyse is professor of sociology of law at the University of Leuven. He has written widely on politics in Belgium and currently is studying both deregulation and the purge of quislings after World War II.

Jon T. Johnsen is associate professor at the Institute for Sociology of Law of the University of Oslo. Since 1978 he also has been director of Juss-Buss, a legal clinic run by law students. His main field of study is legal services; he recently published *Retten til juridisk bistand: En rettspolitisk studie* (Tano, 1987).

Philip S. C. Lewis was a Research Fellow at All Souls College, Oxford, from 1965 to 1988. He founded the Working Group for Comparative Study of Legal Professions and edited (with Robert Dingwall) *The Sociology of Professions: Lawyers, Doctors and Others* (Macmillan, 1983). He has written about the legal profession and legal aid and the sociology of law and is coauthor of *Social Needs and Legal Action* (Martin Robertson, 1973) and author of the eighth edition of *Gatley on Libel and Slander* (Sweet & Maxwell, 1981).

Vittorio Olgiati received his law degree from the University of Milan. He became a researcher of the National Research Council at the Institute of Philosophy and Sociology of Law of the University of Milan in 1976 and was granted tenure there in 1980. He has written widely in scientific and professional journals on the sociology of law and especially the sociology of the legal profession.

Rogelio Pérez Perdomo received a law degree and a doctorate from the Central University of Venezuela, a doctorate in philosophy of law from the University of Paris, and an LL.M. degree from Harvard University. He has been a professor of law at the Central University of Venezuela since 1966. He has written many articles on law and sociology of law and is the author of five books, including *El formalismo jurídico y sus funciones sociales en el siglo XIX venezolano* (Monte Avila, 1978), *Los abogados en Venezuela. Estudio de una élite intelectual y política 1780–1980* (Monte Avila, 1981), and *Justícia y Pobreza en Venezuela* (Monte Avila, 1986).

Valerio Pocar received his law degree from the University of Milan. He taught sociology at the Faculty of Political Science of the University of Messina from 1973 to 1975 and has taught sociology of law at the Faculty of Political Science of the University of Milan since 1976. He has written widely on sociolegal thought, sociology of family law, and the legal profession and is the author of *La sociologia del diritto negli anni '60* (Ed. Meridionali Riuniti, 1975), coauthor of *Per una sociologia del diritto della famiglia* (Ed. Unicopli, 1979), and editor of *Il praticante procuratore. Una ricerca sociológica sull'accesso alla professione di avvocato* (Ed. Unicopli, 1983).

Kahei Rokumoto studied law and political science at the University of Tokyo and sociology at the University of California, Berkeley. He is professor of sociology of law at the faculty of law, University of Tokyo.

Ulrike Schultz is Akademische Oberratin at the FernUniversität in Hagen, Federal Republic of Germany. She specializes in didactics and educational technology for teaching law through media and in schools. She has written about civil law and the legal profession and currently is working on the subject of women's rights and women in law.

Kees Schuyt studied both sociology and law at Leiden, Oslo, and the University of California, Berkeley. He taught sociology of law at the Catholic University of Nijmegen and presently is professor of empirical sociology at Leiden University. From 1983 to 1988 he served on the Scientific Council for Government Policy at the Hague and drafted the proposal on basic education. He has published ten books on civil disobedience, sociology of law, legal aid, tribunals, and the welfare state. His most recent books are *The Divided Society* (1986) and *Philosophy of Social Science* (1987) (both in Dutch).

Carlos Viladás Jene is Professor Titular de Universidad at the Faculty of Law of the University of Barcelona. He also practices business law. He is the author of *Los delitos de quiebra* (Peninsula, 1982) and articles in journals in Spain, France, and England.

# Index

Abel, Richard, 351

Administrative scriveners, in Japan, 164, 165

Admission quotas. *See* Numerus clausus

Advertising: in Australia, 26; in Brazil, 428; in Canada, 26; in England, 26; in Germany, 125, 138, 143; in Italy, 353; in Norway, 77; in Scandinavian countries, 26, 27; in Scotland, 26; in Spain, 374, 375; in U.S., 26; in Venezuela, 390–392

Advocates, 4; in Belgium, 225–226, 230, 233–234, 236–238, 241; black market of, 128; business lawyers and, 135; demand for, 39; development stages of, 90–91; in France, 258–282; geographical distribution of, 79, 85; in Germany, 6, 124–159; growth of, 125, 127–130; income of, 76–80, 136, 141–143; innovation by, 241; Jewish, 6, 128–129, 147; monopolies by, 72–75, 135, 139, 236; in the Netherlands, 200–201; in Norway, 70–91; as notaries, 136–137; professional associations of, 71–72, 77–79, 239–240; role of, 135–136; in Scotland, 18; specialization of, 143–144; women as, 79, 146–147

Age profile, of legal profession: in France, 271; in Germany, 148; in Italy, 348; in Japan, 165; law students and, 68, 129; in the Netherlands, 205–206; in Norway, 68, 79; in Switzerland, 308

Apprenticeship, 11, 15–17; in Australia, 32; in Austria, 16; in Belgium, 16, 226, 237–239; in Brazil, 405–406, 418–419, 424; in Canada, 32; in Colombia, 16; in England, 16–17, 32; entry controls using, 15–17, 237–239, 272, 276–277; in France, 16, 24, 260, 267, 272, 276–277, 280; in Germany, 16, 132; in Italy, 16, 345; in Japan, 161, 162, 167; for judges, 201, 204; legal aid during, 280, 316, 320; in the Netherlands, 16, 201, 204, 205, 210; for notaries, 238; in Scotland, 32; socialization by, 238–239; in Sweden, 16; in Switzerland, 302, 306, 308, 315–316; university replaces, 32; in Venezuela, 16, 381, 384

Argentina, legal profession in, 14

Aubert, Vilhelm, 202–205

Australia, legal profession in: advertising by, 26; apprenticeship of, 32; barristers in, 18; examination of, 15; geographic limitations on, 25; law schools in, 11–12; legal aid and, 26; as private practitioners, 18; as solo practitioners, 39

| | |
|---:|:---|
| Designer: | U.C. Press Staff |
| Compositor: | Asco Trade Typesetting, Ltd. |
| Text: | 11.5/12 Palatino |
| Display: | Palatino |
| Printer: | Edwards Bros., Inc. |
| Binder: | Edwards Bros., Inc. |